Reading STREET

Program Authors

Peter Afflerbach

Camille Blachowicz

Candy Dawson Boyd

Elena Izquierdo

Connie Juel

Edward Kame'enui

Donald Leu

Jeanne R. Paratore

P. David Pearson

Sam Sebesta

Deborah Simmons

Alfred Tatum

Sharon Vaughn

Susan Watts Taffe

Karen Kring Wixson

PEARSON

Glenview, Illinois • Boston, Massachusetts
Chandler, Arizona • Upper Saddle River, New Jersey

We dedicate Reading Street to
Peter Jovanovich.

His wisdom, courage,
and passion for education
are an inspiration to us all.

Accelerated Reader

PEARSON

ISBN-13: 978-0-328-46990-1
ISBN-10: 0-328-46990-4
2 3 4 5 6 7 8 9 10 V064 14 13 12 11 10
CC1

Any Path, Any Pace

"Welcome to Reading Street! Bienvenidos too."

PEARSON

Find Your Place on Reading Street!

Who said so?

The Leading Researchers,

Program Authors

Peter Afflerbach, Ph.D.
Professor
Department of Curriculum and Instruction
University of Maryland at College Park

Camille L. Z. Blachowicz, Ph.D.
Professor of Education
National-Louis University

Candy Dawson Boyd, Ph.D.
Professor
School of Education
Saint Mary's College of California

Elena Izquierdo, Ph.D.
Associate Professor
University of Texas at El Paso

Connie Juel, Ph.D.
Professor of Education
School of Education
Stanford University

Edward J. Kame'enui, Ph.D.
Dean-Knight Professor of Education and Director
Institute for the Development of Educational Achievement and the Center on Teaching and Learning
College of Education
University of Oregon

Donald J. Leu, Ph.D.
*John and Maria Neag Endowed Chair in Literacy and Technology
Director, The New Literacies Research Lab*
University of Connecticut

Jeanne R. Paratore, Ed.D.
Associate Professor of Education
Department of Literacy and Language Development
Boston University

P. David Pearson, Ph.D.
Professor and Dean
Graduate School of Education
University of California, Berkeley

Sam L. Sebesta, Ed.D.
Professor Emeritus
College of Education
University of Washington, Seattle

Deborah Simmons, Ph.D
Professor
College of Education and Human Development
Texas A&M University

Alfred W. Tatum, Ph.D.
Associate Professor and Director of the UIC Reading Clinic
University of Illinois at Chicago

Sharon Vaughn, Ph.D.
*H. E. Hartfelder/Southland Corporation Regents Professor
Director, Meadows Center for Preventing Educational Risk*
University of Texas

Susan Watts Taffe, Ph.D.
Associate Professor in Literacy
Division of Teacher Education
University of Cincinnati

Karen Kring Wixson, Ph.D.
Professor of Education
University of Michigan

Consulting Authors

Jeff Anderson, M.Ed.
Author and Consultant
San Antonio, Texas

Jim Cummins, Ph.D.
Professor
Department of Curriculum, Teaching and Learning
University of Toronto

Lily Wong Fillmore, Ph.D.
Professor Emerita
Graduate School of Education
University of California, Berkeley

Georgia Earnest García, Ph.D.
Professor
Language and Literacy Division
Department of Curriculum and Instruction
University of Illinois at Urbana-Champaign

George A. González, Ph.D.
Professor (Retired)
School of Education
University of Texas-Pan American, Edinburg

Valerie Ooka Pang, Ph.D.
Professor
School of Teacher Education
San Diego State University

Sally M. Reis, Ph.D.
Board of Trustees Distinguished Professor
Department of Educational Psychology
University of Connecticut

Jon Scieszka, M.F.A.
*Children's Book Author
Founder of GUYS READ
Named First National Ambassador for Young People's Literature 2008*

Grant Wiggins, Ed.D.
Educational Consultant
Authentic Education
Concept Development

Lee Wright, M.Ed.
Pearland, Texas

Practitioners, and Authors.

Consultant

Sharroky Hollie, Ph.D.
Assistant Professor
California State University
Dominguez Hills, CA

Teacher Reviewers

Dr. Bettyann Brugger
*Educational Support Coordinator—
Reading Office*
Milwaukee Public Schools
Milwaukee, WI

Kathleen Burke
K–12 Reading Coordinator
Peoria Public Schools, Peoria, IL

Darci Burns, M.S.Ed.
University of Oregon

Bridget Cantrell
District Intervention Specialist
Blackburn Elementary School
Independence, MO

**Tahira DuPree Chase,
M.A., M.S.Ed.**
*Administrator of Elementary
English Language Arts*
Mount Vernon City School District
Mount Vernon, NY

Michele Conner
Director, Elementary Education
Aiken County School District
Aiken, SC

Georgia Coulombe
*K–6 Regional Trainer/
Literacy Specialist*
Regional Center for Training and
Learning (RCTL), Reno, NV

Kelly Dalmas
Third Grade Teacher
Avery's Creek Elementary, Arden, NC

Seely Dillard
First Grade Teacher
Laurel Hill Primary School
Mt. Pleasant, SC

Jodi Dodds-Kinner
Director of Elementary Reading
Chicago Public Schools, Chicago, IL

Dr. Ann Wild Evenson
District Instructional Coach
Osseo Area Schools, Maple Grove, MN

Stephanie Fascitelli
Principal
Apache Elementary, Albuquerque
Public Schools, Albuquerque, NM

Alice Franklin
*Elementary Coordinator, Language
Arts & Reading*
Spokane Public Schools, Spokane, WA

Laureen Fromberg
Assistant Principal
PS100 Queens, NY

Kimberly Gibson
First Grade Teacher
Edgar B. Davis Community School
Brockton, MA

Kristen Gray
Lead Teacher
A.I. Allen Elementary School
Concord, NC

Mary Ellen Hazen
State Pre-K Teacher
Rockford Public Schools #205
Rockford, IL

Patrick M. Johnson
Elementary Instructional Director
Seattle Public Schools, Seattle, WA

Theresa Jaramillo Jones
Principal
Highland Elementary School
Las Cruces, NM

Sophie Kowzun
*Program Supervisor, Reading/
Language Arts, PreK–5*
Montgomery County Public Schools
Rockville, MD

David W. Matthews
Sixth Grade Teacher
Easton Area Middle School
Easton, PA

Ana Nuncio
Editor and Independent Publisher
Salem, MA

Joseph Peila
Principal
Chappell Elementary School
Chicago, IL

Ivana Reimer
Literacy Coordinator
PS100 Queens, NY

Sally Riley
Curriculum Coordinator
Rochester Public Schools
Rochester, NH

Dyan M. Smiley
Independent Educational Consultant

Michael J. Swiatowiec
Lead Literacy Teacher
Graham Elementary School
Chicago, IL

Dr. Helen Taylor
Director of English Education
Portsmouth City Public Schools
Portsmouth, VA

Carol Thompson
Teaching and Learning Coach
Independence School District
Independence, MO

Erinn Zeitlin
Kindergarten Teacher
Carderock Springs Elementary School
Bethesda, MD

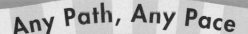
Any Path, Any Pace

UNIT 5

Going Places

In this Teacher's Edition Unit 5, Volume 2

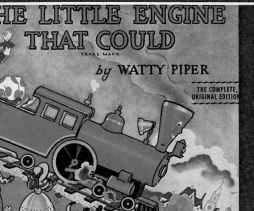

In the **First Stop**
on Reading Street

- **Dear Kindergarten Teacher**

- **Research into Practice on Reading Street**

- **Guide to Reading Street**

- **Assessment on Reading Street**

- **Differentiated Instruction on Reading Street**

- **ELL on Reading Street**

- **Customize Literacy on Reading Street**

- **21st Century Skills on Reading Street**

- **Teacher Resources for Kindergarten**

- **Index**

GO Digital!

See It!

- **Big Question Video**

- **Concept Talk Video**

- **Envision It! Animations**

- **Sing with Me Animations**

Hear It!

- **Sing With Me Animations**

- **eReaders**

- **Grammar Jammer**

- **Leveled Reader Database**

Do It!

- **Story Sort**

- **Letter Tile Drag and Drop**

All Together Now

Key
- **SI** Strategic Intervention
- **OL** On-Level
- **A** Advanced
- **ELL** ELL

Volume 1

Carol Roth
The Little School Bus
illustrated by Pamela Paparone

Volume 2

Look at Us!

Volume 1

Volume 2

Changes All Around Us

Volume 1

Volume 2

Let's Go Exploring

Key
- (SI) Strategic Intervention
- (OL) On-Level
- (A) Advanced
- (ELL) ELL

Volume 1

Volume 2

UNIT 5

Going Places

Volume 1

WEEK 1 • **Max Takes the Train** Animal Fantasy.........7–104

Differentiated Instruction SI OL A ELL ....DI•1–DI•17

WEEK 2 • **Mayday! Mayday!** Nonfiction..................105–210

Differentiated Instruction SI OL A ELL ....DI•18–DI•34

WEEK 3 • **Trucks Roll!** Rhyming Nonfiction 211–310

Differentiated Instruction SI OL A ELL ....DI•35–DI•51

Volume 2

WEEK 4 • **The Little Engine That Could**
Classic Fantasy 311–414

Differentiated Instruction SI OL A ELL ....DI•52–DI•68

WEEK 5 • **On the Move!** Nonfiction 415–512

Differentiated Instruction SI OL A ELL ....DI•69–DI•85

WEEK 6 • **This Is the Way We Go to School** Informational Fiction.................................513–615

Differentiated Instruction SI OL A ELL ....DI•86–DI•102

Customize Literacy...CL•1–CL•31

Putting It Together

Volume 1

Volume 2

Skills Overview

WEEK **1**

WEEK **2**

Key
T Tested
🎯 Target Skill

Max Takes the Train
Animal Fantasy pp. 60–71

Mayday! Mayday!
Nonfiction pp. 158–177

	WEEK 1	WEEK 2
Question of the Week	What are different ways of going places?	What kinds of transportation help us in an emergency?
Amazing Words	*plane, jetway, subway, tunnel, ferryboat, sidecar*	*rescue, pilot, yacht, sailor, mechanic, shimmering*
Phonemic Awareness	**T** 🎯 /j/ **T** 🎯 /w/	**T** 🎯 /ks/
Phonics	**T** 🎯 /j/ Spelled *Jj* **T** 🎯 /w/ Spelled *Ww* **Review** /e/ Spelled *Ee*	**T** 🎯 /ks/ Spelled *Xx* **Review** /j/ Spelled *Jj;* /w/ Spelled *Ww*
High-Frequency Words	**T** *yellow, blue, green*	**T** *yellow, blue, green*
Comprehension	**T** 🎯 **Skill** Realism and Fantasy **Review** Plot	**T** 🎯 **Skill** Cause and Effect **Review** Sequence
Writing	Caption	Rhyme
Conventions	Questions	Question Marks and Capital Letters
Vocabulary	Transportation Words	Position Words
Speaking/Listening	Ask and Answer Questions	Drama: Respond to Literature

Get Ready to Read

Read and Comprehend

Language Arts

How do people and things get from here to there?

WEEK 3	WEEK 4	WEEK 5	WEEK 6
Trucks Roll! Rhyming Nonfiction pp. 264–277	**The Little Engine That Could** Classic Fantasy pp. 363–381	**On the Move!** Nonfiction pp. 468 470	**This Is the Way We Go to School** Informational Fiction pp. 566–583
What kinds of transportation help people do their jobs?	What kind of work do trains do?	How do people in different parts of the world travel?	How do children around the world get to school?
trailers, cabs, haul, steering wheel, truckers, headlight	*engine, tracks, passenger, roundhouse, mountain, valley*	*travel, kayak, llama, dogsled, submarine, double-decker bus*	*cable car, trolley, horse-and-buggy, skis, Metro line, vaporetto*
T /u/	**T** /u/	**T** /v/ **T** /z/	**T** /y/ **T** /kw/
T /u/ Spelled *Uu* **Review** /ks/ Spelled *Xx*	**T** /u/ Spelled *Uu* **Review** Sound-Spellings *Xx, Jj, Ww, Uu*	**T** /v/ Spelled *Vv* **T** /z/ Spelled *Zz* **Review** /u/ Spelled *Uu*	**T** /y/ Spelled *Yy* **T** /kw/ Spelled *Qu* **Review** /v/ Spelled *Vv*; /z/ Spelled *Zz*
T *what, said, was*	**T** *what, said, was*	**T** *where, come*	**T** *where, come*
T Skill Compare and Contrast **Review** Draw Conclusions	**T Skill** Plot **Review** Character	**T Skill** Main Idea **Review** Cause and Effect	**T Skill** Draw Conclusions **Review** Main Idea
Poem	Formal Letter	Invitation	Writing Process: How-to Report
Prepositions	Nouns	Nouns in Sentences	Verbs
Words for Jobs	Time Words	Compound Words	Action Words
Discuss Literature	Sequence	Oral Presentations: Description	Discuss Literary Elements: Plot

Monitor Progress
Make Data-Driven Decisions

Data Management
- Assess
- Diagnose
- Prescribe
- Disaggregate

Classroom Management
- Monitor Progress
- Group
- Differentiate Instruction
- Inform Parents

Don't Wait Until Friday

SUCCESS PREDICTOR	WEEK 1	WEEK 2	WEEK 3	WEEK 4
Phonemic Awareness (Phonemic Awareness)	**T** /j/ **T** /w/	**T** final /ks/	**T** /u/	**T** /u/
Phonics (Sound-Spelling)	**T** /j/ Spelled *Jj* **T** /w/ Spelled *Ww*	**T** /ks/ Spelled *Xx*	**T** /u/ Spelled *Uu*	**T** /u/ Spelled *Uu*
High-Frequency Words (Word Reading)	**T** yellow **T** blue **T** green	**T** yellow **T** blue **T** green	**T** what **T** said **T** was	**T** what **T** said **T** was
Oral Vocabulary/ Concept Development (assessed informally)	plane jetway subway tunnel ferryboat sidecar	rescue pilot yacht sailor mechanic shimmering	trailers cabs haul steering wheel truckers headlight	engine tracks passenger roundhouse mountain valley
Comprehension (Retelling)	**T Skill** Realism and Fantasy **Strategies** Preview and Predict; Retell	**T Skill** Cause and Effect **Strategies** Preview and Predict; Retell	**T Skill** Compare and Contrast **Strategies** Preview and Predict; Retell	**T Skill** Plot **Strategies** Preview and Predict; Retell

Key

T Tested

⊙ Target Skill

WEEK 5	WEEK 6
T ⊙ /v/ **T** ⊙ /z/	**T** ⊙ /y/ **T** ⊙ /kw/
T ⊙ /v/ Spelled *Vv* **T** ⊙ /z/ Spelled *Zz*	**T** ⊙ /y/ Spelled *Yy* **T** ⊙ /kw/ Spelled *Qu*
T where **T** come	**T** where **T** come
travel kayak llama dogsled submarine double-decker bus	cable car trolley horse-and-buggy skis Metro line vaporetto
T ⊙ **Skill** Main Idea **Strategies** Preview and Predict; Retell	**T** ⊙ **Skill** Draw Conclusions **Strategies** Preview and Predict; Retell

GO Digital!

See It!
- **Big Question Video**
- **Concept Talk Video**
- **Envision It! Animations**
- **Sing with Me Animations**

Hear It!
- **Sing with Me Animations**
- **eReaders**
- **Grammar Jammer**
- **Leveled Reader Database**

Do It!
- **Story Sort**
- **Letter Tile Drag and Drop**

UNIT 5

Assessment and Grouping
for Data-Driven Instruction

4-Step Plan for Assessment
1 Diagnose and Differentiate
2 Monitor Progress
3 Assess and Regroup
4 Summative Assessment

STEP 1 Diagnose and Differentiate

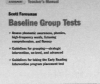

Baseline Group Tests

Diagnose

To make initial grouping decisions, use the Baseline Group Test, the Texas Primary Reading Inventory (TPRI), or another initial placement test. Depending on students' ability levels, you may have more than one of each group.

Differentiate

If... student performance is **SI** **then...** use the regular instruction and the daily Strategic Intervention small group lessons.

If... student performance is **OL** **then...** use the regular instruction and the daily **On-Level** small group lessons.

If... student performance is **A** **then...** use the regular instruction and the daily **Advanced** learners small group lessons.

Small Group Time

SI Strategic Intervention

- Daily small group lessons provide more intensive instruction, more scaffolding, more practice, and more opportunities to respond.
- Reteach lessons in *First Stop* provide instruction of target skills.
- Leveled readers, decodable readers, and other weekly texts build background and provide practice for target skills and vocabulary.

OL On-Level

- Explicit instructional routines teach core skills and strategies.
- Daily On-Level lessons provide more practice and more opportunities to respond.
- Independent activities provide practice for core skills.
- Student Readers and Get Set, Roll! Readers provide additional reading and practice for core skills and vocabulary.

A Advanced

- Daily Advanced lessons provide instruction for accelerated learning.
- Independent Leveled Readers provide additional reading tied to lesson concepts and skills.

Additional Differentiated Learning Options

Reading Street Response to Intervention Kit
- Focused intervention lessons on the five critical areas of reading: phonemic awareness, phonics, vocabulary, comprehension, and fluency

My Sidewalks on Reading Street
- Early Reading Intervention

Don't Wait Until Friday

Use these tools during lesson teaching to **monitor student progress.**

- **Skill and Strategy** instruction during reading

- **Don't Wait Until Friday** boxes to check letter and sound fluency, word reading, retelling, and oral vocabulary

- **Weekly Assessment** on Day 5 to check phonics, high-frequency words, and comprehension

- **Reader's and Writer's Notebook** pages at point of use

Weekly Phonics and High-Frequency Words Assessment

Weekly Comprehension Assessment

Use these tools during lesson teaching to **assess and regroup.**

- **Weekly Assessments** Record results of weekly assessments for phonics and high-frequency words to track student progress.

- **Unit Benchmark Assessment** Administer this assessment to check progress of unit skills.

- **Regroup** We recommend the first regrouping to be at the end of Unit 2. Use weekly assessment information and Unit Benchmark Assessment performance to inform regrouping decisions. Then regroup at the end of each subsequent unit.

Unit 1 Reading Chart in First Stop

Group

Baseline Group Test → **Regroup** Units 1 and 2 → **Regroup** Unit 3 → **Regroup** Unit 4 → **Regroup** Unit 5 → **End of Year**

| Unit 1 Weeks 1–6 | Unit 2 Weeks 7–12 | Unit 3 Weeks 13–18 | Unit 4 Weeks 19–24 | Unit 5 Weeks 25–30 | Unit 6 Weeks 31–36 |

Outside assessments, such as DRA, TPRI, and DIBELS, may recommend regrouping at other times during the year.

Use these tools after lesson teaching to **assess students.**

- **Unit Benchmark Assessments** Use to measure a student's mastery of unit skills.

- **End-of-Year Benchmark Assessment** Use to measure a student's mastery of program skills covered in all six units.

Unit and End-of-Year Benchmark Assessments

Understanding By Design

Grant Wiggins, Ed. D.
Reading Street Author

"We need to go beyond questions answerable by unit facts to questions that burst through the boundaries of the topic. Deep and transferable understandings depend upon framing work around such questions."

Going Places

Reading Street Online

www.ReadingStreet.com

• Big Question Video
• Envision It! Animations
• Story Sort

THE BIG ?

How do people and things get from here to there?

UNIT 5

Small Group Time
Flexible Pacing Plans

Small Group Time

Sometimes you have holidays, programs, assemblies, or other interruptions to the school week. This plan can help you make Small Group Time decisions if you have less time during the week.

Key

SI Strategic Intervention
OL On Level
A Advanced
ELL ELL

SI OL A

5 Day Plan

DAY 1
- Phonemic Awareness
- Phonics
- Reading Practice

DAY 2
- Phonemic Awareness
- Phonics
- Reading Practice

DAY 3
- Phonemic Awareness/ Phonics
- Leveled Reader

DAY 4
- Phonemic Awareness
- Reading Practice

DAY 5
- Phonics
- Reading Practice

4 Day Plan

DAY 1
- Phonemic Awareness
- Phonics
- Reading Practice

DAY 2
- Phonemic Awareness
- Phonics
- Reading Practice

DAY 3
- Phonemic Awareness/ Phonics
- Leveled Reader

DAY 4
- Phonemic Awareness
- Reading Practice

3 Day Plan

DAY 1
- Phonemic Awareness
- Phonics
- Reading Practice

DAY 2
- Phonemic Awareness/ Phonics
- Leveled Reader

DAY 3
- Phonemic Awareness
- Reading Practice

 ELL

5 Day Plan

DAY 1
- Frontload Concept
- Phonemic Awareness/ Phonics
- Comprehension

DAY 2
- Comprehension
- Vocabulary

DAY 3
- Phonemic Awareness/ Phonics
- Conventions

DAY 4
- Phonemic Awareness/ Phonics
- Concepts and Oral Language

DAY 5
- Writing
- Language Workshop

4 Day Plan

DAY 1
- Frontload Concept
- Phonemic Awareness/ Phonics
- Comprehension

DAY 2
- Comprehension
- Vocabulary

DAY 3
- Phonemic Awareness/ Phonics
- Conventions

DAY 4
- Writing
- Language Workshop

3 Day Plan

DAY 1
- Frontload Concept
- Phonemic Awareness/ Phonics
- Comprehension

DAY 2
- Phonemic Awareness/ Phonics
- Conventions

DAY 3
- Writing
- Language Workshop

This Week's ELL Overview

ELL Handbook

- Maximize Literacy and Cognitive Engagement
- Research Into Practice
- Full Weekly Support for Every Selection

   The Little Engine That Could
   - Routines to Support Instruction

- Transfer Activities
- Professional Development

Daily Leveled ELL Notes

ELL notes appear throughout this week's instruction and ELL Support is on the DI pages of your Teacher's Edition. The following is a sample of an ELL note from this week.

English Language Learners

Beginning Build Background Use the picture on Phonics Songs and Rhymes Chart 28 to help children understand the definition of *suds.* Point to the suds in the picture. Explain where suds come from and have children share the word for *suds* in their home language.

Intermediate Support Sound Production Tell children to say /u/ with an open mouth, keeping the tongue down and pushing the air from the back of their throats.

Advanced Survival Vocabulary Explain to children that if they don't understand what someone says and they need the words repeated, they can say *Excuse me?* instead of *What?* Say *Excuse me?* and have children repeat.

Advanced High Vocabulary Children's home languages also have words for people, animals, places, and things. To help them learn English nouns, bring items—apples, hats, dolls, toys, dishes, and so forth—for vocabulary building. As children learn English nouns, have them share the equivalent noun in their home language.

ELL by Strand

The ELL lessons on this week's Support for English Language Learners pages are organized by strand. They offer additional scaffolding for the core curriculum Leveled support notes on these pages address the different proficiency levels in your class. See pages DI•63–DI•68.

ELL Guy
Dr. Jim Cummins

The Three Pillars of ELL Instruction

ELL Strands	Activate Prior Knowledge	Access Content	Extend Language
Vocabulary p. DI•65	Frontload Vocabulary	Provide Scaffolding	Practice
Reading Comprehension p. DI•65	Provide Scaffolding	Set the Scene	Frontload Vocabulary
Phonics, Spelling, and Word Analysis pp. DI•63, DI•66–DI•67	Frontload Words with /u/	Isolate Initial and Medial /u/	Review Initial and Medial /u/
Listening Comprehension p. DI•64	Prepare for the Read Aloud	First Listening	Second Listening
Conventions and Writing pp. DI•66, DI•68	Provide Scaffolding/ Introduce and Model	Practice	Leveled Practice Activities/ Leveled Writing Activities
Concept Development p. DI•63	Read the Concept Literacy Reader	Read the Concept Literacy Reader	Develop Oral Language

This Week's Practice Stations Overview

Six Weekly Practice Stations with Leveled Activities can be found at the beginning of each week of instruction. For this week's Practice Stations, see pp. 318–319.

Practice Stations

Classroom Management Handbook for Differentiated Instruction Practice Stations

Daily Leveled Center Activities

● Below   ■ Advanced

▲ On-Level   ⓔⓛⓛ

Practice Stations Flip Charts

	Listen Up	**Word Work**	**Words to Know**	**Let's Write**	**Read for Meaning**	**Let's Make Art**
Objectives	• Identify words with the short *u*. • Practice saying words with short *u* sound, /u/.	• Identify words with short *u*. • Build words with short *u*.	• Identify and use words for jobs: *pilot, conductor, astronaut, truck driver*.	• Write a poem about transportation.	• Compare by telling how things are alike. • Contrast by telling how things are different.	• Draw or paint a poster for a movie about transportation.
Materials	• *Listen Up* Flip Chart Activity 28 • Picture Cards: *bus, drums, gum, jug, mug, nut, rug, sun, tub, umbrella, up*	• *Word Work* Flip Chart Activity 28 • Alphabet Cards • Picture Cards • Letter Tiles	• *Words to Know* Flip Chart Activity 28 • Picture Cards: *astronaut, jet, train, truck* • Teacher-made Word Cards: *conductor, pilot, truck driver, spaceship* • paper, pencil, crayons	• *Let's Write* Flip Chart Activity 28 • Picture Cards • books showing people using different kinds of transportation • crayons, paper, pencil	• *Read for Meaning* Flip Chart Activity 28 • Little Book *Trucks Roll!* • pencil, crayons, paper	• *Let's Make Art* Flip Chart Activity 28 • variety of books about transportation and jobs that people do • art paper, crayons, finger paint

This Week on Reading Street!

Going Places

Question of the Week
What kind of work do trains do?

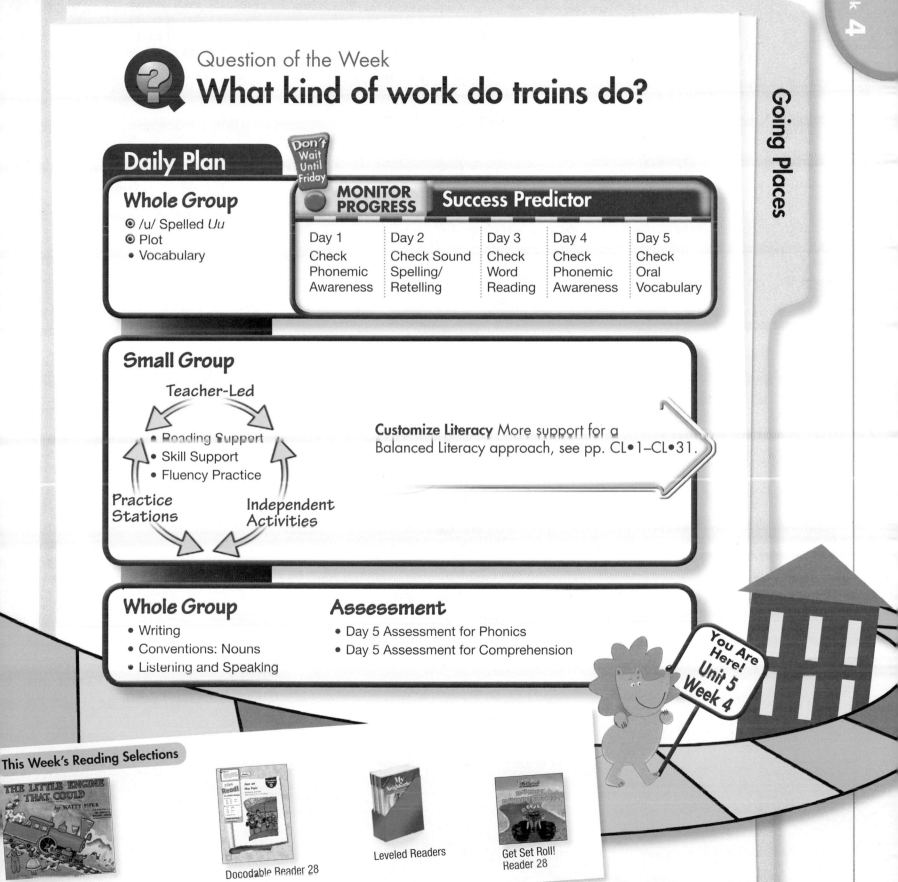

Daily Plan

Whole Group
- /u/ Spelled *Uu*
- Plot
- Vocabulary

Don't Wait Until Friday

MONITOR PROGRESS | **Success Predictor**

Day 1	Day 2	Day 3	Day 4	Day 5
Check Phonemic Awareness	Check Sound Spelling/ Retelling	Check Word Reading	Check Phonemic Awareness	Check Oral Vocabulary

Small Group

Teacher-Led
- Reading Support
- Skill Support
- Fluency Practice

Practice Stations

Independent Activities

Customize Literacy More support for a Balanced Literacy approach, see pp. CL•1–CL•31.

Whole Group
- Writing
- Conventions: Nouns
- Listening and Speaking

Assessment
- Day 5 Assessment for Phonics
- Day 5 Assessment for Comprehension

You Are Here! Unit 5 Week 4

This Week's Reading Selections

THE LITTLE ENGINE THAT COULD by WATTY PIPER

Trade Book
Genre: **Classic Fantasy**

Decodable Reader 28

Leveled Readers

Get Set Roll! Reader 28

Resources on Reading Street!

	Build Concepts	Phonemic Awareness and Phonics	Vocabulary
Whole Group	Talk With Me/ Sing With Me	Student Edition pp. 72–73 Student Edition p. 76	Student Edition p. 77 Student Edition p. 88
Go Digital	• Concept Talk Video • Sing with Me Animations	• eReaders	
Small Group and Independent Practice	Practice Station Flip Chart Leveled Readers	Practice Station Flip Chart Decodable Reader 28 Leveled Readers Get Set, Roll! Reader 28	Practice Station Flip Chart Student Edition p. 77
Go Digital	• eReaders	• eReaders • Letter Tile Drag and Drop	
Customize Literacy	• Leveled Readers	• Decodable Reader	• High-Frequency Word Cards
Go Digital	• Concept Talk Video • Big Question Video • eReaders	• eReaders	• Sing with Me Animations

Question of the Week
What kind of work do trains do?

Comprehension

Student Edition pp. 74–75

Trade Book

- Envision It! Animations

Practice Station Flip Chart

Leveled Readers

Get Set, Roll! Reader 28

- Envision It! Animations
- eReaders

- Leveled Readers

- Envision It! Animations
- eReaders

Fluency

Decodable Reader 28

Kdg. Student Reader K.5.4

Get Set, Roll! Reader 28

- eReaders

Practice Station Flip Chart

Leveled Readers

- eReaders

- Leveled Readers

- eReaders

Conventions and Writing

Reader's and Writer's Notebook

- Grammar Jammer

Practice Station Flip Chart

Reader's and Writer's Notebook

- Grammar Jammer

- *Reader's and Writer's Notebook*

- Grammar Jammer

Week 4

You Are Here!
Unit 5
Week 4

My 5-Day Planner for Reading Street!

Don't Wait Until Friday MONITOR PROGRESS

	Check Phonemic Awareness **Day 1** pages 320–335	Check Sound-Spelling Check Retelling **Day 2** pages 336–353

Get Ready to Read	**Concept Talk,** 320
	Oral Vocabulary, 321 *engine, tracks, passenger, roundhouse, mountain, valley*
	Phonemic Awareness, 322–323
	  ◉ Initial and Medial /u/
	Phonics, 324–325
	  ◉ /u/ Spelled *Uu*
	Handwriting, 326 Letters *U* and *u*
	High-Frequency Words, 327 Introduce *what, said, was*
	READ Decodable Story 28, 328–329
		Concept Talk, 336
		Oral Vocabulary, 337 *engine, tracks*
		Phonemic Awareness, 338–339
		  ◉ Initial and Medial /u/
		Phonics, 340–341
		  ◉ /u/ Spelled *Uu*
		Handwriting, 342 Words with *Uu*
		High-Frequency Words, 343 *what, said, was*
		READ Decodable Reader 28, 344–345

Read and Comprehend	**Listening Comprehension,** 330–331
	  ◉ Plot
		Listening Comprehension, 346
		  ◉ Plot
		READ Trade Book—First Read, 346
		  The Little Engine That Could
		Retell, 347
		Think, Talk, and Write, 348

Language Arts	**Conventions,** 332 Nouns **Writing,** 333 Wonderful, Marvelous Me! **Daily Handwriting,** 333 Letters *U* and *u* **Listening and Speaking,** 334 Sequence **Wrap Up Your Day,** 334 **Extend Your Day!,** 335	**Conventions,** 349 Nouns **Writing,** 350 Respond to Literature **Daily Handwriting,** 350 Letters *U* and *u* **Vocabulary,** 351 Time Words **Wrap Up Your Day,** 352 **Extend Your Day!,** 353

You Are Here! Unit 5 Week 4

Question of the Week
What kind of work do trains do?

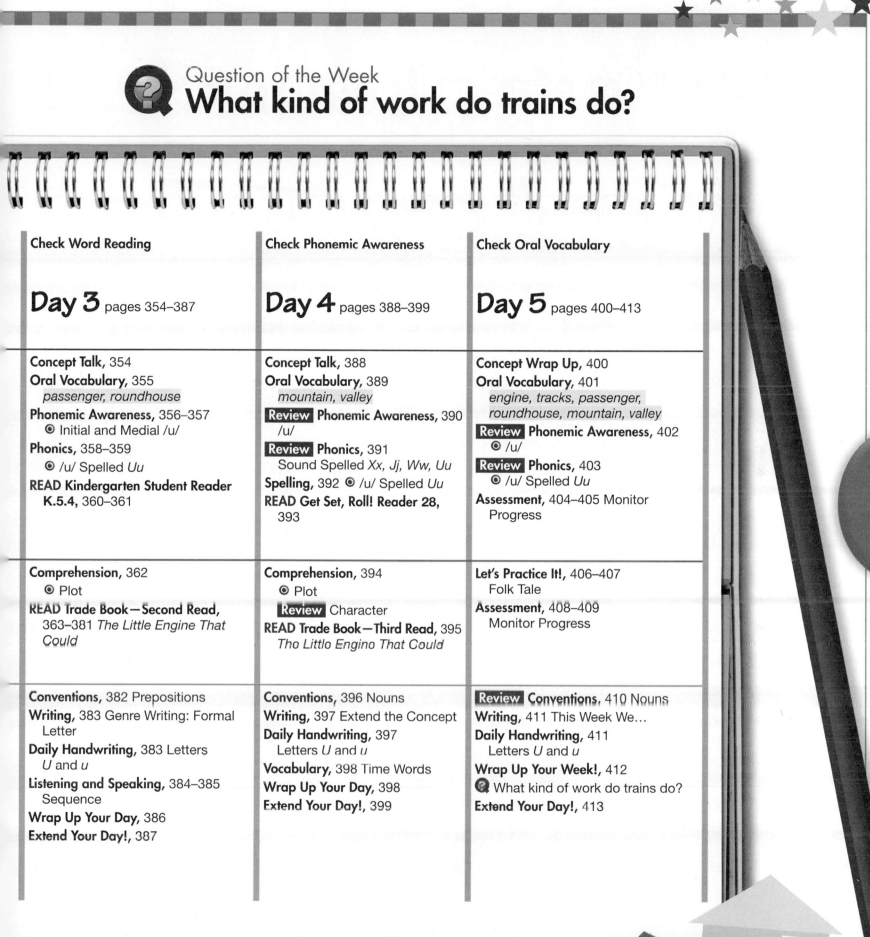

Check Word Reading	Check Phonemic Awareness	Check Oral Vocabulary
Day 3 pages 354–387	**Day 4** pages 388–399	**Day 5** pages 400–413
Concept Talk, 354 **Oral Vocabulary,** 355 *passenger, roundhouse* **Phonemic Awareness,** 356–357 ◉ Initial and Medial /u/ **Phonics,** 358–359 ◉ /u/ Spelled *Uu* **READ Kindergarten Student Reader K.5.4,** 360–361	**Concept Talk,** 388 **Oral Vocabulary,** 389 *mountain, valley* **Review** **Phonemic Awareness,** 390 /u/ **Review** **Phonics,** 391 Sound Spelled *Xx, Jj, Ww, Uu* **Spelling,** 392 ◉ /u/ Spelled *Uu* **READ Get Set, Roll! Reader 28,** 393	**Concept Wrap Up,** 400 **Oral Vocabulary,** 401 *engine, tracks, passenger, roundhouse, mountain, valley* **Review** **Phonemic Awareness,** 402 ◉ /u/ **Review** **Phonics,** 403 ◉ /u/ Spelled *Uu* **Assessment,** 404–405 Monitor Progress
Comprehension, 362 ◉ Plot **READ Trade Book—Second Read,** 363–381 *The Little Engine That Could*	**Comprehension,** 394 ◉ Plot **Review** Character **READ Trade Book—Third Read,** 395 *The Little Engine That Could*	**Let's Practice It!,** 406–407 Folk Tale **Assessment,** 408–409 Monitor Progress
Conventions, 382 Prepositions **Writing,** 383 Genre Writing: Formal Letter **Daily Handwriting,** 383 Letters *U* and *u* **Listening and Speaking,** 384–385 Sequence **Wrap Up Your Day,** 386 **Extend Your Day!,** 387	**Conventions,** 396 Nouns **Writing,** 397 Extend the Concept **Daily Handwriting,** 397 Letters *U* and *u* **Vocabulary,** 398 Time Words **Wrap Up Your Day,** 398 **Extend Your Day!,** 399	**Review** **Conventions,** 410 Nouns **Writing,** 411 This Week We… **Daily Handwriting,** 411 Letters *U* and *u* **Wrap Up Your Week!,** 412 What kind of work do trains do? **Extend Your Day!,** 413

Week 4

Grouping Options for Differentiated Instruction
Turn the page for the small group time lesson plan.

Planning Small Group Time on Reading Street!

SMALL GROUP TIME RESOURCES

DAY 1

Look for this Small Group Time box each day to help meet the individual needs of all your children. Differentiated instruction lessons appear on the DI pages at the end of each week.

Teacher-Led

SI Strategic Intervention	OL On-Level	A Advanced
Teacher-Led • Phonemic Awareness and Phonics **Reread** Decodable Story	**Teacher-Led** • Phonemic Awareness and Phonics **Reread** Decodable Story	**Teacher-Led** • Phonemic Awareness and Phonics **Reread** Decodable Story for Fluency

ELL Place English language learners in the groups that correspond to their reading abilities in English.

Practice Stations
• Listen Up
• Word Work

Independent Activities
• Read Independently
• *Reader's and Writer's Notebook*
• Concept Talk Video

ELL

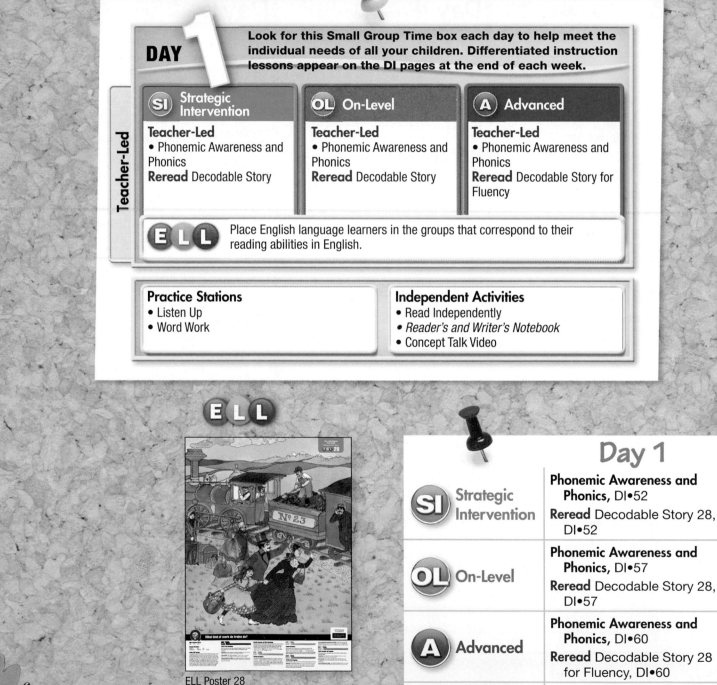

ELL Poster 28

Day 1

SI Strategic Intervention	**Phonemic Awareness and Phonics,** DI•52 **Reread** Decodable Story 28, DI•52
OL On-Level	**Phonemic Awareness and Phonics,** DI•57 **Reread** Decodable Story 28, DI•57
A Advanced	**Phonemic Awareness and Phonics,** DI•60 **Reread** Decodable Story 28 for Fluency, DI•60
ELL English Language Learners	DI•63–DI•64 Frontload Concept Phonemic Awareness and Phonics Comprehension Skill

You Are Here! Unit 5 Week 4

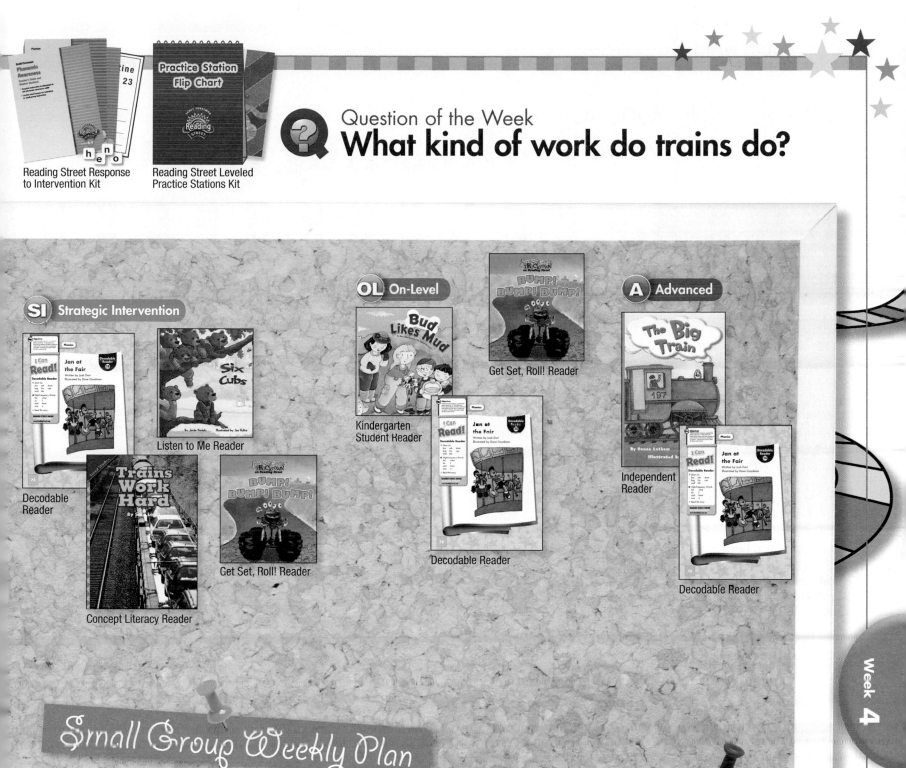

Reading Street Response to Intervention Kit

Reading Street Leveled Practice Stations Kit

SI Strategic Intervention

Decodable Reader

Listen to Me Reader

Concept Literacy Reader

Get Set, Roll! Reader

OL On-Level

Kindergarten Student Reader

Decodable Reader

Get Set, Roll! Reader

A Advanced

Independent Reader

Decodable Reader

Small Group Weekly Plan

Day 2	Day 3	Day 4	Day 5
Phonemic Awareness and Phonics, DI•53 **Reread** Decodable Reader 28, DI•53	**Phonemic Awareness and Phonics,** DI•54 **Read** Concept Literacy Reader K.5.4, DI•54	**Phonemic Awareness and Phonics,** DI•55 **Read** Get Set, Roll! Reader 28, DI•55	**Phonics Review,** DI•56 **Read** Listen to Me Reader K.5.4, DI•56
Phonemic Awareness and Phonics, DI•57 **Reread** Decodable Reader 28	**Phonemic Awareness and Phonics,** DI•58 **Read** Kindergarten Student Reader K.5.4, DI•58	**Review Phonics and High-Frequency Words** **Read** Get Set, Roll! Reader 28, DI•59	**Phonics Review,** DI•59 **Reread** Leveled Books, DI•59
Phonics and Spelling, DI•60 **Reread** Decodable Reader 28 for Fluency, DI•60	**Read** Independent Reader K.5.4 or Kindergarten Student Reader K.5.4, DI•61	**Read** Get Set, Roll! Reader 28 or **Reread** Kindergarten Student Reader K.5.4, DI•62	**Fluency and Comprehension,** DI•62 **Reread** Independent Reader for Fluency, DI•62
DI•65 Comprehension Skill Frontload Vocabulary	DI•66 Review Phonemic Awareness and Phonics Scaffold Conventions	DI•67 Review Phonemic Awareness and Phonics Revisit Concept and Oral Language	DI•68 Language Workshop Writing

Practice Stations for Everyone on Reading Street!

Listen Up!
Words with Short *u*

Objectives
- Identify words with the short *u*.
- Practice saying words with short *u* sound, /u/.

Materials
- *Listen Up!* Flip Chart Activity 28
- Picture Cards: *bus, drums, gum, jug, mug, nut, rug, sun, tub, umbrella, up*

Differentiated Activities

⬤ Find the Picture Card for *umbrella*. Say the sound you hear at the beginning. Find the Picture Card for *tub*. Say the sound you hear in the middle. Draw a picture of a word that has the sound you hear at the beginning of *umbrella*.

▲ Find the Picture Card for *umbrella*. Say the sound you hear at the beginning. Find the Picture Card for *tub*. Say the sound you hear in the middle. Draw a picture of a word with the /u/ sound in the middle.

■ Find the Picture Card for *umbrella*. Say the sound you hear at the beginning. Look at the Picture Card for *tub*. Say the sound you hear in the middle. Draw pictures that show other words with short *u* at the beginning or in the middle.

Word Work
/u/ Spelled *Uu*

Objectives
- Identify words with short *u*.
- Build words with short *u*.

Materials
- *Word Work* Flip Chart Activity 28
- Alphabet Cards: *Uu* and five other cards
- Picture Cards: *drum, duck, tub, rug, mug, bed, ant, van, wig,* and *cat*
- Letter Tiles

Differentiated Activities

⬤ Find the Alphabet Card for the letter *Uu*. Find a Picture Card with the /u/ sound at the beginning or in the middle. Use the Letter Tiles to build a word with the short sound.

▲ Find the Alphabet Card for the letter *Uu*. Find all the Picture Cards with the /u/ sound at the beginning or in the middle. Use the Letter Tiles to build two words with the short *u* sound.

■ Find the Alphabet Card for the letter *Uu*. Find all the Picture Cards with the /u/ sound at the beginning or in the middle. Look around the room. Find other objects that have the /u/ sound. Use the Letter Tiles to spell three words with short *u*.

Technology
- Letter Tile Drag and Drop

Words To Know
Words for jobs

Objectives
- Identify and use words for jobs: *pilot, conductor, astronaut, truck driver.*

Materials
- *Words to Know* Flip Chart Activity 28
- Picture Cards: *astronaut, jet, train, truck*
- Teacher-made word cards: *conductor, pilot, truck driver, spaceship*
- paper, pencil, crayons

Differentiated Activities

⬤ Work with a partner to choose a Picture Card. Say the name of the picture. Find a word card that goes with your picture to name the transportation or the job.

▲ Match all the Picture Cards and word cards so that you have four sets of matched jobs and transportation.

■ Match all the Picture Cards and word cards so that you have four sets of matched jobs and transportation. Then draw a picture of some other kind of transportation and write the job that goes with it.

You Are Here! Unit 5 Week 4

Key

Let's Write!
Poem

Objectives
• Write a poem about transportation.

Materials
• *Let's Write!* Flip Chart Activity 28
• Picture Cards: *bus, van, train, truck, jet, boat, taxi*
• books showing people using different kinds of transportation.
• crayons, paper, pencil

Differentiated Activities

● Look at the Picture Cards and the books. Think about the ways you like to go places. Write a poem about your favorite way to go places. Draw a picture to go with your poem.

▲ Look at the Picture Cards and the books about transportation. Write a four-line poem about different ways to go places. Draw pictures to go with your poem.

■ Write an eight-line poem about different kinds of transportation. Use action words to tell how people go places. Draw pictures to go with your poem.

Read For Meaning
Compare and contrast

Objectives
• Compare by telling how things are alike.
• Contrast by telling how things are different.

Materials
• *Read for Meaning* Flip Chart Activity 28
• Little Book *Trucks Roll!*
• pencil, crayons, paper

Differentiated Activities

When we **compare** we tell how things are alike. When we **contrast** we tell how things are different.

● Read your book. Point to pictures in the selection that show things that are alike. Point to pictures in the selection that show things that are different.

▲ Read your book. Point to two trucks in the selection. Write a sentence that tells how they are alike. Write a sentence that tells how they are different.

■ Read your book. Find two trucks in your book that are similar. Compare by telling how they are alike. Contrast by telling how they are different.

Let's Make Art!

Objectives
• Draw or paint a poster for a movie about transportation.

Materials
• *Let's Make Art!* Flip Chart Activity 28
• variety of books about transportation and jobs that people do
• art paper, crayons, finger paint

Differentiated Activities

● Look at the books. Think about a movie about transportation. Use your art supplies to make a movie poster about transportation.

▲ Look at the books to get ideas about transportation. Think about a movie about different kinds of transportation that people use in jobs. Make a poster to show what the movie is about.

■ Look at the books to get ideas about transportation. Think about a movie about different kinds of transportation that people use in jobs. Make a poster that would make people want to see the movie. Make sure it has an exciting title.

Week 4

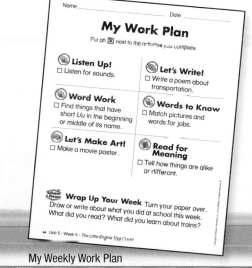

My Weekly Work Plan

Objectives

• Share information and ideas about the concept.

Today at a Glance

Oral Vocabulary
engine, tracks, passenger, round-house, mountain, valley

Phonemic Awareness
◉ Initial and Medial /u/

Phonics
◉ /u/ Spelled *Uu*

Handwriting
U and *u*

High-Frequency Words
what, said, was

Comprehension
◉ Plot

Conventions
Nouns

Writing
Wonderful, Marvelous Me!

Listening and Speaking
Sequence

TRUCKTOWN on Reading Street

Start your engines! Display p. 11 of *Truckery Rhymes.*

• Read aloud "Patty Cake, Patty Cake" and track the print.

• Reread the rhyme and have children chime in as they wish.

• Ask children to identify the rhyming words. (*Dan, can; DD, me*)

Truckery Rhymes

Concept Talk

Question of the Week

What kind of work do trains do?

Introduce the concept

To build concepts and to focus their attention, tell children that this week they will listen, talk, sing, read, and write about **trains.** Write the question of the week and track the print as you read it.

Play the CD that features a conductor giving a tour of a train to a boy and his mom. Are there different kinds of trains? Can you name them?

💿 Background Building Audio

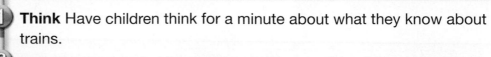

ROUTINE — **Activate Prior Knowledge** — **Team Talk**

1. **Think** Have children think for a minute about what they know about trains.

2. **Pair** Have pairs of children discuss the question of the week. Remind them to take turns speaking. Have children use complete sentences in their discussions about trains.

3. **Share** Call on a few children to share their ideas with the group. Guide discussion and encourage elaboration with prompts such as: Have you ever seen a train? Have you ever traveled on a train?

Routines Flip Chart

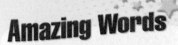
Anchored Talk

Develop oral language

Display Talk with Me Chart 28A. Some of these pictures show different parts of a train. What do you know about trains? Have you ever been on a train? Other pictures show where trains can go. What do these places look like? What do you think it would be like to travel on a train in these places?

We are going to learn six new Amazing Words this week. Listen as I say each word: *engine, tracks, passenger, roundhouse, mountain, valley*. Have children say each word as you point to the picture.

Display Sing with Me Chart 28B. Today we are going to sing a song about a small train engine that helped to bring toys to children. Listen for the Amazing Words *engine, tracks, passenger, roundhouse, mountain,* and *valley*. Read the title and have children describe the picture. Sing the song several times to the tune of "On Top of Old Smoky." Have children stand up and sing with you.

 Sing with Me Audio

Talk with Me/Sing with Me Chart 28A

On the Tracks to the Mountain

On the tracks to the mountain,
chugged a train so sweet,
Taking toys to the valley,
for young ones to meet.

Along came passengers,
on a fast-moving train,
They returned to the roundhouse,
"Too busy!" they claimed.

A small engine came by,
and helped in her way,
To bring toys to children, on this happy day.

Talk with Me/Sing with Me Chart 28B

ELL **Preteach Concepts** Use the Day 1 instruction on ELL Poster 28 to assess and build background knowledge, develop concepts, and build oral vocabulary.

ELL Poster 28

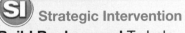
Differentiated Instruction

SI Strategic Intervention

Build Background To help children understand words in the story such as *mountain* and *valley,* use the art. Talk with children about how these places are related.

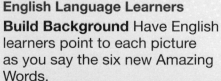 **ELL**

English Language Learners

Build Background Have English learners point to each picture as you say the six new Amazing Words.

ELL Support Additional ELL support and modified instruction is provided in the *ELL Handbook* and in the ELL Support lessons on pp. DI•63–68.

Objectives

◎ Practice initial and medial /u/.

• Identify words with initial and medial /u/.

Check Phonemic Awareness

! SUCCESS PREDICTOR

My Skills Buddy, pp. 72–73

Phonemic Awareness
◉ Initial and Medial /u/

Practice

Today we will practice a sound we have heard before: /u/. Say some words with /u/ with me: /u/, *fun*; /u/, *run*; /u/, *up*; /u/, *Bud.* Display the *umbrella* Picture Card. *Umbrella* begins with /u/ /u/ /u/, *umbrella*. What sound does *umbrella* begin with? Display the *gum* Picture Card. *Gum* has /u/ in the middle. Listen carefully: *gum*. What middle sound does *gum* have? (/u/) Continue with the *up* and *sun* Picture Cards.

Picture Card

Model

Have children look at the picture on pp. 72–73 of *My Skills Buddy*. Tell them they will be listening for a familiar sound—/u/. Some of this picture takes place *underwater*. What sound do you hear at the beginning of *underwater*? I hear /u/ at the beginning of *underwater*. The first sound in *underwater* is /u/. What other things do you see that begin with that sound? What things have the same middle sound as *gum*?

Guide practice

As children name example words from the picture, guide them in identifying that /u/ is the middle sound. Discuss with children some of the bulleted items on

Picture Card

p. 72 of *My Skills Buddy*. Save the other bulleted items for discussion on Day 2.

Corrective feedback

If... children have difficulty naming words with /u/, **then...** say *underwater* again, emphasizing the /u/ sound— /u/ /u/ /u/, *underwater*.

Discriminate sounds

I am going to say two words. Listen carefully to the first sound in each word. One word begins with /u/, and the other word does not: *apple, under. Under* begins with /u/. Repeat these word sets: *apple, under; us, jump; up, sock.*

Now listen to these pairs of words. Which word has the same middle sound as *rug?* Say the following word pairs: *mud, spot; brush, bed; fun, feet.*

Let's listen for /u/. If the word begins with /u/, stand up. If the word has /u/ in the middle, sit on the floor. Listen carefully: *bus* (sit on floor); *up* (stand); *cup* (sit on floor); *mug* (sit on floor); *rug* (sit on floor); *sun* (sit on floor); *us* (stand).

Corrective feedback

If... children cannot discriminate /u/, **then...** have them enunciate /u/ as they say *bus.*

When you say /u/, make sure your lips are unrounded and the muscles in your face are relaxed. See how my lips look when I say *bus.* Now watch my lips when I say *bus.* Say *bus* with me: *bus, bus, bus.*

Sound substitution

If I take away the /u/ in *rug,* what would I have left? (/r/ and /g/) If I change /u/ to /a/, what word will I make? Let's try it: /r/ /a/ /g/, *rag.* The new word is *rag.* Substitute the medial sound in the word *bug* to create the words *bag, beg,* and *big.*

Don't Wait Until Friday

MONITOR PROGRESS ○ Check Phonemic Awareness Words with Initial and Medial /u/

Say *up* and *ant.* Have children identify the word with /u/. Continue with the following word pairs: *hug, hog; cut, cot; jug, jig; rub, rob.*

If... children cannot discriminate /u/ words,

then... use the small-group Strategic Intervention lesson, p. DI•52, to reteach /u/.

Day 1	**Day 2**	**Day 3**	**Day 4**	**Day 5**
Check Phonemic Awareness	Check Sound-Spelling/ Retelling	Check Word Reading	Check Phonemic Awareness	Check Oral Vocabulary

Success Predictor

Differentiated Instruction

Ⓐ **Advanced**

Support Phonemic Awareness
After studying the picture on pp. 72–73 of *My Skills Buddy,* have children draw their own picture. Ask them to include objects that begin with /u/ or have /u/ in the middle.

ELL

English Language Learners
Support Sound Production
Tell children to say /u/ with an open mouth, keeping the tongue down and pushing the air from the back of their throats.

Phonemic Awareness

Success Predictor

Objectives

◎ Associate the sound /u/ with the spelling *u*.

• Blend and read words with /u/.

Skills Trace

◎ **Short *u* Spelled *Uu***

Introduce U5W3D1; U5W4D1; U6W4D1

Practice U5W3D2; U5W3D3; U5W4D2; U5W4D3; U6W4D2; U6W4D3

Reteach/Review U5W3D5; U5W4D4; U5W4D5; U5W5D4; U6W4D5

Assess/Test Benchmark Assessment U5; U6

KEY:

U=Unit   W=Week   D=Day

Phonics — Teach/Model
 ## /u/ Spelled *Uu*

Introduce

Display the *Uu* Alphabet Card. Point to the *umbrella* on the Alphabet Card. *Umbrella* begins with /u/. Say the word with me, *umbrella*. Write *umbrella* on the board and point to the *u*. *Umbrella* begins with /u/ spelled *u*. Now point to the letters *Uu* on the card. The sound for this letter is /u/. The names for these letters are uppercase *U* and lowercase *u*. What is the sound for this letter? What are the names for these letters?

Alphabet Card

Model

Write the word *Bud* on the board. Point to the *u*. When I see this letter, I think of the sound /u/. In this word, I see *u* in the middle. Listen carefully: *Bud*. What middle sound does *Bud* have? *Bud* has /u/ in the middle. The song we will sing is "Bud."

Guide practice

Display Phonics Songs and Rhymes Chart 28. Teach children the song "Bud," sung to the tune of "Mary Had a Little Lamb." Play the CD or sing the song with children several times. Let's look for /u/ words. Here is a word that has *u* in the middle: *mud*. Have children point out the words *Bud, bubbly, tub, suds,* and *full*.

Phonics Songs and Rhymes Audio

Phonics Songs and Rhymes Chart 28

On their own

Have children write uppercase *U* and lowercase *u* on index cards. Display Picture Cards *drum, duck, jug, nut, up,* and *tub* on the board. Have children take turns saying an /u/ word and placing the *Uu* card on the picture.

Blend Words

Review To review sound-spellings, use Alphabet Cards *Aa, Bb, Dd, Ff, Gg, Jj, Mm, Nn, Rr,* and *Ss* and the *ant, bag, dog, fan, gum, jug, mop, nut, rug,* and *sun* Picture Cards. Then use this routine for sound-by-sound blending to have children blend new words.

ROUTINE Sound-by-Sound Blending

1 **Connect** Write the letter *u*. What is the sound for this letter? The sound is /u/. Say it with me: /u/ /u/ /u/. When you see this letter in a word, what sound will you say?

2 **Model** Write *hum* on the board.

- Touch under the letter *h*. What is the sound for this letter? Say it with me: /h/ /h/ /h/. Repeat the routine touching under *u* and *m*.

- Let's blend the sounds together. Listen as I blend the sounds: /h/ /u/ /m/. Say it with me: /h/ /u/ /m/, *hum*. Now say it without me.

- Listen as I use *hum* in a sentence: *I can hum a happy song.* Say it with me. Then have children use *hum* in their own sentences.

3 **Guide Practice** Continue the routine established in step 2 with the words below:

| bug | bus | fun | Gus | mug | rug | run | sun | Jan |

Children should successfully read these words before reading Decodable Story 28 on p. 359 of *Reader's and Writer's Notebook.*

Corrective Feedback If children have trouble reading a word, model blending the sounds to read the word. Then have children say it with you.

Routines Flip Chart

Differentiated Instruction

SI Strategic Intervention

Blending If children have difficulty discriminating the medial sounds, have them say each word without the initial sound.

Teacher Tip

When teaching the blending strategy, make sure that children look at the letters from left to right when blending.

English Language Learners
Pronunciation In Italian, the letter *u* is pronounced like the *oo* sound in *boot.* If children experience difficulty producing the /u/ sound, give them extra practice with words such as *fun, sun,* and *run.*

Objectives
- Write *U* and *u*.
- Learn high-frequency words.

Handwriting

Introduce

Write *Uu* on the board. Words that begin with /u/ are written with an uppercase *U* or lowercase *u*. Which letter is uppercase *U*? Which letter is lowercase *u*?

Model uppercase U

Write *Uncle Bud* on the board. This is the name *Uncle Bud*. We use uppercase letters to begin sentences and for the first letter in a name. Watch as I trace the uppercase *U* with my finger. Follow the stroke instructions below.

Guide practice

Have children write the uppercase *U* in the air. Use your finger to make an uppercase *U* in the air. Now write it on the palm of your hand.

Model lowercase u

Point to the lowercase *u* in *Bud.* This is a lowercase *u*. Watch as I trace a lowercase *u* with my finger. Write another lowercase *u* on the board following the stroke instructions. Again, have children write *u* in the air and on their hands.

Guide practice

Have children use their Write-On Boards to write a row of uppercase *U* and a row of lowercase *u*.

U *u* *U* *u*

D'Nealian™   Ball and Stick

More practice

Use *Reader's and Writer's Notebook*, pp. 357, 358, for additional practice with *u*.

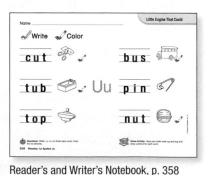

Reader's and Writer's Notebook, p. 357   Reader's and Writer's Notebook, p. 358

High-Frequency Words

Introduce

Use the routine below to teach high-frequency words *what, said,* and *was.*

ROUTINE

Nondecodable Words

1 **Say and Spell** Some words we have to learn by remembering the letters rather than saying the sounds. We will say and spell the words to help learn them. Write *what* on the board. This is the word *what*. It has four letters. The letters in *what* are *w, h, a, t*. Have children say and spell the word, first with you and then without you.

2 **Demonstrate Meaning** I can use the word *what* in lots of sentences. Here is one sentence: *What color is the sun?* Now you use the word in a sentence.

Repeat the routine with the words *said* and *was.*

Add the words *said* and *was* to the Word Wall.

Routines Flip Chart

Academic Vocabulary

Write the following on the board:

noun	preposition
plot	sequence
folk tale	formal letter

Point to the list. This week we are going to learn these important words. They are tools for learning. As we work this week, you will hear them many times. Read the words. Preteach the Academic Vocabulary at point-of-use by providing a child-friendly description, explanation, or example that clarifies the meaning of each term. Then ask children to restate the meaning of the Academic Vocabulary in their own words.

Differentiated Instruction

SI **Strategic Intervention**

Access Content Explain to children that the word *Uncle* is written with an uppercase *U* because *Uncle* is part of *Bud*'s name. When the word *uncle* is written by itself, it is written with a lowercase *u.*

English Language Learners
Formal/Informal English
Explain to children that if they don't understand what someone says and they need the words repeated, they can say *Excuse me?* instead of *What?* Say *Excuse me?* and have children repeat.

Objectives
- Read high-frequency words.
- Decode and read words in context and isolation.

Decodable Story 28
/u/ Spelled *Uu* and High-Frequency Words

Review

Review the following high-frequency words by having children read each word as you point to it on the Word Wall.

are	have	the	like	to	they	see	a

Read Decodable Story 28

Display Decodable Story 28, *Jan and Gus*. Today we will read a story about two pals who like to have fun. Point to the title of the story. The title of the story is *Jan and Gus*. What is the title of the story? We will read lots of /u/ words in this story. Have children read Decodable Story 28 on p. 359 in *Reader's and Writer's Notebook.*

Use the routine for reading decodable books to read Decodable Story 28.

Reader's and Writer's Notebook, pp. 359–360

Reading Decodable Books

1. **Read Silently** Have children whisper read the story page by page as you listen in.

2. **Model Fluent Reading** Have children finger point as you read a page. Then have children reread the page without you.

3. **Read Chorally** Have children finger point as they chorally read the page. Continue reading page by page, repeating steps 1 and 2.

4. **Read Individually** Have children take turns reading aloud a page.

5. **Reread and Monitor Progress** As you listen to individual children reread, monitor progress and provide support.

6. **Reread with a Partner** Have children reread the story page by page with a partner.

Routines Flip Chart

Differentiated Instruction

 **Strategic Intervention**

Support Decoding Before reading *Jan and Gus,* use the *Aa* and *Uu* Alphabet Cards to review the sound-spellings children learned for each letter.

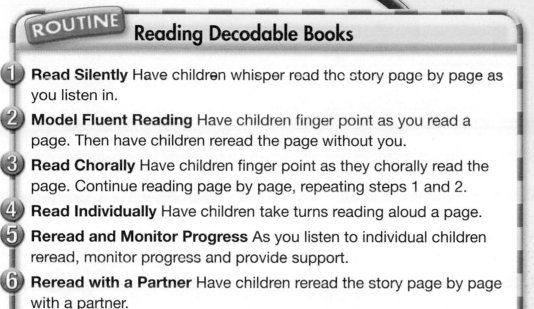

Small Group Time

DAY 1

Break into small groups after reading the Decodable Story and before the comprehension lesson.

Teacher-Led

SI Strategic Intervention	**OL On-Level**	**A Advanced**
Teacher-Led Page DI•52	**Teacher-Led** Page DI•57	**Teacher-Led** Page DI•60
• Phonemic Awareness and Phonics	• Phonemic Awareness and Phonics	• Phonemic Awareness and Phonics
• **Reread** Decodable Story 28	• **Reread** Decodable Story 28, DI•57	• **Reread** Decodable Story 28 for Fluency, DI•60

ELL Place English language learners in the groups that correspond to their reading abilities in English.

Practice Stations
• Visit the Listen Up! Station
• Visit the Word Work Station

Independent Activities
• Read independently
• Concept Talk Video
• *Reader's and Writer's Notebook*

ELL

English Language Learners

Support Decoding Tell children to retell the story using the pictures in the book. If children have difficulty thinking of the word in English, supply words for them to repeat.

Objectives
◎ Identify plot.

Skills Trace
◉ Plot
Introduce U3W2D1; U3W4D1;
U5W4D1; U6W4D1
Practice U3W2D2; U3W2D3;
U3W2D4; U3W4D2; U3W4D3;
U3W4D4; U5W4D2; U5W4D3;
U5W4D4; U6W4D2; U6W4D3;
U6W4D4
Reteach/Review U3W2D5;
U3W4D5; U3W6D4; U4W2D4;
U5W1D4; U5W4D5; U6W2D4;
U6W4D5
Assess/Test Benchmark
Assessment U5; U6

KEY:
U=Unit   W=Week   D=Day

My Skills Buddy, pp. 74–75

Listening Comprehension
⟳ Plot

Introduce
All stories have a beginning, a middle, and an end. The things that happen at the beginning, in the middle, and at the end are called the **plot.** Good readers pay attention to the plot to help them understand what happens.

Envision It!
Have children turn to pp. 74–75 in *My Skills Buddy* and look at the three pictures on the right side. These pictures tell a story.

- What happens in the beginning? (Tortoise and Hare get ready to race.)
- What happens in the middle? (Hare takes a nap during the race, and Tortoise passes him.)
- What happens at the end? (Tortoise wins the race.)

Model
Today I will read a story about a boy and his mom who take the train to the city. Read **"The El"** and model how to identify the plot.

Think Aloud
When I read, I think about what happens in the story. I pay attention to what happens in the beginning, in the middle, and what happens at the end of the story.

Guide practice

After reading, ask children questions about the story's plot.

- What happens in the beginning of the story? (A boy and his mom get on the train to the city.)
- What happens in the middle of the story? (The train travels above and below ground.)
- What happens at the end of the story? (The boy and his mom see a parade in the city.)

More practice

Display Trade Book *Mayday! Mayday!* Page through the story. Help children retell the plot. Have them draw a picture of what happens in the beginning, in the middle, and at the end.

Connect to everyday life

The time we spend at lunch also has a beginning, a middle, and an end. Tell me about the beginning, the middle, and the end of lunchtime.

Academic Vocabulary

plot the events and actions in a story

English Language Learners
Oral Comprehension To prepare English learners for the Read Aloud, use the modified Read Aloud in the ELL Support lesson p. DI•64.

Access Content Help children understand that other languages have words for *beginning, middle,* and *end*. Spanish-speaking children may know these words for *beginning* and *end*: *principio* and *el final.*

Read Aloud

Mom was taking Liam downtown to see a parade. They were going on the elevated train, or "el." Mom put a card in a slot so they could walk, one by one, through the entry gate. They went down the stairs to wait for the train.

The train came to a stop, its doors slid open, and they walked into the car. They found seats near the front. Off they went! Sometimes the train went under the ground. But mostly it traveled on tracks high above the ground.

Liam watched the tall buildings come into view. The train went underground and stopped. Mom and Liam got off and climbed the stairs to get to the street.

Many people were waiting for the parade to start. Liam heard a band playing. Here comes the parade!

Objectives
- Identify and use nouns.
- Write or dictate a story.

Conventions
Nouns

Teach nouns

Remember we have learned about nouns. A noun is a word that names a person, animal, place, or thing. Nouns can name one or more than one. Today we are going to practice finding nouns and telling if the noun is a person, an animal, a place, or a thing.

Model

Display Picture Cards for *drum, elephant,* and *playground. Drum* is a noun. It names something we can play. *Elephant* is a noun that names an animal, and *playground* is a noun for a place. I am a *teacher.* The word *teacher* is a noun for a person. **Write the nouns on the board. Point to each word as you read it.** These are nouns for one. They identify one drum, one elephant, one playground, and one teacher. How can we say these nouns for one as nouns for more than one? We add –s to the end of them and say *drums, elephants, playgrounds,* and *teachers.*

Guide practice

Display the *bubbles* Picture Card. What are these? These are *bubbles.* The word *bubbles* is a noun. Is the noun *bubbles* for one or more than one? Tell me three nouns for things you see in the classroom. **Make a four-column chart on the board and label the columns** *People, Animals, Places,* **and** *Things.* **Write children's nouns for one and more than one in the** *Things* **column. Then have children think of nouns for one and more than one for people, animals, and places. Write those nouns in the appropriate columns. Have children read the chart with you.**

Team Talk Pair children and have them take turns drawing and labeling pictures of people, animals, places, or things. Then have pairs write or dictate a complete sentence about one of their nouns.

Daily Fix-It

Use the Daily Fix-It for more conventions practice.

Writing
Wonderful, Marvelous Me!
I'll Tell You a Story...

Introduce

Talk with children about why people tell stories. Why do you think we tell stories? One reason we tell stories is to have fun. It is fun to write and tell stories. It is also fun to read and listen to stories. We can all have fun when we tell or imagine stories. Do you have fun telling or imagining stories? Encourage children to share their thoughts and ideas about stories, either those you have read together or those children have created.

Model

Today we're going to write a make-believe story about a train trip. I'm going to close my eyes and use my imagination. I have a story in my mind about a dog that takes a train trip. Bud is a brown, furry dog. Draw a picture of a brown, furry dog and write *Bud the dog* underneath. Bud is taking a trip. He is taking the train to Grandma's house. This is Bud's first time on the train. Bud is having so much fun! Draw a picture of a brown, furry dog on a train. Underneath the drawing, write *Bud has fun*. Bud is having fun on the train. What do you think Bud can do on the train?

Guide practice

Encourage children to help you come up with more ideas for your story. Write down their ideas and draw pictures when appropriate.

Independent writing

Now you're going to tell a story about a train trip. Close your eyes and use your wonderful, marvelous imagination. Who is taking a train trip? Where is he or she going? What can he or she do on the train? Have children write or dictate their stories and then illustrate their ideas.

Daily Handwriting

Write *Uncle* and *up* on the board. Review correct letter formation of uppercase *U* and lowercase *u*.

D'Nealian™   Ball and Stick

Have children write *Uncle* and *up* on their Write-On Boards. Remind them to use proper left-to-right and top-to-bottom progression and proper spacing between letters when writing *U* and *u*.

Write Guy
Jeff Anderson

Details, Details

Ask children to notice details in text. Point out a detail that is beyond the obvious (*It was hot* versus *The sun melted my crayons.*). With guidance, children can learn to include *details that matter* rather than obvious details or simply long lists of details.

Academic Vocabulary

noun a word that names a person, animal, place, or thing

Daily Fix-It

bud is in the tub with suds
<u>B</u>ud is in the tub with suds<u>.</u>

This week's practice sentences appear on Teacher Resources DVD-ROM.

Writing Routine

Listening and Speaking
Sequence

Teach
In a story, something happens first, something happens next, and something happens last. The order of events in a story is called sequence. Knowing the order of what happens in a story helps us understand the story better.

Model
When we listen to a story, we listen for the order of events. In *Jan and Gus*, first Jan and Gus are on the rug. Next, they hum on the bus. Last, they run in the mud.

Guide practice
Tell children this short story: *Peg can't find her cat Lucky. She looks in the laundry basket. She looks under the bed. She hears a noise coming from Grandpa's old hat. She sees a black tail move. Peg is glad that she found her cat!* Arrange children in small groups. Have each group discuss one event. Have one child from each group retell the event to the class. Refer to the Rules for Listening and Speaking on pp. 1–2 of *Reader's and Writer's Notebook*. Remind children that good speakers take turns and speak one at a time.

Name _____

Listening Rules

1. Face the person who is speaking.
2. Be quiet while someone is speaking.
3. Pay attention to the speaker.
4. Ask questions if you don't understand.

Listening and Speaking Rules 1

Reader's and Writer's Notebook, pp. 1–2

Wrap Up Your Day

✔ **Concept Talk** This week we are going to talk about trains. The train from our story, "The El," does what kind of work?

✔ **Oral Language** Today we talked about some train and travel words. Let's say the Amazing Words again: *engine, tracks, passenger, roundhouse, mountain, valley.*

✔ **Homework Idea** Send home the Family Times Newsletter Let's Practice It! TR•DVD 55–56.

Preview

DAY 2

Tomorrow we will read about trains and engines.

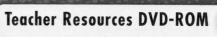

Extend Your Day!

Social Studies
Ordering Trains

Materials: large construction paper, crayons, markers

Discuss the train engines and cars children saw in Talk with Me/Sing with Me Chart 28 or that they heard about in the Background Building Audio CD. Give each child a large sheet of construction paper. Have children draw an engine or train car, filling the length of the paper.

Have children stand with their pictures. Now we are going to put together trains. Arrange children with engines in front and children with cars behind. Now we will drive the trains over the mountain. When your train gets to the end, it waits and rests for the next trip. Allow one train to chug along the length of the room. Instruct children to move aside and rest until the others arrive. When all have arrived, switch some of the engines and repeat the activity.

Conventions
Nouns

Materials: Picture Cards of nouns

Categorize Nouns Give a Picture Card to each child. Say "person" and have children with that type of picture come to the front of the room. Repeat with "things" and "places." Then have children come up with silly sentences using the Picture Cards, such as *The man drove a train in my house.*

Picture Cards

Comprehension
Plot

Story Summary Review the story *Jan and Gus*. Write three sentences summarizing the story.

1. Jan and Gus hum on the bus.

2. Jan and Gus run in the mud.

3. Jan and Gus play on the rug.

Put children in groups of three. Have each child per group illustrate one of the sentences. Invite groups one at a time to show their pictures and allow the class to put them in the right order.

Objectives
- Discuss the concepts to develop oral language.
- Build oral vocabulary.

Today at a Glance

Oral Vocabulary
engine, tracks

Phonemic Awareness
◉ Initial and Medial /u/

Phonics
◉ /u/ Spelled *Uu*

Handwriting
Words with *Uu*

Comprehension
◉ Plot

Conventions
Nouns

Writing
Respond to Literature

Vocabulary
Time Words

TRUCKTOWN on Reading Street

Start your engines! Display p. 11 of *Truckery Rhymes.* Point to "Patty Cake, Patty Cake." Who remembers which truck this rhyme is about? Yes, this rhyme is about Dan. Let's read the rhyme together. Have a child point to the rhyming words as the class reads the rhyme again.

Truckery Rhymes

Concept Talk

 Question of the Week

What kind of work do trains do?

Build concepts

Write the question of the week on the board and track the print as you read it aloud. Have children answer the question in complete sentences. Remind them to speak audibly and clearly when sharing their ideas. To reinforce the concept and focus children's attention, display Talk with Me/Sing with Me Chart 28B. Tell children they are going to sing about a train.

🔘 Sing with Me Audio

Listen for Amazing Words

The Amazing Words *engine* and *tracks* are in the song "On the Tracks to the Mountain." Read the title and tell children to describe the picture. Sing the song several times to the tune of "On Top of Old Smoky." Have children clap when they sing the Amazing Words *engine* and *tracks.*

ELL Reinforce Vocabulary Use the Day 2 instruction on ELL Poster 28 to reinforce the meanings of high-frequency words.

On the Tracks to the Mountain

On the tracks to the mountain,
  chugged a train so sweet,
Taking toys to the valley,
  for young ones to meet.

Along came passengers,
  on a fast-moving train,
They returned to the roundhouse,
  "Too busy!" they claimed.

A small engine came by,
  and helped in her way,
To bring toys to children, on this happy day.

Talk with Me/Sing with Me Chart 28B

ELL Poster 28

Go Digital! 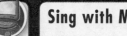 Concept Talk Video | Sing with Me Animations | Sing with Me Audio

Whole Group

Oral Vocabulary
Amazing Words

Amazing Words Oral Vocabulary Routine

Teach Amazing Words

1 Introduce the Word An *engine* is the part of the train that works the hardest. It makes the power to turn the wheels. What's our new Amazing Word for the hardest working part of a train? Say it with me: *engine*.

2 Demonstrate Provide examples to show meaning. *This new engine helps the train.* What is something else that has an *engine*?

Repeat steps 1 and 2.

Introduce the Word A train has to travel on *tracks*. Train *tracks* are special rails that keep the wheels of a train in place. What's our new Amazing Word for the special rails on which a train travels? Say it with me: *tracks*.

Demonstrate *Train tracks are built one piece at a time. It took a long time to make enough tracks to go over a mountain.*

3 Apply Have children use *engine* and *tracks* to tell about a train carrying something from one place to another.

Routines Flip Chart

Use Amazing Words

To reinforce the concept and the Amazing Words, have children supply the appropriate Amazing Word for each sentence.

The _____ pulls the other train cars. (engine)

The train travels on _____. (tracks)

Differentiated Instruction

SI Strategic Intervention

Sentence Production If children have difficulty completing the sentences, use each Amazing Word in the same sentence and ask children to choose the Amazing Word that makes sense. Say the correct sentence together.

English Language Learners
Access Content Have children tell what word in their home language is used for the word *engine*.

Objectives
• Practice initial and medial /u/.

Phonemic Awareness
Initial and Medial /u/

Picture Card

Isolate initial /u/

Display the *up* Picture Card. This picture shows *up*. *Up* begins with /u/. What is this? What sound does *up* begin with? Repeat the routine with the *umbrella* Picture Card.

Model medial /u/

Display the *bus* Picture Card. This is a *bus*. Listen as I say the sounds in *bus:* /b/ /u/ /s/. I hear /u/ in the middle: /b/ /u/ /s/. Say the sounds with me: /b/ /u/ /s/. What sound do you hear in the middle? (/u/) Continue with the following words: *pup, Bud, cub, fuzz, run.*

Picture Card

Guide practice

Have children look at the picture on *My Skills Buddy,* pp. 72–73. Remember that this picture shows things happening *underwater. Underwater* begins with /u/. What other things that begin with /u/ did we see in the picture? Name other things that begin like *underwater.* What things in this picture have /u/ in the middle? Discuss with children those bulleted items on p. 72 not discussed on Day 1.

My Skills Buddy, pp. 72–73

Corrective feedback

If... children cannot discriminate medial /u/,
then... have then enunciate /u/ as they segment /u/ words.

Listen as I segment a word: /k/ /u/ /t/, *cut.* Say it with me: /k/ /u/ /t/, *cut.* What sound do you hear in the middle? I hear /u/ in the middle. Continue with the following words: *hut, cuff, lug, tuck.*

On their own Display Phonics Songs and Rhymes Chart 28, "Bud." Sing the song to the tune of "Mary Had a Little Lamb" several times. Have children join in as they become familiar with the song. This time I want you to raise your hand each time you hear a word that has /u/. Identify the words: *Bud, full, mud, bubbly, tub, suds.*

Bud

Look at Bud, he's full of mud,
full of mud, full of mud.
Look at Bud, he's full of mud.
Get in the bubbly tub!

Look at Bud, he's full of suds,
full of suds, full of suds.
Look at Bud, he's full of suds,
No more mud on Bud!

Phonics Songs and Rhymes
Chart 28

Review

Sound Substitution Listen to the sounds in *tug:* /t/ /u/ /g/. We can make a new word by changing the middle sound. Let's change /u/ to /a/. Say the sounds with me: /t/ /a/ /g/. The new word is *tag.* Continue substituting medial sounds with the following sets of words: *rug, rag; big, bug; duck, dock; fan, fun; him, ham, hum.*

Differentiated Instruction

 **Strategic Intervention**
Support Phonemic Awareness
If children struggle to find words with the appropriate sounds, point to an object in the Phonics Songs and Rhymes Chart 28. Have children name the object and ask if it has a specific sound. For example, point to the tub. After children name it, ask: Does *tub* have /u/?

ELL

English Language Learners
Build Background Use the picture on Phonics Songs and Rhymes Chart 28 to help children understand the definition of *suds.* Point to the suds in the picture. Explain where suds come from and have children share the word for *suds* in their home language.

Objectives
◎ Practice /u/ spelled *Uu*.
• Blend /u/ words.

Check Sound-Spelling
SUCCESS PREDICTOR

Phonics—Teach/Model
/u/ Spelled *Uu*

Alphabet Card

Teach /u/Uu

Point to the *umbrella* on the *Uu* Alphabet Card. What is this? What sound does *umbrella* begin with? *Umbrella* begins with /u/. Write *umbrella* on the board and point to the letter *u* at the beginning. The letter for /u/ is *u*.

Model

Display the *up* Picture Card. What is this? Say the sounds in *up* with me: /u/ /p/, *up*. Where do you hear /u/ in *up*? (at the beginning)

Write *up* on the board. Point to each letter as you say the sounds: /u/ /p/, *up*. Continue the routine with the following words: *jug, us, nut.*

Picture Card

Guide practice

Envision It!

Have children open *My Skills Buddy* to p. 76. Demonstrate using the blending arrows on *My Skills Buddy* p. 76 as you model blending the first word. Put your finger on the red arrow below the *m*. Say the sound that *m* stands for: /m/. Continue with letters *u* and *g*. Now I run my finger along the blue arrow as I blend the letters quickly to read *mug*. Repeat with the word *bug*. Have children work with a partner to blend the rest of the words on the page.

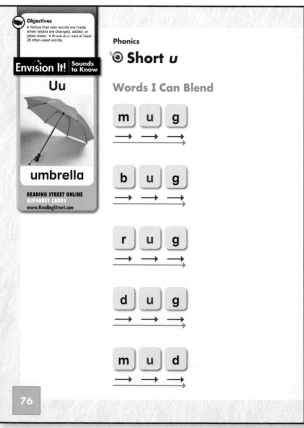

My Skills Buddy, p. 76

Blend Use the following routine to review blending *u* words.

> **ROUTINE** **Sound-by-Sound Blending**
>
> **①** **Connect** Write the letter *m*. What is the sound for this letter? The sound is /m/. Say it with me: /m/ /m/ /m/. When you see this letter in a word, what sound will you say?
>
> **②** **Model** Write the word *mug* on the board.
>
> • Point to *m* and ask: What is the sound for this letter? Say it with me: /m/ /m/ /m/. Repeat the routine for *u* and *g*.
>
> • Listen as I blend the sounds: /m/ /u/ /g/. Say it with me: /m/ /u/ /g/, *mug*. Now say it without me.
>
> • Listen as I use *mug* in a sentence: *Pour the milk in the mug.* Say it with me. Have children use *mug* in a sentence.
>
> **③** **Guide Practice** Continue the routine in step 2 with these words:
>
> | sat | can | get | hop | bug | fun | cup | big | tub |
> |-----|-----|-----|-----|-----|-----|-----|-----|-----|
>
> Have children successfully read all of the words before reading Decodable Reader 28 on pp. 78–85 of *My Skills Buddy*.
>
> **Corrective Feedback** Model blending the sounds to read the word. Then have children say it with you.

Routines Flip Chart

Don't Wait Until Friday

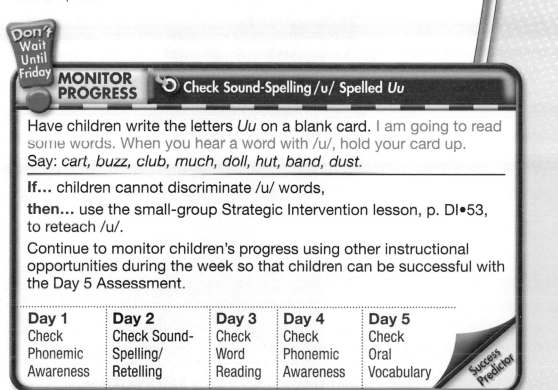

MONITOR PROGRESS ↻ **Check Sound-Spelling /u/ Spelled *Uu***

Have children write the letters *Uu* on a blank card. I am going to read some words. When you hear a word with /u/, hold your card up.
Say: *cart, buzz, club, much, doll, hut, band, dust.*

If... children cannot discriminate /u/ words,

then... use the small-group Strategic Intervention lesson, p. DI•53, to reteach /u/.

Continue to monitor children's progress using other instructional opportunities during the week so that children can be successful with the Day 5 Assessment.

Day 1	Day 2	Day 3	Day 4	Day 5
Check Phonemic Awareness	Check Sound-Spelling/ Retelling	Check Word Reading	Check Phonemic Awareness	Check Oral Vocabulary

Success Predictor

Differentiated Instruction

 **Advanced**

Uu Display the *Uu* Alphabet Card. Have children find *Uu* in words in *Jan at the Fair* before reading.

SI **Strategic Intervention**

Medial /u/ Before children read *Jan at the Fair*, review medial /u/ with the *bus, drum,* and *tub* Picture Cards.

341 **Success Predictor**

Sound-Spelling

Objectives
- Write *U* and *u*.
- Read high-frequency words.

Handwriting
Write Words with *Uu*

Review

Write *Uma* on the board. This is the word *Uma*. I use an uppercase *U* for the first letter in *Uma's* name. Watch me make an uppercase *U*. Write another uppercase *U* on the board using the strokes indicated in the model.

Write *up* on the board. This is the word *up*. I use a lowercase *u* at the beginning of *up*. Watch me make a lowercase *u*. Write another lowercase *u* on the board using the proper strokes.

D'Nealian™   Ball and Stick

Guide practice

Have children use their Write-On Boards to make a row of uppercase *U* and a row of lowercase *u*. Circulate around the room, assisting children when necessary. Continue handwriting with the following words: *us, hug, bun.*

High-Frequency Words

Model reading

Have children turn to p. 77 of *My Skills Buddy*. Read the high-frequency words *what, said,* and *was* together. Then have children point to each word and read it themselves. Read the sentences on the *My Skills Buddy* page together to read the new high-frequency words in context.

Team Talk Pair children and have them take turns reading each of the sentences aloud.

High-Frequency Worrds

Words I Can Read

what

said

was

Sentences I Can Read

1. What is in the tub?
2. "It is a pet," said Bud.
3. Was the pet in mud?

77

My Skills Buddy, p. 77

On their own

Use *Reader's and Writer's Notebook*, p. 361, for additional practice with this week's high-frequency words.

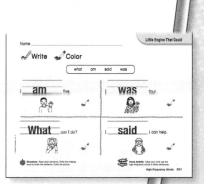

Reader's and Writer's Notebook, p. 361

Decodable Reader 28
🔊 /u/ Spelled *Uu* and High-Frequency Words

Review   Review the previously taught high-frequency words. Have children read each word as you point to it on the Word Wall.

the	what	do	I	said	a	have	was

Have children turn to Decodable Reader 28, *Jan at the Fair,* on p. 78 of *My Skills Buddy*. Today we will read a book about a girl named Jan who goes to the fair. Point to the title of the book. What is the title of this story? The title of this story is *Jan at the Fair*. We will read lots of *u* words in this book.

Use the routine for reading decodable books to read Decodable Reader 28.

My Skills Buddy, pp. 78–85

Act Out   After children read *Jan at the Fair*, have them act out all of the important events in the story—Jan sitting on the bus, Jan hitting the drum, Jan sipping from the red cup, Jan dropping mud in the tub.

 **Reading Decodable Books**

1. **Read Silently** Have children whisper read the book page by page as you listen in.

2. **Model Fluent Reading** Have children finger point as you read a page. Then have children reread the book without you.

3. **Read Chorally** Have children finger point as they chorally read the page. Continue reading page by page, repeating steps 1 and 2.

4. **Read Individually** Have children take turns reading aloud a page.

5. **Reread and Monitor Progress** As you listen to individual children reread, monitor progress and provide support.

6. **Reread with a Partner** Have children reread the book page by page with a partner.

Routines Flip Chart

Differentiated Instruction

A Advanced

Copy /u/ Words Have children copy words with medial /u/ on their Write-On Boards as they read *Jan at the Fair.*

SI Strategic Intervention

Decodable Reader Display the *bus, drum,* and *tub* Picture Cards. Before children read *Jan at the Fair,* have them use the Picture Cards to find these words in the story. Practice blending the sounds in these words with children.

Small Group Time

DAY 2 Break into small groups after reading the Decodable Reader and before the comprehension lesson.

Teacher-Led

SI Strategic Intervention	**OL** On-Level	**A** Advanced
Teacher-Led Page DI•53 • Phonemic Awareness and Phonics • **Reread** Decodable Reader 28	**Teacher-Led** Page DI•57 • Phonemic Awareness and Phonics • **Reread** Decodable Reader 28	**Teacher-Led** Page DI•60 • Phonics and Spelling • **Reread** Decodable Reader 28 for Fluency

 Place English language learners in the groups that correspond to their reading abilities in English.

Practice Stations	**Independent Activities**
• Visit the Word Work Station • Visit the Words to Know Station	• Read independently • Background Building Audio • *Reader's and Writer's Notebook*

ELL

English Language Learners
Vocabulary Development Walk children through *Jan at the Fair.* Have them find the *sub, drum, bug, cup,* and *bus* in the story. Display a word card for each of these words and have a child match each card with an appropriate picture.

Listening Comprehension
🔊 Plot

Review

Envision It!

Have children turn to pp. 74–75 of *My Skills Buddy*. Remind children that all stories have a beginning, middle, and end. This is the plot of the story. Good readers pay attention to the plot because it helps them understand the story.

My Skills Buddy, pp. 74–75

Triple Day Read!

First Read—Trade Book
The Little Engine That Could

Concepts of print

Display *The Little Engine That Could*. Point to the title. The title of this book is *The Little Engine That Could*. The author is Watty Piper.

Preview and predict

Think Aloud

Look at the cover. What do you see? I see a train engine with a smiling face. What do you think this story is about? What makes you think that? Let's read to find out.

Use illustrations

Take children on a picture walk through the book. Have children tell about what they see in each picture.

Introduce genre

A classic is a book that has stood the test of time. It is appealing because it has a theme and characters that readers identify with. Readers of many different generations have enjoyed *The Little Engine That Could*.

Set purpose

Say the question of the week: *What kind of work do trains do?* Listen as I read to learn about some different uses of trains.

Model

Read *The Little Engine That Could* with expression for enjoyment.

DAY 2 Read for enjoyment

DAY 3 Reread using Develop Vocabulary notes

DAY 4 Reread using Guide Comprehension notes

Retell

Check retelling

Have children turn to p. 86 of *My Skills Buddy*. Walk through the retelling boxes as children retell *The Little Engine That Could*. Let's retell what happens in the first box—the beginning of the story. A train is broken and a clown is waving for help. Let's retell what happens in the next box. Continue with the rest of the boxes. After children retell the story as a group, have them draw pictures to retell a favorite part of the story. Have them write or dictate a word or sentence to go with their picture.

My Skills Buddy, p. 86

Top-Score Response A top-score response describes events in sequence with details.

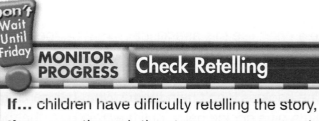

MONITOR PROGRESS Check Retelling

Don't Wait Until Friday

If... children have difficulty retelling the story,

then... go through the story one page at a time, and ask children to tell what happens in their own words.

Day 1	Day 2	Day 3	Day 4	Day 5
Check Phonemic Awareness	Check Sound-Spelling/ Retelling	Check Word Reading	Check Phonemic Awareness	Check Oral Vocabulary

Success Predictor

Differentiated Instruction

SI Strategic Intervention

Talk About It Have children tell about something that was hard for them to do at first. Have them explain how they finally learned to do it.

A Advanced

Write Have children write or dictate a short letter thanking the Little Blue Engine for doing such a good job.

Retelling Plan

☑ **Week 1** Assess Advanced students.

☑ **Week 2** Assess On-Level students.

☑ **Week 3** Assess Strategic Intervention students.

☑ **This week assess Advanced students.**

☐ **Week 5** Assess On-Level students.

☐ **Week 6** Assess Strategic Intervention students.

Retelling

Success Predictor

Think, Talk, and Write

Discuss concepts

We're learning about what kind of work a train can do. Think about how you would feel if you were one of the trains that the little clown asked for help.

• What kind of train would you want to be? Why?

• Would you help the clown? Why?

• How did the Little Blue Engine feel at the end of the story?

Confirm predictions

Ask children to recall their predictions before you read *The Little Engine That Could.*

• What did you think the story would be about?

• Was your prediction correct?

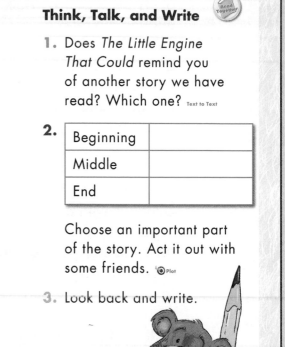

My Skills Buddy, p. 87

Have children turn to p. 87 of *My Skills Buddy.* Read the questions and directives and have children respond.

Text to text

1. Does *The Little Engine That Could* remind you of another story we have read? Which one? Can you think of other characters in stories that work very hard to meet their goals? What can we learn from these characters?

◉ Plot

2. Let's make a chart like this and fill it in. What happens at the beginning of the story *The Little Engine That Could?* (A train breaks down.) What happens in the middle of the story? (The toys on the train ask some engines for help. The engines won't help them.) What happens at the end of the story? (A little blue engine helps pull the train over the mountain.) Have children act out an important part of the story with friends.

Look back and write

3. Let's look back at our story and write about it. We remember that the dolls and toys ask a passenger train for help. Listen for what the passenger car says to them. Read pp. 16–17 of *The Little Engine That Could.* Now let's write our ideas. Discuss with children what the passenger train looks like and record children's responses on chart paper. (Possible responses: This train has sleeping cars. People can eat in the dining car. The parlor car has soft chairs.)

Conventions
Nouns

Review

Remind children of what they learned about nouns and verbs. *Which word,* noun *or* verb, *is the action part of a sentence?* (*verb*) An action word is a *verb*. *Which word,* noun *or* verb, *is used to name a person, animal, place, or thing?* (*noun*) A person, animal, place, or thing is a *noun*. Nouns can name one or more than one.

Guide practice

Display pp. 4–5 of *The Little Engine That Could.* *What are some nouns on these pages?* Record children's responses on the board. Then display pp. 6–7 and 8–9 of *The Little Engine That Could.* Have children identify more nouns on the pages. Read the final list of nouns with children, pointing to each word as you say it. Have them tell if each noun names a person, animal, place, or thing. Then have them say the noun for more than one.

On their own

Use *Reader's and Writer's Notebook,* p. 362, for more practice with nouns.

Daily Fix-It

Use the Daily Fix-It exercise for more conventions practice.

Reader's and Writer's Notebook, p. 362

Differentiated Instruction

A **Advanced**

Conventions Remind children that nouns can name one or more than one person, animal, place, or thing. I am going to say some nouns. If a noun names one person, place, or thing, raise one hand. If a noun names more than one person, place, or thing, raise both hands. Say the following words: *train, tracks, cars, engine.*

Daily Fix-It

can it go up the hil
Can it go up the hill?

This week's practice sentences appear on Teacher Resources DVD-ROM.

English Language Learners

Vocabulary Children's home languages also have words for people, animals, places, and things. To help them learn English nouns, bring items—apples, hats, dolls, toys, dishes, and so forth—for vocabulary building. As children learn English nouns, have them share the equivalent noun in their home language.

Objectives
- Write sentences related to the selection.
- Identify and use time words.

Writing
Respond to Literature

Discuss   Display *The Little Engine That Could*. Discuss with children what the little train is carrying.

Model   In the story, the train is carrying toys over the mountain to bring to good boys and girls. But the train gets stuck. If you were waiting for toys from the train, would you be excited? I will write a sentence about what I would like to get from the train.

> **I will get my doll.**

Guide practice   Invite children to help you write more sentences about the kinds of toys that are on the train.

> **I want to spin the top.**
> **I will read the book.**

Independent writing   Have children write or dictate about the toys on the train. Then have them illustrate their sentence.

I will get my doll.

Daily Handwriting

Write *Uncle* and *us* on the board. Review correct letter formation of uppercase *U* and lowercase *u*.

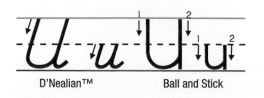
D'Nealian™   Ball and Stick

Have children write *Uncle* and *us* on their Write-On Boards. Remind children to use proper left-to-right and top-to-bottom progression when writing *U* and *u*.

Vocabulary
Time Words

Model Have children turn to p. 88 of *My Skills Buddy.* Direct them to the calendar. We are going to learn words for the days of the week. Point to the calendar on the page. This is a calendar. Use the first Vocabulary bullet on p. 88 to guide the discussion. We have a calendar like this in our class. Remember, we have calendars to tell the month (point to *April*), the week (point to a week), and the day (point to a day). There are seven days in every week, and we have different names for each of these days. Point to *Monday* on the calendar. This day is called *Monday*. Listen for the word *day* in the word: *Monday*. The word *day* is part of each day's name. Let's learn the names for the other days. Point to each day as you name it: *Tuesday, Wednesday, Thursday, Friday, Saturday, Sunday.*

Guide practice Write the words *Monday, Tuesday, Wednesday, Thursday, Friday, Saturday,* and *Sunday* on the board. Point to each word as you read it.

Let's play a game about days. Write each word on a sheet of construction paper. I will give one of these days to seven different players: one player for each day of the week. Say each word as you give it to a child. Have these children stand in correct order. I will say the name of a player. Then I want everybody to tell me what day the player is holding. Let's try one together: *(Name). (Name)* has *Monday.* Repeat the routine for the other days of the week. Then repeat the game with new players until every child has had a chance to play.

On their own Assign children one day of the week. Have them draw what they like to do on that day and label their pictures with the correct day name. Use the pictures to assemble a calendar on the board. Have children describe their pictures to the class, using this sentence frame: *I like to (activity) on (day).*

My Skills Buddy, p. 88

English Language Learners
Access Content Have children say the days of the week in their home language.

Build Background In languages including Spanish, French, Polish, and Vietnamese, the names of days and months are not usually capitalized. Explain to children that in English, names for days are like names for people: They always begin with capital (uppercase) letters.

Objectives
• Review skills learned and practiced today.

Wrap Up Your Day

✔ **Concept Talk** Today we read about a little engine. How does the engine help the toys? Have you ever helped someone with a problem?

✔ **Conventions** We see many different kinds of nouns every day. How many nouns can you find in the classroom?

✔ **Vocabulary Skill** Today we talked about the seven days of the week: *Monday, Tuesday, Wednesday, Thursday, Friday, Saturday, Sunday*. What day is today?

✔ **Homework Idea** Have children find nouns for a person and a thing in their homes and draw a picture of each.

Preview
DAY 3
Tomorrow we will read about another train trip.

Extend Your Day!

Social Studies
Alphabet Train
Materials: construction paper, crayons

Make a classroom train by cutting out a large engine. Use sheets of paper for the train cars, and write a letter of the alphabet on each.

Take It by Train Give each child a lettered train car. Have children draw something that begins with that letter. I want you to think of things that train cars may carry. For example, if I have the *Aa* car, I may have it carry *apples*. I will draw apples on my train car. Provide assistance for children with difficult letters such as *q* and *x*. When all the pictures are done, tape the train cars in alphabetical order.

Travel by Train Where can our train travel? Up a mountain? across a field? near a river? Make a two-column chart with land and water features on one side and position words on the other. Have children dictate sentences that tell where the train traveled with its cargo. Then have them share their pictures with the class.

Phonics
/u/ Spelled *Uu*
Materials: paper, markers, crayons

Make a List Have children list words that have *Uu*. After you have created a list on the board, have children write a large *U* in the middle of a sheet of paper. Then have them copy several words from the list onto their papers. Have children illustrate each of their words using markers or crayons.

Comprehension
Plot
Materials: paper, markers, crayons

The Little Engine That Could Remind children that *The Little Engine That Could* starts with a train breaking down. Have children retell what happens in the middle and at the end of the story. Write the responses on the board. Then give each child a sheet of paper folded in three parts. Have children label the first part *Beginning*, the middle part *Middle*, and the last part *End*. Children should then draw pictures that show what happens in each part of the story.

Objectives
- Share information and ideas about the concept.
- Build oral vocabulary.

Today at a Glance

Oral Vocabulary
passenger, roundhouse

Phonemic Awareness
◉ Initial and Medial /u/

Phonics
◉ /u/ Spelled *Uu*

Comprehension
◉ Plot

Conventions
Prepositions

Writing
Formal Letter

Listening and Speaking
Sequence

TRUCKTOWN on Reading Street

Start your engines! Display p. 11 of *Truckery Rhymes*. Do you know the original "Patty Cake, Patty Cake"? Recite it first, and then have children repeat it with you:

> Patty Cake, Patty Cake, baker's man
> Bake me a cake as fast as you can.
> Roll it, pat it, mark it with a *B*,
> Put it in the oven for baby and me.

Truckery Rhymes

Concept Talk

Question of the Week

What kind of work do trains do?

Write and read the question of the week as you track the print. Talk with children about what trains do. Remind children to take turns and answer the question in complete sentences.

Listen for Amazing Words

Let's Sing Display Sing with Me Chart 28B. Remind children that yesterday they sang "On the Tracks to the Mountain" and listened for the words *engine* and *tracks*. Today we are going to listen for the Amazing Words *passenger* and *roundhouse*. Sing the song several times to the tune of "On Top of Old Smoky." Have children sing with you. Have them clap when they hear the Amazing Words *passenger* and *roundhouse*.

💿 Sing with Me Audio

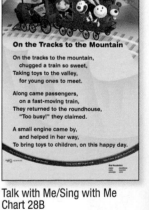

On the Tracks to the Mountain

On the tracks to the mountain,
    chugged a train so sweet,
Taking toys to the valley,
    for young ones to meet.

Along came passengers,
    on a fast-moving train,
They returned to the roundhouse,
    "Too busy!" they claimed.

A small engine came by,
    and helped in her way,
To bring toys to children, on this happy day.

Talk with Me/Sing with Me Chart 28B

Oral Vocabulary
Amazing Words

Amazing Words

engine	tracks
passenger	roundhouse
mountain	valley

Teach Amazing Words

Amazing Words — Oral Vocabulary Routine

1 **Introduce the Word** A *passenger* is a person who rides on a train, on a bus, in a car, or in an airplane. What's our new Amazing Word for a person who rides on a train? Say it with me: *passenger*.

2 **Demonstrate** Provide examples to show meaning. *The passenger sits on the bus.*

Repeat steps 1 and 2.

Introduce the Word A *roundhouse* is a special building that is round on the outside. Inside the *roundhouse*, trains turn around and wait for their next turn to make a trip. What's our new Amazing Word for the place where trains wait? Say it with me: *roundhouse*.

Demonstrate *My train waits in the roundhouse.*

3 **Apply** Have children use *passenger* and *roundhouse* in complete sentences. Have them illustrate the words.

Routines Flip Chart

Use Amazing Words

To reinforce the concept and the Amazing Words, have children supply the appropriate Amazing Word for each sentence.

> **The trains turn around in the _____.** (roundhouse)
>
> **The _____ rides a train into the city.** (passenger)

 **Expand Vocabulary**
Use the Day 3 instruction on ELL Poster 28 to help children expand vocabulary.

 Poster 28

Differentiated Instruction

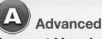 **Advanced**
Support Vocabulary Have children make up a story about passengers on a train trip. Have them tell the story orally or with pictures.

English Language Learners
Access Content Have children tell what word in their home language is used for the word *passenger*. Tell children to show the shape of a *roundhouse* with their hands, and explain to them that a *roundhouse* is like a train's home.

Objectives

◎ Practice initial and medial /u/.
- Discriminate initial and medial /u/.
- Segment words.
- Substitute medial sounds.

Phonemic Awareness
↻ Initial and Medial /u/

Review

Initial /u/ Display the *umbrella* Picture Card. This is an *umbrella. Umbrella* begins with /u/: /u/, *umbrella*. What sound does *umbrella* begin with? Continue the routine with the following words: *under, up, us.*

Medial /u/ Display the *nut* Picture Card. This is a *nut*. Listen to the sounds in *nut:* /n/ /u/ /t/. How many sounds do you hear? (three) Where do you hear /u/? Is /u/ the first sound in *nut*, /n/ /u/ /t/? (no) Is /u/ the last sound in *nut*, /n/ /u/ /t/? (no) The /u/ in *nut* is in the middle. Continue the routine with the following words: *puff, sub, luck, bud.*

Picture Card

Discriminate sounds

Listen to the beginning sound in *us. Us* begins with /u/. Now listen to these two words: *down, under.* Which word begins with the same sound as *us?* Does *down* begin with /u/? (no) Does *under* begin with /u/? (yes) *Us* and *under* both begin with /u/.

I am going to say three words. Repeat the two words that have /u/ in the middle. Listen carefully: *cot, jug, bun.* Which two words have /u/ in the middle? (*jug* and *bun*) Say *jug* and *bun* with me: *jug, bun.* Continue the routine with these sets of words: *dump, doll, dust; tub, sun, tent; hen, hut, suds.*

Picture Card

On their own

Display the *duck, egg, jug,* and *mop* Picture Cards. Have children choose one of the pictures to draw. Have them write a *u* on their paper if the word has /u/.

Segment

How many sounds do you hear in the word *tug*? Hold up a finger for each sound. Listen carefully: /t/ /u/ /g/. How many sounds do you hear? There are three sounds in *tug*. Continue with these words: *run, dug, cut, sun.*

Corrective feedback

If... children do not grasp the concept of segmenting words into sounds,

then... review the sounds of individual phonemes before moving on to segmenting words.

Substitute medial sounds

Listen to this word: *fun*, /f/ /u/ /n/, *fun*. Say it with me: /f/ /u/ /n/, *fun*. I can make a new word by changing the middle sound in *fun* to /a/. Listen: /f/ /a/ /n/, *fan*. Say it with me as I blend the new sounds: /f/ /a/ /n/, *fan*. Continue substituting medial sounds with the following words: *mud, mad; tag, tug.*

Differentiated Instruction

 **Strategic Intervention**

Segment Use a segmentation cheer to segment a word sound by sound. Say a word and tell children to give you the beginning sound, middle sound, and ending sound. Then say the word together.

![ELL]

English Language Learners
Access Content Have children share words in their home language that start with or include /u/.

Phonics — Teach/Model

 /u/ Spelled *Uu*

Review   **/u/Uu** Display the *Uu* Alphabet Card and point to the *umbrella*. What sound do you hear at the beginning of *umbrella*? What letter spells that sound? **Point to the letters *Uu*.** What is the sound for this letter? What are the names of these letters?

Review   **Letter Names and Sounds** Use Alphabet Cards to review the following letter names and sounds: *Aa, Bb, Dd, Ee, Ff, Gg, Ii, Mm, Nn, Oo, Pp, Rr, Ss, Tt, Xx.*

Alphabet Card

Blend sounds   Write *bug* on the board. Say the sound of each letter with me: /b/ /u/ /g/. Now blend the sounds as I point to each letter: /b/ /u/ /g/. What is the word? (*bug*) Now that we know *u* and *g* spell *-ug*, we can read more words that end with *-ug*. Write *rug* on the board. Say the sounds with me: /r/ *-ug*. What is the new word? The new word is *rug*. Continue with *mug, hug, plug, dug,* and *tug*. Then use the *-um* family: *gum, sum, glum, drum*.

More practice   Use *Reader's and Writer's Notebook,* p. 363 for additional practice with /u/.

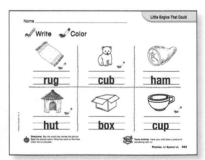

Reader's and Writer's Notebook, p. 363

Sound-Spelling Display the *Ww* Alphabet Card. What sound do you hear at the beginning of *water-melon*? What letter spells that sound? The letter *w* spells /w/. Review the following letters with Alphabet Cards: *Aa, Bb, Dd, Ee, Gg, Hh, Ii, Mm, Rr, Ss.*

High-Frequency Words Write *what* on the board. This is the word *what*. What is this word? Continue the routine with *said, was, little, have,* and *to.*

Alphabet Card

Differentiated Instruction

 Strategic Intervention

Support High-Frequency Words Remind children that high-frequency words are not words they can sound out. Children should memorize these words so they know them when they come across them in a story.

Don't Wait Until Friday

MONITOR PROGRESS ↺ Check Word Reading High-Frequency Words

Write *what, said,* and *was* on the board. Have children take turns reading the words.

Practice reading these words from Kindergarten Student Reader K.5.4, *Bud Likes Mud.*

| Bud | pup | Jem | Rex | Jan | dig | mud | run |
| jump | big | tub | suds | fill | fits | tugs | rags |

If... children cannot read the high-frequency words,
then... write the words on cards for them to practice at home.

If... children cannot segment words into sounds,
then... review the sounds of individual phonemes before moving on to segmenting words.

If... children can successfully blend sounds to read the words,
then... have them read Kindergarten Student Reader K.5.4, *Bud Likes Mud.*

Day 1	Day 2	Day 3	Day 4	Day 5
Check Phonemic Awareness	Check Sound-Spelling/ Retelling	Check Word Reading	Check Phonemic Awareness	Check Oral Vocabulary

Success Predictor

Word Reading

Success Predictor

Objectives
- Read /u/ words.
- Read high-frequency words.

Kindergarten Student Reader K.5.4
 /u/ Spelled *Uu* and
High-Frequency Words

Review

Review the previously taught high-frequency words. Have children read each word as you point to it on the Word Wall.

is	little	he	a	with	like	to	the
said	they	what	was	my	look	here	we	do

Teach rebus words

Write the word *garden* on the board. This is the word *garden*. Name the letters with me: *g, a, r, d, e, n; garden.* What is a garden? Look for the word *garden* in the book we read today. A picture above the word will help you read it.

Read Kindergarten Student Reader K.5.4

Display the Kindergarten Student Reader K.5.4. Today we are going to read a new book. Point to the title of the book. The title of this book is *Bud Likes Mud*. The author's name is Ben Ollie. Hector Borlasca illustrated the book.

Use the reading decodable books routine to read the Kindergarten Student Reader.

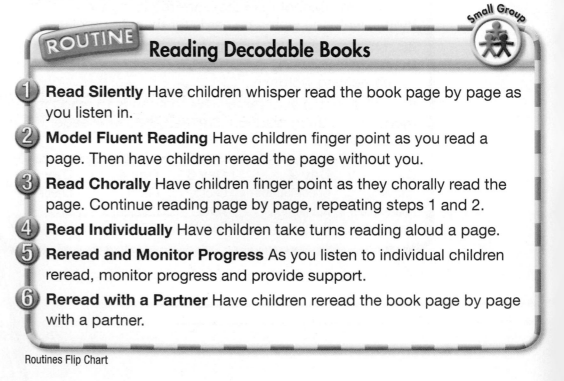

ROUTINE **Reading Decodable Books** *Small Group*

1. **Read Silently** Have children whisper read the book page by page as you listen in.

2. **Model Fluent Reading** Have children finger point as you read a page. Then have children reread the page without you.

3. **Read Chorally** Have children finger point as they chorally read the page. Continue reading page by page, repeating steps 1 and 2.

4. **Read Individually** Have children take turns reading aloud a page.

5. **Reread and Monitor Progress** As you listen to individual children reread, monitor progress and provide support.

6. **Reread with a Partner** Have children reread the book page by page with a partner.

Routines Flip Chart

Bud is a little pup.
He is a fun little pup.
Jem, Rex, and Jan have fun with Bud.

2

Bud likes to dig in the mud.
Mom said, "Do not dig in the mud."
But Bud likes to dig.

3

Jem, Rex, and Jan run and jump.
They run and jump for fun.
Bud digs in the garden.

4

Kindergarten Student Reader K.5.4

What was in my garden?
Look at it! Did Bud dig here?

5

Look at Bud!
We will get the big tub.
Mom will get the suds.

6

We fill the tub with lots of suds.
Bud fits in the tub.
He tugs at the rags.

7

We had fun!
Do not dig in the garden, Bud!

8

Differentiated Instruction

(A) Advanced

Support Retelling Have children retell *Bud Likes Mud* in front of the class to practice their retelling and speaking skills.

Teacher Tip

You may wish to have children use the high-frequency words in sentences so that they may better understand the words.

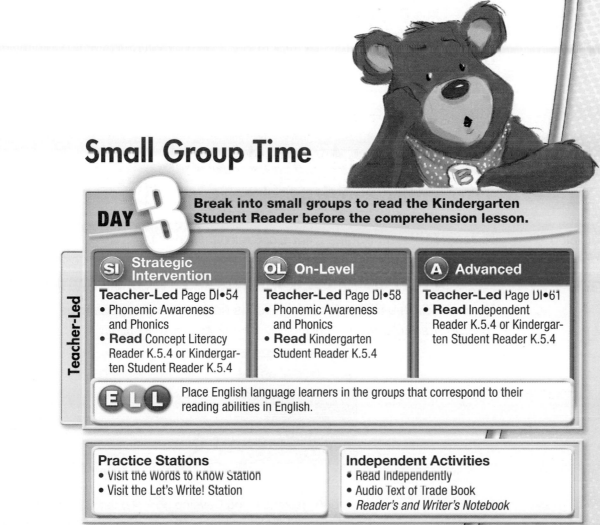

Small Group Time

DAY 3

Break into small groups to read the Kindergarten Student Reader before the comprehension lesson.

Teacher-Led

SI Strategic Intervention	**OL** On-Level	**A** Advanced
Teacher-Led Page DI•54	**Teacher-Led** Page DI•58	**Teacher-Led** Page DI•61
• Phonemic Awareness and Phonics	• Phonemic Awareness and Phonics	• **Read** Independent Reader K.5.4 or Kindergarten Student Reader K.5.4
• **Read** Concept Literacy Reader K.5.4 or Kindergarten Student Reader K.5.4	• **Read** Kindergarten Student Reader K.5.4	

ELL Place English language learners in the groups that correspond to their reading abilities in English.

Practice Stations
• Visit the Words to Know Station
• Visit the Let's Write! Station

Independent Activities
• Read Independently
• Audio Text of Trade Book
• *Reader's and Writer's Notebook*

ELL

English Language Learners

Access Content Have children act out the action words *dig, fill,* and *tug* from Kindergarten Student Reader K.5.4.

Objectives
- Recall and retell a selection.
◎ Practice plot.
- Develop and use vocabulary.
- Develop and apply comprehension skills.

Comprehension

Retell the story

Have children turn to p. 86 of *My Skills Buddy* and use the retelling boxes to retell the story *The Little Engine That Could*.

Envision It!

Think Aloud Direct students to the first retell box. This is when the train breaks down. Tell me about the trains that the clown asks for help.

Continue reviewing the retelling boxes and having children retell the story.

My Skills Buddy, p. 86

Review

◎ **Plot** Display illustrations in *The Little Engine That Could*. Let's review the plot in this story.

- What happens at the beginning of the story? (A train breaks down. It is carrying toys and dolls.)

- What happens in the middle of the story? (The toys and dolls ask other engines for help.)

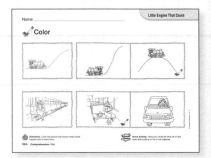

- What happens at the end of the story? (The Little Blue Engine helps the train over the mountain.)

More practice Use *Reader's and Writer's Notebook*, p. 364, for additional practice with plot.

Reader's and Writer's Notebook, p. 364

Second Read—Trade Book
The Little Engine That Could

Develop vocabulary

Reread *The Little Engine That Could*. Follow the Day 3 arrow beginning on p. 363, and use the Develop Vocabulary notes to prompt conversations about the story.

Have children use the Amazing Words *engine, tracks, passenger, roundhouse, mountain,* and *valley* to talk about the story.

DAY **2**
Read for enjoyment

DAY **3**
Reread using Develop Vocabulary notes

DAY **4**
Reread using Guide Comprehension notes

Develop Vocabulary

DAY 3

Open-ended
What do you see riding on the train? (toys, animals)

- The train is carrying toys and animals. Where do you think it is going?

Chug, chug, chug. Puff, puff, puff. Ding-dong, ding-dong. The little train rumbled over the tracks. She was a happy little train

Trade Book, p. 3

Guide Comprehension

DAY 4

Inferential
How do you think the Little Red Engine feels at the beginning of the trip? How can you tell? (The Little Red Engine is happy. She is smiling.)

Develop Vocabulary, continued

DAY 3

Wh- question

What are some of the toys you see here? (stuffed animals, dolls)

- The train is carrying dolls and many stuffed animals. What animals do you see?

Develop Vocabulary load, dolls

for she had such a jolly load to carry. Her cars were filled full of good things for boys and girls.

There were toy animals—giraffes with long necks, Teddy

bears with almost no necks at all, and even a baby elephant. Then there were dolls—dolls with blue eyes and yellow curls, dolls with

Trade Book, pp. 4–5

Guide Comprehension, continued

DAY 4

Recall

Where is the little train going? (The little train is taking good things to boys and girls. She is going over a river on a bridge.)

Distancing

What are some of the toys you see here? (stuffed animals, dolls, a clown, a kite, an airplane, tops, a fire truck, and books)

• There are dolls, books, games, and other toys. Which toys would you like to play with?

brown eyes and brown bobbed heads, and the funniest little toy clown you ever saw. And there were cars full of toy engines,

airplanes, tops, picture puzzles, books, and every kind of thing boys or girls could want.

Trade Book, pp. 6–7

Compare and Contrast

How are the things on the little train alike? (They are all things children can play with.) How are the things on the little train different? (some are indoor toys, some are outdoor toys; some are books, some are dolls, etc.)

Develop Vocabulary, continued

DAY 3

Wh- question
What kinds of food do you see here? (oranges, apples, milk, spinach, peppermints, lollypops)

• There are some foods here that are healthy and some that are not so healthy. Which ones are best for you? (oranges, apples, milk, spinach)

But that was not all. Some of the cars were filled with all sorts of good things for boys and girls to eat—big golden oranges, red-cheeked apples, bottles of creamy milk for their breakfasts,

fresh spinach for their dinners, peppermint drops, and lollypops for after-meal treats.

Trade Book, pp. 8–9

Guide Comprehension, continued

DAY 4

Distancing
Why is the little train bringing both toys and food to the boys and girls? (Children need both toys and food to be healthy and happy.)

Open-ended

What happens to the train at the beginning of the story? (The train stops moving.)

- The train stops moving. What do you think will happen next to the toys?

The little train was carrying all these wonderful things to the good little boys and girls on the other side of the mountain. She

puffed along merrily. Then all of a sudden she stopped with a jerk. She simply could not go another inch. She tried and she tried, but her wheels would not turn.

Trade Book, pp. 10–11

Open-ended

How do you think the toys feel when the train stops? (They are surprised. They wonder what happened.)

Develop Vocabulary, continued

DAY 3

Open-ended
What is the clown doing? (waving a red flag)

• The clown is waving a red flag. Why is he doing that? (to signal for help)

What were all those good little boys and girls on the other side of the mountain going to do without the wonderful toys to play with and the good food to eat?

"Here comes a shiny new engine," said the funny little clown who jumped out of the train. "Let us ask him to help us."
So all the dolls and toys cried out together:

Trade Book, pp. 12–13

Guide Comprehension, continued

DAY 4

Wh- question
Who does the clown flag down?
(The clown flags down the Shiny New Engine.)

Wh- question

What do you think the clown is doing? (asking for help)

- The clown is asking the Shiny New Engine for help. How does the clown want the Shiny New Engine to help? (He asks the Shiny New Engine to help pull their train over the mountain.)

Develop Vocabulary toys

"Please, Shiny New Engine, won't you please pull our train over the mountain? Our engine has broken down, and the boys and girls on the other side won't have any toys to play with or good food to eat unless you help us."

Trade Book, pp. 14–15

Distancing

The dolls and toys ask the Shiny New Engine to help them. How do you ask someone for help? (I always say "please" and explain why I need help. Then I say "thank you" after they help me.)

Develop Vocabulary, continued

DAY 3

Wh- question
Why is the Shiny New Engine leaving? (He won't help them.)

- The Shiny New Engine won't pull the train. How do the toys look now?

Develop Vocabulary sleeping cars, dining car

Expand Vocabulary berths

But the Shiny New Engine snorted: "I pull you? I am a Passenger Engine. I have just carried a fine big train over the mountain, with more cars than you ever dreamed of. My train had sleeping cars, with comfortable berths; a dining-car where waiters bring whatever hungry people want to eat; and parlor cars in which people sit in soft arm-chairs and look out of big plate-glass windows. I pull the likes of you? Indeed not!" And off

Trade Book, pp. 16–17

Guide Comprehension, continued

DAY 4

Compare and Contrast
How are the Little Red Engine and the Shiny New Engine alike? (They both pull train cars.) How are the Little Red Engine and the Shiny New Engine different? (The Little Red Engine carries cars of toys and the Shiny New Engine carries cars of passengers.)

Recall

What is the clown waving at now? (another engine)

- The toys are trying to get another engine to stop.
  Did they give up after one engine said no? (No;
  they are trying again.)

he steamed to the roundhouse, where engines live when they are
not busy.

How sad the little train and all the dolls and toys felt!
Then the little clown called out, "The Passenger Engine is not

Trade Book, pp. 18–19

Recall

Where does the Shiny New Engine go? (The Shiny
New Engine goes to the roundhouse to wait for his
next trip.)

Develop Vocabulary, continued

DAY 3

Open-ended

Another engine is coming. Is it big and strong or small and weak? (big and strong)

- This engine is big and strong. Do you think it can pull the train?

the only one in the world. Here is another engine coming, a great big strong one. Let us ask him to help us."

The little toy clown waved his flag and the big strong engine came to a stop.

"Please, oh, please, Big Engine," cried all the dolls and toys together. "Won't you please pull our train over the mountain? Our engine has broken down, and the good little boys and girls

Trade Book, pp. 20–21

Guide Comprehension, continued

DAY 4

Wh- question

Why does the Big Engine stop? (He sees the clown waving the red flag.)

Recall

Does this engine help the train? (no)

- This engine does not help. How many engines have the toys asked for help so far? (two)

Expand Vocabulary freight

on the other side won't have any toys to play with or good food to eat unless you help us."

But the Big Strong Engine bellowed: "I am a Freight Engine.

I have just pulled a big train loaded with big machines over the mountain. These machines print books and newspapers for grown-ups to read. I am a very important engine indeed. I won't pull the likes of you!" And the Freight Engine puffed off

Trade Book, pp. 22–23

Plot

Name the major events of the story so far. What happens before the Big Strong Engine leaves? (First, the little train breaks. Next, the toys ask the Shiny New Engine for help. He does not help. Then the toys ask the Big Strong Engine for help. He does not help, either.)

Develop Vocabulary, continued

DAY 3

Open-ended

What does this next engine look like? (old and tired)

- The engine is old and tired. Do you think this tired, old engine can help the train over the mountain?

indignantly to the roundhouse.

The little train and all the dolls and toys were very sad.

"Cheer up," cried the little toy clown. "The Freight Engine is

not the only one in the world. Here comes another. He looks very old and tired, but our train is so little, perhaps he can help us."

So the little toy clown waved his flag and the dingy, rusty old

Trade Book, pp. 24–25

Guide Comprehension, continued

DAY 4

Inferential

Why is the clown excited? (He thinks the Rusty Old Engine will help.)

Wh- question

Why can't the Rusty Old Engine help? (He is too tired.)

- The Rusty Old Engine is too tired to help. How do the toys feel now?

Develop Vocabulary wheels

engine stopped.

"Please, Kind Engine," cried all the dolls and toys together. "Won't you please pull our train over the mountain? Our engine has broken down, and the boys and girls on the other side won't

have any toys to play with or good food to eat unless you help us."

But the Rusty Old Engine sighed: "I am so tired. I must rest my weary wheels. I cannot pull even so little a train as yours over the mountain. I can not. I can not. I can not."

Trade Book, pp. 26–27

Monitor and Fix Up

How do the toys feel? How do you know? If you don't understand how the toys feel, what could you do? (If I don't understand what is read, I look at the pictures to help me understand the story. I see the dolls are crying, so I know they are sad.)

Develop Vocabulary, continued

Wh- question

How do the toys look now? (excited, happy)

DAY 3

- The toys look excited and happy.
  Why are they happy and excited?

And off he rumbled to the roundhouse chugging, "I can not. I can not. I can not."

Then indeed the little train was very, very sad, and the dolls and toys were ready to cry.

But the little clown called out, "Here is another engine coming, a little blue engine, a very little one, maybe she will help us."

The very little engine came chug, chugging merrily along. When she saw the toy clown's flag, she stopped quickly.

Trade Book, pp. 28–29

Guide Comprehension, continued

DAY 4

Recall

Which trains have the toys asked for help so far, and in what order? (First, they asked the Shiny New Engine. Then they asked the Big Strong Engine. Last, they asked the Rusty Old Engine.)

Open-ended

What are the toys doing now? (asking the Little Blue Engine for help)

- The toys are asking for the Little Blue Engine to pull the train. Does she look strong enough to pull the train?

"What is the matter, my friends?" she asked kindly.

"Oh, Little Blue Engine," cried the dolls and toys. "Will you pull us over the mountain? Our engine has broken down and the

good boys and girls on the other side won't have any toys to play with or good food to eat, unless you help us. Please, please, help

Trade Book, pp. 30–31

Inferential

How do you know the the toys are polite? (They always say "please" when they are asking for help.)

Develop Vocabulary, continued

DAY 3

Wh- question

Is the Little Blue Engine leaving like the other engines? (no)

- The Little Blue Engine says she's not very big, but she doesn't say no. How do you think the toys feel about that?

Develop Vocabulary switching

us, Little Blue Engine."

"I'm not very big," said the Little Blue Engine. "They use me only for switching trains in the yard. I have never been over the mountain."

"But we must get over the mountain before the children awake," said all the dolls and the toys.

The very little engine looked up and saw the tears in the dolls' eyes. And she thought of the good little boys and girls on the other side of the mountain who would not have any toys or good

Trade Book, pp. 32–33

Guide Comprehension, continued

DAY 4

Open-ended

How do you think the author feels about trying to help others? (I think the author feels it is important to help others.)

Distancing

The Little Blue Engine decides to try. What does she say over and over again? (**"I think I can."**)

- The Little Blue Engine tries very hard and says, "I think I can." Have you ever had to try very hard to do something?

food unless she helped.

Then she said, "I think I can. I think I can. I think I can." And she hitched herself to the little train.

She tugged and pulled and pulled and tugged and slowly,

slowly, slowly they started off.

The toy clown jumped aboard and all the dolls and the toy animals began to smile and cheer.

Puff, puff, chug, chug, went the Little Blue Engine. "I think I can—I think I can—I think I can—I think I can—I think I can—

Trade Book, pp. 34–35

Draw Conclusions

How do you know that the toys were happy? (**They smile and cheer. People smile when they are happy.**)

Develop Vocabulary, continued

DAY 3

Distancing

How do the toys feel when they reach the top of the mountain? (happy)

• The Little Blue Engine and toys are very happy. How do you feel when someone helps you?

I think I can—I think I can—I think I can—I think I can."

Up, up, up. Faster and faster and faster and faster the little engine climbed, until at last they reached the top of the mountain.

Down in the valley lay the city.

"Hurray, hurray," cried the funny little clown and all the dolls and toys. "The good little boys and girls in the city will be happy because you helped us, kind, Little Blue Engine."

Trade Book, pp. 36–37

Guide Comprehension, continued

DAY 4

Open-ended

What words could you use to describe the Little Blue Engine? (The Little Blue Engine is kind, helpful, determined, and brave.)

Distancing

Do you think the Little Blue Engine enjoys helping the toys? (Yes, it makes her happy.)

- The Little Blue Engine is happy to reach her goal. How do you feel when you are able to do something hard?

Continue with **DAY 3**

Conventions p. 382

And the Little Blue Engine smiled and seemed to say as she puffed steadily down the mountain,

"I thought I could. I thought I could. I thought I could.
I thought I could.
I thought I could.
I thought I could."

Trade Book, pp. 38–39

Open-ended

What do you think helps the Little Blue Engine pull the train over the mountain? (The Little Blue Engine has a good attitude. She tells herself over and over again, "I think I can. I think I can.")

Skip to **DAY 4**

Conventions p. 396

Conventions
Prepositions

Review

Write this sentence on the board:

> **The mug is on the desk.**

Remind children of what they learned about prepositions. A preposition is a word that tells us more about a noun in a sentence. It tells how the noun is related to the other parts of a sentence. *Mug* is the noun. Point to *on* and *mug* as you read the sentence. *On* is the preposition in this sentence. *On* tells us where to find the mug: **on** *the desk*. Underline the word *on*.

Guide practice

Write the following sentences on the board:

> **Ann reads under the tree.**
>
> **Bugs crawl on rocks.**
>
> **Ducks fly over this lake.**

Read the first sentence. Which word tells us about where Ann reads? (*under*) Point to *under*. *Under* is the preposition. What does the preposition tell us about where Ann reads? (It tells that she reads under the tree.) Read the second sentence. Which word tells us where bugs crawl? (*on*) What kind of word is this? (preposition) Read the third sentence. Which word is a preposition? (*over*)

Team Talk Pair children and have them draw pictures of an apple *in, on,* or *under* a desk. Have children label their pictures with the appropriate prepositions and then take turns telling where the apple can be found in their pictures in complete sentences.

On their own Use *Reader's and Writer's Notebook,* p. 365, for more practice with prepositions.

Daily Fix-It Use the Daily Fix-It for more conventions practice.

Reader's and Writer's Notebook, p. 365

Writing
Formal Letter

Teach
What are the parts of a letter? A letter has a greeting, something to share, a closing, and a signature. What makes letters different from each other is the reason they are written and to *whom* they are sent. Informal letters are friendly. We send them to people we know. We send formal letters to people we do not know very well, such as leaders or business people. We write them to share ideas, to ask for something, or to express our feelings.

Model
Let's write a formal letter to the Little Blue Engine's company telling about the good job she did. First, I will write a greeting. Since I don't know the company owner's name, I use this greeting: (say and write the greeting: *Dear Sir or Madam,*). Next, I will share my message. Say and write the following sentences: *The Little Blue Engine works hard. She is helpful. She does a good job*. Next, I write a formal closing: (say and write: *From,*). The last thing I write is my name: (say and write your name).

Guide practice
Have children suggest ideas for a formal letter to the school principal. Choose one of these suggestions and guide children in writing a class letter.

Independent writing
Have children turn to p. 366 of *Reader's and Writer's Notebook*. Have children write or dictate a formal letter about a toy or game they like to someone who works at a toy company.

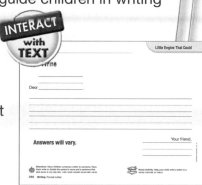

Reader's and Writer's Notebook, p. 366

Daily Handwriting

Write *Uncle* and *suds* on the board. Review correct letter formation of uppercase *U* and lowercase *u.*

D'Nealian™   Ball and Stick

Have children write *Uncle* and *suds* on their Write-On Boards. Remind children to use proper left-to-right and top-to-bottom progression and proper spacing between letters when writing *U* and *u.*

Differentiated Instruction

SI Strategic Intervention

Physical Response Help children understand the prepositions *in, on, over,* and *under* by acting out the words. I am going to say some sentences. Act out the preposition in each sentence. Have children put their hands in their pockets for *in*, on their desks for *on,* under their desks for *under*, and over their heads for *over.* Use the following sentences: *We are in school. Bud hid under the table. The pup naps on the rug. I see over the fence.*

Academic Vocabulary

preposition word that shows how a noun is related to other words in that sentence

formal letter a piece of writing sent to someone the writer does not know well or at all

Daily Fix-It

can you do hard work
Can you do hard work?

This week's practice sentences appear on Teacher Resources DVD-ROM.

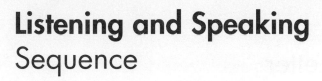
Listening and Speaking
Sequence

Review   Remind children that good speakers take turns and speak one at a time when sharing ideas and information with the class. Remind students of the importance of listening for sequence in a story. When we listen to a story, we listen for the order in which things happen. We call this the sequence of a story. We look for what happens first, next, and last.

Model   Pick up AlphaBuddy and have him act out tying a shoe. Discuss how children learn to tie their shoes. First, someone shows you how to tie a shoelace. Next, they show you again and let you try to help. Later, they let you try and if you cannot do it, they help you finish. Finally, you can do it by yourself.

Guide practice   Have children turn to p. 88 of *My Skills Buddy.* Use the first Listening and Speaking bullet to guide the discussion. When you are trying to do a job that is hard to do, what happens? Can you do the job the first time? Do you need to try several times before you can do it?

Tell children to discuss things that they have learned to do, first by trying repeatedly, and later doing it easily. For boys and girls it is just as hard to tie shoelaces as it is for a train to pull a big load up a mountain.

My Skills Buddy, p. 89

Independent practice

Have children turn to p. 89 of *My Skills Buddy.* Use the Listening and Speaking bullets on p. 88 of *My Skills Buddy* to guide the discussion. Do you remember which engine tried first to pull the train up the mountain? Help children recall that the first engine broke trying to pull the train up the mountain. Then have children come to the front of the class one at a time to tell one thing that happens next, until someone tells the last event in the story. Refer children to the Rules for Listening and Speaking from p. 1 of *Reader's and Writer's Notebook.* Remind children to take turns, speaking one at a time, when retelling the story's sequence of events. Remind children to face the speaker when listening to events from the story.

Name _____

🐻 Listening Rules

1. Face the person who is speaking.
2. Be quiet while someone is speaking.
3. Pay attention to the speaker.
4. Ask questions if you don't understand.

Listening and Speaking Rules 1

Reader's and Writer's Notebook, p. 1

Be a Good Listener

1. Face the speaker who is speaking.
2. Be quiet while someone is speaking.
3. Pay attention to the speaker.
4. Ask questions if you don't understand.
5. Take turns speaking and listening.

English Language Learners

Support Listening Comprehension According to Dr. Georgia Earnest García of the University of Illinois at Urbana-Champaign: "Beginning English language learners benefit from the repeated readings of predictable texts with illustrations, especially when the teacher has provided a brief preview of each text to introduce the topic of the story and preview new vocabulary."

Objectives
- Review skills learned and practiced today.
- Write one's own name.

Wrap Up Your Day

✔ **Concept Talk** Today we read about a good helper, the Little Blue Engine. How can you be a good helper?

✔ **Respond to Literature** Today we read about a pup that digs in the garden. Have you ever seen a muddy dog take a bath?

✔ **Conventions** Write the following sentence on the board: *The pup digs in mud*. Have children copy and illustrate the sentence. Then have them circle the preposition. (*in*)

✔ **Homework Idea** Have children draw and label a picture of a pup.

Preview DAY 4

Tomorrow we will read about one of our Trucktown friends.

Extend Your Day!

Science
Motion

Materials: balls of various sizes, smooth and rough ground surfaces

A Body in Motion In the gym or on the playground, have children observe carefully as you roll a ball toward a barrier.

- Describe the way the ball moved. Was it rolling quickly or slowly?
- What happened when the ball hit the wall?
- Why did the ball change direction?

Roll a different-sized ball with similar force toward the barrier and compare the results.

Resistance Move to an open space. Have children predict what will happen if you roll a ball here. Will the ball change direction? Will it keep rolling forever? Will the ball move differently if you roll it on smooth ground or on the grass? Arrange children into groups and give each group a ball. Tell them to take turns rolling the balls with the same force on both smooth and rough surfaces. Discuss the outcome.

Language Arts
Letter Train

Materials: construction paper, colored paper rectangles, crayons, glue

Write Your Name Give each child one paper rectangle for each letter in his or her first name. These rectangles are train cars. Each car will carry one letter of your name. Instruct children to write one letter of their name on each rectangle. Model the process on the board.

All Aboard! Have children glue the rectangles to the paper, moving from left to right. Instruct children to connect their train cars with lines and to decorate their trains.

Phonemic Awareness
/u/ Words

Materials: Picture Cards

Identify /u/ Words Separate /u/ Picture Cards from the rest of the deck. Display sets of three Picture Cards—two /u/ cards and one other card. Identify the picture on each card and have children tell you the sounds. Choose a volunteer to pick the two cards with /u/.

Picture Cards

Objectives

- Discuss the concept to develop oral language.
- Build oral vocabulary.

Today at a Glance

Oral Vocabulary
mountain, valley

Phonemic Awareness
Initial and Medial /u/

Phonics
Sounds Spelled *Xx, Jj, Ww, Uu*

Comprehension
◉ Plot

Conventions
Nouns

Writing
Extend the Concept

Vocabulary
Time Words

TRUCKTOWN on Reading Street

Start your engines!

- Display "Patty Cake, Patty Cake" and lead the group in saying the rhyme a few times.
- Have the group clap the rhythm as they recite the rhyme.
- When children master the rhythm, have them march around the room as they say the rhyme.

Truckery Rhymes

Concept Talk

Question of the Week

 What kind of work do trains do?

Build concepts

Write the question of the week on the board. Read the question as you track the print. Have children answer the question in complete sentences. Display Sing with Me Chart 28B.

Listen for Amazing Words

We are going to sing this song again. Listen for the Amazing Words *mountain* and *valley*. Sing the song several times with children to the tune of "On Top of Old Smoky." Have them stamp their feet when they hear *mountain* and *valley*.

 Sing with Me Audio

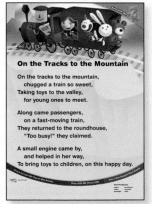

On the Tracks to the Mountain

On the tracks to the mountain,
chugged a train so sweet,
Taking toys to the valley,
for young ones to meet.

Along came passengers,
on a fast-moving train,
They returned to the roundhouse,
"Too busy!" they claimed.

A small engine came by,
and helped on her way,
To bring toys to children, on this happy day.

Talk with Me/Sing with Me Chart 28B

ELL **Produce Oral Language** Use the Day 4 instruction on ELL Poster 28 to extend and enrich language.

ELL Poster 28

Oral Vocabulary
Amazing Words

Amazing Words

engine	tracks
passenger	roundhouse
mountain	valley

Teach Amazing Words

> **Amazing Words** **Oral Vocabulary Routine**
>
> **1** **Introduce the Word** A *mountain* is a very tall hill. It sometimes has trees and snow. What is our new Amazing Word for a very tall hill? Say it with me: *mountain*.
>
> **2** **Demonstrate** *Some mountains are so tall they have snow on them all year.* Have you ever been on a *mountain*?
>
> Repeat steps 1 and 2.
>
> **Introduce the Word** A *valley* is the low land between two hills or mountains. What is our new Amazing Word for the low land between hills or mountains? Say it with me: *valley*.
>
> **Demonstrate** *If you live in a valley, you are between two big hills or mountains. Some valleys have rivers.*
>
> **3** **Apply** Tell children to use *mountain* and *valley* in complete sentences. Have them illustrate the words.

Routines Flip Chart

Use Amazing Words

To reinforce the concept and the Amazing Words, have children supply the appropriate Amazing Word for each sentence.

> **Snow covered the top of the _____.** (mountain)
>
> **The _____ is surrounded by hills.** (valley)

Differentiated Instruction

SI Strategic Intervention

Amazing Words Help children understand the relationship between a mountain and a valley by drawing on the board a simple valley surrounded by two mountains. Point to the two mountain peaks. These are mountains. Point to the valley. This is the valley. Valleys are between mountains or hills. You need at least two mountains or hills to make a valley.

English Language Learners
Access Content Have children share how they say *mountain* and *valley* in their home languages.

Phonemic Awareness
Review /u/

Review

Display the *up* Picture Card. This arrow is pointing *up*. *Up* begins with /u/. What sound does *up* begin with? Continue the routine with the words *under* and *us*. Then display the *duck* Picture Card. This is a *duck*. Where do you hear /u/ in the word *duck*? The middle sound in *duck* is /u/. What is the middle sound in *duck*? Repeat the routine with the *mug* and *tub* Picture Cards.

I am going to say three words. Tell me which words have /u/: *skunk, bank, tub*. I hear /u/ in *skunk* and *tub*. Let's try some more. Listen carefully to each set of words and tell me which words have /u/: *suds, sock, pup.* Continue the activity with the following sets of words: *mug, trunk, tank; bunch, camp, plug.*

Picture Card

Corrective feedback

If... children cannot discriminate /u/,
then... have them say /u/ several times, /u/, /u/, /u/.

When you say /u/, your tongue is lifted up halfway in your mouth. Have children practice saying /u/, and then repeat the discrimination activity.

Picture Card

Phonics
Sounds Spelled *Xx, Jj, Ww, Uu*

Review Display the *Xx* Alphabet Card. This is an *x-ray*. *X-ray* begins with /ks/. What letter spells this sound /ks/? Yes, the letter *x*. Repeat the routine with the *Jj, Ww,* and *Uu* Alphabet Cards.

Write the word *win* on the board. Help me blend this word. Listen as I say each sound: /w/ /i/ /n/. Now let's blend the sounds together to read the word: /w/ /i/ /n/, *win*. What is the word? (*win*) Let's try some more. Repeat the routine with *jar, jug, wax,* and *up*.

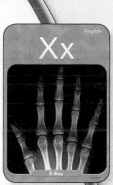

Xx
X-Ray

Alphabet Card

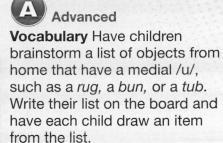

MONITOR PROGRESS **Check Phonemic Awareness**

Phoneme Segmentation I am going to say a word. I want you to tell me the sounds in the word.

tub	rug	sub	mud	bus	duck	sun	mug

If... children cannot identify the sounds in the word,

then... use the small-group Strategic Intervention lesson, p. DI•55, to reteach segmentation skills.

Continue to monitor children's progress using other instructional opportunities during the week so that they can be successful with the Day 5 Assessment. See the Skills Trace on p. 324.

Day 1	Day 2	Day 3	Day 4	Day 5
Check Phonemic Awareness	Check Sound-Spelling/ Retelling	Check Word Reading	Check Phonemic Awareness	Check Oral Vocabulary

Success Predictor

Don't Wait Until Friday

Differentiated Instruction

A Advanced

Vocabulary Have children brainstorm a list of objects from home that have a medial /u/, such as a *rug*, a *bun*, or a *tub*. Write their list on the board and have each child draw an item from the list.

ELL

English Language Learners

Support Phonics Speakers of Spanish, Tagalog, and some Asian languages may have a hard time distinguishing the short vowel in words such as *mud* and *mad*, or *pup* and *pop*. Have children practice pronouncing word pairs: *hut, hat; cup, cap; luck, lock; rub, rob*.

391

Phonemic Awareness

Success Predictor

Objectives
- Spell words.
- Blend and segment words.
- Read decodable text.
- Read high-frequency words.

Spelling
↻ /u/ Spelled *Uu*

ROUTINE **Spell Words**

Spell words

1 **Review Sound-Spellings** Display the *Uu* Alphabet Card. This is an *umbrella. Umbrella* begins with /u/. What is the letter for /u/? (*u*) Continue the routine with the following Alphabet Cards: *Cc, Pp, Rr, Bb, Hh, Gg.*

2 **Model** Today we are going to spell some words. Listen to the three sounds in *cup:* /k/ /u/ /p/.

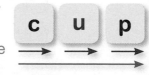

- What is the first sound in *cup?* (/k/) What is the letter for /k/? (*c*) Write *c* on the board.

- What is the middle sound you hear? (/u/) What is the letter for /u/? (*u*) Write *u* on the board.

- What is the last sound in *cup?* (/p/) What is the letter for /p/? (*p*) Write *p* on the board.

- Point to *cup.* Help me blend the sounds of the letters together to read this word: /k/ /u/ /p/. The word is *cup.* Repeat with the word *tub.*

3 **Guide Practice** Now let's spell the word *rub* together. Listen to the sounds in *rub:* /r/ /u/ /b/. What is the first sound in *rub?* (/r/) What is the letter for /r/? (*r*) Write *r* on the board. Now write *r* on your paper. What is the middle sound in *rub?* (/u/) What is the letter for /u/? (*u*) Write *u* on the board. Now write *u* on your paper. What is the last sound in *rub?* (/b/) What is the letter for /b/? (*b*) Write *b* on the board. Now write *b* on your paper. Now we can blend the sounds of the letters together to read the word: /r/ /u/ /b/. What is the word? (*rub*) Continue spell and blend practice with the words *hut* and *pup.*

4 **On Your Own** This time I am going to say a word. I want you to write the word on your paper. First say the word slowly in your head and then write the letter for each sound you hear. Listen carefully. Write the word *hug.* Give children time to write the word. How do you spell the word *hug?* Listen to the sounds: /h/ /u/ /g/. The first sound is /h/. What is the letter for /h/? Did you write *h* on your paper? The middle sound is /u/. What is the letter for /u/? Did you write *u* on your paper? The last sound is /g/. What is the letter for /g/? Did you write *g* on your paper? Name the letters in *hug. Hug* is spelled *h, u, g.* Continue the activity with the following words: *gum, bud, bug, but, dug, nut, hum.*

Routines Flip Chart

Get Set, Roll! Reader 28
⟳ Practice /u/ Spelled *Uu*

Review

Review the high-frequency words *have, they, what, said,* and *was*. Have children read each word as you point to it on the Word Wall.

Teach rebus words

Write *road* on the board. This word is *road.* Name the letters with me: *r, o, a, d.* When we read our book today, we will see the word *road* with a picture above it. The picture above the word will help you read it.

Read Get Set, Roll! Reader 28

Display Get Set, Roll! Reader 28, *Bump! Bump! Bump!* Today we will read a book about a bumpy road. Point to the title of the book. What is the title of the book? (*Bump! Bump! Bump!*) We will read some words with /u/ in this book.

Use the routine for reading decodable books found in the Routines Flip Chart to read Get Set, Roll! Reader 28.

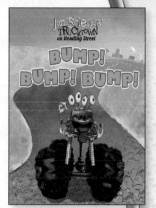

Get Set, Roll! Reader 28

Small Group Time

DAY 4

Break into small groups to read the Get Set, Roll! Reader before the comprehension lesson.

Teacher-Led

SI Strategic Intervention	**OL** On-Level	**A** Advanced
Teacher-Led Page DI•55 • Phonemic Awareness and Phonics • **Read** Get Set, Roll! Reader 28	**Teacher-Led** Page DI•59 • **Read** Get Set, Roll! Reader 28	**Teacher-Led** Page DI•62 • **Read** Get Set, Roll! Reader 28 or **Reread** Kindergarten Student Reader K.5.4

ELL Place English language learners in the groups that correspond to their reading abilities in English.

Practice Stations
• Visit the Let's Write! Station
• Visit the Read for Meaning Station

Independent Activities
• Read independently
• Audio Text of the Trade Book
• *Reader's and Writer's Notebook*

Differentiated Instruction

A Advanced

Practice High-Frequency Words Have children copy the high-frequency words *have, they, what, said,* and *was* on their Write-On Boards. Have them use the Word Wall as reference.

English Language Learners

Frontload Reader Take a picture walk with children to preview the reader before starting the routine.

Comprehension
◉ Plot

Practice plot

 Envision It!

Have children turn to the Literary Elements pictures on p. 75 of *My Skills Buddy.* As you look at the pictures, remind children that all stories have a beginning, a middle, and an end.

Team Talk Pair children and have them take turns describing the beginning, middle, and end of their day yesterday. Tell them that this is the plot of that day.

My Skills Buddy, pp. 74–75

Character

Review

Direct children to the Literary Elements picture on p. 74 of *My Skills Buddy.*

Characters are the animals or people in a story. Good readers pay attention to the characters so they know who the story is about. We can understand the characters better when we identify their traits. Traits are the qualities of the characters, such as *shy, smart,* or *silly.* Review the story "The Tortoise and the Hare."

• How can we describe the tortoise? (determined, stubborn, slow)
• How can we describe the hare? (proud, bragging, fast)

More practice

For more practice with character, use *Reader's and Writer's Notebook,* p. 367.

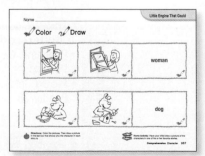

Reader's and Writer's Notebook, p. 367

Third Read—Trade Book
The Little Engine That Could

Guide comprehension

Display *The Little Engine That Could.* The characters in the story are train engines and toys. Remember, what these characters say and do is important to the plot of a story.

- How does the Little Red Engine act as she carries good things for children? (happy, jolly)

- How do the big engines act when they refuse to help the little train? (selfish, mean) What do they do? (leave without helping)

- The clown keeps getting new ideas to help the train. What does this tell about the clown? (He is trying hard; he is helping.) How does he act? (sometimes jumping and waving, sometimes slumping sadly)

Reread *The Little Engine That Could.* Return to p. 363. Follow the Day 4 arrow and use the Guide Comprehension notes to give children the opportunity to gain a more complete understanding of the story.

Differentiated Instruction

A **Advanced**

Support Comprehension Have children retell a story with which they are familiar. Then have them describe the traits of the characters in the story.

SI **Strategic Intervention**

Support Comprehension Some children may find it difficult to understand that an object can be a character. Explain to children that objects can be characters in fantasy stories. If an object acts and talks like a person, it can be a character. Explain that this is similar to when animals act like people in stories.

DAY **2**
Read for enjoyment

DAY **3**
Reread using Develop Vocabulary notes

DAY **4**
Reread using Guide Comprehension notes

Objectives
- Practice nouns.
- Write or dictate sentences about trains.

Conventions
Nouns

Review

Remind children of what they learned about nouns. A person, animal, place, or thing is a noun. We can name one or more than one. What are some nouns you see in the classroom? **Point to a book.** *Book* is a noun that names a thing. **Point to a child and say his or her name.** (*Child's name*) is a noun that names a person. **Point to your state on a map.** (*Your state*) is a noun that names a place. **Point to AlphaBuddy.** AlphaBuddy is a bear. *Bear* is a noun that names an animal. How can we say *book* and *bear* as nouns for more than one? Yes, *books* and *bears*.

Classroom is a noun for the place we are sitting right now. I can use the noun *classroom* in a sentence: *We learn in a classroom.* What are some words that name people and things in our classroom? Let's write our nouns on the board.

Guide practice

Write and read the following sentences:

> **Judy can hit the ball with her bat.**
>
> **Pam got a plum and two books at the store.**
>
> **The boy took his dogs to the park.**

Which words are nouns? **As children identify nouns, underline them.** I will reread the sentences. Clap when you hear a noun that names a person. **Reread the sentences.** (*Judy, Pam, boy*) Now, pat your head when you hear a noun that names a place. **Reread the sentences.** (*store, park*) Now, stomp your foot when you hear a noun that names a thing. **Reread the sentences.** (*ball, bat, plum, books*) Now, jump when you hear a noun that names an animal. **Reread the sentences.** (*dogs*) Which nouns name more than one? Circle the nouns for more than one as children identify them.

On their own

Use *Reader's and Writer's Notebook,* p. 368, for more practice with nouns.

Daily Fix-It

Use the Daily Fix-It for more conventions practice.

Reader's and Writer's Notebook, p. 368

Writing
Extend the Concept: Text to World

Discuss different trains

We just read a story about many different types of trains and engines. We read about a train that carries toys and food and about trains that carry passengers. In reading about trains in a story, we learned about the work trains do in real life.

Ask children to think about trains they have seen in person, in books, or on television. Have them describe what these trains looked like from the outside and what they may have carried. Children who have traveled on trains can describe what they look like on the inside. Guide children in comparing the trains they have seen with the trains from the story.

Guide practice

Use children's contributions to the discussion to write sentences.

> **Trains are on tracks.**
>
> **Some trains carry food.**
>
> **We can go on some trains.**

Encourage children to help you write more sentences. Have them read the sentences with you.

Independent writing

Have children draw pictures of trains. Tell them to draw the item that their train carries on the sides of the cars. Then help children label their pictures with the name of that item.

Daily Handwriting

Write uppercase *U* and lowercase *u* on the board. Review correct letter formation with children.

D'Nealian™   Ball and Stick

Have children write a row each of uppercase *U* and lowercase *u* on their Write-On Boards. Remind them to use proper left to right and top-to-bottom progression when writing *U* and *u*.

Differentiated Instruction

SI Strategic Intervention

Build Background Provide photographs and drawings of trains for children with limited experience with them. Be sure to include representations of a wide variety of trains: long-distance passenger trains, commuter trains and subways, and freight trains.

Daily Fix-It

i will take the train
I will take the train.

This week's practice sentences appear on Teacher Resources DVD-ROM.

English Language Learners
Support Writing As children write or dictate, supply English words if needed to express their ideas.

Vocabulary
Time Words

Teach

Write the words *Monday, Tuesday, Wednesday, Thursday, Friday, Saturday,* and *Sunday* on the board. Point to each word as you read it. These words name the days of the week. Have children turn to p. 88 of *My Skills Buddy.* Use the last two Vocabulary bullets in the discussion. Direct children to *Monday* on the calendar. What day is this: *Monday* or *Tuesday?* (Monday) Then direct them to *Thursday.* This is today's name. What day is today? (Thursday) Repeat with the other days of the week.

My Skills Buddy, p. 88

(**Team Talk**) Pair children and have them take turns describing what they like to do on different days in complete sentences.

Wrap Up Your Day

✔ **Oral Language** Sing "On the Tracks to the Mountain" with me. Blow a make-believe train whistle when you hear our Amazing Words: *engine, tracks, passenger, roundhouse, mountain, valley.*

✔ **Phonemic Awareness** I will say a sentence. Clap when you hear a word with /u/. *Uncle Gus put his plump skunk in the tub.*

✔ **Homework Idea** Have children search through magazines at home for nouns. Ask them to cut out a picture of *one* person, animal, or thing. Have them write or dictate a label for their picture. Then have them draw *more than one* of that noun. Have them write or dictate a label for the plural noun.

Preview DAY 5

Tell children that tomorrow they will review some of the books and stories they have read this week.

Extend Your Day!

Social Studies
Mountains

Materials: topographical map of the United States, outline maps of the United States (one per child), crayons

Map Reading Display a map of the United States. Review the colors for the land and water areas and identify the mountains. Help children find various mountain ranges on the map.

Show children where your state is and its proximity to a mountain range. Give children an outline map and have them draw the various mountain ranges. Then have them locate where

they live. Have them make a route for the train to follow to go over the mountains to get to their state, just like the train in the story *The Little Engine That Could.*

Phonics
Blending

Materials: pre-cut construction paper train cars, construction paper engine, tape

Blending Train Tape the construction paper engine to the board. Let's make a train to help blend words. Write the letters *b, u,* and *g* on three separate train cars. Tape them behind the engine, forming a train. The first train car has a *b, /b/.* The middle train car has a *u, /u/.* The last train car has a *g, /g/.* Blend the letters on the train cars with me: /b/ /u/ /g/. What word does this train spell? (*bug*) Replace letters to blend new words (bag, big, bug, but).

Comprehension
Plot

Materials: construction paper, markers, crayons

Beginning, Middle, End Review Get Set, Roll! Reader 28, *Bump! Bump! Bump!* What happens at the beginning of this story? What happens in the middle of this story? What happens at the end of this story? After the discussion, have children illustrate the major events of the story. Fold your paper into three parts. Draw what happens at the beginning of the story in the top part. Draw what happens in the middle of the story in the middle part, and draw what happens at the end in the bottom part.

Objectives
- Review the concepts.
- Build oral vocabulary.

Today at a Glance

Oral Vocabulary
engine, tracks, passenger, roundhouse, mountain, valley

Phonemic Awareness
◉ Initial and Medial /u/

Phonics
◉ /u/ Spelled *Uu*

Comprehension
◉ Plot

Conventions
Nouns

Writing
This Week We…

Check Oral Vocabulary
SUCCESS PREDICTOR

TRUCKTOWN on Reading Street

Start your engines!

- Display "Patty Cake, Patty Cake" and lead the group in saying the rhyme a few times.
- Have half the group recite the rhyme while the other half acts it out.
- Then have the groups change roles.

Truckery Rhymes

Concept Wrap Up

 Question of the Week

What kind of work do trains do?

Listen for Amazing Words

Write the question of the week on the board. Track the print as you read it to children. Have them use Amazing Words in their responses (*engine, tracks, passenger, roundhouse, mountain, valley*) and remind them to use complete sentences. Display Sing with Me Chart 28B. Let's sing "On the Tracks to the Mountain." I want you to listen to the Amazing Words we learned this week. Remind children that the words *engine, tracks, passenger, roundhouse, mountain,* and *valley* are in the song. Sing the song several times to the tune "On Top of Old Smoky." Tell children to sing along and clap each time they sing an Amazing Word.

 Sing with Me Audio

E L L Check Concepts and Language Use Day 5 instruction on ELL Poster 28 to monitor children's understanding of the lesson concept.

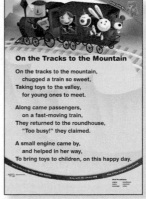

On the Tracks to the Mountain

On the tracks to the mountain,
chugged a train so sweet,
Taking toys to the valley,
for young ones to meet.

Along came passengers,
on a fast-moving train,
They returned to the roundhouse,
"Too busy!" they claimed.

A small engine came by,
and helped in her way,
To bring toys to children, on this happy day.

Sing with Me Chart 28B

E L L Poster 28

Oral Vocabulary
Amazing Words

Review

Let's Talk Display Talk with Me Chart 28A. We learned six new Amazing Words this week. Let's say the Amazing Words as I point to the pictures on the chart. Point to each picture and give children the chance to say the appropriate Amazing Word before offering it.

My train waits at the _____. (roundhouse)

Trains ride on _____. (tracks)

The _____ makes a train move. (engine)

A _____ train carries people. (passenger)

This _____ is tall and snowy. (mountain)

Lin lives in a _____ between two hills. (valley)

Amazing Words

engine	tracks
passenger	roundhouse
mountain	valley

Talk with Me/Sing with Me Chart 28A

It's Friday

MONITOR PROGRESS   ⟳ Check Oral Vocabulary

Demonstrate Word Knowledge Monitor the Amazing Words by asking the following questions. Have children use the Amazing Word in their answer.

- **Where does a train turn around?** (roundhouse)
- **Which part of the train works the hardest?** (engine)
- **What word means "a very tall hill"?** (mountain)
- **What are the special rails a train rides on?** (tracks)
- **What is the low land between two big hills?** (valley)
- **What is a person who rides in a train, bus, or car?** (passenger)

If... children have difficulty using the Amazing Words,

then... reteach the words using the Oral Vocabulary Routine on the Routine Flip Chart.

Day 1	Day 2	Day 3	Day 4	Day 5
Check Phonemic Awareness	Check Sound-Spelling/ Retelling	Check Word Reading	Check Phonemic Awareness	**Check Oral Vocabulary**

Success Predictor

Differentiated Instruction

A   **Advanced**

Amazing Words Have children write or dictate their own sentence using one of this week's Amazing Words, such as *The tracks go over the mountain.* Remind them to use a capital letter and period.

Oral Vocabulary   **Success Predictor**

Objectives
◎ Review initial and medial /u/.
◎ Review /u/ spelled *Uu*.

Phonemic Awareness Review

/u/

Isolate initial and medial /u/

Display the *up* Picture Card. What is the first sound in *up?* Say the word with me: /u/ /u/ /u/, *up*. Continue to review initial /u/ with the *umbrella* Picture Card.

Display the *nut* Picture Card. What is the middle sound in *nut?* Say it again: *nut,* /n/ /u/ /t/. Continue isolating medial /u/ with these Picture Cards: *duck, gum, jug, rug, tub.*

Discriminate initial and medial sounds

I am going to say some words with /u/. When you hear /u/ at the beginning of the word, put your hands up. When you hear /u/ in the middle of the word, clap your hands. Listen carefully: *under.* Do you hear /u/ at the beginning or in the middle of *under?* (beginning) I hear /u/ at the beginning of *under,* so I put my hands up. Continue the routine with *cut, cup, us, mug,* and *uncle.*

Picture Card

Picture Card

Phonics Review
/u/ Spelled *Uu*

Teach /u/Uu
Display the *Uu* Alphabet Card. This is an *umbrella*. What sound do you hear at the beginning of *umbrella*? What letter spells that sound?

High-frequency words
Write *what* on the board. This is the word *what*. What is this word? Continue with *said* and *was*.

Apply phonics in familiar text
Let's Reread Have children reread one of the books specific to the target letter sounds. You may wish to review the decodable words, rebus words, and high-frequency words that appear in each book.

Alphabet Card

Differentiated Instruction

A Advanced

Support Comprehension
After children reread one of the stories, have them retell the beginning, middle, and end in a few words.

Decodable Reader 28
My Skills Buddy, p. 78

Kindergarten Student
Reader K.5.4

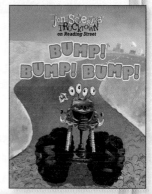

Get Set, Roll!
Reader 28

Small Group Time

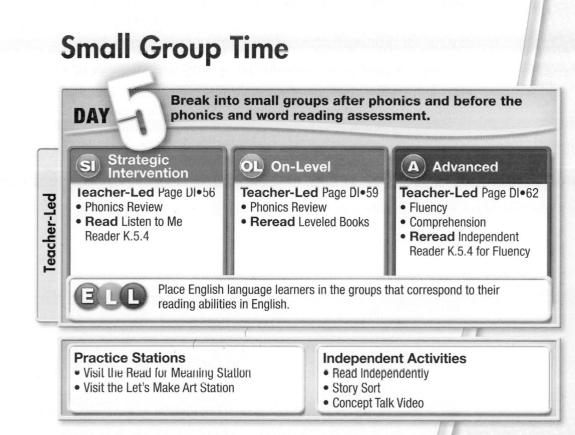

DAY 5 Break into small groups after phonics and before the phonics and word reading assessment.

Teacher-Led

SI Strategic Intervention	**OL** On-Level	**A** Advanced
Teacher-Led Page DI•56 • Phonics Review • **Read** Listen to Me Reader K.5.4	**Teacher-Led** Page DI•59 • Phonics Review • **Reread** Leveled Books	**Teacher-Led** Page DI•62 • Fluency • Comprehension • **Reread** Independent Reader K.5.4 for Fluency

E L L Place English language learners in the groups that correspond to their reading abilities in English.

Practice Stations
• Visit the Read for Meaning Station
• Visit the Let's Make Art Station

Independent Activities
• Read Independently
• Story Sort
• Concept Talk Video

Assess

◎ Read words with /u/.
• Read high-frequency words.
• Read sentences.

Assessment
Monitor Progress

/u/ Spelled Uu

Whole Class Give each child an index card. Have children write *u* on the card. I am going to say some words. If it is a word with /u/, hold up your *u* card. Listen carefully. Use the following words: *under, bump, igloo, duck, pond, bus, soccer, funny, gift, buddy.*

MONITOR PROGRESS	Word and Sentence Reading

If... children cannot complete the whole-class assessment,
then... use the Reteach lesson in *First Stop*.

If... you are unsure of a child's grasp of this week's skills,
then... use the assessment below to obtain a clearer evaluation of the child's progress.

/u/ Spelled Uu and high-frequency words

One-on-One To facilitate individual progress monitoring, assess some children on Day 4 and the rest on Day 5. While individual children are being assessed, the rest of the class can reread this week's books and look for words with /u/.

Word reading

Use the word lists on reproducible p. 405 to assess a child's ability to read words with /u/ and high-frequency words. We're going to read some words. I'll read the first word, and you read the rest. The first word is *mug*, /m/ /u/ /g/. For each child, record any decoding problems.

Sentence reading

Use the sentences on reproducible p. 405 to assess a child's ability to read words in sentences. Have the child read two sentences aloud. Have each child read different sentences. Start over with sentence one if necessary.

Record scores

Monitor children's accuracy by recording their scores using the Word and Sentence Reading Chart for this unit in *First Stop*.

Name _____

Read the Words

mug	☐	club	☐
cub	☐	what	☐
was	☐	rub	☐
nut	☐	plus	☐
said	☐	drum	☐
bug	☐	dust	☐

Read the Sentences

1. What is in the cup, Gus?

2. He said, "I dug in the mud."

3. Was a bug on the rug?

4. Was the pup a gift for Russ?

5. Dad said, "I can see dust on the drum."

Note to Teacher: Children read each word. Children read two sentences.

Scoring for Read the Words: Score 1 point for each correct word.

/u/*Uu* (*mug, cub, nut, bug, club, rub, plus, drum, dust*) _____ /__9__
High-Frequency Words (*was, said, what*) _____ /__3__

MONITOR PROGRESS
- /u/ Spelled *Uu*
- High-frequency words

Objectives
- Recognize a folk tale.
- Identify the common elements of folk tales.

My Skills Buddy, pp. 90–91

Let's Practice It!
Folk Tale

Teach

Tell children that today they will listen to a well-known folk tale. A folk tale is a story that has been passed down through retelling. Review features of a folk tale with children.

- A folk tale tells a story.
- A folk tale often teaches a lesson.
- A folk tale has some real parts and some make-believe parts.

Have children turn to pp. 90–91 of *My Skills Buddy*. I am going to read a folk tale called "Queen of the Forest." Look at the pictures as I read. Read the text of "Queen of the Forest." As you read, direct children to look at the appropriate picture.

Guide practice

Discuss the features of a folk tale and the bulleted text on *My Skills Buddy* p. 90.

- A folk tale tells a story. What happens at the beginning, middle, and end of "The Queen of the Forest"? (beginning—Fox is attacked by Tiger; middle—Fox tells Tiger she is "Queen of the Forest" and tricks Tiger into believing it; end—Fox runs away)

- A folk tale often teaches a lesson. What lesson do we learn from "The Queen of the Forest"? (Cleverness can help us solve our problems.)

- A folk tale has real and make-believe parts. Which parts of this folk tale are real? (Tigers are strong. Animals are afraid of tigers.) Which are make-believe? (Animals act like people.)

Differentiated Instruction

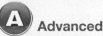 **Advanced**

Folk Tale Have children name and retell other folk tales they have heard with a clever fox. Then have them discuss if they have heard of other clever animals in folk tales, such as coyotes or spiders.

Academic Vocabulary

folk tale a story that has been passed down through retelling

The Queen of the Forest

Long, long ago, in a forest in China, there lived a mighty tiger. All the other animals would flee in terror at the mere mention of her name. She was the Queen of the Forest.

One day, a fox was trotting through the forest when the tiger leaped out and grabbed her. Fox had to think of something quick.

"How dare you attack me!" Fox declared. "I am Queen of the Forest!"

Tiger was amazed. "Nonsense!" she sputtered. "You are not Queen!"

"Yes, I am," said Fox calmly. "All the other animals flee in terror when they see me. I'll show you. Just follow me."

Fox walked into the forest with Tiger close behind her. They came upon a herd of deer. When the deer saw Tiger behind Fox, they ran away. Fox and Tiger came upon a flock of birds. When the birds saw Tiger behind Fox, they flew away. Fox and Tiger came upon a group of monkeys. When the monkeys saw Tiger behind Fox, they scampered away.

Fox said to Tiger, "See how all the animals run away? Now do you believe I am Queen of the Forest?"

"Yes, now that I have seen it with my own eyes, I do believe you are Queen." Tiger bowed low to Fox and then walked off into the forest.

As soon as Tiger was out of sight, Fox ran away as fast as she could.

Objectives
◎ Review plot.

Assess
◉ Identify plot.

Comprehension Assessment
Monitor Progress

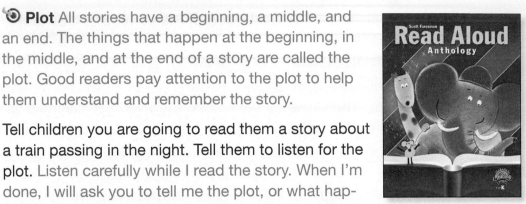

Read Aloud Anthology

Review

◉ **Plot** All stories have a beginning, a middle, and an end. The things that happen at the beginning, in the middle, and at the end of a story are called the plot. Good readers pay attention to the plot to help them understand and remember the story.

Read "Hiawatha Passing"

Tell children you are going to read them a story about a train passing in the night. Tell them to listen for the plot. Listen carefully while I read the story. When I'm done, I will ask you to tell me the plot, or what happens at the beginning, in the middle, and at the end of the story. Read "Hiawatha Passing" on p. 68 of the *Read Aloud Anthology.*

Check plot

After you read the story, ask children to identify the plot.

- What happens at the beginning of the story? (A boy wakes up to a strange sound in the night.)

- What happens in the middle of the story? (The boy looks outside the window to see what makes the sound. He sees a train speeding through the valley.)

- What happens at the end of the story? (The train sound stops and the boy goes back to sleep.)

Corrective feedback

If... children cannot identify plot,

then... reteach plot using the Reteach lesson in *First Stop*.

Assess plot

Use the blackline master on p. 409. Make one copy for each child. Have children color the left-hand picture to show the beginning of the story. Then have them color the picture that shows what the boy discovers in the middle of the story.

Plot

Color the boy in his bed. Then color the picture that shows what he finds out in the middle of the story.

Note to Teacher: Have children color the picture of the boy and what he discovers in the middle of the story.

Objectives
- Practice nouns.
- Write about books and songs.

Conventions
Nouns

Review   Remind children of what they learned about nouns. A noun is a word that names a person, an animal, a place, or a thing. Nouns can also name more than one person, animal, place, or thing.

Model   Make a four-column chart on the board with the headings *People, Animals, Places,* and *Things.* Choose a letter of the alphabet and give an example of a noun that begins with that letter. I choose the letter *b. Bus* is a word that names a thing. *Bus* is a noun that begins with *b.* Write *bus* in the *Things* column and read it with children. *Bears* is a noun that names more than one animal. Write *bears* in the *Animals* column and read it with children. *Boys* is a noun that names more than one person. Write *boys* in the *People* column. *Backyard* is a noun that names a place. Write *backyard* in the *Places* column.

Guide practice   Continue the activity with children choosing letters and naming other nouns. After children say a word, ask: Does this noun name a person, an animal, a place, or a thing? Write the noun in the correct column. Reread the final list with children. Have children identify nouns for one and more than one. Then have them change a noun from one to more than one and from more than one to one.

On their own   Have children draw a picture of a noun for one or a noun for more than one on a sheet of paper. Help them label their pictures. Have children share their drawings with the class. Then have each child tape his or her drawing to the board under the correct column—*People, Animals, Places,* or *Things.*

Daily Fix-It   Use the Daily Fix-It exercise for more conventions practice.

Writing
This Week We...

Review

Display *The Little Engine That Could,* Sing with Me Chart 28B, Phonics Songs and Rhymes Chart 28, Decodable Reader 28 from *My Skills Buddy,* Kindergarten Student Reader K.5.4, and Get, Set, Roll! Reader 28. This week we learned about trains. We read new books, and we sang new songs. Which book or song was your favorite? Let's share our ideas with each other. Remind children to use complete sentences when sharing ideas.

Team Talk Pair children and have them take turns telling which book or song was their favorite and why.

Model

Today we will write sentences that tell about what happened in our stories and songs.

> **The red engine has toys in its cars.**
>
> **The toys are for boys and girls.**
>
> **The red engine stops on the tracks.**

Guide practice

Continue writing sentences with children. Then read the sentences with children. Have children identify the nouns.

On their own

Have each child write a noun that names something about trains. Collect all the nouns. Randomly pass the nouns out to children. Have each child read and illustrate the noun. Have them tell if their noun names a person, an animal, a place, or a thing.

Daily Handwriting

Write uppercase *U* and lowercase *u* on the board. Review correct letter formation with children.

D'Nealian™   Ball and Stick

Have children write a row each of uppercase *U* and lowercase *u* on their Write-On Boards. Remind them to use proper left-to-right and top-to-bottom progression.

Wrap Up Your Week!

Question of the Week
What kind of work do trains do?

Illustrate plot   This week we talked about the different kinds of work done by trains.

• Make a story map like the one shown and fill it with children's responses about the story *The Little Engine That Could.*

• Have children draw their favorite event from the story map.

• Have children write or dictate a phrase or sentence about their picture.

• Help children arrange the pictures to show the order of story events.

Amazing Words

You've learned
0 0 6
words this week!

You've learned
1 6 8
words this year!

Story Map: *The LIttle Engine That Could*
Beginning
Middle
End

Next Week's Question
How do people in different parts of the world travel?

Discuss next week's question. Talk with children about whether they think people ride trains in other parts of the world.

Preview
NEXT WEEK

Tell children that next week they will read about people on the move.

Extend Your Day!

Social Studies
Land, Air, Water

Materials: paper, scissors, hole punch, yarn

Transportation Words Brainstorm with children different ways in which people travel or transport things. Make a list of the words as children respond.

Forms of Transportation Tell children things can move three ways: by land, air, and water. Create a three-column chart with the labels: *Land, Air,* and *Water.* Have children contribute forms of transportation. Write them in the correct column.

Transportation Books Divide the class into three groups— Land, Air, and Water Transportation. Have each group draw pictures of forms of transportation in their category. Tell the groups that their pages will be a chapter in a class book. Have each group write a sentence for each page and label their chapter by their category. Help children make a cover, punch holes, and tie yarn to make the class book.

Land	Air	Water
car	jet	boat
motorcycle	plane	yacht
bike	helicopter	ferry

Art
Beautiful Butterflies

Materials: butterfly cutouts, colored tissue paper, glue, paintbrushes, markers

Noun Butterflies *Butterfly* is a noun. We are going to make beautiful butterflies to show off nouns that we know. Give each child a large butterfly cutout, bits of colored tissue paper, a paintbrush, and watered-down glue. Have children glue small pieces of tissue paper on the butterfly. Have them write or dictate a noun and glue it to their butterflies.

Drama
Puppet Show

Materials: train patterns, crayons, craft sticks, glue

Dramatize *The Little Engine That Could* Have each child use the train patterns to make one of the trains from *The Little Engine That Could.* When children have finished, have groups of children act out the story.

Weekly Assessment

Use the whole-class assessment on pages 404–405 and 408–409 in this Teacher's Edition to check:

✔ 🔊 **Short *u* Spelled *Uu***

✔ 🔊 **Comprehension Skill** *Plot*

✔ **High-Frequency Words** *what said was*

Teacher's Edition, Day 5

Managing Assessment

Use the Assessment Handbook for:

✔ **Observation Checklists**

✔ **Record-Keeping Forms**

✔ **Portfolio Assessment**

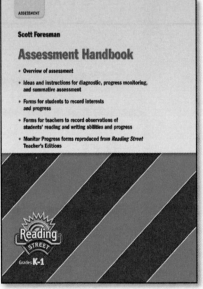

Assessment Handbook

Teacher Notes

Small Group Time

Pacing Small Group Instruction

5 Day Plan

DAY 1	• Phonemic Awareness/ Phonics • Decodable Story 28
DAY 2	• Phonemic Awareness/ Phonics • Decodable Reader 28
DAY 3	• Phonemic Awareness/ Phonics • Concept Literacy Reader K.5.4 or Kindergarten Student Reader K.5.4
DAY 4	• Phonemic Awareness/ Phonics • Get Set, Roll! Reader 28
DAY 5	• Phonics Review • Listen to Me Reader K.5.4

3 or 4 Day Plan

DAY 1	• Phonemic Awareness/ Phonics • Decodable Story 28
DAY 2	• Phonemic Awareness/ Phonics • Decodable Reader 28
DAY 3	• Phonemic Awareness/ Phonics • Concept Literacy Reader K.5.4 or Kindergarten Student Reader K.5.4
DAY 4	• Phonemic Awareness/ Phonics • Get Set, Roll! Reader 28

3 Day Plan: Eliminate the shaded box.

DAY 1

Phonemic Awareness•Phonics

■ **Isolate /u/** Display the *duck* Picture Card. This is a *duck. Duck* has /u/ in the middle. Say it with me: /d/ /u/ /k/, *duck.* Repeat with *hug* and *cut.*

■ **Connect /u/ to *Uu*** I am going to say three words. I want you to tell me which word has /u/. Listen carefully: *cat, cut, cot.* Which word has /u/? *Cut* has /u/. *Cat* and *cot* do not have /u/. Write the letters *Uu* on the board. The letter *u* can stand for /u/ in words. Continue the procedure with the following sets of words: *hut, hit, hot; Ron, ran, run; bit, but, bat.*

Decodable Story 28

■ **Review** Review the previously taught high-frequency words by writing each of the words and having children say the words with you.

are	they	like	to	have	the	see

If... children have difficulty reading the words,
then... say a word and have children point to the word and say the word. Repeat several times, giving assistance as needed.

■ **Read** Have children read *Jan and Gus* orally. Then have them reread the story several times individually.

Reader's and Writer's Notebook, pp. 359–360

Objectives
• Identify the common sounds that letters represent.
• Read at least 25 high-frequency words from a commonly used list.

SI *Strategic Intervention*   **DAY 2**

More Reading
Use Leveled Readers or other text at children's instructional level.

Phonemic Awareness•Phonics

■ **Discriminate /u/** Display Phonics Songs and Rhymes Chart 28. Sing the song "Bud" to the tune of "Mary Had a Little Lamb" with children. Ask them to clap when they hear a word with /u/.

■ **Connect /u/ to Uu** Display the *Uu* Alphabet Card. What letter is this? This is the letter *U.* What sound did we learn for this letter? Say it with me: /u/ /u/ /u/. Look at the picture. Say the word with me: *umbrella.* Does *umbrella* begin with /u/? What other words do you know that begin with /u/?

Decodable Reader 28

■ **Review** Review the high-frequency words by writing *what* on the board. This is the word *what.* What word is this? Continue with the following words: *the, do, said, was, I, have, a.*

> **If...** children have difficulty reading the words,
> **then...** say a word and have children point to the word. Repeat several times, giving assistance as needed.

■ **Read** Display the cover of *Jan at the Fair* on p. 78 of *My Skills Buddy.* Ask a volunteer to read the first page of the story. Have children tell what Jan does at the fair. Continue through the story in this manner.

My Skills Buddy

SI Strategic Intervention

DAY 3

Phonemic Awareness•Phonics

■ **Isolate /u/** Display the *bus* Picture Card. This is a *bus. Bus* has /u/ in the middle. Say it with me: /b/ /u/ /s/, *bus.* Repeat the routine with the *duck* and *gum* Picture Cards.

■ **Connect /u/ to *Uu*** Hum a verse to a song. I am humming. *Hum* has /u/ in the middle. Say it with me: /h/ /u/ /m/, *hum.* Write *hum* on the board. Point to the letter *u.* The letter *u* can stand for /u/. Demonstrate for children how to hum. When you hear a word that has /u/, I want you to *hum.* Use the following words: *hut, hit, cap, cup, gum, gem, mad, mud.*

■ **Blend Sounds** Write *sub* on the board. Have children blend the sound of each letter to read the word: /s/ /u/ /b/, *sub.* Change *s* to *t.* We changed one letter to make a new word. Let's blend the sound of each letter to read the word: /t/ /u/ /b/, *tub.* Continue with *cub, bus,* and *fun.*

■ **Review High-Frequency Words** Write *said* on the board. Have volunteers say the word and use it in a sentence. Continue with the words *what, was, blue, yellow,* and *green.*

■ To practice phonics and high-frequency words, have children read Kindergarten Student Reader K.5.4. Use the instruction on pp. 360–361.

For a complete lesson plan and additional practice, see the **Leveled Reader Teaching Guide**.

Concept Literacy Reader K.5.4

■ **Preview and Predict** Display the cover of the Concept Literacy Reader K.5.4. Point to the title. The title of the book is *Trains Work Hard.* What do you think this book is about? Have children tell about the picture and what they think the book might be about.

■ **Set a Purpose** We talked about the title of the book. Let's read the book to learn about trains. Have children read the Concept Literacy Reader.

■ **Read** Provide corrective feedback as children read the book orally. During reading, ask them if they are able to confirm any of the predictions they made prior to reading.

If... children have difficulty reading the book individually,

then... read a sentence aloud as children point to each word. Then have the group reread the sentences as they continue pointing to the words.

■ **Retell** Have children retell the content as you page through the book. Help them identify what the book is about. Also call attention to the fact that trains can carry many different things.

Concept Literacy Reader K.5.4

Phonemic Awareness•Phonics

- **Segmenting** Say *sun.* I hear three sounds in *sun,* /s/ /u/ /n/. How many sounds do you hear in *hut?* What are they? (three, /h/ /u/ /t/) Continue with *bus, but, not, club,* and *dug.*

- **Connect /u/ to *Uu*** Draw a sun on the board and write the word below the picture. Have children name the picture and spell the word. Ask children what letter stands for /u/ in the middle of the word. Continue with the pictures and words for *bus, cup,* and *rug.*

- **Decorate the Cup** Give children a paper cup. Have children draw pictures of /u/ words on the cup. Have children share their decorated cups with the class by naming their /u/ words.

Get Set, Roll! Reader 28

- **Review** Review the following high-frequency words with children prior to reading the story: *said, was, what, they, have.*

- **Teach Rebus Words** Write the word *road* on the board. This is the word *road.* Name the letters with me: *r, o, a, d, road.* Cars, buses, and trucks travel on roads. What else can travel on a road? Look for this word in the story we will read today. There will be a picture above the word to help you read it.

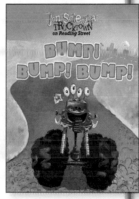

Get Set, Roll! Reader 28

- **Read** Display Get Set, Roll! Reader 28, *Bump! Bump! Bump!* Today we will read a story about a bumpy road. The title of the story is *Bump! Bump! Bump!* Look at the picture and think about the title. What do you think this story will be about?

   If... children have difficulty reading the story individually, **then...** read a sentence aloud as children point to each word. Then have the group reread the sentences as they continue pointing to the words.

- **Reread** Use echo reading of Get Set, Roll! Reader 28 to model fluent reading. Use your oral reading to model for children where to pause, when to change pitch, and which words to stress. Then have children reread orally three to four times, or until they can read with few or no mistakes.

Objectives
- Identify the common sounds that letters represent.
- Read at least 25 high-frequency words from a commonly used list.
- Predict what might happen next based on the cover.

Small Group Time

More Reading

Use Leveled Readers or other text at children's instructional level.

SI Strategic Intervention

DAY 5

Phonics Review

■ **Recognize *Uu*** Write *Uu* on the board. What is the sound we have learned for *Uu*? That's right, /u/. Tell children you will tell them a story and they should listen for /u/. When you say a word with /u/, the children should point up and repeat the word. Tell a simple story, emphasizing /u/ words and pausing to give children a chance to point up and repeat the words. *Bud* the *pup* likes to play in the *mud*. No, *Bud,* no! *Bud* the *pup* likes to chase the *bugs*. No, *Bud,* no! *Bud* the *pup* likes to *tug* on the *rug*. No, *Bud,* no! *Bud* the *pup* likes to *rub* in the *tub*. Yes, *Bud,* yes!

Listen to Me Reader K.5.4

■ **Preview and Predict** Display the cover of the book. The title of this story is *Six Cubs.* Let's count the cubs. Point to each cub as children count to six. This story is written by Jamie Daniels. It is illustrated by Joe Kulka. What do you think the six cubs will do in the story? Tell me your ideas.

■ **Teach Rebus Words** Write the word *bees* on the board. This is the word *bees.* Say the letters with me: *b, e, e, s, bees.* The letter *s* at the end of the word means there is more than one bee. What sound do bees make? Repeat the routine with the word *tree.* Look for the words *bees* and *trees* in the story today. There will be a picture above the word to help you read it.

Listen to Me Reader K.5.4

■ **Set a Purpose** Review children's ideas. Point out that after they read, they will know more about the six cubs. Tell children that you will read the story with them. Follow along with your finger as I read. Then we will take turns reading this page. Repeat this routine through all of the pages. Guide children to decode words.

■ **Reread for Fluency** Use echo reading of Listen to Me Reader K.5.4 to model reading fluently. Use your oral reading to model for children when to pause, when to change pitch, and which words to stress. Then have children reread orally three to four times, or until they can read with few or no mistakes.

Objectives
• Identify the common sounds that letters represent.
• Predict what might happen next based on the title.

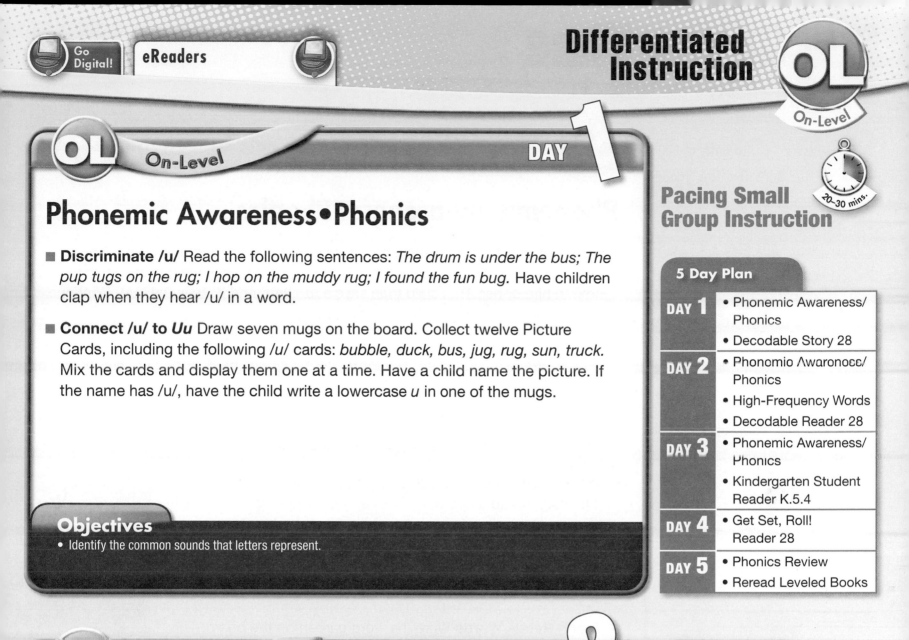
OL On-Level — DAY 1

Phonemic Awareness•Phonics

■ **Discriminate /u/** Read the following sentences: *The drum is under the bus; The pup tugs on the rug; I hop on the muddy rug; I found the fun bug.* Have children clap when they hear /u/ in a word.

■ **Connect /u/ to Uu** Draw seven mugs on the board. Collect twelve Picture Cards, including the following /u/ cards: *bubble, duck, bus, jug, rug, sun, truck.* Mix the cards and display them one at a time. Have a child name the picture. If the name has /u/, have the child write a lowercase *u* in one of the mugs.

Objectives
• Identify the common sounds that letters represent.

Pacing Small Group Instruction

20–30 mins.

5 Day Plan	
DAY 1	• Phonemic Awareness/ Phonics • Decodable Story 28
DAY 2	• Phonemic Awareness/ Phonics • High-Frequency Words • Decodable Reader 28
DAY 3	• Phonemic Awareness/ Phonics • Kindergarten Student Reader K.5.4
DAY 4	• Get Set, Roll! Reader 28
DAY 5	• Phonics Review • Reread Leveled Books

OL On-Level — DAY 2

Phonemic Awareness•Phonics

■ **Fill the Cup** Place a large paper cup on a table. Label it with *Uu*. We learned the sound /u/ for *Uu*. Give children small circles of paper. Have them draw a picture of a /u/ word on the paper circle and write the letter *u* beneath the picture. Then have children take turns naming their picture and putting the paper circle in the cup to "fill the cup." The following list of objects could be used: *cup, mug, sun, bug, tub, hut, umbrella, cub.*

■ **High-Frequency Words** Display the following word cards: *said, what, was, green, yellow, blue.* Say the word *was* and select a child to point to the word. Have children say the word and use it in a sentence. Continue with the other words.

Objectives
• Read at least 25 high-frequency words from a commonly used list.

3 or 4 Day Plan	
DAY 1	• Phonemic Awareness/ Phonics • Decodable Story 28
DAY 2	• Phonemic Awareness/ Phonics • High-Frequency Words • Decodable Reader 28
DAY 3	• Phonemic Awareness/ Phonics • Kindergarten Student Reader K.5.4
DAY 4	• Get Set, Roll! Reader 28

3 Day Plan: Eliminate the shaded box.

More Practice

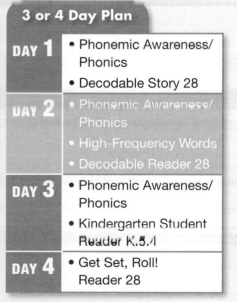

For additional practice with this week's phonics skills, have children reread the Decodable Story (Day 1) and the Decodable Reader (Day 2).

Phonemic Awareness•Phonics

■ **Pass the Cup** Have children stand in a circle. Give a cup to one child. At a signal to begin, the child says a word with /u/ and passes the cup to the child next to him or her. That child then says a /u/ word and passes the cup. Continue around the circle until many *u* words are given.

■ **Connect /u/ to *Uu*** The sound we learned for *Uu* is /u/. When I say a word with /u/, trace a *u* in the air. Say these words: *elbow, mud, sock, sun, hut, hop, bunny, bed,* and *up.*

Kindergarten Student Reader K.5.4

■ **Preview and Predict** Display the cover of the book. The title of this story is *Bud Likes Mud.* Look at the cover and think about the title. What do you think will happen in this story?

■ **Set a Purpose** Review the list of things children think might happen in the story. Remind children they will read to find out about Bud.

■ **Teach Rebus Words** Write the word *garden* on the board. This is the word *garden.* Say the letters with me: *g, a, r, d, e, n, garden.* What can you grow in a *garden?* Look for the word *garden* in our story today. There will be a picture above the word to help you read it.

Kindergarten Student Reader K.5.4

■ **Read** Have children follow along as they read the story with you. After reading pp. 2–3, ask children to tell about Bud and what he likes to do. Continue with each page. Ask the following questions:

• Who doesn't want Bud to dig in the mud?

• Where does Bud dig?

• How does Bud get clean?

■ **Summarize** Have children retell the story to a partner and tell what happens at the end.

■ **Text to Self** Help children make personal connections to the story as they tell about something they like to do outside.

Objectives

• Identify the common sounds that letters represent.
• Predict what might happen next based on the cover.
• Respond to questions about text.

 **OL** On-Level | DAY **4**

Get Set, Roll! Reader 28

■ **Review** Review the high-frequency words *have, they, what, said,* and *was* by writing each word on the board and saying the word with children.

■ **Review Rebus Words** Write the word *road* on the board. This is the word *road.* Name the letters with me: *r, o, a, d, road.* What forms of transportation travel on a *road?* Remember, there will be a picture above this word to help you read it.

■ **Read** Display Get Set, Roll! Reader 28, *Bump! Bump! Bump!* Point to the title of the story. What is the title of the story? *Bump! Bump! Bump!* is the title of the story. Look at the picture. What do you think will happen in this story? We will read some words with /u/ in this story. Let's read the story together.

Objectives
• Read at least 25 high-frequency words from a commonly used list.
• Predict what might happen next based on the cover.

OL On-Level | DAY **5**

Phonics Review

■ **Make a *U* Album** Give children a white sheet of paper. Have children write the letters *Uu* on the paper and draw pictures whose names have /u/. When children are finished, combine all pages. Punch holes along the side and tie the sheets together using yarn. Make a cover page titled, *Our U Album.* Go through the album with children naming the letters and pictures on each page.

Objectives
• Identify the common sounds that letters represent.

More Reading
Use Leveled Readers or other text at children's instructional level to develop fluency.

Small Group Time

Pacing Small Group Instruction

5 Day Plan

DAY 1	• Phonemic Awareness/ Phonics • Decodable Story 28
DAY 2	• Phonics • Spelling • Decodable Reader 28
DAY 3	• Independent Reader K.5.4 or Kindergarten Student Reader K.5.4
DAY 4	• Get Set, Roll! Reader 28 or Kindergarten Student Reader K.5.4
DAY 5	• Fluency/Comprehension • Independent Reader K.5.4

3 or 4 Day Plan

DAY 1	• Phonemic Awareness/ Phonics • Decodable Story 28
DAY 2	• Phonics • Spelling • Decodable Reader 28
DAY 3	• Independent Reader K.5.4 or Kindergarten Student Reader K.5.4
DAY 4	• Get Set, Roll! Reader 28 or Kindergarten Student Reader K.5.4

3 Day Plan: Eliminate the shaded box.

More Practice

For additional practice with this week's phonics skills and to develop fluency, have children reread the Decodable Story (Day 1) and the Decodable Reader (Day 2).

A — Advanced — DAY 1

Phonemic Awareness•Phonics

■ **Report the Weather** Give children two blank cards. Have them draw a picture of a sun on one and an umbrella on the other and label each with the letter *u*. Review both words with children. These words are both spelled with the letter *u*. The sound we learned for *u* is /u/. What is the weather like when the sun comes out? (warm/hot and sunny) Say *sun* with me: /s/ /u/ /n/, *sun*. What do you need when it rains? (an umbrella) Say *umbrella* with me: /u/ /u/ /u/, *umbrella*. Tell children to hold up the *sun* card when you say a word with /u/ in the middle and the *umbrella* card when the word begins with /u/. Use the following word list: *mug, tug, uncle, up, cut, pup, under, hum, cub, usher, hunt, umpire*.

Objectives
• Identify the common sounds that letters represent.

A — Advanced — DAY 2

Phonics•Spelling

■ **Connect /u/ to *Uu*** Display the *duck* Picture Card and the *Uu* Alphabet Card. What is this picture? What is the name of this letter? What is the sound for this letter? Do you hear /u/ in the word *duck*? Have volunteers write the letter *u* on the board. Continue with these Picture Cards: *bus, drum, gum, jug*.

■ **Spell Sounds** Give each child the following letter tiles: *b, c, d, m, n, r, s, u*. Listen to the sounds in the word *cub*: /k/ /u/ /b/, *cub*. What is the letter for /k/ in *cub*? It is *c*. Place your *c* tile in front of you. (Children have also learned the letter *k* for /k/. Review this if a child suggests *k*.) Continue with the remaining sounds. Repeat the routine with the following words: *bus, sun, drum*.

Objectives
• Identify the common sounds that letters represent.
• Use letter-sound correspondences to spell consonant-vowel-consonant (CVC) words.

A Advanced

DAY **3**

For a complete lesson plan and additional practice, see the **Leveled Reader Teaching Guide**.

Independent Reader K.5.4

- **Practice High-Frequency Words** Write *what* on the board. Have volunteers say the word and use it in a sentence. Continue with the words *said* and *was*.

- **Activate Prior Knowledge** Remind children that trains travel on tracks from place to place. Encourage children to share what they know about trains. What is the name of the person who drives the train? What is the sound a train makes as it passes by?

Independent
Reader K.5.4

- **Plot** Display the cover of *The Big Train.* Have children tell what happens in the beginning, the middle, and at the end of the story.

- **Reread for Fluency** After rereading with children, model reading fluently for them. I am going to read this book aloud. I will read the words with no mistakes. I want you to read it aloud with me. Try to read the words just as I do.

Use echo reading of Independent Reader K.5.4 to model reading fluently. Use your oral reading to model for children where to pause, when to change pitch, and which words to stress. Then have children reread orally three to four times, or until they can read with few or no mistakes.

- For more practice with phonics and high-frequency words and to develop fluency, have children read Kindergarten Student Reader K.5.4. Use the instruction on pp. 360–361.

More Reading

Use Leveled Readers or other text at children's instructional level.

Objectives
- Read at least 25 high-frequency words from a commonly used list.
- Identify elements of a story including key events.

Small **Group Time**

More Reading

Use Leveled Readers or other text at children's instructional level.

A Advanced

DAY 4

Kindergarten Student Reader K.5.4

- **Revisit Rebus Words** Write the word *garden* on the board. This is the word *garden.* Say the letters with me: *g, a, r, d, e, n, garden.* What can you tell me about a *garden?*

- **Reread** Use Kindergarten Student Reader K.5.4 to practice reading fluently.

- **Text to World** Ask children to think about mud. What is mud? How is mud made? Do you like mud?

- **Read** Have children read Get Set, Roll! Reader 28, *Bump! Bump! Bump!* Use the instruction on p. 393.

Kindergarten Student Reader K.5.4

Objectives
- Read at least 25 high-frequency words from a commonly used list.
- Predict what might happen next based on the illustrations.

A Advanced

DAY 5

Fluency•Comprehension

- **Reread for Fluency** Use the Independent Reader K.5.4 to model reading fluently for children. I am going to read this selection aloud. I will read the words with no mistakes. I want you to read it aloud with me. Try to read the words just as I do.

- **Comprehension** After children have finished reading, have them retell what happens in the selection. Then have children draw a picture of their favorite part.

Independent Reader K.5.4

Objectives
- Read at least 25 high-frequency words from a commonly used list.
- Identify elements of a story including key events.

Concept Development

■ **Read the Concept Literacy Reader** To build background and vocabulary, read *Trains Work Hard,* pausing to discuss each page. Model sentence patterns and vocabulary that describe the pictures. This is a train. The train runs on tracks. This train carries passengers from place to place. On a second reading, invite children to talk about the different work that different trains do. This train carries logs. It hauls very heavy loads.

■ **Develop Oral Language** Revisit *Trains Work Hard,* reviewing the different ways that trains work. Then have children recite this chant with you several times to the tune of "Baa, Baa, Black Sheep":

> Choo-Choo train, choo-choo train,
> Have you any logs?
> Yes, sir, yes, sir,
> Three cars full.

Continue the chant using *food, bikes,* and *coal* in place of *logs.*

Phonemic Awareness/Phonics

■ **Frontload Words with /u/** Have children look at the picture on pp. 72–73 of *My Skills Buddy.* This picture shows animals in the sea. Some creatures are on the shore. Some are underwater. Listen to the word *underwater.* What sound does *underwater* begin with? *Underwater* begins with /u/; *underwater,* /u/. Then use this routine to introduce picture words with initial and medial /u/: *Under, under* starts with /u/. Who can find something that starts with /u/? (Pause for an answer.) Repeat the routine with other words in the picture that have initial or medial /u/, including *cup, bug, sun, tub, duck, umbrella, bus, bun, hug,* and *nut.*

■ **Connect /u/ to Uu** Use letter tiles to display the words *under* and *bug* or write them on the board. Tell children that some words have /u/ at the beginning, and others have /u/ in the middle. This word is *under:* /u/ /n/ /d/ /r/, *under.* Say the word with me. Have children write the word *under* and circle the letter that makes /u/. Write and read aloud the following sentence: *Russ the bug was under the tub.* Point to the *u* in *Russ.* What letter is this? Yes, this is *u.* Continue with *bug, under,* and *tub.*

Content Objective
• Develop content knowledge related to work that trains do.

Language Objectives
• Understand and use grade-level content area vocabulary.

• Recognize the sounds of English.

Concept Literacy Reader K.5.4

Daily Planner

DAY 1	• Concept Development • Phonemic Awareness/ Phonics • Listening Comprehension
DAY 2	• Comprehension • Vocabulary
DAY 3	• Phonemic Awareness/ Phonics • Conventions
DAY 4	• Phonemic Awareness/ Phonics • Concepts and Oral Language
DAY 5	• Language Workshop • Writing

Support for English Language Learners

Content Objective
- Understand plot.

Language Objective
- Learn and use academic vocabulary.

My Skills Buddy, pp.74–75

Listening Comprehension: Plot

- **Frontload Vocabulary** Discuss the illustrations on pp. 74–75 in *My Skills Buddy* to frontload vocabulary. What animals do you see in the pictures? (a tortoise and a hare) Does a tortoise move quickly or slowly? (slowly) Does a hare move quickly or slowly? (quickly) In the big picture, what is the hare doing? (sleeping) What is the tortoise doing? (walking)

- **Provide Scaffolding** Look at the illustrations on p. 74. Point to and explain the *Characters* and *Setting* keys. Then point to the *Plot* key on p. 75. Explain what is happening in each picture. Help children understand that in the beginning of the story, the tortoise and the hare are having a race. In the middle of the story, the hare falls asleep. At the end of the story, the tortoise wins the race.

- **Prepare for the Read Aloud** The modified Read Aloud below prepares children for listening to the oral reading "The El" on p. 331.

Read Aloud

The El

Mom and Liam went to a parade. They took the elevated train. It is called the "el." Mom had a special card. They went through the entry gate. They went down the stairs to wait for the train.

The train stopped. The doors opened. Mom and Liam walked into the car. They found seats near the front. The train went under the ground. It also went high above the ground.

Liam saw tall buildings. The train went underground and stopped. Mom and Liam got off the train. They climbed stairs to the street.

Many people were waiting for the parade to start. Liam heard a band playing. Here comes the parade!

- **First Listening** Write the title of the Read Aloud on the board. This is about Liam and his mom. They go to a parade. Listen to find out how they get there. After reading, ask children to recall the names of the characters and the events. How do they get on the train? Where are the train tracks?

- **Second Listening** Write the words *beginning, middle,* and *end* on the board. As you listen to the story, think about what happens in the beginning, in the middle, and at the end. After reading, point to each word on the board and ask children to tell what happens then in the story.

Objectives
- Understand the main points of spoken language ranging from situations in which language is familiar to unfamiliar. • Understand implicit ideas in increasingly complex spoken language commensurate with grade-level learning expectations.

Comprehension

■ **Provide Scaffolding** Display *The Little Engine That Could* Lead a detailed picture walk through the story, naming what you see in the illustrations and describing what is happening. Use gestures and facial expressions to convey meaning. Focus on the following:

• **Set the Scene** Use the cover of the Trade Book to help children understand that this story is about a train. A train can be small or big. A train carries a load. Some trains carry people. Some carry heavy loads, like logs and coal. What do you know about trains? Allow children to use their prior knowledge to discuss trains and the work they do.

• **Frontload Vocabulary** Use the illustrations to introduce unfamiliar words in the text. Include some of the nouns. Look at this picture on page 4. The train is rumbling down the tracks. What is the train going over? These nouns can be included: *cars* (p. 4); *dolls* (p. 5); *clown* (p. 6); *tops, books* (p. 7); *food* (p. 15).

Vocabulary: Time Words

■ **Frontload Vocabulary** Have children turn to p. 88 of *My Skills Buddy.* Talk about each picture, using time words *Monday, Tuesday, Wednesday, Thursday, Friday, Saturday,* and *Sunday.* For example, point to the calendar. This is a calendar. The first day of this month is Friday. Do you come to school on Friday? Which day comes before Friday? Which day comes after Friday? Then invite children to talk about the pictures using the time words.

■ **Provide Scaffolding** Write the words *Monday, Tuesday, Wednesday, Thursday, Friday, Saturday,* and *Sunday* on the board and on large cards. Read the words aloud. These words name the days of the week. Hold up the *Monday* card. What do you do on Monday? Invite children to tell something they do on Monday. Then say a sentence about the activity and have children repeat the sentence: I learn new words on Monday. Repeat with the other days of the week.

■ **Practice** Have children work in pairs. Assign one of the time words (*Monday, Tuesday, Wednesday, Thursday, Friday, Saturday,* or *Sunday*) to each pair. Have one child act out something he or she does on that day. Then have the partner say a sentence about what the first child is doing: *Sonya Li is playing the recorder on Thursday.*

Content Objective
• Develop background knowledge.

Language Objective
• Learn and use words for jobs.

Use Learning Strategies
Remind children that if they have trouble using time words, they can consult a calendar or ask their partner for help.

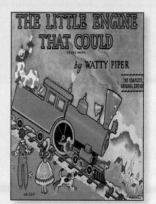

Trade Book

Support for English Language Learners

Content Objective
• Use learning strategies.

Language Objectives
• Connect /u/ with *Uu.*
• Use prepositions.

 **Transfer Skills**

Pronouncing /u/ In Italian, the letter *u* is pronounced like /oo/ in *boot.* If children experience difficulty producing the /u/ sound, give them extra practice with words such as *fun, sun,* and *run.*

Use Learning Strategies
Help children understand that nouns name a person, place, or thing. On the board, write a list of nouns and verbs. Point to a word and ask children whether the word names a person, a place, or a thing. If the word names none of these, help students see that the word names an action and is a verb.

Phonemic Awareness/Phonics

■ **Isolate Initial and Medial /u/** Write on the board and say the following sentence: *The bug ran up the cup.* Underline the words that have /u/. Repeat the sentence, emphasizing the /u/ sounds as you read the words aloud. Point to the letter *u.* What letter is this? Yes, this is *u.* Next, segment and blend *bug, up,* and *cup* as you point to the words.

■ **/u/ Spelled *Uu*** Write the word *pup* on the board. As you read it aloud, track the sounds and letters with your fingers. Let's write new words by changing the first letter. Write *sup* on the board. What is the new word? Confirm that it is *sup,* and segment and blend each sound as you point to the corresponding letter: /s/ /u/ /p/, *sup.*

Conventions: Nouns

■ **Provide Scaffolding** Point to the image on pp. 4–5 of *The Little Engine That Could.* The train carries toys. Write *toys* on the board. The word *toys* tells us what the train carries. *Toys* names a thing. It is a noun. Have children look for other *things* or *toys* in the picture and name a thing. Write their nouns on the board. The word *bear* is a noun. *Bear* names a thing.

■ **Practice** What are some other nouns in this story? Page through the Trade Book and have children name different naming words they see. Include the nouns. Make a list of these words on the board. Have children say sentences using the nouns they find in the pictures.

Leveled LS Support

Beginning/Intermediate For each noun, have a child tell something about the word. Have the class repeat each sentence.

Advanced/Advanced-High Have students look through the illustrations in the Trade Book and name nouns and verbs. While you create a list on the board, have children tell what type of word they have found. For example, using the illustration on p. 24, a child may say: *All the animals ran. Ran names what the animals did.* It *is a verb.*

Objectives
• Develop repertoire of learning strategies commensurate with grade-level learning expectations. • Decode (sound out) words using a combination of skills. • Use visual and contextual support to develop grasp of language structures needed to comprehend increasingly challenging language.

Phonemic Awareness/Phonics

■ **Review Initial and Medial /u/** To review /u/ in words, begin by asking the following questions: Can a pup tug on a rug? Can a bug jump up on a mug? As children answer, have them emphasize the words that have initial or medial /u/: *pup, tug, bug, jump, up, mug.* Ask children to say /u/ in these words. Compare words such as *sup* and *cup.* Help children notice the same sounds (/u/ and /p/) and different sounds (/s/ and /k/).

■ **/u/ Spelled *Uu*** Have children read the words *up, tug, chug, puff, us, jump, fun,* and *but* as you run your hand under each word. Have children point out the initial and medial /u/ and read the words. Check each child's progress. Monitor pronunciation for clarity but not for perfection.

Concepts and Oral Language

■ **Revisit Talk with Me Chart 28A** Display the chart. Have children describe each image on the page. Help them by describing how trains do work.

■ **Develop Oral Language** Introduce language patterns that help describe the pictures on Talk with Me Chart 28A. Write this sentence frame on the board: *The ___ is ___* Let's use this sentence pattern to talk about the first picture. *The train is black. The train is in the roundhouse.* Have children use the same sentence pattern to talk about the other pictures. Then add this sentence frame: *The ___ has ___.* Now I will use a new pattern to talk about the pictures. *The man has a hat.* Have children use this pattern to talk about the pictures. Then add this sentence frame: *The ___ are ___* Now I will use a new pattern to talk about the pictures. *The tracks are long.* Continue with another sentence frames of your choice.

 Beginning Have children repeat the sentences that other children make up. Let them take a turn pointing to a picture on the chart.

Intermediate Ask questions to help children notice more details about the pictures, such as *Where is the train going? What is the train carrying?*

Advanced/Advanced-High Organize children into pairs and have them create their own sentence frames. Encourage pairs to use nouns and prepositions to complete their sentences about trains.

Content Objectives
- Develop oral language.
- Use learning strategies.

Language Objectives
- Connect /u/ with *Uu.*
- Learn English language patterns.

Use Learning Strategies
Work with children to create a list of nouns that name people, places, or things in the pictures in the Talk with Me Chart.

Talk with Me Chart 28A

Language Opportunity
Show the Concept Talk Video. Then use the Concept Talk Video Routine (*ELL Handbook,* p. 48) to have children respond orally to questions about the video to reinforce concept attainment.

Objectives
• Speak using grade-level content area vocabulary in context to build academic language proficiency. • Respond orally to information in a wide variety of print, electronic, audio, and visual media to build and reinforce concept attainment.

Support for English Language Learners

Content Objectives
- Understand *The Little Engine That Could.*
- Practice plot.

Language Objectives
- Express opinions through speaking and writing.
- Write using grade-level vocabulary.

Monitor and Self-Correct
Remind children that if they don't know how to write the words, they should ask for help.

Home Language Support
Invite children to share ideas in their home languages before creating their songs.

 **E L L** English Language Learners

Language Workshop: Talk About the Songs

■ **Introduce and Model** Turn to p. 3 of *The Little Engine That Could.* Who rides on the train? The little train carries toys. What number is on the train? Write 7 on the board, and count to 7 with children. Page through the book and count some of the toys. Explain that these numbers tell how many toys there are.

■ **Practice** A song has words that you can sing. They often rhyme, like a poem. But they don't have to rhyme. A song has a rhythm and a beat. Explain that you will be writing a song together. Write the song below on the board:

> The little red engine carries toys,
> Carries toys, carries toys.
> The little red engine carries toys
> All around the mountain.

Sing the song to the tune of "The Wheels on the Bus." Repeat the song and stress the rhythm. Then have children sing the song with you. Have them march to the beat.

Writing: Write a Song

■ **Prepare for Writing** We read a song. Now let's write our own song.

■ **Create Songs About *The Little Engine That Could*** Write the following song frame on a sheet of paper and make a copy for each child.

> The little red engine carries _____,
> Carries _____, carries _____.
> The little red engine carries _____
> All _____ the _____.

Have children complete the song by writing or dictating words in the blanks. (Possible answers: *bears, giraffes, dolls, food*) Then have children illustrate their songs. When children are finished with the first three lines, help them use a preposition to write the last line of the song. Have them share their songs.

 Beginning/Intermediate Write the words *dolls, elephants, clown,* and *tracks* and have children choose the correct word to put in each blank.

Advanced/Advanced-High Encourage children to copy and complete the song frame on their own.

Objectives
• Monitor written language production and employ self-corrective techniques or other resources. • Distinguish intonation patterns of English with increasing ease. • Learn new expressions heard during classroom instruction and interactions. • Write using content-based grade-level vocabulary.

This Week's ELL Overview

ELL Handbook

- Maximize Literacy and Cognitive Engagement
- Research Into Practice
- Full Weekly Support for Every Selection

  ### On the Move!
  - Routines to Support Instruction

- Transfer Activities
- Professional Development

Daily Leveled ELL Notes

ELL notes appear throughout this week's instruction and ELL Support is on the DI pages of your Teacher's Edition. The following is a sample of an ELL note from this week.

English Language Learners

Beginning Connect Sound-Spelling Have children write the words *sip* and *zip* on their Write-On Boards. Use the *Ss* and *Zz* Alphabet Cards to distinguish the two sounds. Then have children read the words.

Intermediate Support High-Frequency Words Explain to children that the word *where* is often used at the beginning of a question. A question that begins with *where* asks about the location of someone or something. Have children practice saying questions that begin with *where.*

Advanced Visual Support Scaffold understanding of today's Amazing Word *kayak* by pointing to the image of a *kayak* on Talk with Me Chart 29A. Then use hand motions to show how a person would get a kayak to move.

Advanced High Extend Language Explain to children the difference between the words *come* and *go.* Tell them that the word *go* means to move away from something and the word *come* means to go toward something. Have children practice saying each word in a sentence.

ELL by Strand

The ELL lessons on this week's Support for English Language Learners pages are organized by strand. They offer additional scaffolding for the core curriculum. Leveled support notes on these pages address the different proficiency levels in your class. See pages DI•80–DI•85.

ELL Guy
Dr. Jim Cummins

The Three Pillars of ELL Instruction

ELL Strands	Activate Prior Knowledge	Access Content	Extend Language
Vocabulary p. DI•82	Frontload Vocabulary	Provide Scaffolding	Practice
Reading Comprehension p. DI•82	Provide Scaffolding	Set the Scene	Frontload Vocabulary
Phonics, Spelling, and Word Analysis pp. DI•80, DI•83–DI•84	Frontload Words with /v/ and /z/	Isolate Final /v/ and /z/	Review Initial and Medial /u/
Listening Comprehension p. DI•81	Prepare for the Read Aloud	First Listening	Second Listening
Conventions and Writing pp. DI•83, DI•85	Provide Scaffolding/ Introduce and Model	Practice	Leveled Practice Activities/ Leveled Writing Activities
Concept Development p. DI•80	Read the Concept Literacy Reader	Read the Concept Literacy Reader	Develop Oral Language

This Week's Practice Stations Overview

Six Weekly Practice Stations with Leveled Activities can be found at the beginning of each week of instruction. For this week's Practice Stations, see pp. 422–423.

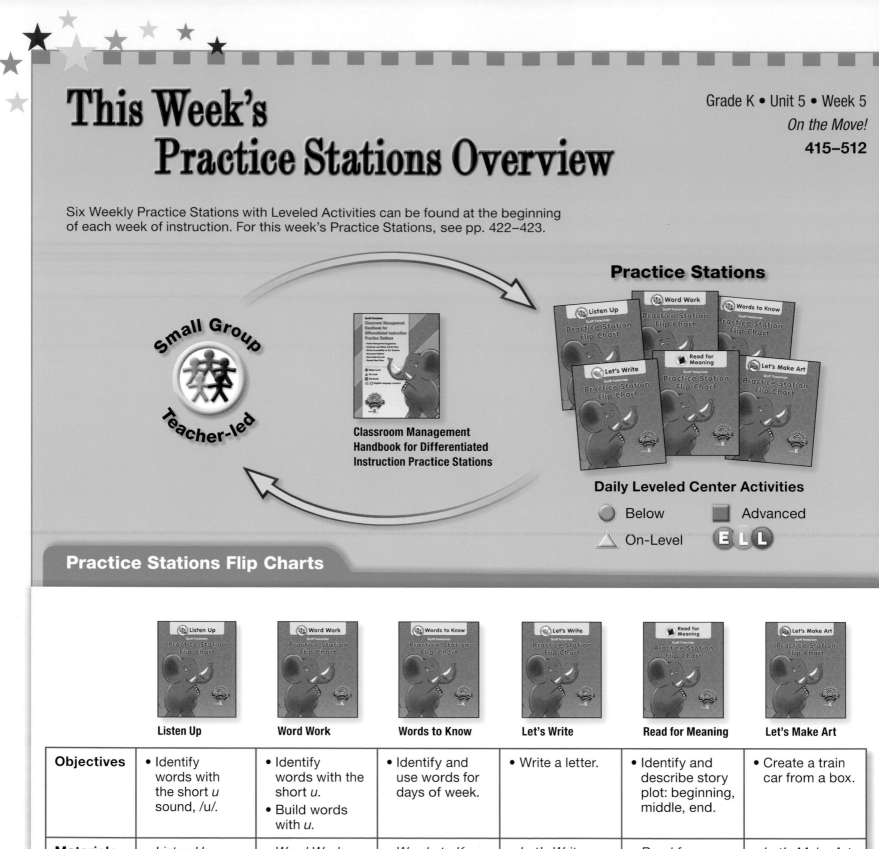

Small Group Teacher-led

Classroom Management Handbook for Differentiated Instruction Practice Stations

Practice Stations

Daily Leveled Center Activities

○ Below   ▢ Advanced   △ On-Level   ⓔⓛⓛ

Practice Stations Flip Charts

	Listen Up	Word Work	Words to Know	Let's Write	Read for Meaning	Let's Make Art
Objectives	• Identify words with the short *u* sound, /u/.	• Identify words with the short *u*. • Build words with *u*.	• Identify and use words for days of week.	• Write a letter.	• Identify and describe story plot: beginning, middle, end.	• Create a train car from a box.
Materials	• *Listen Up* Flip Chart Activity 29 • Picture Cards: *bus, jug, mug, rug, tub* • Letter Tiles	• *Word Work* Flip Chart Activity 29 • Picture Cards • Letter Tiles	• *Words to Know* Flip Chart Activity 29 • Teacher-made Word Cards: *Monday, Tuesday, Wednesday, Thursday, Friday, Saturday, Sunday* • Teacher-made calendar • paper, pencils	• *Let's Write* Flip Chart Activity 29 • Little Book *On the Move!* • Teacher-made chart of a letter including address, greeting, body, closing, and signature • paper, pencils	• *Read for Meaning* Flip Chart Activity 29 • Trade Book *The Little Engine That Could* • pencil, crayons, paper	• *Let's Make Art* Flip Chart Activity 29 • Trade Book *The Little Engine That Could* • small boxes • art paper • crayons • safety scissors • glue sticks • paper

This Week on Reading Street!

Going Places

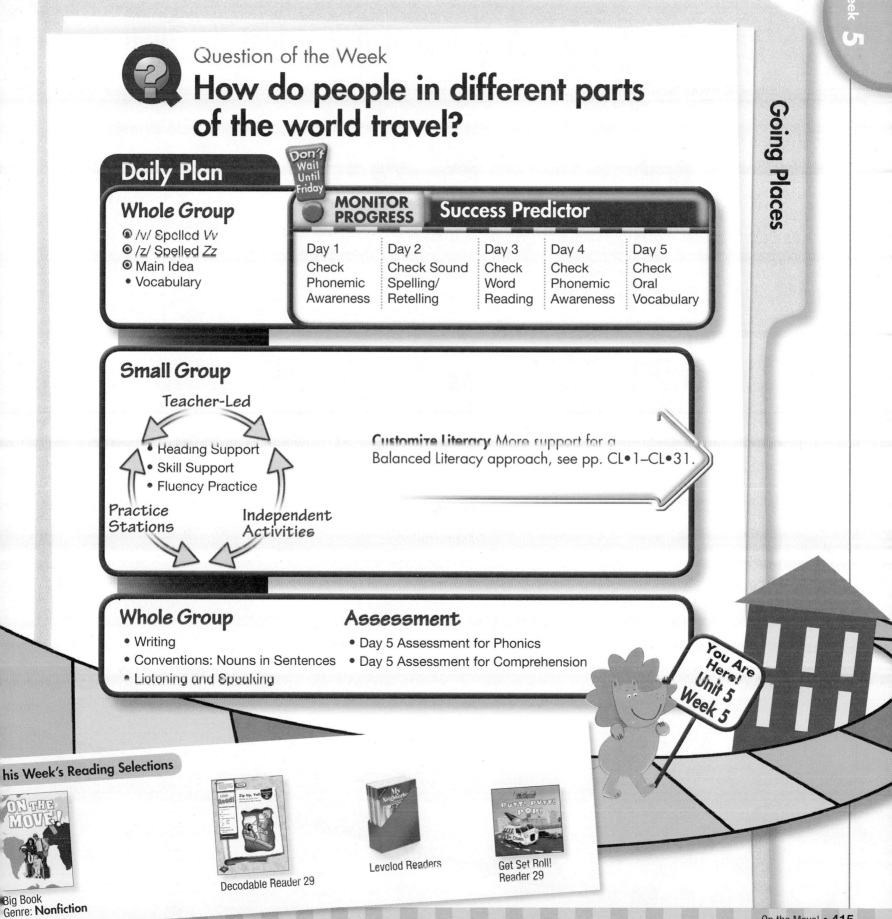

Question of the Week

How do people in different parts of the world travel?

Daily Plan

Don't Wait Until Friday

Whole Group

- /v/ Spelled Vv
- /z/ Spelled Zz
- Main Idea
- Vocabulary

MONITOR PROGRESS | **Success Predictor**

Day 1	Day 2	Day 3	Day 4	Day 5
Check Phonemic Awareness	Check Sound Spelling/ Retelling	Check Word Reading	Check Phonemic Awareness	Check Oral Vocabulary

Small Group

Teacher-Led

- Reading Support
- Skill Support
- Fluency Practice

Practice Stations

Independent Activities

Customize Literacy More support for a Balanced Literacy approach, see pp. CL•1–CL•31.

Whole Group

- Writing
- Conventions: Nouns in Sentences
- Listening and Speaking

Assessment

- Day 5 Assessment for Phonics
- Day 5 Assessment for Comprehension

You Are Here! Unit 5 Week 5

This Week's Reading Selections

ON THE MOVE!

Big Book
Genre: **Nonfiction**

Zip Up, Val!
Decodable Reader 29

My Neighborhood
Leveled Readers

PUTT! PUTT! POP!
Get Set Roll!
Reader 29

Resources on Reading Street!

	Build Concepts	Phonemic Awareness and Phonics	Vocabulary
Whole Group	Talk With Me/ Sing With Me	Student Edition pp. 92–93 Student Edition p. 96	Student Edition p. 97 Student Edition p. 108
Go Digital	• Concept Talk Video • Sing with Me Animations	• eReaders	
Small Group and Independent Practice	Practice Station Flip Chart Leveled Readers	Practice Station Flip Chart Decodable Reader 29 Leveled Readers Get Set, Roll! Reader 29	Practice Station Flip Chart Student Edition p. 97
Go Digital	• eReaders	• eReaders • Letter Tile Drag and Drop	
Customize Literacy	• Leveled Readers	• Decodable Reader	• High-Frequency Word Cards
Go Digital	• Concept Talk Video • Big Question Video • eReaders	• eReaders	• Sing with Me Animations

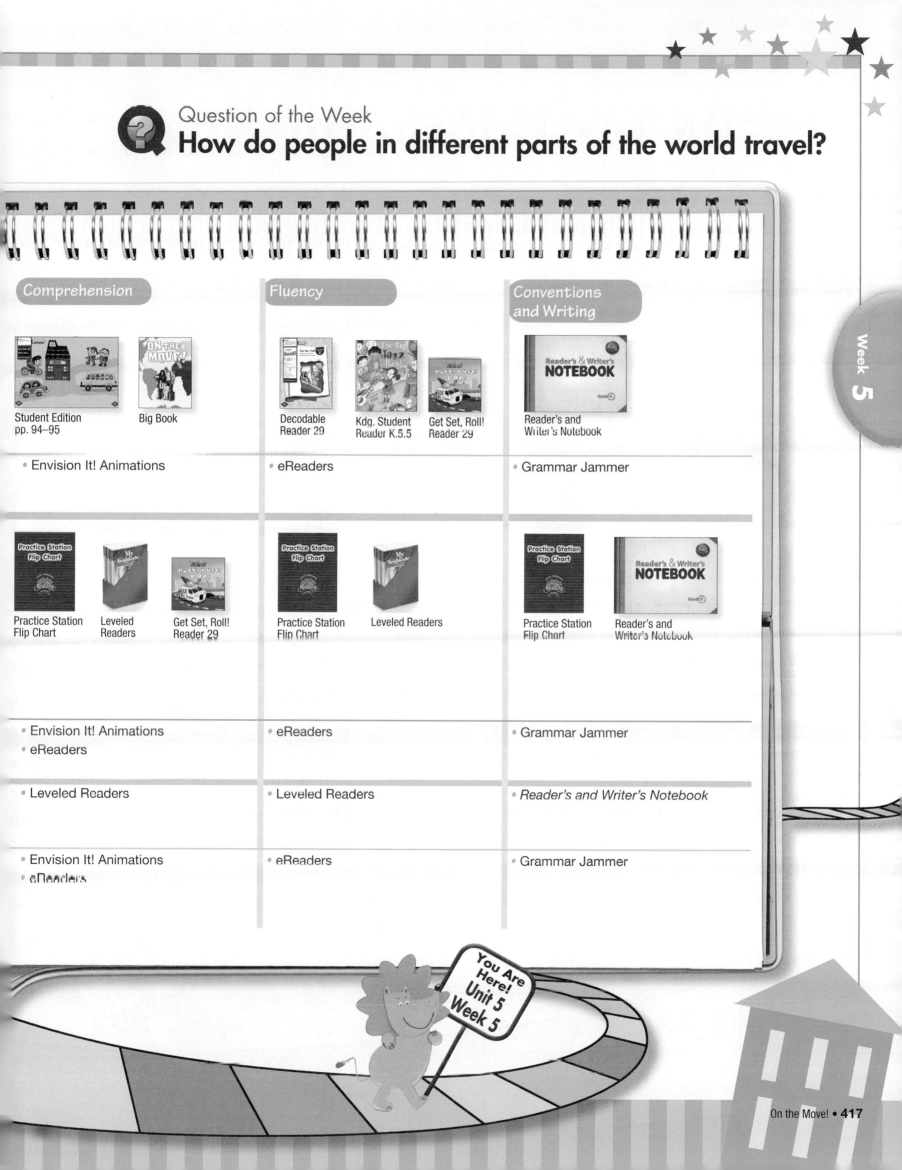

Question of the Week
How do people in different parts of the world travel?

Comprehension

Student Edition
pp. 94–95

Big Book

- Envision It! Animations

Practice Station
Flip Chart

Leveled Readers

Get Set, Roll!
Reader 29

- Envision It! Animations
- eReaders

- Leveled Readers

- Envision It! Animations
- eReaders

Fluency

Decodable
Reader 29

Kdg. Student
Reader K.5.5

Get Set, Roll!
Reader 29

- eReaders

Practice Station
Flip Chart

Leveled Readers

- eReaders

- Leveled Readers

- eReaders

Conventions and Writing

Reader's and
Writer's Notebook

- Grammar Jammer

Practice Station
Flip Chart

Reader's and
Writer's Notebook

- Grammar Jammer

- *Reader's and Writer's Notebook*

- Grammar Jammer

You Are
Here!
Unit 5
Week 5

My 5-Day Planner for Reading Street!

MONITOR PROGRESS
Don't Wait Until Friday

	Check Phonemic Awareness **Day 1** pages 424–439	Check Sound-Spelling Check Retelling **Day 2** pages 440–457

Get Ready to Read	**Concept Talk,** 424
	Oral Vocabulary, 425
	  travel, kayak, llama, dogsled, submarine,
	  double-decker bus
	Phonemic Awareness, 426–427
	  ◉ Initial /v/ and /z/
	Phonics, 428–429
	  ◉ /v/ Spelled *Vv*, /z/ Spelled *Zz*
	Handwriting, 430 Letters *V, v, Z* and *z*
	High-Frequency Words, 431 Introduce *where, come*
	READ Decodable Story 29, 432–433
		Concept Talk, 440
		Oral Vocabulary, 441 *travel, kayak*
		Phonemic Awareness, 442–443
		  ◉ Initial /v/ and /z/
		Phonics, 444–445
		  ◉ /v/ Spelled *Vv*, /z/ Spelled *Zz*
		Handwriting, 446 Words with *Vv* and *Zz*
		High-Frequency Words, 447 *where, come*
		READ Decodable Reader 29, 448–449

Read and Comprehend	**Listening Comprehension,** 434–435
	  ◉ Main Idea
		Listening Comprehension, 450
		  ◉ Main Idea
		READ Big Book—First Read, 450
		  On the Move!
		Retell, 451
		Think, Talk, and Write, 452

Language Arts	**Conventions,** 436 Nouns in Sentences **Writing,** 437 Wonderful, Marvelous Me! **Daily Handwriting,** 437 Letters *V, v, Z* and *z* **Listening and Speaking,** 438 Oral Presentation—Description **Wrap Up Your Day,** 438 **Extend Your Day!,** 439	**Conventions,** 453 Nouns in Sentences **Writing,** 454 Respond to Literature **Daily Handwriting,** 454 Letters *V, v, Z* and *z* **Vocabulary,** 455 Compound Words **Wrap Up Your Day,** 456 **Extend Your Day!,** 457

You Are Here! Unit 5 Week 5

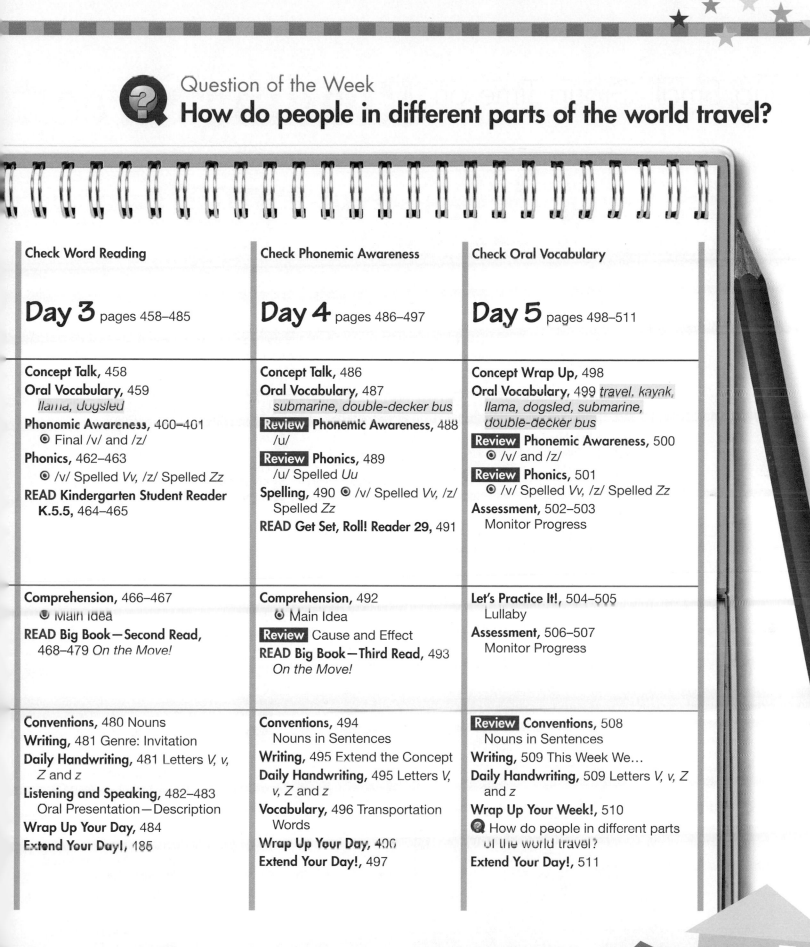

Question of the Week
How do people in different parts of the world travel?

Check Word Reading	Check Phonemic Awareness	Check Oral Vocabulary
Day 3 pages 458–485	**Day 4** pages 486–497	**Day 5** pages 498–511
Concept Talk, 458 **Oral Vocabulary,** 459 *llama, dogsled* **Phonemic Awareness,** 460–461 ⊙ Final /v/ and /z/ **Phonics,** 462–463 ⊙ /v/ Spelled *Vv*, /z/ Spelled *Zz* **READ Kindergarten Student Reader K.5.5,** 464–465	**Concept Talk,** 486 **Oral Vocabulary,** 487 *submarine, double-decker bus* **Review Phonemic Awareness,** 488 /u/ **Review Phonics,** 489 /u/ Spelled *Uu* **Spelling,** 490 ⊙ /v/ Spelled *Vv*, /z/ Spelled *Zz* **READ Get Set, Roll! Reader 29,** 491	**Concept Wrap Up,** 498 **Oral Vocabulary,** 499 *travel, kayak, llama, dogsled, submarine, double-decker bus* **Review Phonemic Awareness,** 500 ⊙ /v/ and /z/ **Review Phonics,** 501 ⊙ /v/ Spelled *Vv*, /z/ Spelled *Zz* **Assessment,** 502–503 Monitor Progress
Comprehension, 466–467 ⊙ Main Idea **READ Big Book—Second Read,** 468–479 *On the Move!*	**Comprehension,** 492 ⊙ Main Idea **Review** Cause and Effect **READ Big Book—Third Read,** 493 *On the Move!*	**Let's Practice It!,** 504–505 Lullaby **Assessment,** 506–507 Monitor Progress
Conventions, 480 Nouns **Writing,** 481 Genre: Invitation **Daily Handwriting,** 481 Letters *V, v, Z* and *z* **Listening and Speaking,** 482–483 Oral Presentation—Description **Wrap Up Your Day,** 484 **Extend Your Day!,** 485	**Conventions,** 494 Nouns in Sentences **Writing,** 495 Extend the Concept **Daily Handwriting,** 495 Letters *V, v, Z* and *z* **Vocabulary,** 496 Transportation Words **Wrap Up Your Day,** 496 **Extend Your Day!,** 497	**Review Conventions,** 508 Nouns in Sentences **Writing,** 509 This Week We… **Daily Handwriting,** 509 Letters *V, v, Z* and *z* **Wrap Up Your Week!,** 510 How do people in different parts of the world travel? **Extend Your Day!,** 511

Week 5

Grouping Options for Differentiated Instruction
Turn the page for the small group time lesson plan.

Planning Small Group Time on Reading Street!

SMALL GROUP TIME RESOURCES

DAY 1

Look for this Small Group Time box each day to help meet the individual needs of all your children. Differentiated instruction lessons appear on the DI pages at the end of each week.

Teacher-Led

SI Strategic Intervention	**OL On-Level**	**A Advanced**
Teacher-Led • Phonemic Awareness and Phonics **Reread** Decodable Story	**Teacher-Led** • Phonemic Awareness and Phonics **Reread** Decodable Story	**Teacher-Led** • Phonemic Awareness and Phonics **Reread** Decodable Story for Fluency

ELL Place English language learners in the groups that correspond to their reading abilities in English.

Practice Stations
• Listen Up
• Word Work

Independent Activities
• Read Independently
• *Reader's and Writer's Notebook*
• Concept Talk Video

ELL

ELL Poster 29

Day 1

SI Strategic Intervention	**Phonemic Awareness and Phonics,** DI•69 **Reread** Decodable Story 29, DI•69
OL On-Level	**Phonemic Awareness and Phonics,** DI•74 **Reread** Decodable Story 29, DI•74
A Advanced	**Phonemic Awareness and Phonics,** DI•77 **Reread** Decodable Story 29 for Fluency, DI•77
ELL English Language Learners	DI•80–DI•81 Frontload Concept Phonemic Awareness and Phonics Comprehension Skill

You Are Here!
Unit 5
Week 5

Question of the Week
How do people in different parts of the world travel?

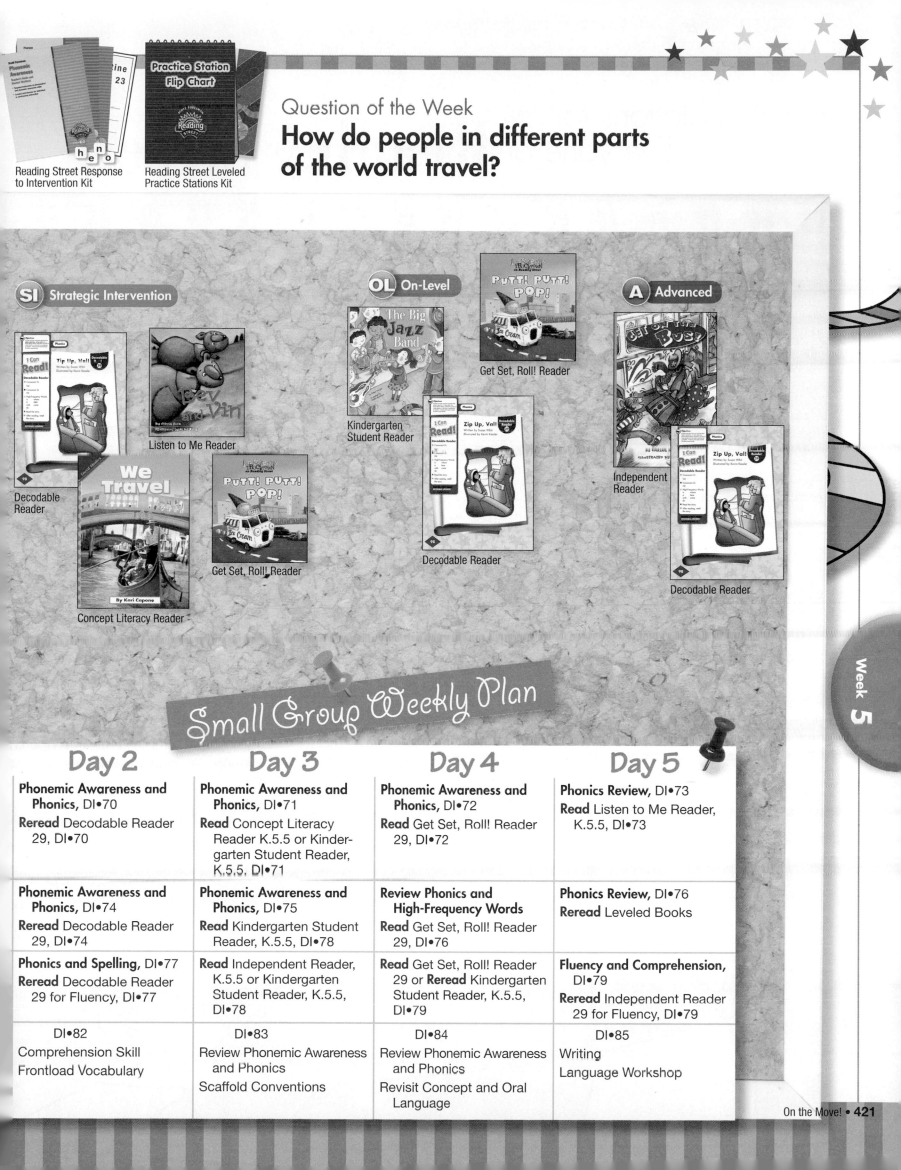

SI Strategic Intervention

Decodable Reader

Listen to Me Reader

We Travel
By Kari Capone
Concept Literacy Reader

PUTT! PUTT! POP!
Get Set, Roll! Reader

OL On-Level

The Big Jazz Band
Kindergarten Student Reader

Zip Up, Val!
Decodable Reader

PUTT! PUTT! POP!
Get Set, Roll! Reader

A Advanced

GET ON THE BUS!
Independent Reader

Zip Up, Val!
Decodable Reader

Small Group Weekly Plan

Day 2	Day 3	Day 4	Day 5
Phonemic Awareness and Phonics, DI•70 **Reread** Decodable Reader 29, DI•70	**Phonemic Awareness and Phonics,** DI•71 **Read** Concept Literacy Reader K.5.5 or Kindergarten Student Reader, K.5.5, DI•71	**Phonemic Awareness and Phonics,** DI•72 **Read** Get Set, Roll! Reader 29, DI•72	**Phonics Review,** DI•73 **Read** Listen to Me Reader, K.5.5, DI•73
Phonemic Awareness and Phonics, DI•74 **Reread** Decodable Reader 29, DI•74	**Phonemic Awareness and Phonics,** DI•75 **Read** Kindergarten Student Reader, K.5.5, DI•78	**Review Phonics and High-Frequency Words** **Read** Get Set, Roll! Reader 29, DI•76	**Phonics Review,** DI•76 **Reread** Leveled Books
Phonics and Spelling, DI•77 **Reread** Decodable Reader 29 for Fluency, DI•77	**Read** Independent Reader, K.5.5 or Kindergarten Student Reader, K.5.5, DI•78	**Read** Get Set, Roll! Reader 29 or **Reread** Kindergarten Student Reader, K.5.5, DI•79	**Fluency and Comprehension,** DI•79 **Reread** Independent Reader 29 for Fluency, DI•79
DI•82 Comprehension Skill Frontload Vocabulary	DI•83 Review Phonemic Awareness and Phonics Scaffold Conventions	DI•84 Review Phonemic Awareness and Phonics Revisit Concept and Oral Language	DI•85 Writing Language Workshop

Week 5

Practice Stations for Everyone on Reading Street!

Listen Up!
Short *u*

Objectives
• Identify words with the short *u* sound, /u/.

Materials
• *Listen Up!* Flip Chart Activity 29
• Picture Cards: *bus, jug, mug, rug, tub, fox, cat, lamp, van, bat*

Differentiated Activities

⬤ Find the Picture Card for *tub*. Say the sound you hear in the middle. Draw a picture of another word that has the /u/ sound you hear in the middle of *tub*.

▲ Find the Picture Card for *tub*. Say the sound you hear at the beginning, in the middle, and at the end. Then sort the Picture Cards into two piles, things with the sound /u/ and things without it.

⬛ Find the Picture Card for *tub*. Say the sound you hear at the beginning, in the middle, and at the end. Then think of words that rhyme with *tub* and make up a short poem.

Word Work
/u/ spelled *Uu*

Objectives
• Identify words with the short *u*.
• Build words with the short *u*.

Materials
• *Word Work* Flip Chart Activity 29
• Picture Cards: *bus, jug, mug, rug, tub, fox, cat, lamp, van, bat*
• Letter Tiles

Differentiated Activities

⬤ Find the Picture Card for the word *tub*. Use the Letter Tiles to build the word *tub*. Say the name for each letter and say *tub*.

▲ Find the Picture Card for the word *tub*. Use the Letter Tiles to build the word *tub*. Take away the letter *t* and replace it with the letter *c*. Read the word you made.

⬛ Find the Picture Card for the word *tub*. Use the Letter Tiles to build the word *tub*. Use the Letter Tiles to make other words with the sound /u/ in the middle.

Technology
• Letter Tile Drag and Drop

Words To Know
Words for time

Objectives
• Identify and use words for time: *Monday, Tuesday, Wednesday, Thursday, Friday, Saturday, Sunday*.

Materials
• *Words to Know* Flip Chart Activity 29
• Teacher-made word cards: *Monday, Tuesday, Wednesday, Thursday, Friday, Saturday, Sunday.*
• Teacher-made calendar with the days of the week across the top: *Sunday, Monday, Tuesday, Wednesday, Thursday, Friday, Saturday.*
• paper, pencils

Differentiated Activities

⬤ Match the word cards for *Monday, Tuesday, Wednesday, Thursday, Friday, Saturday, Sunday* with the words on the calendar. Recite the days of the week in order.

▲ Match the word cards for *Monday, Tuesday, Wednesday, Thursday, Friday, Saturday, Sunday* with the words on the calendar. Tell about something you do each day of the week.

⬛ Match the word cards for *Monday, Tuesday, Wednesday, Thursday, Friday, Saturday, Sunday* with the words on the calendar. Write sentences about something you do using the words *Monday, Tuesday, Wednesday, Thursday, Friday, Saturday, or Sunday*.

You Are Here! Unit 5 Week 5

Key

⬤ Below-Level Activities

▲ On-Level Activities

■ Advanced Activities

Practice Station Flip Chart

Let's Write!
Letter

Objectives
• Write a letter.

Materials
• *Let's Write!* Flip Chart Activity 29
• Little Book *On the Move!*
• Teacher-made chart of a letter including address, greeting, body, closing, and signature
• paper, pencil

Differentiated Activities

⬤ Look at the book. Think about different kinds of transportation. Draw a picture or write a letter to your principal that tells about what you are learning.

▲ Look at the book. Think about different kinds of transportation. Write a letter to your principal that tells about what you are learning. Use the chart to help you write the letter.

■ Look at the book. Think about different kinds of transportation. Write a letter to your principal that tells about what you are learning. Use the chart to help you. Be sure to include all the parts of a formal letter.

Read For Meaning
Plot

Objectives
• Identify and describe story plot: beginning, middle, end.

Materials
• *Read for Meaning* Flip Chart Activity 29
• Trade Book *The Little Engine That Could*
• pencil, crayons, paper

Differentiated Activities

The **plot** is what happens in the story. A good way to understand the plot is to think about what happens at the **beginning**, in the **middle**, and at the **end**.

⬤ Read your book. Find a picture that shows something that happens at the beginning. Tell what you see.

▲ Read your book. Draw a picture that shows what happens in the story. Write a sentence that tells what happens. Tell if it happens in the beginning, the middle, or the end of the story.

■ Read your book. Draw a picture that shows what happens in the story. Write three sentences that tell what happens in the beginning, in the middle, and at the end.

Let's Make Art!

Objectives
• Create a train car from a box.

Materials
• *Let's Make Art!* Flip Chart Activity 29
• Trade Book *The Little Engine That Could*
• small boxes
• art paper
• crayons
• safety scissors
• glue sticks
• construction paper

Differentiated Activities

⬤ Look at the pictures of the train in your story. Choose a box and use the art supplies to make the box look like one of the train cars.

▲ Look at the pictures of the train in your story. Look at the different lines, shapes, and colors. Choose a box and use the art supplies to make a train car of your own.

■ Look at the pictures of the train in your story. Choose a box and use the art supplies to make a train car of your own. Be sure and show what the train car is used for.

Week 5

Name _____ Date _____

My Work Plan
Put an ☒ next to the activities you complete.

Listen Up!
☐ Listen for sounds.

Let's Write!
☐ Make a letter.

Word Work
☐ Build words with short *u*.

Words to Know
☐ Match words for time with words on a calendar.

Let's Make Art!
☐ Make a train car.

Read for Meaning
☐ Tell what happens in the beginning, middle, and end of a story.

Wrap Up Your Week Turn your paper over. Draw or write about what you did at school this week. What did you read? What did you learn about how people travel?

Unit 5 • Week 5 • *On the Move!*

My Weekly Work Plan

Objectives
- Share information and ideas about the concept.

Today at a Glance

Oral Vocabulary
travel, kayak, llama, dogsled, double-decker bus, submarine

Phonemic Awareness
◉ Initial /v/ and /z/

Phonics
◉ /v/ Spelled *Vv*
◉ /z/ Spelled *Zz*

Handwriting
V, v, Z, and *z*

High-Frequency Words
where, come

Comprehension
◉ Main Idea

Conventions
Nouns in Sentences

Writing
Wonderful, Marvelous Me!

Listening and Speaking
Oral Presentation: Description

TRUCKTOWN on Reading Street

Start your engines! Display p. 14 of *Truckery Rhymes.*

- Read aloud "Jack and Kat" and track the print.
  - Reread the rhyme and have children say it with you.
  - Ask children to identify the rhyming words. (*down, Trucktown*)

Truckery Rhymes

Concept Talk

Question of the Week

 How do people in different parts of the world travel?

Introduce the concept

To build concepts and to focus their attention, tell children that this week they will talk, sing, read, and write about **transportation used around the world.** Write the question of the week and track the print as you read it.

Play the CD that features a story about llamas. What do you think riding on a llama would be like?

🔘 Background Building Audio

ROUTINE **Activate Prior Knowledge** **Team Talk**

1. **Think** Have children think for a minute about transportation.

2. **Pair** Have pairs of children discuss the question of the week. Remind them to take turns speaking. Have children use complete sentences in their discussions about transportation around the world.

3. **Share** Call on a few children to share their ideas with the group. Guide discussion and encourage elaboration with prompts such as: How can people travel in the air?

Routines Flip Chart

Anchored Talk

Develop oral language

Display Talk with Me Chart 29A. What do you see in the pictures? These pictures show different ways people travel around the world. Do you like to travel? Where have you gone on a trip? How did you get to your destination? This week we will talk about how people around the world travel in different ways.

We are going to learn six new Amazing Words. Listen as I say each word: *travel, kayak, llama, dogsled, double-decker bus, submarine.* Say the Amazing Words with me as I point to the pictures.

Display Sing with Me Chart 29B. Today we are going to sing a song about different ways to travel. Read the title. Have children describe the pictures. Sing the song several times to the tune of "Do Your Ears Hang Low?" Listen for the Amazing Words *travel, kayak, llama, dogsled, double-decker bus,* and *submarine.* Have children stand up and sing with you.

Sing with Me Audio

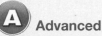
Talk with Me/Sing with Me Chart 29A

Talk with Me/Sing with Me Chart 29B

ELL Preteach Concepts Use the Day 1 instruction on ELL Poster 29 to assess and build background knowledge, develop concepts, and build vocabulary.

ELL Poster 29

Amazing Words

travel	kayak
llama	dogsled
double-decker bus	submarine

Differentiated Instruction

A **Advanced**

Support Discussion Have children create a story about traveling to a faraway place. Tell them to describe the transportation they would use.

ELL

English Language Learners
Build Background Use the art in the chart to help children understand words such as *llama* and *submarine.*

ELL Support Additional ELL support and modified instruction is provided in the *ELL Handbook* and in the ELL Support Lessons on pp. DI•80–85.

Objectives

◎ Learn initial /v/.
◎ Learn initial /z/.
• Discriminate words with initial /v/ and /z/.

Check Phonemic Awareness
SUCCESS PREDICTOR

My Skills Buddy, pp. 92–93

Phonemic Awareness
Initial /v/ and /z/

Introduce

Today we will learn two new sounds. Listen carefully to the first sound: /v/ /v/ /v/. Say it with me: /v/ /v/ /v/. Display the *van* Picture Card. *Van* begins with /v/ /v/, *van*. What sound does *van* begin with? Continue the routine with the words *vacuum* and *victory*. Repeat the routine for /z/ with the *zebra, zipper,* and *zoo* Picture Cards.

Picture Card

Model

Have children look at the picture on pp. 92–93 of *My Skills Buddy.* The word *victory* begins with /v/. What things do you see in the picture with names that begin with /v/? The word *zero* begins with /z/. What do you see in the picture that begins with /z/?

Guide practice

As children name examples of words from the picture, guide them in stating that /v/ or /z/ is the beginning sound. Discuss with children some of the bulleted items on p. 92 of *My Skills Buddy.* Save the other bulleted items for discussion on Day 2.

Picture Card

Corrective feedback

If... children have difficulty naming words with /v/ or /z/, **then...** say *vest* and *zero* again, stretching the beginning sound.

Discriminate sounds

I am going to say two words. Listen carefully to the first sound in each word. One word begins with /v/, and the other does not: *very, light. Very* begins with /v/. Continue the routine with the following word sets: *math, vest; lake, vet; umbrella, volcano; vase, toad.*

Now listen to more words. One word will begin with /z/. I want you to tell me which word begins with /z/. Listen carefully: *zoo, museum.* Which word begins with /z/? *Zoo* begins with /z/. Now try it with me. Continue the routine with the following word sets: *zipper, button; zip, tie; well, zoom; zero, city.*

Corrective feedback

If... children cannot discriminate initial /v/ or /z/,

then... have them enunciate /v/ as they say *very* and /z/ as they say *zoo.*

When you say the first sound in *very,* you will feel your throat move quickly. Put your hand on your neck as you say /v/. When you say *zoo,* put your hand on your neck and feel it move quickly as you buzz like a bee.

Segment

Review segmentation. Listen to the sounds in the word *van:* /v/ /a/ /n/. Say it with me: /v/ /a/ /n/, *van.* How many sounds do you hear? Continue with the following words: *vest, zip, zap, vet.*

Don't Wait Until Friday

MONITOR PROGRESS — ↻ Check Phonemic Awareness /v/ and /z/

I will say some words. Clap if the word begins with /v/, and wiggle your fingers if the word begins with /z/. Use the following words: *violet, zone, zing, valley, vote.*

If... children cannot discriminate initial /v/ or /z/,

then... use the small-group Strategic Intervention lesson, p. DI•69, to reteach /v/ and /z/.

Day 1	Day 2	Day 3	Day 4	Day 5
Check Phonemic Awareness	Check Sound-Spelling/Retelling	Check Word Reading	Check Phonemic Awareness	Check Oral Vocabulary

Differentiated Instruction

A **Advanced**

Initial /v/ and /z/ First have children brainstorm a list of words that begin with /v/ and /z/. Then have children create silly sentences or stories that have words that begin with those sounds.

ELL

English Language Learners

Support Phonemic Awareness Speakers of Japanese, Korean, and Spanish may have a hard time distinguishing the /b/ and /v/ sounds. Show how the lips and teeth are used differently to produce each sound. Provide additional practice with /v/ words.

In Latin American Spanish, the letter *z* is pronounced /s/, so speakers may pronounce *zip* as *sip.* The /z/ sound may also be challenging for speakers of Cantonese, Hmong, and Korean. Provide extra practice with words beginning with /z/.

Success Predictor

Objectives

◎ Associate the sound /v/ with the spelling v.

◎ Associate the sound /z/ with the spelling z.

• Recognize uppercase V and lowercase v.

• Recognize uppercase Z and lowercase z.

Skills Trace

◎ /v/ Spelled Vv; /z/ Spelled Zz

Introduce U5W5D1

Practice U5W5D2; U5W5D3

Reteach/Review U5W5D5; U5W6D4

Assess/Test Benchmark Assessment U5

KEY:
U=Unit   W=Week   D=Day

Phonics—Teach/Model
/v/ Spelled Vv and /z/ Spelled Zz

Introduce

Display the *Vv* Alphabet Card. Point to the *volcano* on the Alphabet Card. *Volcano* begins with /v/. Say the word with me, *volcano.* Write *volcano* on the board and point to the *v. Volcano* begins with /v/ spelled *v.* Now point to the letters *Vv* on the card. The sound for this letter is /v/. The names of these letters are uppercase *V* and lowercase *v.* What is the sound for this letter? What are the names of these letters? Repeat the routine with the *Zz* Alphabet Card.

Alphabet Card

Model

Write this sentence on the board: *Zak sat in the van.* Point to the *Z* in *Zak.* When I see this letter, I think of the sound /z/. The first word is *Zak*—/z/ Zak. Point to the *v* in *van.* When I see this letter, I think of the sound /v/. This word is *van*—/v/, van. I know that when I see a *z,* the sound will be /z/ and when I see a *v,* the sound will be /v/.

Alphabet Card

Guide practice

Display Phonics Songs and Rhymes Chart 29. We are going to sing a new song today. Teach children the song, "I Want My Car to Vroom," sung to the tune of "A Sailor Went to Sea, Sea, Sea." Play the CD and sing the song several times. I hear words that begin with /v/ and /z/. When you hear a word that begins with /v/ or /z/, clap your hands. As you sing the song, point to words that begin with v and z.

Phonics Songs and Rhymes Audio

On their own

Have children look around the room to find uppercase V and Z and lowercase v and z. When they spot *Vv,* they should make a v with their fingers. If they spot *Zz,* they should make a z in the air with their fingers.

I Want My Car to Vroom

I want my car to vroom, vroom, vroom.
It zips around the room, room, room.
Oh, can you see it zoom, zoom, zoom,
Zig, zag, and vroom, vroom, vroom?

I want my plane to vroom, vroom, vroom.
It veers around the room, room, room.
Oh, can you see it zoom, zoom, zoom,
Zip and zap and vroom, vroom, vroom?

Phonics Songs and Rhymes Chart 29

Blend Words

To review sound-spellings, use Alphabet Cards *Aa, Cc, Ee, Ii, Ll, Pp, Ss,* and *Tt* and the *ant, cap, egg, inch, lamp, pig, six,* and *tub* Picture Cards. Then use this routine for sound-by-sound blending to have children blend new words.

 **ROUTINE** **Sound-by-Sound Blending**

1 Connect Write the letter *v* on the board. What is the sound for this letter? The sound is /v/. Say it with me: /v/ /v/ /v/. When you see this letter in a word, what sound will you say? Repeat with *z.*

2 Model Write *van* on the board.

- Touch under the letter *v:* What is the sound for this letter? Say it with me: /v/ /v/ /v/. Repeat the routine for *a* and *n.*

- Let's blend the sounds together. Listen as I blend the sounds: /v/ /a/ /n/. Say it with me: /v/ /a/ /n/, *van.* Now say it without me.

- Listen as I use *van* in a sentence. *I like to ride in a van.* Say it with me. Then have children use *van* in their own sentences.

3 Guide Practice Continue the routine established in step 2 with the words below:

Val	Zap	Zip	Vic	vest	top	red	up	tag

Children should successfully read these words before reading Decodable Story 29 on pp. 371–372 of *Reader's and Writer's Notebook.*

Corrective Feedback If children have trouble reading a word, model blending the sounds to read the word. Then have children say it with you.

Routines Flip Chart

Differentiated Instruction

SI Strategic Intervention

/z/ Spelled *Zz* Have children draw pictures of things that begin with /z/. Then have them label their drawings with the letter for that sound. Use the *zoo* and *zebra* Picture Cards or pp. 92–93 of *My Skills Buddy* to generate ideas. Have children repeat the activity with /v/ spelled *Vv.*

Teacher Tip

If a computer is available, have children go to the keyboard and type the letters *v* and *z.*

 **ELL**

English Language Learners

Connect Sound-Spelling Have children write the words *sip* and *zip* on their Write-On Boards. Use the *Ss* and *Zz* Alphabet Cards to distinguish the two sounds. Then have children read the words.

Objectives
- Write *V*, *v*, *Z*, and *z*.
- Learn high-frequency words.

Handwriting

Introduce

Write *Vv* on the board. Words that begin with /v/ are written with uppercase *V* or a lowercase *v*. Which letter is uppercase *V*? Which letter is lowercase *v*? Repeat the routine with *Zz*.

Model uppercase *V* and *Z*

Write *Vic* on the board. Point to the uppercase *V*. This is an uppercase *V*. We use uppercase letters to begin sentences and for the first letters in a name. Watch as I trace the uppercase *V* with my finger. Follow the stroke instructions pictured below. Repeat with the name *Zelda*.

Guide practice

Have children write the uppercase *V* in the air. Use your finger to make an uppercase *V* in the air. Now write it on the palm of your hand. Repeat with uppercase *Z*.

Model lowercase *v* and *z*

Write *vase* on the board. Point to the lowercase *v*. This is a lowercase *v*. Watch as I trace a lowercase *v* with my finger. Write another lowercase *v* on the board following the stroke instructions. Again, have children write *v* in the air and on their hands. Repeat the procedure with lowercase *z* and the word *zero*.

Guide practice

Have children use their Write-On Boards to write a row each of uppercase *V* and *Z* and a row each of lowercase *v* and *z*.

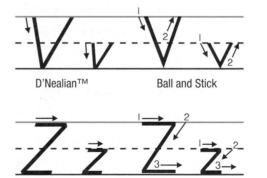

D'Nealian™   Ball and Stick

D'Nealian™   Ball and Stick

More practice

Use *Reader's and Writer's Notebook*, pp. 369, 370, for additional practice with initial *v* and *z*.

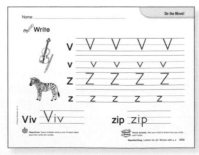

Reader's and Writer's Notebook, p. 369

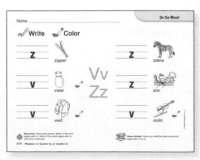

Reader's and Writer's Notebook, p. 370

High-Frequency Words

Introduce Use the routine below to teach high-frequency words *where* and *come*.

> **ROUTINE** **Nondecodable Words**
>
> **1** **Say and Spell** Some words we have to learn by remembering the letters rather than saying the sounds. We will say and spell the words to help learn them. Write *where* on the board. This is the word *where*. It has five letters. The letters in *where* are *w, h, e, r,* and *e.* Have children say and spell the word, first with you and then without you.
>
> **2** **Demonstrate Meaning** I can use the word *where* in lots of sentences. Here is one sentence: *Where is my coat?* Now you use the word in a sentence.
>
> Repeat the routine with the word *come*.
>
> Add the words *where* and *come* to the Word Wall.

Routines Flip Chart

Academic Vocabulary

Write the following words on the board:

main idea	**compound word**
lullaby	**noun**
sentence	**invitation**

Point to the list. This week we are going to learn these important words. They are tools for learning. As we work this week, you will hear them many times. Read the words. Preteach the Academic Vocabulary at point-of-use by providing a child-friendly description, explanation, or example that clarifies the meaning of each term. Then ask children to restate the meaning of the Academic Vocabulary in their own words.

Decodable Story 29
/v/ Spelled Vv, /z/ Spelled Zz, and High-Frequency Words

Review

Review the following high-frequency words by having children read each word as you point to it on the Word Wall.

come	a	they	go	to	look
for	see	is	like	the	he

Read Decodable Story 29

Display Decodable Story 29. Today we will read a story about a girl named Val and the shopping trip she takes with her mom. What is the title of the story? Point to the title of the story. The title of the story is *Val's Top.* What sound do you hear at the beginning of *Val?* We will read /v/ and /z/ words in this story. Have children read Decodable Story 29 on pp. 371–372 in *Reader's and Writer's Notebook.*

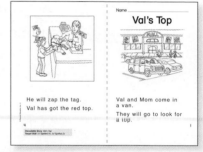

Reader's and Writer's Notebook, pp. 371–372

Use the routine for reading decodable books to read Decodable Story 29.

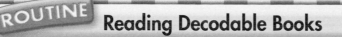

ROUTINE Reading Decodable Books

1. **Read Silently** Have children whisper read the story page by page as you listen in.

2. **Model Fluent Reading** Have children finger point as you read a page. Then have children reread the page without you.

3. **Read Chorally** Have children finger point as they chorally read the page. Continue reading page by page, repeating steps 1 and 2.

4. **Read Individually** Have children take turns reading aloud a page.

5. **Reread and Monitor Progress** As you listen to individual children reread, monitor progress and provide support.

6. **Reread with a Partner** Have children reread the story page by page with a partner.

Routines Flip Chart

Small Group Time

DAY 1

Break into small groups after reading the Decodable Story and before the comprehension lesson.

Teacher-Led

SI Strategic Intervention	**OL On-Level**	**A Advanced**
Teacher-Led Page DI•69 • Phonemic Awareness and Phonics • **Reread** Decodable Story 29	**Teacher-Led** Page DI•74 • Phonemic Awareness and Phonics • **Reread** Decodable Story 29, DI•74	**Teacher-Led** Page DI•77 • Phonemic Awareness and Phonics • **Reread** Decodable Story 29 for Fluency, DI•77

ELL Place English language learners in the groups that correspond to their reading abilities in English.

Practice Stations
• Visit the Listen Up! Station
• Visit the Word Work Station

Independent Activities
• Read independently
• Concept Talk Video
• *Reader's and Writer's Notebook*

Differentiated Instruction

SI Strategic Intervention

Support Decoding Before children read *Val's Top*, review /v/ and /z/ with the following Picture Cards: *van, vacuum, zebra, zoo.*

 **ELL**

English Language Learners

Visual Support Remind children to use the pictures of the story to help them understand or decode words in the text.

Objectives

• Identify and describe main idea.

KEY:

U=Unit   W=Week   D=Day

My Skills Buddy, pp. 94–95

Listening Comprehension
🎯 Main Idea

Introduce

All stories are about a big idea. This is the most important idea that the author wants to write about. The most important idea of a selection is called the **main idea.** Good readers look for the main idea because it helps them understand what the selection is all about.

Envision It!

Have children turn to pp. 94–95 in *My Skills Buddy* and look at the picture.

• How do the children get to school? (by car, by bus, by bike, or by foot)

• What is the main idea of this picture? (Children come to school in different ways.)

Model

Today we are going to read a selection about transportation in London. Read **"Traveling in London"** and model how to find the main idea.

Think Aloud

When I read, I look for the most important idea the author is writing about. I can figure out the main idea if I think about the details. This selection tells that people in London travel in cars, double-decker buses, and the subway. The main idea of this selection is that people in London travel in different ways.

Guide practice

Reread **"Traveling in London."** Have children tell about the different ways people travel in London. What is the main idea of this selection? (People in London travel in different ways.)

More practice

Display the Big Book *Then and Now.* Page through the selection. Help children recall the main idea. What does the selection tell about? (It tells about things in the past and things today.) What is the main idea of the selection? (Many things have changed over time, but some things have stayed the same.)

Connect to everyday life

Think of some things you do, such as playing a game like soccer. What is the game all about?

Academic Vocabulary

main idea the big idea that tells what the selection is mainly about; the most important idea of a text

Traveling in London

London is a huge city in England, a country across the Atlantic Ocean. People in London can travel in many different ways. Many people drive cars. Some people take taxicabs. Many people take buses. London was once famous for its red double-decker buses. When you got on one of those buses, you climbed narrow stairs to get to the top deck.

Like many big cities, London has a subway system. Subways are trains that travel in underground tunnels. People go from the street down stairs to the subway station. There they buy tickets and get on the trains. They can look at big maps to see which train to take to get where they want to go.

English Language Learners
Oral Comprehension To prepare English learners for the Read Aloud, use the teaching routine in the *ELL Handbook* p. DI•81.

Objectives

- Introduce nouns in sentences.
- Write sentences using nouns.
- Write or dictate about learning something.

Conventions
Nouns in Sentences

Teach nouns

Remind children that nouns are naming words. We use nouns to name people, animals, places, or things. Nouns can name one or more than one. Today we are going to use nouns in sentences.

Model

Display the *taxi* Picture Card. What is this picture? This is a taxi. A taxi is a kind of transportation. It names a thing. It is a noun. I can use the word *taxi* in a sentence: *I like to ride in a taxi.* The word *taxi* names one thing. I can also say this sentence: *There are many taxis.* The word *taxis* names more than one thing.

Guide practice

Have on display these other transportation Picture Cards: *boat, bus, train, truck, van, wagon.* These are different kinds of transportation. They are nouns that name things. What is a sentence you can say for each word? Write the sentences children say on the board. Read each sentence with children, pointing to the noun.

Have children use the transportation Picture Cards to say sentences with nouns for more than one. Write those sentences on the board. Read each sentence, pointing to the noun for more than one.

Team Talk Pair children and have them take turns saying sentences with nouns for one and more than one. Then have them identify the noun in each sentence they say. Then have children write one of their sentences.

Daily Fix-It

Use the Daily Fix-It for more conventions practice.

Writing
Wonderful, Marvelous Me!
I Just Learned...

Introduce Talk with children about learning. We learn about reading and writing in school, but we also learn about sharing and following rules. What other things do we learn in school? We also learn things at home. What do we learn at home? Encourage children to share their thoughts and ideas about what they learn at school and at home.

Model Today we're going to tell about something wonderful and marvelous that we've learned. I'm going to close my eyes and think. I love traveling to new places, but I am not good at reading a map. Draw a simple map. Write the word *map* underneath. The first time I read a map, I wasn't sure what all the lines were for. But my friend told me that the lines were roads. Write the word *road* on the map. She also told me that the compass shows directions. Draw a compass on the map. Write the word *compass* underneath. Now I know how to use a map. I use it whenever I go on a trip.

Independent writing Now you're going to tell about something you just learned. Maybe it's something you know, like the name of our president. Maybe it's something you can do, like jumping rope. Close your eyes and think about something wonderful and marvelous that you've learned. Have children write or dictate their ideas and then illustrate them.

Daily Handwriting

Write *Vic, Zeke, vent,* and *zone* on the board. Review correct letter formation of uppercase *V* and *Z* and lowercase *v* and *z*.

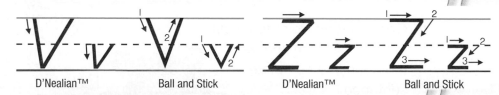

D'Nealian™   Ball and Stick   D'Nealian™   Ball and Stick

Have children write *Vic, Zeke, vent,* and *zone* on their Write-On Boards. Remind children to use proper left-to-right and top-to-bottom progression and proper spacing between letters when writing *V, v, Z,* and *z.*

Write Guy
Jeff Anderson

Show Off—in a Good Way

Post children's successful sentences. Celebrate them as writers. Select a sentence of the week, and write it large! Children can learn from each others' successes.

Academic Vocabulary

noun a word that names a person, animal, place, or thing

sentence a group of words that expresses a complete thought, begins with an uppercase letter, and ends with a punctuation mark

Daily Fix-It

The dog ran to nick
The dog ran to <u>Nick.</u>

This week's practice sentences appear on Teacher Resources DVD-ROM.

Writing Routine

Day 1 Wonderful, Marvelous Me!
Day 2 Respond to Literature
Day 3 Genre Writing
Day 4 Extend the Concept
Day 5 This Week We...

Objectives
- Understand the purpose of a description.
- Practice descriptions.
- Speak loudly and clearly.
- Face the speaker when listening.
- Take turns speaking.

Listening and Speaking
Oral Presentation—Description

Teach

When I stand in front of the class and tell you about something that is beautiful, fascinating, or funny, I am giving a description. I give a description to share information about what I see, hear, smell, taste, or feel.

Model

I am going to describe a funny car I saw. It was very small, too small for more than one person to be in. It had yellow, blue, red, and green dots all over it. The horn was loud, and the car squirted water. When the door opened, first one, then two, then a whole lot of people dressed in funny clothes tumbled out of the car. What did I just describe to you? **(a clown car)**

Guide practice

Divide the class into smaller groups. Have children take turns telling about a trip they took or something interesting they saw. Tell them to speak loudly and clearly and to allow everyone a turn to share his or her description. When I listen, I must face the speaker. Refer children to the Rules for Listening and Speaking on pp. 1–2 of *Reader's and Writer's Notebook.* Remind them to speak loudly and clearly and to take turns when presenting and to face the speaker when they are listening.

Name _____

🎧 Listening Rules

1. Face the person who is speaking.
2. Be quiet while someone is speaking.
3. Pay attention to the speaker.
4. Ask questions if you don't understand.

Listening and Speaking Rules 1

Reader's and Writer's Notebook, p. 1

Wrap Up Your Day

✔ **Oral Language** Today we talked about the way people travel in different countries. Say the Amazing Words with me: *travel, kayak, llama, dogsled, double-decker bus, submarine.*

✔ **Conventions** Point to a noun in the classroom and use the noun in a complete sentence.

✔ **Homework Idea** Send home the Family Times Newsletter on Let's Practice It! TR DVD•57–58.

Preview DAY 2

Tomorrow we will read about different types of transportation.

Extend Your Day!

Social Studies
Movement

Materials: map of the United States, construction paper, markers.

Landmarks Show a map of the United States to children. Start with California and point to the various states traveling across the country to New York. Point out the state where the children live. As each state is named, make a list on the board and tell children something they might see or experience in that state.

California—cable cars, ocean, redwood forest

Texas—rivers, plains, Alamo

Tennessee—country music, mountains

Pennsylvania—Liberty Bell, mountains

New York—skyscrapers, Statue of Liberty

All Aboard Let's take a trip on a train. I am the conductor, and you are the passengers. To get on the train, you must have a ticket. Give each child a sheet of paper as a ticket. Have children write on it the name of a state they want to visit. Point to a state on the map, say its name, and children with tickets for that state line up and "board" the train. Continue until all children have boarded.

Vocabulary
Way to Go

Materials: map or globe, drawing paper, drawing and writing tools

How We Travel Discuss ways of travel. Point out where children live, and tell them to plan a trip anywhere in the world. They can travel on land, in the air, and on or under water. I will visit London, England. Show where London is. I could take a plane to London, but it is a long flight, so I will fly to New York, and then take a submarine to London! Point to the places as you discuss your trip.

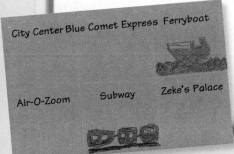

City Center Blue Comet Express Ferryboat

Air-O-Zoom   Subway   Zeke's Palace

Listening and Speaking
What Is It?

Giving Descriptions Have children play a game of "I am thinking of." Begin by modeling for them.

I am thinking of something in this room. It is round and has black and white spots. You play with it outside. You can kick it, but you shouldn't touch it with your hands. What is it? (a soccer ball)

Have children give descriptions of various items around the classroom for others to guess. The one who guesses correctly is the next one to give a description of another object in the room.

Objectives
- Discuss the concepts to develop oral language.
- Build oral vocabulary.

Today at a Glance

Oral Vocabulary
travel, kayak

Phonemic Awareness
◉ Initial /v/ and /z/

Phonics
◉ /v/ Spelled *Vv*
◉ /z/ Spelled *Zz*

Handwriting
Words with *Vv* and *Zz*

Comprehension
◉ Main Idea

Conventions
Nouns in Sentences

Writing
Respond to Literature

Vocabulary
Transportation Words

TRUCKTOWN on Reading Street

Start your engines! Display p. 14 of *Truckery Rhymes*. Point to "Jack and Kat." Who is this rhyme about? Let's read the rhyme together. Have children point to the rhyming words as the class reads the rhyme again. Give additional children the opportunity to say the rhyme aloud and track the print.

Truckery Rhymes

Concept Talk

Question of the Week

How do people in different parts of the world travel?

Build concepts

Write the question of the week on the board and track the print as you read it aloud. Have children answer the question in complete sentences. To reinforce the concept and focus children's attention, display Sing with Me Chart 29B. Tell children they are going to sing about the ways different people go places.

 Sing with Me Audio

Listen for Amazing Words

The Amazing Words *travel* and *kayak* are in the song "How Do You Go?" Read the title and have children describe the picture. Sing the song several times to the tune of "Do Your Ears Hang Low?" until children become familiar with the song. Have them clap when they hear *travel* and *kayak*.

Talk with Me/Sing with Me Chart 29B

ELL Reinforce Vocabulary Use the Day 2 instruction on ELL Poster 29 to reinforce the meanings of high-frequency words.

ELL Poster 29

Oral Vocabulary
Amazing Words

Amazing Words

Oral Vocabulary Routine

Teach Amazing Words

1. **Introduce the Word** When we *travel,* we go from one place to another. What's our new Amazing Word that means "to go from place to place"? Say it with me: *travel.*

2. **Demonstrate** Provide examples to show meaning. *When we travel, we usually go to a place that is far from home.* Where are some places you would like to *travel?*

   Repeat steps 1 and 2.

   Introduce the Word A *kayak* is a small boat that looks like a canoe and has a small opening in the center where a person sits. What's our new Amazing Word for a small canoe with an opening in the center? Say it with me: *kayak.*

   Demonstrate *You can paddle a kayak to get from place to place in the water.* Have you ever seen a *kayak?*

3. **Apply** Encourage children to use *travel* and *kayak* in complete sentences. Have them show you how they would travel in a kayak.

Routine Flip Chart

Use Amazing Words

To reinforce the concept and the Amazing Words, have children supply the appropriate Amazing Word for each sentence.

People can use a _____ to travel in the water. (kayak)

I like to _____ by car when I go to visit my aunt. (travel)

Amazing Words

travel	kayak
llama	dogsled
double-decker bus	submarine

Differentiated Instruction

SI Strategic Intervention

Sentence Completion
If children have difficulty completing the sentences, model saying the complete sentence and then have children repeat it after you.

E L L

English Language Learners
Visual Support Scaffold understanding of today's Amazing Word *kayak* by pointing to the image of a *kayak* on Talk with Me Chart 29A. Then use hand motions to show how a person would get a kayak to move.

Objectives
- Practice initial /v/ and /z/.
- Discriminate words that begin with /v/ or /z/.
- Segment words into sounds.

Phonemic Awareness
Initial /v/ and /z/

Isolate /v/

Display the *vest* Picture Card. Listen to the sounds in *vest:* /v/ /e/ /st/. What is the first sound in *vest?* Say the word with me: /v/ /e/ /st/, *vest. Vest* begins with /v/. Continue with the word *vet* and *Val.*

Isolate /z/

Listen to the sound in this word: /z/ /a/ /p/. This is the word *zap.* What is the first sound in *zap?* The first sound is /z/. Say the word with me: /z/ /a/ /p/, *zap. Zap* begins with /z/. Continue with the words *zip* and *zest.*

Picture Card

Guide practice

Model

Have children look at the picture on *My Skills Buddy* pp. 92–93. Remember that there are things in this picture that begin with /v/, such as *violin,* and /z/, such as *zero.* What things in the picture have names that begin with /v/ and /z/? Discuss with children those bulleted items on p. 92 not discussed on Day 1.

My Skills Buddy, pp. 92–93

Corrective feedback

If... children cannot discriminate /v/ or /z/, **then...** have then enunciate /v/ and /z/ as they segment /v/ and /z/ words.

Listen as I segment a word, /v/ /e/ /t/. Say it with me: /v/ /e/ /t/. What sound do you hear at the beginning of *vet?* I hear /v/ at the beginning of *vet.* Continue with the following words: *zip, Val, zap.*

On their own Display the Phonics Songs and Rhymes Chart 29, "I Want My Car to Vroom." Remind children of the tune: "A Sailor Went to Sea, Sea, Sea." Sing the song several times. When you hear a word that begins with /v/ or /z/, clap your hands.

Review **Segmentation** I am going to say a word. Tell me all of the sounds in the word. Say the following words: *zap, zip, van, vest.*

I Want My Car to Vroom

I want my car to vroom, vroom, vroom.
It zips around the room, room, room.
Oh, can you see it zoom, zoom, zoom,
Zig, zag, and vroom, vroom, vroom?

I want my plane to vroom, vroom, vroom.
It veers around the room, room, room.
Oh, can you see it zoom, zoom, zoom,
Zip and zap and vroom, vroom, vroom?

Phonics Songs and
Rhymes Chart 29

Differentiated Instruction

SI **Strategic Intervention**

Support Phonemic Awareness
If children have difficulty identifying or remembering things on pp. 92–93 of *My Skills Buddy* that begin with /v/ or /z/, point to the images and have children say the word. If children do not say a /v/ or /z/ word, use questions to direct them to the word.

ELL

English Language Learners
Language Transfer Some languages substitute /f/, /b/, and /w/ for /v/. Point out how the upper teeth touch the bottom lip and children should hear their voice when they produce /v/. Have children practice saying *van, vine, live,* and *have.*

ELL Support For additional support for language transfer, see Linguistic Contrastive Analysis in the *ELL Handbook.*

Objectives
◎ Practice /v/ spelled *Vv*.
◎ Practice /z/ spelled *Zz*.
• Blend /v/ and /z/ words.

Check Sound-Spelling
SUCCESS PREDICTOR

Phonics—Teach/Model
/v/ Spelled Vv and /z/ Spelled Zz

Teach /v/Vv and /z/Zz

Point to the *volcano* on the *Vv* Alphabet Card. What is this? What sound does *volcano* begin with? *Volcano* begins with /v/. Write *volcano* on the board and point to the letter *v*. The letter for /v/ is *v*. Repeat with the *Zz* Alphabet Card.

Alphabet Card

Model

Display the *van* Picture Card. What is this? Say the sounds in *van* with me: /v/ /a/ /n/, *van*. Where do you hear /v/ in *van*? (at the beginning)

Write *van* on the board. Point to each letter as you the say the sounds, /v/ /a/ /n/, *van*. Continue the routine with the following words: *vest, zip, zap*.

Alphabet Card

Guide practice

Envision It!

Have children open *My Skills Buddy* to p. 96. Demonstrate using the blending arrows on *My Skills Buddy*, p. 96, as you model blending the first word. Put your finger on the red arrow below the *v*. Say the sound that *v* stands for: /v/. Continue with letters *a* and *n*. Now I run my finger along the blue arrow as I blend the letters quickly to read *van*. Repeat with the word *Val*. Explain to children that when the last letter of *van* is changed to *l*, a new word is created. Have children work with a partner to blend the rest of the words on the page.

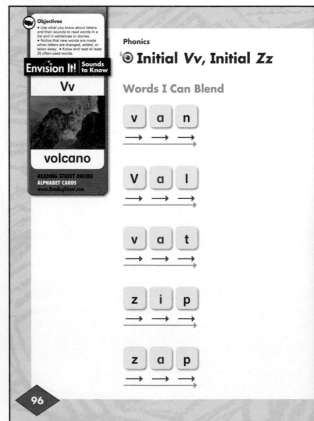

My Skills Buddy, p. 96

Blend   Use the routine to blend *v* and *z* words.

ROUTINE   Sound-by-Sound Blending

(1) Connect Write the letter *v*. What is the sound for this letter? The sound is /v/. Say it with me: /v/ /v/ /v/. When you see this letter in a word, what sound will you say?

(2) Model Write the word *van* on the board.

- Point to *v* and ask: What is the sound for this letter? Say it with me: /v/ /v/ /v/. Repeat the routine with *a* and *n*.

- Let's blend the sounds together. Listen as I blend the sounds: /v/ /a/ /n/. Say it with me: /v/ /a/ /n/, *van*. Now say it without me.

- Listen as I use *van* in a sentence: *I ride in a van to school.* Say it with me. Have children use *van* in a sentence.

(3) Guide Practice Continue the routine established in step 2.

| Val | vat | zip | vet |

Have children successfully read all of the words before reading Decodable Reader 29 on pp. 98–105 of *My Skills Buddy*.

Corrective Feedback If children have difficulty blending words, model blending the sounds to read the word. Then have children say it with you.

Routines Flip Chart

Don't Wait Until Friday

MONITOR PROGRESS   ↻ Check Sound-Spelling   /v/ Spelled Vv; /z/ Spelled Zz

Have children write *Vv* and *Zz* on separate cards. I am going to say some words. If the word begins with /v/, hold up your *Vv* card. If the word begins with /z/, hold up your *Zz* card. Say: *zebra, zone, vanilla, volleyball, zing, visit, vitamin, zippy.*

If... children cannot discriminate /v/ or /z/,

then... use the small-group Strategic Intervention lesson, p. DI•70, to reteach /v/ and /z/.

Continue to monitor children's progress using other instructional opportunities during the week so that children can be successful with the Day 5 Assessment.

Day 1	Day 2	Day 3	Day 4	Day 5
Check Phonemic Awareness	Check Sound-Spelling/ Retelling	Check Word Reading	Check Phonemic Awareness	Check Oral Vocabulary

Differentiated Instruction

(A) Advanced

Support Blending Provide additional /v/ and /z/ words children can use to practice blending. Write the words on the board and have children copy them on their Write-On Boards. Then have them say the sound for each letter and then blend the sounds.

Success Predictor

Success Predictor

Sound-Spelling

Objectives
- Write *V, v, Z,* and *z*.
- Read high-frequency words.

Handwriting
Write Words with *Vv* and *Zz*

Review

Write *Zak* on the board. This is the name *Zak*. I use an uppercase *Z* for the first letter in *Zak's* name. Watch me make an uppercase *Z*. Write another *Z* on the board using the strokes indicated in the model. Repeat with the name *Velma*.

Write *zip* on the board. This is the word *zip*. I use a lowercase *z* for the first letter in the word. Watch me make a lowercase *z*. Write another *z* on the board using the strokes indicated in the model. Repeat with the word *vent*.

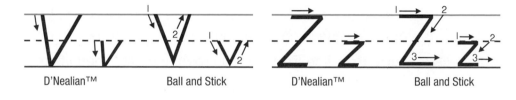

D'Nealian™   Ball and Stick   D'Nealian™   Ball and Stick

Guide practice

Have children use their Write-On Boards to make a row each of uppercase *V* and *Z* and a row each of lowercase *v* and *z*. Circulate around the room, assisting children when necessary. Then have children write the following words: *Val, Zel, zap, van*.

High-Frequency Words

Model reading

Have children turn to p. 97 of *My Skills Buddy.* Read the high-frequency words *where* and *come* together. Then have children point to each word and read it themselves. Read the sentences on *My Skills Buddy* page together to read the new high-frequency words in context.

Team Talk Pair children and have them take turns reading each of the sentences aloud.

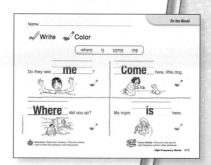

High-Frequency Words

Words I Can Read

where

come

Sentences I Can Read

1. Where is Zak?
2. He will come in a van.
3. Val can not come.

97

My Skills Buddy, p. 97

On their own

Use *Reader's and Writer's Notebook,* p. 373, for additional practice with this week's high-frequency words.

Reader's and Writer's Notebook, p. 373

Differentiated Instruction

SI **Strategic Intervention**

Practice Handwriting Have children draw a picture of a van. Then have them write as many uppercase *V* and lowercase *v* as they can inside the van. Have children draw a zoo. Tell them to write as many uppercase *Z* and lowercase *z* as they can in the zoo.

ELL

English Language Learners

Extend Language Explain to children the difference between the words *come* and *go.* Tell them that the word *go* means to move away from something and the word *come* means to go toward something. Have children practice saying each word in a sentence.

Decodable Reader 29

 /v/ Spelled Vv, /z/ Spelled Zz, and High-Frequency Words

Review Review the previously taught high-frequency words. Have children read each word as you point to it on the Word Wall.

is	where	a	here	with	come	do

Have children turn to Decodable Reader 29, *Zip Up, Val!* on p. 98 of *My Skills Buddy.* Today we will read a story about a girl named Val who takes a trip. **Point to the title.** The title of the story is *Zip Up, Val!* What is the title of the story? **Point to the name of the author.** The author's name is Susan Whit. What does an author do?

Use the routine for reading decodable books to read Decodable Reader 29.

My Skills Buddy, pp. 98–105

ROUTINE Reading Decodable Books

1. **Read Silently** Have children whisper read the book page by page as you listen in.

2. **Model Fluent Reading** Have children finger point as you read a page. Then have children reread the book without you.

3. **Read Chorally** Have children finger point as they chorally read the page. Continue reading page by page, repeating steps 1 and 2.

4. **Read Individually** Have children take turns reading aloud a page.

5. **Reread and Monitor Progress** As you listen to individual children reread, monitor progress and provide support.

6. **Retell** After reading, have children retell the story to demonstrate comprehension.

Differentiated Instruction

SI Strategic Intervention

Build Background Have children tell about an article of clothing they wear when it's cold that can zip. Why does the piece of clothing need to be able to zip?

Small Group Time

DAY 2 Break into small groups after reading the Decodable Reader and before the comprehension lesson.

Teacher-Led

SI Strategic Intervention	**OL** On-Level	**A** Advanced
Teacher-Led Page DI•70	**Teacher-Led** Page DI•74	**Teacher-Led** Page DI•77
• Phonemic Awareness and Phonics	• Phonemic Awareness and Phonics	• Phonics and Spelling
• **Reread** Decodable Reader 29	• **Reread** Decodable Reader 29	• **Reread** Decodable Reader 29 for Fluency

ELL Place English language learners in the groups that correspond to their reading abilities in English.

Practice Stations
• Visit the Word Work Station
• Visit the Words to Know Station

Independent Activities
• Read independently
• Background Building Audio
• *Reader's and Writer's Notebook*

English Language Learners
Recognize /v/ and /z/ Words
Ask children to name the word in the book's title that begins with /v/ and the one that begins with /z/. Have children point to and name the letters.

Objectives

◎ Practice main idea.
• Preview and predict.
• Retell a selection.

Check Retelling
SUCCESS PREDICTOR

Listening Comprehension
Main Idea

Review

Envision It!

Have children turn to pp. 94–95 of *My Skills Buddy.* Remind them that the most important idea in a selection is the **main idea.** Good readers pay attention to the main idea of a selection because it helps them understand what they are reading.

My Skills Buddy, pp. 94–95

First Read—Big Book
On the Move!

Concepts of print	Display the cover of *On the Move!* The title of this book is *On the Move!* The author is Donna Latham. What does an author do? (writes the book)
Preview and predict	*Think Aloud* Display *On the Move!* What do you see on the cover? I see a family and a map in the background. What do you think this book will be about? Let's read to find out.
Use photographs	Take children on a walk through the book. Have children tell about what they see in each photograph.
Introduce genre	An informational text teaches readers about things that happen in the world. In this selection we will learn about different types of transportation people use around the world.
Set purpose	Remind children of the question of the week: *How do people in different parts of the world travel?* Have children listen as you read for different forms of transportation used around the world.
Model	Read *On the Move!* with expression for enjoyment.

DAY 2
Read for enjoyment

DAY 3
Reread using Develop Vocabulary notes

DAY 4
Reread using Guide Comprehension notes

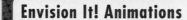
Retell

Check retelling

Envision It!

Have children turn to p. 106 of *My Skills Buddy.* Walk through the retelling boxes as children retell *On the Move!* Let's retell what happens in the first box— the beginning of the selection. People get on an airplane. Let's retell what happens in the next box. Continue with the rest of the boxes. After children retell the selection as a group, have them draw a picture to retell their favorite part of the selection. Have them write or dictate a word or sentence to go with their picture.

My Skills Buddy, p. 106

Top-Score Response A top-score response identifies the topic and details.

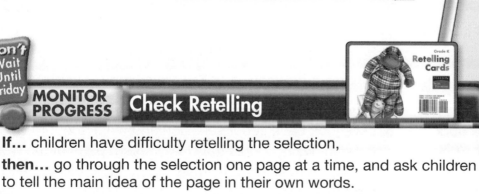

MONITOR PROGRESS Check Retelling

If... children have difficulty retelling the selection,

then... go through the selection one page at a time, and ask children to tell the main idea of the page in their own words.

Day 1	Day 2	Day 3	Day 4	Day 5
Check Phonemic Awareness	Check Sound-Spelling/ Retelling	Check Word Reading	Check Phonemic Awareness	Check Oral Vocabulary

Success Predictor

Differentiated Instruction

SI **Strategic Intervention**

Retell Have children add motions that show how forms of transportation move as they retell *On the Move!*

Retelling Plan

☑ **Week 1** Assess Advanced students.

☑ **Week 2** Assess On-Level students.

☑ **Week 3** Assess Strategic Intervention students.

☑ **Week 4** Assess Advanced students.

☑ **This week assess On-Level students.**

☐ **Week 6** Assess Strategic Intervention students.

English Language Learners Professional Development

Retelling As a way for children to show they have understood what they have read, have them "dictate what they remember from their reading to the teacher. Students can then illustrate their summaries and label the illustrations with vocabulary from the reading."
—Dr. Georgia Earnest García

Objectives
- Practice main idea.
- Confirm predictions.
- Practice nouns in sentences.

Think, Talk, and Write

Discuss concept

We're learning about ways people travel all over the world. Think about what it would be like to ride on those forms of transportation.

- Which forms of transportation in the selection have you tried before?
- Which form of transportation would you like to try? Why?
- Choose a form of transportation we read about. Where would you travel in it?

Confirm predictions

Ask children to recall their predictions before you read *On the Move!*

- What did you think this selection would be about?
- Was your prediction correct?

Have children turn to p. 107 of *My Skills Buddy.* Read the questions and directives and have children respond.

Think, Talk, and Write

1. When might someone take a plane to travel? When would they take a bus?

   Text to World

2. What is the selection *On the Move!* mostly about?

   Main Idea

3. Look back and write.

107

My Skills Buddy, p. 107

Text to world

1. When might someone take a plane to travel? When would someone take a bus? How far can a bus travel?

Main idea

2. What is the selection *On the Move!* mostly about? (different ways people travel) What do the pictures show? (a boat, a car, a plane)

Look back and write

3. Let's look back at our selection and write about it. We learned about the different ways people travel in different parts of the world. Listen for how two different kinds of animals help people travel. Read pp. 12–13 of *On the Move!* Now let's write our ideas. Discuss with children how certain animals help people travel. Record children's responses on chart paper. (Possible responses: Llamas carry people on a trail. Dogs pull people on a sled.)

Conventions
Nouns in Sentences

Review

Remind children what they learned about nouns. Nouns are words that name people, animals, places, and things. Nouns can name one or more than one. This week we are learning to use nouns in sentences.

Guide practice

Show Picture Cards for zoo and tiger. These pictures show nouns. They show a tiger and a zoo. I can use these nouns in a sentence: *I saw tigers at the zoo.* Write the sentence on the board. Read it with children. I will circle the nouns in the sentence. Which noun in the sentence tells about one place? Which noun in the sentence tells about more than one animal?

Display pp. 8–9 of *On the Move!* Guide children to identify nouns in the sentences on the pages. Have them tell if the noun names one or more than one person, animal, place, or thing. Write the nouns children identify on the board. Then have children use one of the nouns on the board in a sentence.

On their own

Use *Reader's and Writer's Notebook,* p. 374, for more practice with nouns in sentences.

Daily Fix-It

Use the Daily Fix-It exercise for more conventions practice.

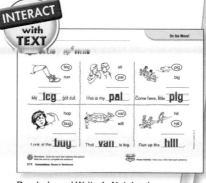

Reader's and Writer's Notebook, p. 374

INTERACT with TEXT

Differentiated Instruction

 Strategic Intervention

Discuss Concept As a model, tell children where you would travel and what form of transportation you would use.

A **Advanced**

Look Back and Write Allow children to write their own responses about how llamas and dogs help people travel.

Daily Fix-It

the dog can sit on the mat
The dog can sit on the mat.

This week's practice sentences appear on Teacher Resources DVD-ROM.

Objectives
- Write sentences about transportation.
- Identify compound words.
- Write *V, v, Z,* and *z.*

Writing
Respond to Literature

Discuss   Display *On the Move!* Discuss with children the different forms of transportation used around the world.

Model   *On the Move!* is about different forms of transportation. We learned about cars, planes, rafts, and many other forms of transportation. Can you think of other forms of transportation? **List children's responses.** I am going to write a sentence about one of these forms of transportation:

> **Submarines move in the water.**

Guide practice   Invite children to help you write more sentences about the different forms of transportation.

> **I can ride a camel in the desert.**
>
> **Dogs pull a sled in the snow.**

Independent writing   Have children write or dictate their own sentences about transportation in *On the Move!* Then have them illustrate their sentences.

The book was about transportation. Double-decker buses move on land.

Daily Handwriting

Write *Val, Zoe, zero,* and *vet* on the board. Review correct letter formation of uppercase *V* and *Z* and lowercase *v* and *z.*

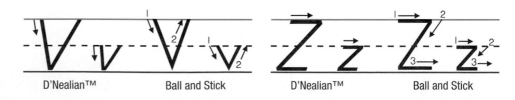

D'Nealian™   Ball and Stick   D'Nealian™   Ball and Stick

Have children write *Val, Zoe, zero,* and *vet* on their Write-On Boards. Remind children to use proper left-to-right and top-to-bottom progression with writing *V, v, Z,* and *z.*

Vocabulary
Compound Words

Model Have children turn to p. 108 of *My Skills Buddy.* Incorporate the first two Vocabulary bullets on the page into the discussion. Direct them to the picture of the dog. This is a *dog.* Direct children to the picture of the sled. This is a *sled.* Point to the plus sign. This plus sign tells us that when we put the shorter words *dog* and *sled* together, we make the longer word *dogsled.* *Dogsled* is a compound word made up of two shorter words, *dog* and *sled.* Repeat the procedure with *raincoat* and *mailbox.*

My Skills Buddy, p. 108

Guide practice Write the words *dogsled, raincoat,* and *mailbox* on the board. Point to each compound word as you read it.

> dogsled   raincoat   mailbox

Let's practice our new words. We can figure out the meanings of compound words if we know what the shorter words mean. Read the word *raincoat.* What are the shorter words in *raincoat?* Yes, the words are *rain* and *coat.* What does the word *rain* mean? What does the word *coat* mean? What do you think the word *raincoat* means? Repeat the routine with *dogsled* and *mailbox.*

On their own Have children choose one word part from the compound words *dogsled, raincoat,* and *mailbox.* Tell them to draw a picture of that part. Then have children find a partner who drew a picture of the other word part that completes their compound word.

Differentiated Instruction

 **Advanced**

Build Vocabulary Write the word *raincoat* on the board. Have children think of other compound words that use the shorter word *rain,* such as *rainbow, raindrop,* and *rainfall.*

English Language Learners Expand Vocabulary Have children say the compound words in their home languages. Explain that although these words may only be one word in their home language, the words are compound words in English and are made up of two shorter words.

Objectives
- Review skills learned and practiced today.
- Identify shorter words in compound words.
- Use nouns in complete sentences.

Wrap Up Your Day

✔ **Concept Talk** Today we read about forms of transportation in *On the Move!* What are some of the forms of transportation we read about?

✔ **Conventions** Remember, nouns are words that name people, places, animals, and things. What are some nouns in *On the Move!?* How can you use that noun in a complete sentence?

✔ **Vocabulary Skill** Today we talked about the compound words *dogsled, raincoat,* and *mailbox.* What are the shorter words that make up each of these compound words?

✔ **Homework Idea** Have children draw a picture of a way they travel around town. Have each child write a sentence about his or her picture.

Preview
DAY 3

Tomorrow we will read *On the Move!* again. What are some ways we can get from place to place?

Extend Your Day!

Social Studies
Physical Traits of Geography

Materials: pictures of mountains, oceans, beaches, prairies, etc. (one for each child); paper; crayons

What Does It Look Like? Discuss with children that different forms of transportation can help us go to places that are far away and look different from where we live.

Show children pictures of different places and discuss what the pictures show about that type of geography.

Give each child a picture with a number on the back. On a sheet of paper, have the children write or dictate three words that describe the picture and draw their own version of it. On the other side of the paper, have them write the same number that is on the back of the picture.

Gather the numbered pictures and display them around the room. Then collect the children's drawings. Have the class try to match the draw ings to the pictures. (Verify by looking at the number the child wrote on the back of his or her picture.) Attach the drawings to the side of the pictures.

Phonics
Very Fine V Vine

Materials: drawing of a long vine, cutout drawings of leaves (one for each child), crayons

Vv Give each child a cutout of a leaf to color green. Have each child write or dictate a word that begins with *v* on the leaf. Attach the leaves to a drawing of a long vine. Call the display *Very Fine V Vine.* Have children point to and read the words on the vine.

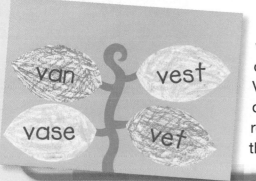

Art
Visiting Places

Materials: large craft paper, scissors, markers or paint, Big Book *On the Move!*

Favorite Place Trace children's bodies on sheets of craft paper large enough to fit each child. Then have each child draw or paint a background on the paper and draw clothes appropriate for a place from the book *On the Move!* that he or she would like to visit. Help each child cut out a face hole. Children can poke their heads through the face hole as they tell why they want to visit that place.

Objectives
- Share information and ideas about the concept.
- Build oral vocabulary.

Today at a Glance

Oral Vocabulary
llama, dogsled

Phonemic Awareness
◉ Final /v/ and /z/

Phonics
◉ /v/ Spelled *Vv*
◉ /z/ Spelled *Zz*

Comprehension
◉ Main Idea

Conventions
Nouns

Writing
Invitation

Listening and Speaking
Oral Presentation—Description

TRUCKTOWN on Reading Street

Start your engines! Display p. 14 of *Truckery Rhymes.* Do you know the original "Jack and Kat"? It's called "Jack and Jill." Recite it first, and then have children repeat after you:

> Jack and Jill went up a hill
> To fetch a pail of water.
> Jack fell down and broke his crown,
> And Jill came tumbling after.

Truckery Rhymes

Concept Talk

Question of the Week

How do people in different parts of the world travel?

Write the question of the week on the board. Read the question as you track the print. Talk with children about transportation. Remind children to speak clearly and to take turns speaking.

Listen for Amazing Words

Let's Sing Display Sing with Me Chart 29B. Remind students that yesterday they sang "How Do You Go?" and listened for the words *travel* and *kayak.* Today we are going to listen for the Amazing Words *llama* and *dogsled.* Sing the song several times to the tune of "Do Your Ears Hang Low?" Have children clap when they hear the Amazing Words *llama* and *dogsled.*

 Sing with Me Audio

How Do You Go?

Do you travel to and fro
  to get where you want to go?
Can you drive a big car or a boat you row?
Can you climb up on a llama and go real slow?
How do you go?

Talk with Me/Sing with Me Chart 29B

Oral Vocabulary
Amazing Words

Amazing Words

travel	kayak
llama	dogsled
double-decker bus	submarine

Teach Amazing Words

Amazing Words — Oral Vocabulary Routine

1 Introduce the Word A *llama* is an animal with long, shaggy fur that is the size of a pony. The *llama* lives in South America. What's our new Amazing Word for a South American animal with shaggy fur? Say it with me: *llama*.

2 Demonstrate Provide examples to show meaning. *The llama can climb mountains and carry a person on its back.* Have you ever seen a *llama* at the zoo?

Repeat steps 1 and 2.

Introduce the Word A *dogsled* is a sled that carries one or two people and is pulled across the snow by many dogs. A *dogsled* is used in Alaska and northern Canada. What's our new Amazing Word for a sled pulled by dogs? Say it with me: *dogsled*.

Demonstrate *Alaska and northern Canada are cold and snowy like Antarctica, so a dogsled can be used almost all year to move people and things.*

3 Apply Have children use *llama* and *dogsled* in complete sentences. Have them illustrate the words.

Routines Flip Chart

Use Amazing Words

To reinforce the concept and the Amazing Words, have children supply the appropriate Amazing Word for each sentence.

A _____ **can climb in the mountains.** (llama)

The dogs pulled the _____ **over the snow.** (dogsled)

 **Expand Vocabulary**
Use the Day 3 instruction on ELL Poster 29 to help children expand vocabulary.

 Poster 29

Differentiated Instruction

SI Strategic Intervention
Sentence Production Use Talk with Me Chart 29A to help children complete the Amazing Word sentences.

ELL

English Language Learners
Access Content Have children say *llama* in their home languages or use words to describe the animal.

Objectives

◎ Isolate final /v/ and /z/.
- Discriminate final sounds.
- Blend sounds to say /v/ and /z/ words.
- Substitute medial sounds.

Phonemic Awareness
↻ Final /v/ and /z/

Review

Initial /v/ and /z/ Display the *vest* Picture Card. Listen as I say this word: *vest*. What is the first sound in *vest*? Say it with me: /v/ /v/ /v/, *vest*. Display the *zebra* Picture Card. Listen as I say this word: *zebra*. What is the first sound in *zebra*? Say it with me: /z/ /z/ /z/, *zebra*. Today we will hear /v/ and /z/ at the ends of words.

Picture Card

Teach final /v/ and /z/

Display the *five* Picture Card. This is the number *five*. I hear /v/ at the end of *five*. Repeat for final /z/ in the word *fuzz*. Practice final /v/ and /z/ with these words: *Bev, buzz, jazz, give.*

Discriminate final sounds

I will say two words. Tell me which one ends with /v/: *like, live.* The word *live* ends with /v/. Continue with the following words: *love, pool; wave, lake; glove, hand.*

Listen to these two words: *fizz, first.* Which word ends with /z/? The word *fizz* ends with /z/. Continue with these words: *buzz, beam; man, maze; jazz, jump.*

Picture Card

On their own

Listen to these sound words: *zap, buzz, rap, bam.* Choose a word that begins or ends with /z/. Draw a picture of something that can make that sound. Label your drawing with the letter *z*.

Picture Card

Blend

Display the *van* Picture Card. Listen to the sounds in this word: /v/ /a/ /n/. We can blend the sounds in this word. Say the sounds with me: /v/ /a/ /n/, *van*. We have blended the sounds to say the word *van*. Listen as I blend the sounds in this word: /z/ /i/ /p/, *zip*. Blend the sounds with me: /z/ /i/ /p/, *zip*. We have blended the sounds to say the word *zip*. Continue the routine with the following words: *Bev, zest, zing, vat, vent, fizz, fuzz*.

Corrective feedback

If... children cannot blend words,
then... provide practice segmenting words and then blending the sounds, such as *zip*, /z/ /i/ /p/, *zip*.

Substitute medial sounds

Listen to this word: *zap*, /z/ /a/ /p/, *zap*. Say it with me: /z/ /a/ /p/, *zap*. I can make a new word by changing the middle sound in *zap* to /i/. Listen: /z/ /i/ /p/, *zip*. Say it with me as I blend the new sounds: /z/ /i/ /p/, *zip*. Continue substituting medial sounds with these words: *vet, vat, zig, zag*.

Teacher Tip

Use sound discrimination activities that focus on words with final /v/ and final /z/ to check children's ability to discriminate sounds in the final position.

Objectives
◎ Practice /v/ spelled *Vv*.
◎ Practice /z/ spelled *Zz*.
• Read /v/ and /z/ words.
• Read high-frequency words.

Check Word Reading
SUCCESS PREDICTOR

Phonics—Teach/Model
 /v/ Spelled Vv and /z/ Spelled Zz

Review **/v/Vv, /z/Zz** Display the *Vv* Alphabet Card and point to the *volcano.* What sound do you hear at the beginning of *volcano?* What letter spells that sound? Point to the letters *Vv.* What is the sound we learned for this letter? What are the names of these letters? Repeat with the *Zz* Alphabet Card.

Alphabet Card

Review **Letter Names and Sounds** Use Alphabet Cards to review the following letter names and sounds: *Aa, Bb, Ee, Ff, Ii, Mm, Ss, Tt, Uu.*

Blend sounds Write *jazz* on the board. Point to each letter as you say the sound: /j/ /a/ /z/. Explain that sometimes when /z/ comes at the end of a word, it is spelled with two *z*'s. When I blend these sounds together, I make the word *jazz.* Say the sounds with me: /j/ /a/ /z/. Now blend the sounds together: /j/ /a/ /z/, *jazz.* Repeat the blending routine with *buzz, Bev, vest, zip, fuzz, zap,* and *fizz.*

Alphabet Card

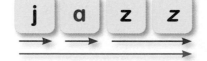

More practice Use *Reader's and Writer's Notebook,* p. 375, for additional practice with /v/ and /z/.

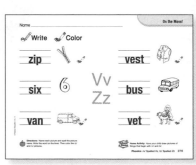

Reader's and Writer's Notebook, p. 375

Review

Sound-Spelling Display the *Tt* Alphabet Card. What sound do you hear at the beginning of *turtle*? What letter spells that sound? Yes, the letter *t* spells /t/. Review the following sounds and letters with Alphabet Cards: *Aa, Bb, Dd, Ee, Ff, Gg, Hh, Ii, Jj, Ll, Mm, Nn, Oo, Pp, Rr, Ss.*

Alphabet Card

Review

High-Frequency Words Write *where* on the board. This is the word *where*. What is this word? Continue the routine with *come, what, said,* and *was.*

Differentiated Instruction

 Strategic Intervention

Support Sound-Spelling Explain to children that when a word ends with /z/, it often is spelled with two *z*'s, such as *buzz, fuzz,* and *fizz.*

Don't Wait Until Friday

MONITOR PROGRESS   Check Word Reading   High-Frequency Words

Write *come, where, what, said,* and *was* on the board. Have children take turns reading the words.

Practice reading these words from Kindergarten Student Reader K.5.5, *The Big Jazz Band.*

zip	Jan	van	get	glad
jazz	band	big	fun	stops

If... children cannot read the high-frequency words,
then... write the words on cards for them to practice at home.

If... children cannot blend sounds to read the words,
then... provide practice blending the words in chunks, /z/ -ip.

If... children can successfully blend sounds to read the words,
then... have them read Kindergarten Student Reader K.5.5, *The Big Jazz Band.*

Day 1	Day 2	Day 3	Day 4	Day 5
Check Phonemic Awareness	Check Sound-Spelling/ Retelling	Check Word Reading	Check Phonemic Awareness	Check Oral Vocabulary

Success Predictor

Objectives
- Read /v/ and /z/ words.
- Read high-frequency words.

Kindergarten Student Reader K.5.5
/v/ Spelled Vv, /z/ Spelled Zz, and High-Frequency Words

Review

High-Frequency Words Review the previously taught high-frequency words. Have children read each word as you point to it on the Word Wall.

the	they	see	come	was
with	where	said	go	was

Read Kindergarten Student Reader K.5.5

Display Kindergarten Student Reader K.5.5. Today we are going to read a new story about a trip to see a jazz band. Point to the title of the book. The title of the book is *The Big Jazz Band.* The author is Diego Vargas. The story was illustrated by Hector Borlasca.

Use the reading decodable books routine to read the Kindergarten Student Reader.

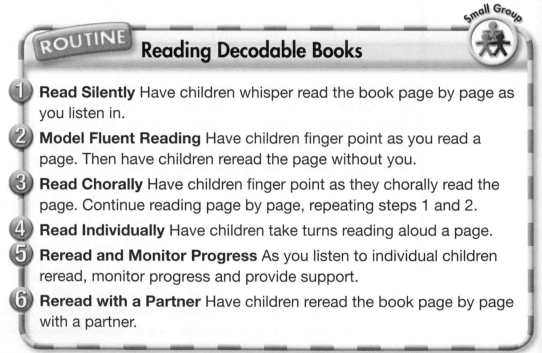

ROUTINE **Reading Decodable Books**

Small Group

1. **Read Silently** Have children whisper read the book page by page as you listen in.

2. **Model Fluent Reading** Have children finger point as you read a page. Then have children reread the page without you.

3. **Read Chorally** Have children finger point as they chorally read the page. Continue reading page by page, repeating steps 1 and 2.

4. **Read Individually** Have children take turns reading aloud a page.

5. **Reread and Monitor Progress** As you listen to individual children reread, monitor progress and provide support.

6. **Reread with a Partner** Have children reread the book page by page with a partner.

Routines Flip Chart

Jan and Dad zip up.
Jan and Dad get in the van.

2

They see Jem and Dad.
"Can you come with us?
You will like it."

3

Jem and Dad get in the van.
Jan is glad Jem can come.

4

Kindergarten Student Reader K.5.5

Dad sees Bev.
Dad stops the van next to a bus.

5

"Come with me," said Bev.
"You will like it.
You will see a big jazz band."

6

The jazz band is big.
Jan and Jem have fun.
Do you like it?

7

Where did you go?
We went to see a big jazz band.
It was fun.

8

Differentiated Instruction

SI Strategic Intervention

Access Content Explain to children that jazz is a type of music with a strong beat. Sometimes jazz musicians make up music as they play.

Small Group Time

DAY 3 Break into small groups to read the Kindergarten Student Reader before the comprehension lesson.

Teacher-Led

SI Strategic Intervention	**OL** On-Level	**A** Advanced
Teacher-Led Page DI•71 • Phonemic Awareness and Phonics • **Read** Concept Literacy Reader K.5.5 or Kindergarten Student Reader K.5.5	**Teacher-Led** Page DI•75 • Phonemic Awareness and Phonics • **Read** Kindergarten Student Reader K.5.5	**Teacher-Led** Page DI•78 • **Read** Independent Reader K.5.5 or Kindergarten Student Reader K.5.5

ELL Place English language learners in the groups that correspond to their learning abilities in English.

Practice Stations
• Visit the Words to Know Station
• Visit the Let's Write! Station

Independent Activities
• Read independently
• Audio Text of Big Book
• *Reader's and Writer's Notebook*

Objectives

- Recall and retell a selection.
- ◎ Practice main idea.
- Develop and use vocabulary.
- Develop and apply comprehension skills.

Comprehension

Retell the selection

Have children turn to p. 106 of *My Skills Buddy* and use the retelling boxes to retell the selection *On the Move!*

Think Aloud Direct students to the first retell box. This is when the family gets on an airplane. Tell me about the other forms of transportation.

Continue reviewing the retelling boxes and having children retell the selection.

My Skills Buddy, p. 106

Review

Main Idea Display photographs from *On the Move!* Let's review the main idea of the selection.

- What kinds of transportation do we learn about in this selection? (airplane, car, truck, train, kayak, llama, dogsled, raft, camel, airboat, submarine, double-decker bus, bike, helicopter)

- What kinds of animals are used for transportation? (llama, camels, dogs)

- What is the big idea of this selection? (People around the world use different forms of transportation.)

More practice

Use *Reader's and Writer's Notebook,* p. 376, for additional practice with main idea.

Reader's and Writer's Notebook, p. 376

Second Read—Big Book
On the Move!

Develop vocabulary

Reread *On the Move!* Follow the Day 3 arrow beginning on p. 468, and use the Develop Vocabulary notes to prompt conversations about the selection.

Have children use the Amazing Words *travel, kayak, llama, dogsled, double-decker bus,* and *submarine* to talk about the selection.

DAY 2
Read for enjoyment

DAY 3
Reread using Develop Vocabulary notes

DAY 4
Reread using Guide Comprehension notes

Develop Vocabulary

DAY 3

Wh- question
What is the girl looking at on this page? (a map)

- The girl is looking at a map. What is the girl thinking about?

Develop Vocabulary water, land, air

Where is the place you want to go?
What ways to get there do you know?

When we must get from here to there,
We travel by water, land, and air.

2

3

Big Book, pp. 2–3

Guide Comprehension

DAY 4

Open-ended
What kind of transportation would you like to travel in? (Children may say they like to travel in an airplane because they want to be up high or on a boat because they like water.)

Distancing

What form of transportation is the family going on? **(a plane)**

• The family is getting ready to get on a plane. Have you ever been on a plane? Tell us about it.

Everybody, pile on in!
Buckle up, and let's begin!

4

Everybody, wave good-bye!
We're on the move; come on let's fly!

5

Big Book, pp. 4–5

Open-ended

Why do so many people like to travel by airplane? (People like to travel fast and airplanes go fast. Other people might like to be high up in the sky.)

Develop Vocabulary, continued

DAY 3

Open-ended

Where does an airplane travel? (in the sky)

- The airplane travels in the sky, and we can see the city below the plane. Why does everything look so small when you are on a plane?

Develop Vocabulary airplane

Expand Vocabulary quest

Around the world, we're on a quest.
We'll find the ways to travel best.

6

Do you like this view way up high?
Our airplane vrrrrooms right through the sky.

7

Big Book, pp. 6–7

Guide Comprehension, continued

DAY 4

Wh- question

What do you think when you see an airplane overhead? (I think about what it would feel like to be in the airplane going somewhere. I would like to look out and see the tiny area below.)

Open-ended

How many wheels does this truck have?
(eight wheels)

• This truck has eight wheels. Where do you
  think this truck is going?

To home or school, in a city or town,
A car zigs and zags and zooms around.

8

Eight big wheels and a heavy load,
A truck rumbles and rambles down the road.

9

Big Book, pp. 8–9

Wh- **question**

What makes the truck different from the car?
(The truck is bigger and has more wheels. The
truck can carry more things than the car can.)

Develop Vocabulary, continued

DAY 3

Distancing

Point to the picture of the train track.
What is this train traveling on? (a track)

- A train goes quickly along a track. Have you ever been on a train?

Clickety-clack, along the track!
A quick train zips you there and back.

10

Splashing, dashing winning raves.
A kayak veers above the waves.

11

Big Book, pp. 10–11

Guide Comprehension, continued

DAY 4

Wh- question

Which travels faster, the kayak or the train? How do you know? (The train travels faster because an engine pulls the train and the engine is stronger and faster than the man.)

Wh- question

What kind of animal is this? (llama)

- A llama can go places where there isn't a road. **Point to the mountains in the picture.** Where can a llama go that a car or bus cannot go?

Develop Vocabulary trail

Where there's no road, where there's no rail,
A sure-footed llama moves up the trail.

12

Over frozen ground and chunky snow,
A dogsled is the very best way to go.

13

Big Book, pp. 12–13

Main Idea

What can you learn about transportation used around the world from these pages? (In some places, people use animals to travel.)

Develop Vocabulary, continued

DAY 3

Open-ended
What kind of a boat is this? (a raft)

- The people are on a raft that is bouncing around in the water. How hard would it be to stay on this raft?

Develop Vocabulary camel

On rushing waters of purest white,
A raft bounces and bobs, so hold on tight!

14

Desert winds are blowing sand,
As a camel ambles over the land.

15

Big Book, pp. 14–15

Guide Comprehension, continued

DAY 4

Open-ended
Which would you rather ride, a camel or a raft? Why? (I would want to ride on a raft because I like water.)

Wh- question

What is the best way to travel in a swamp? (in an airboat)

- The people are traveling through the swamp on an airboat. Look at the picture. How is an airboat different from other kinds of boats?

Develop Vocabulary ocean

Expand Vocabulary romp, swamp

Through murky waters in a squishy swamp,
An airboat is the very best way to romp.

The ocean sparkles in the sun's warm glow,
As a submarine vanishes down below.

16

17

Big Book, pp. 16–17

Inferential

What do you think it would be like to travel underwater in a submarine? (It would be fun to be underwater and see the sea creatures.)

Develop Vocabulary, continued

DAY 3

Open-ended

What kind of bus can carry many people? (a double-decker bus)

- A double-decker bus can carry twice as many people as a regular bus. Look at the picture. How is a double-decker bus different from a regular bus?

To carry many people take this advice.
A double-decker bus is twice as nice.

18

It's a beautiful day, but it's too far to hike.
So strap on your helmet, and pedal your bike.

19

Big Book, pp. 18–19

Guide Comprehension, continued

DAY 4

Wh- question

Where would you travel on your bike? (I would ride my bike to the park, on a bike path, or around my neighborhood.)

Distancing

What allows a helicopter to stay in the sky?
(whirling propellers)

• A helicopter uses its propellers to help it fly in the sky. What are other forms of transportation that fly in the sky?

Whirling propellers allow it to hover.
A helicopter ride is a time to discover.

20

We've flown around from here to there.
We've seen travel by water, land, and air.

21

Big Book, pp. 20–21

***Wh-* question**

Look at the picture on page 21. Which kind of transportation do you like best and why?
(I like the airplane because it travels in the air. It would be fun to look out the windows and see how small everything looks.)

Develop Vocabulary, continued

DAY 3

Distancing
What is this picture showing? (a map)

- This is a map of the world. What color is the land where we live?

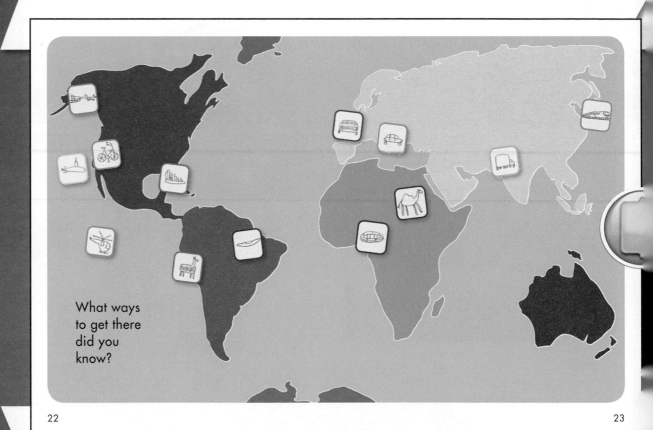

What ways to get there did you know?

22   23

Big Book, pp. 22–23

Guide Comprehension, continued

DAY 4

Open-ended
You know what land we live in. Where else would you like to visit or live? (I want to visit Australia because interesting animals live there.)

Recall

These are some more facts about things we heard about when we read today. What are the pictures showing? (a train, a llama, and a submarine)

- We read about a train, a llama, and a submarine. Which one of these forms of transportation travels the fastest?

Continue with **DAY** 3

Conventions p. 480

Fun Facts From Here to There

The Shinkansen, or bullet trains, of Tokyo, Japan, travel at great speeds on land. These electric trains zip along railways at 186 miles (300 kilometers) per mile. This one is passing Mount Fuji.

A kayak rides the waves. But a submarine moves under them off San Diego, California! A sub is made to move quickly underwater. It has a long shape that might remind you of a loaf of bread. Have you wondered how people see out of submarines underwater? A sail sticks out of the sub's middle. Inside is a periscope, used to peek outside.

In a day, a llama can carry 130 pounds (60 kilograms). It can travel 20 miles (32 kilometers) over the mountains of South America. The llama, a member of the camel family, is a pack animal. Steady on its feet, it carries people and things. But don't overwork a llama, or you'll get a bit of drama! When a llama needs a break, it will lie down on the trail and refuse to take one more step.

Big Book, p. 24

Wh- question

What are some other facts you know about different kinds of transportation? (Trains carry a lot of people. A llama gives a bumpy ride. The llama is an animal and the train and kayak are not.)

Skip to **DAY** 4

Conventions p. 494

Objectives
• Review nouns.
• Dictate or write an invitation.

Conventions

Nouns

Review

Write the words *boy, pen, park,* and *cat* on the board. Remind children what they learned about nouns. A noun is a naming word. A noun names a person, place, animal, or thing. Nouns can name one or more than one. Point to and read the word *boy* on the board. This is a noun that names a person. Point to and read the word *pen* on the board. This is a noun that names a thing. Point to and read the word *park* on the board. This is a noun that names a place. Point to and read the word *cat* on the board. This is a noun that names an animal. We usually add *-s* to nouns to show more than one. How can we say these nouns for more than one? As children say the words, write them on the board. Then read the nouns for more than one with children.

Guide practice

AlphaBuddy is going to say some words. Listen for the nouns he says. Have AlphaBuddy say these words: *teacup, helicopter, dance, where, yacht, feather, pilot, play, dog, house.* When children identify a noun, write the word on the board. Point to each noun as you read it. After you read each noun, ask children if it names a person, animal, place, or thing.

Team Talk Pair children and have them take turns choosing a noun from the board and saying the noun for more than one. Then have children write a sentence using a noun for one or for more than one.

On their own

Use *Reader's and Writer's Notebook,* p. 377, for more practice with nouns.

Daily Fix-It

Use the Daily Fix-It for more conventions practice.

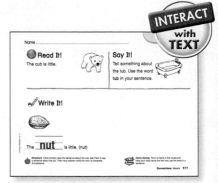

Reader's and Writer's Notebook, p. 377

Writing
Invitation

Teach

Write the following invitation on the board:

> **What:** Book Fair
>
> **Where:** school library
>
> **When:** Saturday
>
> **Time:** 1 o'clock

This is an invitation. An invitation is a polite way to ask someone to come someplace or to do something. An invitation gives details about when, where, and what time an event will happen. **Point to each line as you read the details.** What are other events for which we can make an invitation? **Write children's suggestions on the board.**

Model

Write a blank version of the invitation above on the board. Let's imagine we are planning a class trip to the zoo. We want to invite some chaperones for our trip. **Point to the first line.** This line tells the event. I will write *Trip to the Zoo* on this line.

Guide practice

Have children help you continue to complete the invitation for the class trip. Write the information on the appropriate lines.

Independent writing

Have children turn to p. 378 of *Reader's and Writer's Notebook.* Have them draw a picture of a class play and complete the invitation.

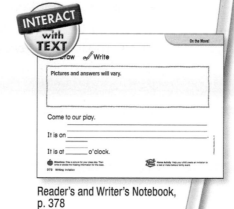

INTERACT with TEXT

Draw ✏ Write

Pictures and answers will vary.

Come to our play.

It is on _____

It is at _____ o'clock.

Reader's and Writer's Notebook, p. 378

Daily Handwriting

Write *Zak, zing, Vic,* and *vote* on the board. Review correct letter formation of uppercase *V* and *Z* and lowercase *v* and *z.*

Have children write *Zak, zing, Vic,* and *vote* on their Write-On Boards. Remind children to use proper left-to-right progression and proper spacing between letters when writing *V, Z, v,* and *z.*

D'Nealian™   Ball and Stick

D'Nealian™   Ball and Stick

Objectives

- Practice oral presentations.
- Speak loudly and clearly.
- Speak one at a time.
- Face the speaker when listening.

Listening and Speaking
Oral Presentation—Description

Review   Remember that when we describe something, we tell what it is like. If I were going to describe this chair, I might say it is white and smooth, and that it is comfortable to sit in.

Model   When I describe something in an oral presentation, I use words that tell more about it. **Display pp. 4–5 of *On the Move!*** I am going to tell you three things about this airplane. This airplane is big. It is white. It has tiny windows.

Guide practice   Have children turn to p. 109 of *My Skills Buddy.* Use the first Listening and Speaking bullet on p. 108 of *My Skills Buddy* to guide the discussion. These pictures show two different animals from *On the Move!* that people use for transportation. Let's choose one animal and use words to describe it. Discuss with children what kinds of words can describe the animal. Then have them describe the other animal.

My Skills Buddy, p. 109

Independent practice

Have children come to the front of the class to give an oral presentation that describes their favorite food. Remind children that when they give descriptions to the class, they need to speak loudly and clearly to make sure everyone can hear them and understand them. Tell them to speak one at a time. Remind them that good listeners show they are listening by facing the speaker. Refer children to their Rules for Listening and Speaking from pp. 1–2 of *Reader's and Writer's Notebook.*

Name

🌀 Speaking Rules

1. Speak clearly.
2. Tell only important ideas.
3. Choose your words carefully.
4. Take turns speaking.
5. Speak one at a time.

Reader's and Writer's Notebook, p. 2

Be a Good Speaker

1. Speak loudly and clearly.
2. Tell only important ideas.
3. Choose your words carefully.
4. Speak one at a time.

Differentiated Instruction

SI Strategic Intervention

Access Content Remind children that words that describe things are called adjectives. There are adjectives for color, shape, and size. Have children tell adjectives they know.

English Language Learners
Access Content Allow English language learners to join in the activity when they are ready, or let them discuss the questions in their home languages and then help them express them in English.

Objectives
- Review skills learned and practiced today.
- Read, write, and say nouns for one and more than one.

Wrap Up Your Day

✔ **Concept Talk** Today we reread the selection about different forms of transportation. Tell me what kinds of transportation we read about and where you would see each type.

✔ **Respond to Literature** Today we read about listening to a jazz band. Have you ever heard jazz music? Do you like it?

✔ **Conventions** Have children say a noun for one and a noun for more than one and write or dictate them on a sheet of paper. Then have the children draw a picture of the nouns.

✔ **Homework Idea** Have children draw and label a picture of a van with people riding inside.

Preview DAY 4

Tomorrow we will read about one of our Trucktown friends.

Extend Your Day!

Social Studies
The Best Way to Go

Materials: Big Book *On the Move!*, photographs of a desert, mountain, polar area, city, and town

Go by Camel Display p. 15 of *On the Move!*
In some parts of the world, a camel is the best way to travel. In the desert, how do people dress differently than we do? Why?

Go by Llama Display p. 12 of *On the Move!*
In some parts of the world, a llama is the best way to travel. In the mountains, how do people dress differently than we do? Why?

Go by Dogsled Display p.13 of *On the Move!*
In some parts of the world, a dogsled is the best way to travel. In polar regions, how do people dress differently than we do? Why?

Display pictures of a desert, mountain, polar region, city, and town. Have children draw themselves in one of the areas using transportation and wearing clothing that is best for that region.

High-Frequency Words
Come with Me

Destination Unknown Have children act out forms of transportation suggested by the dialogue below. Let several children take a turn to be "Leader." List all of the responses on the board as they are named to avoid duplication.

Leader: Come with me.
Class: Where are we going?
  Leader: We are going to _____.
    Class: How will we get there?
    Leader: We will go by _____.

Phonemic Awareness
Can You Name It?

Rhyme Time Tell children they will complete rhymes with words that have /v/ or /z/. Say the following rhymes. Have children supply the missing words and draw a picture of the /v/ or /z/ word. Then have children make up their own rhymes using words with /v/ or /z/.

This is our home. We can dip and dive. We are flying insects that live in a _____. (hive)

It takes a rocket to get to the moon. Sit down, take a ride, and you will _____! (zoom)

You'll find camels there and monkeys too. There are dolphins and foxes. It must be the _____. (zoo)

Objectives
- Discuss the concept to develop oral language.
- Build oral vocabulary.

Today at a Glance

Oral Vocabulary
double-decker bus, submarine

Phonemic Awareness
Initial and Medial /u/

Phonics
/u/ Spelled *Uu*

Comprehension
◉ Main Idea

Conventions
Nouns in Sentences

Writing
Extend the Concept

Vocabulary
Compound Words

TRUCKTOWN on Reading Street

Start your engines!

- Display "Jack and Kat" and lead the group in saying the rhyme a few times.
- Have the group clap the rhythm as they recite the rhyme.
- When children master the rhythm, have them march around the room as they say the rhyme.

Truckery Rhymes

Concept Talk

Question of the Week

How do people in different parts of the world travel?

Build concepts	Write the question of the week on the board. Read the question as you track the print. Tell children to respond in complete sentences. Display Sing with Me Chart 29B.
Listen for Amazing Words	We are going to sing this song again. Listen for the Amazing Words *double-decker bus* and *submarine*. Sing the song several times with children to tune of "Do Your Ears Hang Low?" Have them clap when they hear *double-decker bus* and *submarine*.

💿 Sing with Me Audio

ELL Produce Oral Language Use the Day 4 instruction on ELL Poster 29 to extend and enrich language.

Talk with Me/Sing with Me Chart 29B

ELL Poster 29

 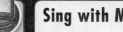
Oral Vocabulary
Amazing Words

Amazing Words

travel	kayak
llama	dogsled
double-decker bus	submarine

Teach Amazing Words

Amazing Words — Oral Vocabulary Routine

1. **Introduce the Word** A *double-decker bus* is a bus with two levels of seats, an upstairs and a downstairs. What's our new Amazing Word for a bus with an upstairs and a downstairs? Say it with me: *double-decker bus.*

2. **Demonstrate** *I like to sit on the top level of a double-decker bus.* Have you ever seen a *double-decker bus?*

   Repeat steps 1 and 2.

   Introduce the Word A *submarine* is a long boat that travels underwater. A *submarine* has no windows. Sailors use a special tool called a periscope to see outside. What's our new Amazing Word for a boat that travels underwater? Say it with me: *submarine.*

   Demonstrate *Navies and scientists use submarines to travel underwater.* Why might a scientist want to see what's under the ocean?

3. **Apply** Have children use *double-decker bus* and *submarine* in complete sentences as they talk about the modes of transportation in *On the Move!*

Routines Flip Chart

Use Amazing Words

To reinforce the concept and the Amazing Words, have children supply the appropriate Amazing Word for each sentence.

You can ride on the top of a _____. (double-decker bus)

A _____ can travel all around the world underwater. (submarine)

Differentiated Instruction

A Advanced

Access Content Have children recall the location where a double-decker bus is used. Then have them draw a picture of one.

Objectives
• Review /u/ spelled *Uu*.

Check Phonemic Awareness
SUCCESS PREDICTOR

Phonemic Awareness
Review /u/

Review

Display the *umbrella* Picture Card. This is an *umbrella*. *Umbrella* begins with /u/. What sound do you hear at the beginning of *umbrella?* Say it with me: /u/ /u/ /u/, *umbrella*. Continue with *uncle, ugly, under,* and *up*. Then display the *mug* Picture Card. This is a *mug*. Where do you hear /u/ in the word *mug? Mug* has /u/ in the middle. What is the middle sound in *mug?*

I am going to say three words. Tell me which words begin with /u/: *apple, upstairs, upper. Upstairs* and *upper* begin with /u/. *Apple* begins with /a/. Let's try some more. **Continue** the activity with the following sets of words: *understand, upon, ice; hat, umpire, unknown; unless, open, utter*.

Picture Card

Corrective feedback

If... children cannot discriminate /u/,
then... have them say /u/ several times /u/, /u/, /u/.

When you say /u/, your mouth drops open and you make the /u/ sound from the back of the throat. **Have** children practice saying /u/.

Picture Card

Phonics
/u/ Spelled *Uu*

Review

Display the *Uu* Alphabet Card. This is an *umbrella*. *Umbrella* begins with /u/. What letter spells the sound /u/? Yes, the letter *u*.

Write the word *up* on the board. Help me blend this word. Listen as I say each sound: /u/ /p/. Now let's blend the sounds together to read the word, /u/ /p/, *up*. What is the word? (*up*) Repeat the routine with *zip*, *cut*, *van*, *run*, and *vet*.

Alphabet Card

Differentiated Instruction

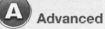 **Advanced**

Connect Sound-Spelling Have children make a list of initial and medial /u/ words. Then have them make silly sentences using the words.

Don't Wait Until Friday

MONITOR PROGRESS — Check Phonemic Awareness

Phoneme Segmentation I am going to say a word. Tell me all the sounds you hear in the word.

Bev	buzz	fizz	fuzz	jazz

If... children cannot identify the sounds in the word,

then... use the small-group Strategic Intervention lesson, p. DI•72, to reteach segmentation skills.

Continue to monitor children's progress using other instructional opportunities during the week so that they can be successful with the Day 5 Assessment. See the Skills Trace on p. 428.

Day 1	Day 2	Day 3	Day 4	Day 5
Check Phonemic Awareness	Check Sound-Spelling/ Retelling	Check Word Reading	Check Phonemic Awareness	Check Oral Vocabulary

Success Predictor

Phonemic Awareness

Success Predictor

Objectives
- Spell words.
- Blend and segment words.
- Read decodable text.
- Read high-frequency words.

Spelling
/v/ Spelled Vv, /z/ Spelled Zz

> **ROUTINE** Spell Words

Spell words

1 **Review Sound-Spellings** Display the *Vv* Alphabet Card. This is a *volcano. Volcano* begins with /v/. What is the letter for /v/? (*v*) Continue the routine with the following Alphabet Cards: *Aa, Ee, Gg, Ii, Jj, Nn, Ss, Tt, Zz.*

2 **Model** Today we are going to spell some words. Listen to the three sounds in *van:* /v/ /a/ /n/.

- What is the first sound in *van?* (/v/) What is the letter for /v/? (*v*) Write *v* on the board.
- What is the middle sound you hear? (/a/) What is the letter for /a/? (*a*) Write *a* on the board.
- What is the last sound you hear? (/n/) What is the letter for /n/? (*n*) Write *n* on the board.
- Point to *van.* Help me blend the sound of each letter together to read this word: /v/ /a/ /n/. The word is *van.* Repeat with the word *zip.*

3 **Guide Practice** Now let's spell some words together. Listen to this word: /b/ /e/ /v/. What is the first sound in *Bev?* (/b/) What is the letter for /b/? (*b*) Write *B* on the board. Now you write an uppercase *B* on your paper. What is the middle sound in *Bev?* (/e/) What is the letter for /e/? (*e*) Write *e* on the board. Now you write *e* on your paper. What is the last sound in *Bev?* (/v/) What is the letter for /v/? (*v*) Write *v* on the board. Now you write *v* on your paper. We can blend the sound of each letter together to read the word: /b/ /e/ /v/. What is the word? (*Bev*) Continue spell and blend practice with the following words: *zig, zag, vest, jazz, vet, fizz.*

4 **On Your Own** This time I am going to say a word. I want you to write it on your paper. Remember, first say the word slowly in your head, and then write the letter for each sound. Write the word *zap.* **Give children time to write the word.** How do you spell the word *zap?* Listen to the sounds: /z/ /a/ /p/. The first sound is /z/. What is the letter for /z/? Did you write *z* on your paper? What is the letter for /a/? Did you write *a* on your paper? What is the letter for /p/? Did you write *p* on your paper? Name the letters in *zap. Zap* is spelled *z, a, p.* Continue the activity with the following words: *Val, Vic, zest, vat.*

Routines Flip Chart

Get Set, Roll! Reader 29
🔄 /v/ Spelled Vv, /z/ Spelled Zz

Review

Review the high-frequency words *the, to, a, is, of, he, me, look,* and *said.* Have children read each word as you point to it on the Word Wall.

Teach rebus words

Write the word *vroom* on the board. This is the word *vroom.* Name the letters with me: *v, r, o, o, m.* Look for the word *vroom* in the story we read today. There will be a picture above the word to help you read it.

Read Get Set, Roll! Reader 29

Display Get Set, Roll! Reader 29. Today we will read a book about Izzy the ice cream truck. **Point to the title of the book.** What is the title of the book? (*Putt! Putt! Pop!*) We will read words with /v/ and /z/ in this book.

Use the routine for reading decodable books found in the Routines Flip Chart to read Get Set, Roll! Reader 29.

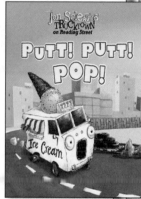

Get Set, Roll! Reader 29

Differentiated Instruction

Ⓐ Advanced

Access Content Explain to children that the words *putt, vroom,* and *pop* are words that tell sounds. Have children think of other words that can tell sounds, such as *buzz* or *bam.*

Small Group Time

DAY 4 — Break into small groups to read the Get Set, Roll! Reader before the comprehension lesson.

Teacher-Led

SI Strategic Intervention	**OL** On-Level	**Ⓐ** Advanced
Teacher-Led Page DI•72	**Teacher-Led** Page DI•76	**Teacher-Led** Page DI•79
• Phonemic Awareness and Phonics	• **Read** Get Set, Roll! Reader 29	• **Read** Get Set, Roll! Reader 29 or **Reread** Kindergarten Student Reader K.5.5
• **Read** Get Set, Roll! Reader 29		

ELL Place English language learners in the groups that correspond to their reading abilities in English.

Practice Stations
• Visit the Let's Write Station
• Visit the Read for Meaning Station

Independent Activities
• Read independently
• Audio Text of the Big Book
• *Reader's and Writer's Notebook*

Comprehension
↻ Main Idea

Practice main idea

Envision It!

Have children turn to the Main Idea picture on pp. 94–95 of *My Skills Buddy.* As you look at the picture, remind children that the main idea is the most important idea.

Team Talk Pair children and have them discuss the main idea of going to school. We go to school every day. What kinds of things do we do at school? What is the main reason we go to school?

My Skills Buddy, pp. 94–95

Cause and Effect

Review

Direct children to the Cause and Effect picture on pp. 34–35 of *My Skills Buddy*.

In a story, things often happen because of something else. A cause is what makes something happen. What happens is called the effect. Look at these pictures. The first picture shows the cause of what happens in the second picture.

• What happens in the first picture? (The dog jumps on the table.)

• What happens in the second picture? (The paint spills on the floor.)

• What causes the paint to spill? (the dog jumping on the table)

• Is the paint spilling the cause or the effect? (the effect)

More practice

Use *Reader's and Writer's Notebook,* p. 379, for additional practice with cause and effect.

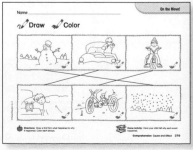

Reader's and Writer's Notebook, p. 379

 Triple Day Read!

Third Read—Big Book
On the Move!

Guide comprehension

Display *On the Move!* There are reasons why different people travel in different ways.

- Why doesn't everybody in the world travel by land? (Some places are too far, and other places are across the ocean.)

- Why does a truck need more wheels than a car? (Trucks are longer, bigger, and heavier.)

- Why do camels carry people in the desert but llamas do not? (Camels live there but llamas do not.)

- Why do some buses have two levels and other buses only have one? (Some buses must carry twice as many people.)

Reread *On the Move!* Return to p. 468. Follow the Day 4 arrow and use the Guide Comprehension notes to give children the opportunity to gain a more complete understanding of the selection.

DAY **2**
Read for enjoyment

DAY **3**
Reread using Develop Vocabulary notes

DAY **4**
Reread using Guide Comprehension notes

Differentiated Instruction

SI Strategic Intervention

Practice Cause and Effect Tell children different situations and have them identify the cause and the effect. For example, *It is raining outside, so you take an umbrella.* What happens in this situation? (You take an umbrella.) What event causes you to take that action? (It is raining.)

Objectives
- Practice nouns in sentences.
- Write or dictate sentences about transportation.

Conventions
Nouns in Sentences

Review
Remind children of what they learned about nouns in sentences. Sentences have nouns. Nouns are words that name people, animals, places, and things. Nouns can name one or more than one.

Model
Classroom is a noun for the place we are sitting right now. I can use the noun *classroom* in a sentence: *We learn in a classroom.* What are some words that name people and things in our classroom? Write children's nouns on the board.

Guide practice
Read the list of nouns with children. Which words are nouns for one? Which words are nouns for more than one? Let's use these nouns in a sentence. Have children say nouns in sentences.

Write and read the following sentences on the board: Have children listen for nouns in sentences. Raise your hand when you know the noun in the sentence.

> **The boy runs fast.**
>
> **The dog runs faster.**
>
> **The _____ runs fastest.**

Have the children provide a noun for the last sentence.

On their own
Use *Reader's and Writer's Notebook,* p. 380, for more practice with nouns in sentences.

Daily Fix-It
Use the Daily Fix-It for more conventions practice.

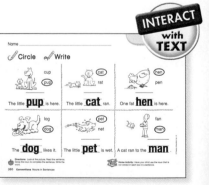

Reader's and Writer's Notebook, p. 380

Writing
Extend the Concept: Text to World

Discuss transportation

We just learned about different forms of transportation people use around the world. Some forms of transportation we know about and have seen, and others we have just learned about.

Guide practice

Ask children to think about the forms of transportation they read about in *On the Move!* Talk with children about where people use those forms of transportation, where the transportation can take them, and how it can take them.

Use children's contributions to the discussion to write sentences.

An airplane...	**can take me to Florida.**
	can fly over a state.
A dogsled...	**is used to travel over snow.**
	can pull people in Alaska.

Independent practice

Have children write or dictate their own sentences about different forms of transportation or they may copy a sentence from the board. Invite children to read their sentences to the class.

Daily Handwriting

Write uppercase *V* and *Z* and lowercase *v* and *z* on the board. Review correct letter formation with children.

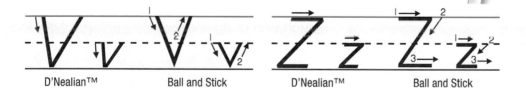

D'Nealian™   Ball and Stick   D'Nealian™   Ball and Stick

Have children write a row each of uppercase *V* and *Z* and a row each of lowercase *v* and *z* on their Write-On Boards. Remind them to use proper left-to-right and top-to-bottom progression when writing *V, v, Z,* and *z.*

Differentiated Instruction

SI Strategic Intervention

Support Discussion Have children classify the forms of transportation into groups about where they travel, such as in the air, on land, in water, and underwater. Discuss with children how this information affects where these forms of transportation can be used.

Daily Fix-It

he is on a Camel.
He is on a camel.

This week's practice sentences appear on Teacher Resources DVD-ROM.

English Language Learners
Support Writing Allow children with the same home language to share their ideas in that language and discuss how to express them in English before writing.

Vocabulary
Transportation Words

train   truck   airplane   boat

Teach

Write the words *train, truck, airplane,* and *boat* on the board. Point to each word as you read it. These are transportation words. Have children turn to p. 28 of *My Skills Buddy.* Incorporate the second Vocabulary bullet on the page in the discussion. Which form of transportation is used in the air? Which is used on water? Which ones are used on land? Have children say the word and point to the picture as they answer the questions.

My Skills Buddy, p. 28

Team Talk Pair children and have them take turns using one of the transportation words to tell an adventure story. Remind them to tell the story in complete sentences.

Wrap Up Your Day

✔ **Oral Language** Ask the person sitting across from you what his or her favorite part of *On the Move!* is. Ask the person to use one of our Amazing Words in his or her answer. Listen and answer when that person asks you the same question.

✔ **Homework Idea** Tell children to ask a family member a question and bring the answer back to share with the class.

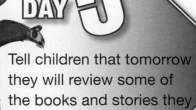

Preview DAY 5

Tell children that tomorrow they will review some of the books and stories they have read this week.

Extend Your Day!

Social Studies
Working Together
Materials: paper airplane

Transportation Moves All forms of transportation have one thing in common: They move people and things from here to there. But how do they move?

It Takes Force Discuss how objects cannot move by themselves. Lift the paper airplane and drop it to the floor. Then pick it up and throw it so that it flies. Tell children to describe what happened each time. For an object to move, something must move it. I moved the paper airplane. What moves a real airplane?

Airplanes and cars use a motor to make them move. What forms of transportation get their power from people or animals? Record the information in a chart.

motor	person	animal
car	bike	dogsled
plane	skate-board	horse-drawn carriage
train	wagon	

Have children draw a picture of something in motion. Have them show the picture and tell whether a motor, person, or animal moves it.

Phonemic Awareness
Name It

What Is It? Tell children that you will describe something that begins with either /v/ or /z/, and they will guess what it is.

I am an animal. I am black and white. I look like a horse, but I am wild. What am I? (zebra)

Carrots, potatoes, and broccoli are just one kind of me. It is always good to eat me. What am I? (vegetables)

You use me to clean the rugs. I suck things up inside me. What am I? (vacuum)

Have children think of other things that begin with /v/ or /z/ and make up clues for classmates to guess the word they thought of.

Comprehension
Cause and Effect

This Cause Discuss the various kinds of land areas in the book, such as mountain, desert, and swamp. Write each on the board.

The Effect Distribute paper and have children choose a land area you have discussed, or select another one, to illustrate. Have them draw the land area and then the transportation that could be used on that landform.

Objectives
- Review the concepts.
- Build oral vocabulary.

Today at a Glance

Oral Vocabulary
travel, kayak, llama, dogsled, double-decker bus, submarine

Phonemic Awareness
◉ Initial and Final /v/ and /z/

Phonics
◉ /v/ Spelled *Vv*
◉ /z/ Spelled *Zz*

Comprehension
Main Idea

Conventions
Nouns in Sentences

Writing
This Week We…

Check Oral Vocabulary
SUCCESS PREDICTOR

TRUCKTOWN on Reading Street

Start your engines!

- Display "Jack and Kat" and lead the group in saying the rhyme a few times.
- Have half the group recite the rhyme while the other half acts it out.
- Then have the groups change roles.

Truckery Rhymes

Concept Wrap Up

Question of the Week

How do people in different parts of the world travel?

Listen for Amazing Words

Write the question of the week on the board. Track the print as you read it to children. Have them use the Amazing Words in their responses (*travel, kayak, llama, dogsled, double-decker bus, submarine*). Display Sing with Me Chart 29B. Let's sing "How Do You Go?" I want you to listen for the Amazing Words we learned this week. Remind children that the words *travel, kayak, llama, dogsled, double-decker bus,* and *submarine* are in the song. Sing the song several times to the tune of "Do Your Ears Hang Low?" Have children pretend to travel on the transportation as they sing the Amazing Words. Then discuss how people travel. Remind children to speak one at a time.

Sing with Me Chart 29B

 Sing with Me Audio

ELL Check Concepts and Language Use Day 5 instruction on ELL Poster 29 to monitor children's understanding of the lesson concept.

ELL Poster 29

Oral Vocabulary
Amazing Words

Review

Let's Talk Display Talk with Me Chart 29A. We learned six new Amazing Words this week. Let's say the Amazing Words as I point to the pictures on the chart. Point to each picture and give children the chance to say the appropriate Amazing Word before offering it.

> The children _____ every summer. (travel)
>
> A _____ travels under the water. (submarine)
>
> An animal the size of a pony with long, shaggy fur is called a _____. (llama)
>
> Do you think it is easy to paddle a _____? (kayak)
>
> What kind of dog pulls a _____? (dogsled)
>
> London used the _____ at one time. (double-decker bus)

Amazing Words

travel	kayak
llama	dogsled
double-decker bus	submarine

Talk with Me/Sing with Me Chart 29A

Differentiated Instruction

SI Strategic Intervention

Access Content Have children draw a picture of each Amazing Word. Then have them show their drawings to a partner. Tell the partner to use the Amazing Word in a sentence.

It's Friday

MONITOR PROGRESS ○ **Check Oral Vocabulary**

Demonstrate Word Knowledge Monitor the Amazing Words by asking the following questions. Have children use the Amazing Word in their answer.

- **What do most people like to do when they take a vacation?** (travel)
- **What kind of transportation travels under the water?** (submarine)
- **What kind of bus can you ride on the top of?** (double-decker bus)
- **What kind of boat is like a canoe?** (kayak)
- **What kind of transportation is pulled by dogs?** (dogsled)
- **What animal can people ride through the mountains?** (llama)

If… children have difficulty using the Amazing Words,

then… reteach unknown words using the Oral Vocabulary Routine, on the Routines Flip Chart.

Day 1	Day 2	Day 3	Day 4	Day 5
Check Phonemic Awareness	Check Sound-Spelling/ Retelling	Check Word Reading	Check Phonemic Awareness	Check Oral Vocabulary

Success Predictor

Oral Vocabulary

499

Success Predictor

Objectives
- Review initial and final /v/ and /z/.
- Review /v/ spelled *Vv*.
- Review /z/ spelled *Zz*.

Phonemic Awareness Review
/v/ and /z/

Isolate initial and final /v/ and /z/

Display the *van* Picture Card. What is the first sound in *van*? Say the word with me: /v/ /v/ /v/, *van*. *Van* begins with /v/. Review initial /v/ with these Picture Cards: *vacuum, vase, vest*. Display the *five* Picture Card. What is the last sound in *five? Five* ends with /v/. Review final /v/ with these words: *live, save, wave*.

Display the *zipper* Picture Card. What is the first sound in *zipper*? Say the word with me: /z/ /z/ /z/, *zipper*. *Zipper* begins with /z/. Review initial /z/ with these Picture Cards: *zebra, zoo*. Say the word *buzz*. What is the last sound in *buzz? Buzz* ends with /z/. Review final /z/ with these words: *jazz, quiz, size*.

Discriminate final sounds

Show children how to make a *v* sign with their index and middle fingers and make *z* in the air with their index finger. I am going to say some words. I want you to listen for /v/ or /z/ at the end. If you hear /v/, make the *v* sign. If you hear /z/, make a *z* in the air. Let's try one together: *have*. Do you hear /v/ at the end of *have*? Did you make the *v* sign? Listen again: *buzz*. What sound did you hear at the end? Did you make a *z* in the air? Continue with the following words: *gaze, live, fizz, fuzz, love, glove, Bev, jazz*.

Picture Card

Picture Card

Picture Card

Phonics Review
/v/ Spelled Vv and /z/ Spelled Zz

Teach /v/Vv, /z/Zz

Display the *Vv* Alphabet Card. This is a *volcano*. What sound do you hear at the beginning of *volcano*? What letter spells that sound? Repeat with *Zz*.

High-frequency words

Write *where* on the board. This is the word *where*. What is this word? Repeat the routine for the word *come*.

Apply phonics in familiar text

Let's Reread Have children reread one of the books specific to the target letter sounds. You may wish to review the decodable words and high-frequency words that appear in each book prior to rereading.

Decodable Reader 29
My Skills Buddy, p. 98

Kindergarten Student
Reader K.5.5

Get Set, Roll!
Reader 29

Differentiated Instruction

SI Strategic Intervention

Support Reading Remind children to use their fingers to follow the words across the page as they reread Decodable Reader 29, Kindergarten Student Reader K.5.5, and Get Set, Roll! Reader 29.

Alphabet Card

Alphabet Card

Small Group Time

DAY 5 Break into small groups after phonics and before the phonics and word reading assessment.

Teacher-Led

SI Strategic Intervention	**OL** On-Level	**A** Advanced
Teacher-Led Page DI•73 • Phonics Review • **Read** Listen to Me Reader K.5.5	**Teacher-Led** Page DI•76 • Phonics Review • **Reread** Leveled Books	**Teacher-Led** Page DI•79 • Fluency and Comprehension • **Reread** Independent Reader K.5.5 for Fluency

ELL Place English language learners in the groups that correspond to their reading abilities in English.

Practice Stations	**Independent Activities**
• Visit the Read for Meaning Station • Visit the Let's Make Art Station	• Read independently • Story Sort • Concept Talk Video

Assess

◉ Read words with /v/ and /z/.
- Read high-frequency words.
- Read sentences.

Assessment
Monitor Progress

/v/ Spelled Vv and /z/ spelled Zz

Whole Class Have children number a sheet of paper from 1 to 6. Say the following words. If children hear /v/, have them write a *v* next to the number. If they hear /z/, have them write a *z* next to the number.

1. zip   2. jazz   3. vest   4. van   5. buzz   6. fizz

MONITOR PROGRESS	Check Word and Sentence Reading

If... children cannot complete the whole-class assessment,

then... use the Reteach lesson in *First Stop*.

If... you are unsure of a child's grasp of this week's skills,

then... use the assessment below to obtain a clearer evaluation of the child's progress.

Success Predictor

/v/ Spelled Vv, /z/ spelled Zz, and high-frequency words

One-on-One To facilitate individual progress monitoring, assess some children on Day 4 and the rest on Day 5. While individual children are being assessed, the rest of the class can reread this week's books and look for words with /v/ and /z/.

Word reading

Use the word lists on reproducible p. 503 to assess a child's ability to read words that begin and end with /v/ and /z/ and high-frequency words. We're going to read some words. I'll read the first word, and you read the rest. The first word is *zip, /z/ /i/ /p/.* For each child, record any decoding problems.

Sentence reading

Use the sentences on reproducible p. 503 to assess a child's ability to read words in sentences. Have each child read two sentences aloud. Have each child read different sentences. Start over with sentence one if necessary.

Record scores

Monitor children's accuracy by recording their scores using the Word and Sentence Reading Chart for this unit in *First Stop*.

Name _____

Read the Words

zip ☐   frizz ☐

van ☐   Val ☐

where ☐   come ☐

jazz ☐   zap ☐

Bev ☐   vest ☐

buzz ☐   vet ☐

Read the Sentences

1. Where is the van for the jazz band?

2. Did you see where Buzz left his vest?

3. Come and look at the fuzz, Val.

4. I see where the vet is, Zak.

5. Mom will come and zip up my vest.

Note to Teacher: Children read each word. Children read two sentences.

Scoring for Read the Words: Score 1 point for each correct word.

/v/Vv (van, Bev, Val, vest, vet) _____ /___5___
/z/Zz (zip, jazz, buzz, frizz, zap) _____ /___5___
High-Frequency Words (where, come) _____ /___2___

MONITOR PROGRESS
- /v/Vv
- /z/Zz
- High-frequency words

My Skills Buddy, pp. 110–111

Let's Practice It!
Lullaby

Teach

Tell children that today they will listen to a lullaby. A lullaby is type of song. Review the features of a lullaby with children. Have children discuss the purpose for singing and listening to lullabies.

- A lullaby is often about a baby.
- People sing lullabies to babies to help them sleep.
- People and babies listen to lullabies to help them fall asleep.
- A lullaby often has rhyming words.

Have children turn to pp. 110–111 of *My Skills Buddy*. I am going to read a lullaby called "All the Pretty Little Horses." Look at the pictures as I read. Read the text of "All the Pretty Little Horses." As you read, direct children to look at the appropriate picture.

Guide practice

Discuss the features of a lullaby with children and the bulleted text on *My Skills Buddy*, p. 110.

- A lullaby is often about a baby. How do you know this is a lullaby? (The words are telling a baby not to cry and to go to sleep.)

- People sing lullabies to babies. What does this lullaby promise to the baby when it wakes up? (all the pretty little horses)

- A lullaby often has rhyming words. What words rhyme in this lullaby? (*bye, cry; bays, grays*)

- What other words rhyme with *bye*? (*my, sigh, tie*)

- Why do we sing lullabies to babies? (Lullabies are meant to help a baby go to sleep. When we sing, it makes the words soothing.)

- What words or phrases repeat in this lullaby? (*Go to sleep, my little baby. Hush-a-bye, don't you cry.*)

All the Pretty Little Horses

Go to sleep, baby child.
Go to sleep, my little baby.
Hush-a-bye, don't you cry.
Go to sleep, my little baby.

When you wake, you will have
All the pretty little horses.
Blacks and bays, sorrels and grays,
All the pretty little horses.

Blacks and bays, sorrels and grays,
All the pretty little horses.
Hush-a-bye, don't you cry.
Go to sleep, my little baby.

Differentiated Instruction

SI Strategic Intervention

Access Content Tell children that when they sing a lullaby, their voice should be soft and soothing. Have them practice singing short phrases of "All the Pretty Little Horses" after you sing them.

Teacher Tip

Before reading the lullaby, tell children the definitions of *bay* and *sorrel*.

bay a horse with a reddish brown body and a black mane and tail

sorrel a horse with a light orange-brown body and a white mane and tail

Objectives
◎ Review main idea.

Assess
◉ Identify main idea.

Comprehension Assessment
Monitor Progress

Read Aloud Anthology

Review | **Main Idea** The main idea is the most important idea in a story. Good readers pay attention to the main idea to help them understand what they are reading.

Read "Man on the Moon" | Tell children that you are going to read them a selection about astronauts landing on the moon. Tell them to think about the main idea of the selection as you read. Listen carefully as I read the selection. When I am done, I will ask you to tell me the main idea. Read "Man on the Moon" on p. 70 of *Read Aloud Anthology*.

Check main idea | After you read the selection, ask children to identify the main idea.

- Who are the people in "Man on the Moon"? (astronauts Michael Collins, Buzz Aldrin, and Neil Armstrong)

- What did they use to get to the moon? (the Apollo II rocket and the *Columbia* spacecraft)

- What did the people on Earth do? (watched on television)

- What did the astronauts do once they landed on the moon? (They took pictures, collected rocks, and planted an American flag.)

- What is "Man on the Moon" all about? (It is about the first time people landed on the moon.)

Corrective feedback | **If...** children cannot identify main idea,
then... reteach main idea using the Reteach lesson in *First Stop*.

Assess main idea | Use the blackline master found on p. 507. Copy one page for each child. Have them color the picture that shows the main idea of "Man on the Moon."

Name _____

Main Idea

Color the picture that shows the main idea of "Man on the Moon."

Note to Teacher: Have children color the picture that shows the correct main idea.

Objectives
- Review nouns in sentences.
- Write about forms of transportation.

Conventions
Nouns in Sentences

Review   Remind children of what they learned about nouns in sentences. Nouns are words that name one or more than one person, animal, place, or thing. Nouns are used in sentences.

Model   Let's talk about the people, places, animals, and things we learned this week. Draw a four-column chart on the board and write a label in each section: *People, Animals, Places, Things.* Who are some people we talked about this week? We have talked about astronauts, Val, Jan, and her dad. I will write these names in my *People* column. Continue with the remaining columns, naming animals, places, and things children have read and heard about this week such as *llamas, camels, moon, desert, submarine,* and *kayak.* All of these words are nouns for one or more than one.

Guide practice   Have children choose a noun from the chart to dictate sentences as you write them on the board. After you have some sentences, read each sentences with children, pointing to each word. All of these sentences have nouns.

On their own   Have children copy and illustrate one of the sentences from the board.

Daily Fix-It   Use the Daily Fix-It exercise for more conventions practice.

Writing
This Week We...

Review

Display *On the Move!,* Sing with Me Chart 29B, Phonics Songs and Rhymes Chart 29, Decodable Reader 29 from *My Skills Buddy,* Kindergarten Student Reader K.5.5, and Get Set, Roll! Reader 29. This week we learned about transportation around the world. We read new books, and we sang new songs. Which book or song was your favorite? Let's share our ideas with each other.

Team Talk Pair children and have them take turns telling which book or song was their favorite and why.

Model

Today we will write a list of the forms of transportation in our songs and books. The girl in *On the Move!* first got on an airplane. I will write *airplane* on the list.

> **Transportation**
> 1. airplane

Guide practice

Continue the list with children. Then read through the list and have children tell a place each form of transportation can take them.

> **Transportation**
> 1. airplane   2. submarine
> 3. bike   4. boat

On their own

Have children write a sentence about a form of transportation.

Daily Handwriting

Write uppercase *V* and *Z* and lowercase *v* and *z* on the board. Review correct letter formation with children.

Have children write a row of uppercase *V* and *Z* and lowercase *v* and *z* on the Write-On Boards. Remind them to use proper left-to-right and top-to-bottom progression.

V v V v
D'Nealian™   Ball and Stick

Z z Z z
D'Nealian™   Ball and Stick

Differentiated Instruction

SI Strategic Intervention

Support Conventions Have children identify nouns by looking through familiar books and picking out their favorite places or things.

Daily Fix-It

a man can go to the moon
A man can go to the moon.

This week's practice sentences appear on Teacher Resources DVD-ROM.

Objectives
- Review weekly concept.
- Review main idea.

Wrap Up Your Week!

Question of the Week
How do people in different parts of the world travel?

Amazing Words

You've learned
0 0 6
words this week!

You've learned
1 7 4
words this year!

Illustrate main idea

This week we have read about different kinds of transportation used by people in different parts of the world.

- Make a chart like the one pictured or use Graphic Organizer 27 and ask children to identify the main idea of *On the Move!* Write their responses in the top box.

- Fill in the other boxes with things they remember from the selection.

- Have children write or dictate a sentence about a form of transportation. Then have them illustrate their sentence.

> **There are many ways people travel.**

Next Week's Question
How do children around the world get to school?

Discuss next week's question. Talk with children about forms of transportation children can take to school.

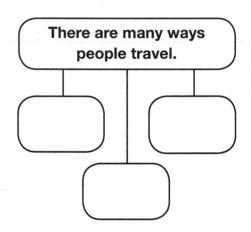

Preview
NEXT WEEK

Tell children that next week they will read about how children around the world get to school.

Extend Your Day!

Social Studies
Transportation

Materials: chart paper, construction paper

On the Move Have children brainstorm the main ways to move things from place to place. There are three main ways that machines help move people and things. If we wanted to travel someplace far, what is the fastest way to get there? (plane) If we need to go someplace close, what is the fastest way to get there? (car, bus, or train) If we need to travel across a lake or river, what is the best way to get there? (boat)

Making a Map On chart paper, have children help you make a simple map showing a river, bridges, train tracks, and roads. Include places to go, such as stores, school, a park, an airport, and houses. Have children make a vehicle they would like to ride in. I want to get from the post office to my home. I will ride on a bus. This is how I will go. Use a paper bus and make your route. Describe your route as you go. Have children take turns getting from one point to another and describing the route they take.

Literature
What Happens Next?

Materials: drawing paper, drawing tools

Complete the Story I am going to read you a story. I want you to use your imagination and draw a picture of the ending.

One day a little boat was traveling down the river. He was singing and looking at all of the pretty trees on the riverbank. He had never gone so far without his parents, but he felt very brave. Before he knew it, the river had grown very wide. He almost couldn't see the other side. All he saw was a giant ocean with high waves...

Science
What Do I Wear?

Materials: old magazines, scissors, four boxes

Seasonal Clothing Remind children that the weather is different in different parts of the world and during different seasons. Who can tell me the names of the four seasons? What is the weather like in each of the seasons?

Have children look through the magazines and cut out pictures of clothing. Set up four boxes labeled *Spring, Summer, Fall,* and *Winter*. Have children take turns holding up a picture, naming and describing the article of clothing, and placing it in the appropriate season box.

Weekly Assessment

Use the whole-class assessment on pages 502–503 and 506–507 in this Teacher's Edition to check:

✔ 🔊 **/v/ Spelled** *Vv*

✔ 🔊 **/z/ Spelled** *Zz*

✔ 🔊 **Comprehension Skill** *Main Idea*

✔ **High-Frequency Words** *where come*

Teacher's Edition, Day 5

Managing Assessment

Use the Assessment Handbook for:

✔ **Observation Checklists**

✔ **Record-Keeping Forms**

✔ **Portfolio Assessment**

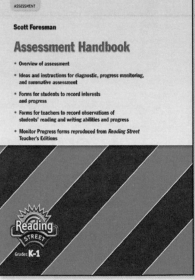

Assessment Handbook

Teacher Notes

Small Group Time

Pacing Small Group Instruction

20–30 mins.

5 Day Plan

DAY 1	• Phonemic Awareness/ Phonics • Decodable Story 29
DAY 2	• Phonemic Awareness/ Phonics • Decodable Reader 29
DAY 3	• Phonemic Awareness/ Phonics • Concept Literacy Reader K.5.5 or Kindergarten Student Reader K.5.5
DAY 4	• Phonemic Awareness/ Phonics • Get Set, Roll! Reader 29
DAY 5	• Phonics Review • Listen to Me Reader K.5.5

3 or 4 Day Plan

DAY 1	• Phonemic Awareness/ Phonics • Decodable Story 29
DAY 2	• Phonemic Awareness/ Phonics • Decodable Reader 29
DAY 3	• Phonemic Awareness/ Phonics • Concept Literacy Reader K.5.5 or Kindergarten Student Reader K.5.5
DAY 4	• Phonemic Awareness/ Phonics • Get Set, Roll! Reader 29

3 Day Plan: Eliminate the shaded box.

SI Strategic Intervention

DAY 1

Phonemic Awareness•Phonics

- **Isolate /v/ and /z/** Display the *vacuum* Picture Card. This is a *vacuum. Vacuum* begins with /v/. Say it with me: /v/ /v/ /v/, *vacuum*. Repeat with *van* and *vase.* Display the *zoo* Picture Card. *Zoo* begins with /z/. Say it with me: /z/ /z/ /z/, *zoo.*

- **Connect /v/ to Vv and /z/ to Zz** I am going to say three words. I want you to tell me which word begins with /v/. Listen carefully: *vest, best, nest.* Say the words with me: *vest, best, nest.* Which word begins with /v/? *Vest* begins with /v/. *Best* and *nest* do not begin with /v/. Write *Vv* on the board. The letter *v* stands for /v/ in words. Continue discriminating /v/ with the following sets of words: *van, ban, pan; met, bet, vet; boy, violet, puppy.* Repeat the routine with /z/ with these sets of words: *zip, tip, flip; zoo, blue, crew; zebra, lion, tiger.*

Decodable Story 29

- **Review** Review the previously taught high-frequency words by writing each of the words and having children say the words with you.

come	they	go	to	look	for	like

    If... children have difficulty reading the words,
    then... say a word and have children point to the word and say the word. Repeat several times, giving assistance as needed.

- **Read** Have children read *Val's Top* orally. Then have them reread the story several times individually.

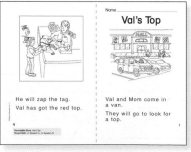

Reader's and Writer's Notebook, pp. 371–372

Objectives
- Identify the common sounds that letters represent.
- Read at least 25 high-frequency words from a commonly used list.

SI Strategic Intervention DAY 2

Phonemic Awareness•Phonics

More Reading

Use Leveled Readers or other text at children's instructional level.

■ **Discriminate /v/ and /z/** Display Phonics Songs and Rhymes Chart 29. Sing "I Want My Car to Vroom, Vroom, Vroom" to the tune of "A Sailor Went to Sea, Sea, Sea" several times with children. Show children how to drive by pushing on an imaginary pedal and holding an imaginary wheel. Have children pretend to drive when they hear a /v/ or /z/ word.

■ **Connect /v/ to *Vv* and /z/ to *Zz*** Review the *Vv* and *Zz* Alphabet Cards. Then ask children to name words that have /v/ and /z/. List the words as they say them. Have children echo read the list of words. Then ask children to take turns circling the *v* and *z* in the words on the list.

Decodable Reader 29

■ **Review** Review the high-frequency words by writing *is* on the board. This is the word *is*. What word is this? Continue with the following words: *where, a, here, with, come, do.*

> **If...** children have difficulty reading the words,
> **then...** say a word and have children point to the word. Repeat several times, giving assistance as needed.

■ **Read** Display the cover of *Zip Up, Val!* on p. 98 of *My Skills Buddy*. Ask a volunteer to read the first page of the story. Have children tell why Val has to zip up. What does Val do so she does not have to zip up?

My Skills Buddy

Objectives
• Identify the common sounds that letters represent.
• Read at least 25 high-frequency words from a commonly used list.
• Retell a main event from a story read aloud.

SI *Strategic Intervention*

DAY **3**

Phonemic Awareness•Phonics

- **Discriminate /z/** Show the *zipper* Picture Card. This is a *zipper. Zipper* begins with /z/. Say it with me: /z/ /z/ /z/, *zipper.* Show children how to buzz like a bee. When you hear a word that begins or ends with /z/, buzz like a bee. Use the following words: *snail, zag, zoo, seal, jazz, zebra.*

- **Connect /v/ to *Vv* and /z/ to *Zz*** Display the *Vv* Alphabet Card. What letter is this? This is the letter *V.* What sound does this letter stand for? Say it with me: /v/ /v/ /v/. What is this picture? **(a volcano)** Say the word with me: /v/ /v/ /v/, *volcano.* Continue with the *Zz* Alphabet Card.

- **Blend Sounds** Write *van* on the board. Have children blend the sound of each letter to read the word: /v/ /a/ /n/, *van.* Have you seen a *van?* Repeat the routine with the following words: *zip, zap, vet.*

- **Review High-Frequency Words** Write *come* on the board. Have volunteers say the word and use it in a sentence. Continue with the words *where, was, what, was.*

- To practice phonics and high-frequency words, have children read Kindergarten Student Reader K.5.5. Use the instruction on pp. 464–465.

For a complete lesson plan and additional practice, see the **Leveled Reader Teaching Guide**.

Concept Literacy Reader K.5.5

- **Preview and Predict** Display the cover of the Concept Literacy Reader K.5.5. Point to the title. The title of the book is *We Travel.* What do you think this book is about? Have children tell about the picture and what they think the book might be about.

- **Set a Purpose** We talked about the title of the book. Let's read the book to learn about the different ways we can travel. Have children read the Concept Literacy Reader.

- **Read** Provide corrective feedback as children read the book orally. During reading, ask them if they are able to confirm any of the predictions they made prior to reading.

If... children have difficulty reading the book individually,

then... read a sentence aloud as children point to each word. Then have the group reread the sentences as they continue pointing to the words.

- **Retell** Have children retell the content as you page through the book. Help them identify what the book is about. Also call attention to where we can use these forms of transportation to travel.

Concept Literacy Reader K.5.5

DAY 4

Phonemic Awareness•Phonics

■ **Segmenting** Say *fuzz.* I hear three sounds in *fuzz,* /f/ /u/ /z/. How many sounds do you hear in *vet?* What are they? (three, /v/ /e/ /t/) Repeat with *zap, Liz, and vat.*

■ **Vegetables!** Display pictures of vegetables. These are *vegetables. Vegetable* begins with /v/. Say it with me: /v/ /v/ /v/, *vegetable.* Do you eat *vegetables?* Give children paper. Have them draw a picture of their favorite vegetables.

■ **Connect /v/ to *Vv* and /z/ to *Zz*** Write uppercase *V* on the board. Name the letter as you write it several times. Have children trace the letter in the air. Then write a lowercase *v* on the board. What sound does this letter stand for? Name the letter and ask a volunteer to write the lowercase letter *v* on the board. Ask children to name words that begin with /v/. Repeat with the letters *Zz.*

Get Set, Roll! Reader 29

■ **Review** Review the following high-frequency words with children: *the, to, a, is, he, of, me, look, said.*

■ **Teach Rebus Words** Write the word *vroom* on the board. This is the word *vroom.* Name the letters with me: *v, r, o, o, m, vroom. Vroom* is a made-up word. We can use the word *vroom* as a sound. Look for this word in the story we will read today. There will be a picture above the word to help you read it.

Get Set, Roll! Reader 29

■ **Read** Display Get Set, Roll! Reader 29, *Putt! Putt! Pop!* Today we will read a story about Izzy the ice cream truck. The title of the story is *Putt! Putt! Pop!* Look at the picture and think about the title. What do you think this story will be about?

> **If...** children have difficulty reading the story individually,
> **then...** read a sentence aloud as children point to each word. Then have the group reread the sentences as they continue pointing to the words.

■ **Reread** Use echo reading of Get Set, Roll! Reader 29 to model fluent reading. Use your oral reading to model for children where to pause, when to change pitch, and which words to stress. Then have children reread orally three to four times, or until they can read with few or no mistakes.

Objectives
• Identify the common sounds that letters represent.
• Read at least 25 high-frequency words from a commonly used list.
• Predict what might happen next based on the cover.

More Reading

Use Leveled Readers or other text at children's instructional level.

Phonics Review

■ **Discriminate /v/ and /z/** Draw six vases on the board. Gather about twelve Picture Cards, including the following cards: *vacuum, van, vase, zebra, zipper, zoo.* Mix the cards and display them one at a time. Have a child name the picture. If the name has /v/ or /z/, have the child write a lowercase *v* or *z*, depending on the Picture Card, in one of the vases.

Listen to Me Reader K.5.5

■ **Preview and Predict** Display the cover of the book. The title of this story is *Bev and Vin.* It is written by Olivia Suez. It is illustrated by Ariel Pang. What are Bev and Vin doing? Tell me what you think this story will be about.

Listen to Me Reader K.5.5

■ **Set a Purpose** Review children's ideas. Point out that after they read, they will know more about Bev and Vin. Tell children that you will read the story with them. Follow along with your finger as I read. Then we will take turns reading this page. Repeat this routine through all of the pages. Guide children to decode words.

■ **Reread for Fluency** Use echo reading of Listen to Me Reader K.5.5 to model reading fluently. Use your oral reading to model for children when to pause, when to change pitch, and which words to stress. Then have children reread orally three to four times, or until they can read with few or no mistakes.

Objectives

• Identify the common sounds that letters represent.
• Predict what might happen next based on the cover.

OL On-Level — **DAY 1**

Phonemic Awareness•Phonics

■ **Recognize /v/ and /z/** Tell children you will say some sentences and they should listen for words with /v/. Say the following sentences: *Valerie* has a *very* nice *vest*. *Victor vacuums* in the *valley*. The *violin* and *vase* were in the *van*. The *vine* had many *vegetables*. Have children use their arms to make a *V* above their heads when they hear /v/ words. Continue with the following sentences for /z/: *Zip* went to the *zoo* to see the *zebra*. *Zane* has a *zero* on his *zipper*. *Zinnia* likes *zesty zucchini*. Tell children to take one finger and make a *Z* in the air when they hear /z/ words.

Objectives
• Isolate the initial sound in spoken one-syllable words.
• Identify the common sounds that letters represent.

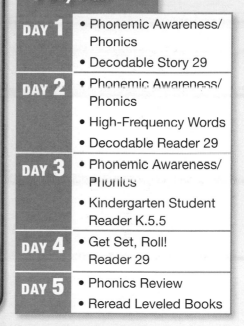

Pacing Small Group Instruction
20–30 mins.

5 Day Plan

DAY 1	• Phonemic Awareness/ Phonics • Decodable Story 29
DAY 2	• Phonemic Awareness/ Phonics • High-Frequency Words • Decodable Reader 29
DAY 3	• Phonemic Awareness/ Phonics • Kindergarten Student Reader K.5.5
DAY 4	• Get Set, Roll! Reader 29
DAY 5	• Phonics Review • Reread Leveled Books

OL On-Level — **DAY 2**

Phonemic Awareness•Phonics

■ **Make a *V* and *Z* Bulletin Board** Give children two pieces of construction paper to make a picture of something that starts with /v/ and something that starts with /z/. Have them cut out their pictures and attach them to a bulletin board. Label the bulletin board with an uppercase *V* and *Z*. Have children take turns naming their pictures, emphasizing /v/ as in /v/ /v/ /v/, *vase* or /z/ as in /z/ /z/ /z/, *zoo*.

■ **High-Frequency Words** Display the following word cards: *come, where, said, was, what.* Say the word *was* and select a child to point to the word. Have children say the word and use it in a sentence. Continue with the other words.

Objectives
• Read at least 25 high-frequency words from a commonly used list.

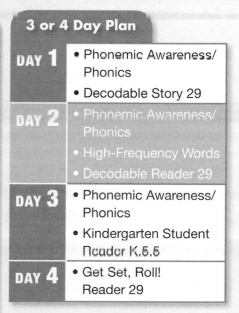

3 or 4 Day Plan

DAY 1	• Phonemic Awareness/ Phonics • Decodable Story 29
DAY 2	• Phonemic Awareness/ Phonics • High-Frequency Words • Decodable Reader 29
DAY 3	• Phonemic Awareness/ Phonics • Kindergarten Student Reader K.5.5
DAY 4	• Get Set, Roll! Reader 29

3 Day Plan: Eliminate the shaded box.

More Practice

For additional practice with this week's phonics skills, have children reread the Decodable Story (Day 1) and the Decodable Reader (Day 2).

OL On-Level

DAY 3

Phonemic Awareness•Phonics

■ **Be a Bee!** Show children how to buzz by saying *zzzz* like a bee. Tell children that you will say some words. If the words begin or end with /z/, they should buzz like a bee. Use these words: *zebra, real, fizz, vacuum, bag, fuzz, spider, zipper, zoo, very, bug.* What letter spells /z/?

■ **Be a Voter!** Explain to children that when we raise our hands to make a choice, we vote. Let's vote on words that begin or end with /v/. I will say a word. If you think the word begins or ends with /v/, raise your hand and vote. Use these words: *love, leaf, visit, trip, vest, hat, dove, wave, wish, van.* What letter spells /v/?

Kindergarten Student Reader K.5.5

Kindergarten Student Reader K.5.5

■ **Preview and Predict** Display the cover of the book. The title of this story is *The Big Jazz Band.* Look at the cover. What kinds of instruments are the children playing? What do you think will happen in this story?

■ **Set a Purpose** Review the list of things children think might happen in the story. Remind children they will read to find out about the jazz band.

■ **Read** Have children follow along as they read the story with you. After reading p. 2, ask children to tell what Jan and Dad are doing. Continue with each page. Ask the following questions:

  • Who do Jan and Dad pick up?

  • Where are they going?

  • How many people are in the jazz band?

■ **Summarize** Have children retell the story to a partner and tell who Jan tells about his trip to see the jazz band.

■ **Text to Self** Help children make personal connections to the story as they tell about a special trip they took.

Objectives
• Identify the common sounds that letters represent.
• Predict what might happen next based on the cover.
• Respond to questions about text.

Get Set, Roll! Reader 29

■ **Review** Review the high-frequency words *said, look, me, he, of, is, a, to,* and *the* by writing each word on the board and saying the word with children.

■ **Review Rebus Words** Write the word *vroom* on the board. This is the word *vroom*. Name the letters with me: *v, r, o, o, m, vroom.* Remember, there will be a picture above this word to help you read it.

■ **Read** Display Get Set, Roll! Reader 29, *Putt! Putt! Pop!* Today we will read a story about Izzy the ice cream truck. **Point to the title of the story.** *Putt! Putt! Pop!* is the title of the story. Look at the picture. What do you think will happen in this story? Let's read the story together.

Objectives
• Read at least 25 high-frequency words from a commonly used list.
• Predict what might happen next based on the cover.

Phonics Review

■ **Listen for /v/ and /z/** Give each child two blank cards. Have them write *Vv* on one card and *Zz* on the other card. I am going to say some words. If the word begins with /v/, raise your *Vv* card. If the word begins with /z/, raise your *Zz* card. Listen carefully: *Val zips.* Did you raise your *Vv* card for *Val?* Did you raise your *Zz* card for *zips?* **Continue with these sentences:** *Vans zoom; Vests zip; We vacuum the zoo.* Use these sentences for final /v/ and /z/: *Leave the bee to buzz; I will give a quiz.*

Objectives
• Identify the common sounds that letters represent.

More Reading

Use Leveled Readers or other text at children's instructional level to develop fluency.

Small Group Time

20–30 mins.

5 Day Plan

DAY 1	• Phonemic Awareness/ Phonics • Decodable Story 29
DAY 2	• Phonics • Spelling • Decodable Reader 29
DAY 3	• Independent Reader K.5.5 or Kindergarten Student Reader K.5.5
DAY 4	• Get Set, Roll! Reader 29 or Kindergarten Student Reader K.5.5
DAY 5	• Fluency/Comprehension • Independent Reader K.5.5

3 or 4 Day Plan

DAY 1	• Phonemic Awareness/ Phonics • Decodable Story 29
DAY 2	• Phonics • Spelling • Decodable Reader 29
DAY 3	• Independent Reader K.5.5 or Kindergarten Student Reader K.5.5
DAY 4	• Get Set, Roll! Reader 29 or Kindergarten Student Reader K.5.5

3 Day Plan: Eliminate the shaded box.

More Practice

For additional practice with this week's phonics skills, have children reread the Decodable Story (Day 1) and the Decodable Reader (Day 2).

A Advanced **DAY 1**

Phonemic Awareness•Phonics

■ **Design a Van** Divide children into groups of four. Give children construction paper, glue, and scissors. Tell children to make a van. Remind them to make the body of the van and the wheels and windows. Help children write the word *van* on their picture. What did you make? (a van) What sound does *van* begin with? Yes, *van* begins with /v/. Say it with me: /v/ /v/ /v/, *van*. Let's draw some pictures of things that begin with /v/ or /z/ on our vans.

Objectives
• Isolate the initial sound in spoken one-syllable words.

A Advanced **DAY 2**

Phonics•Spelling

■ **Connect /v/ to Vv and /z/ to Zz** Display the *Vv* Alphabet Card. What is the name of this letter? What is the sound for this letter? Can you make the letter *v* using your index and middle fingers? Repeat with the *Zz* Alphabet Card.

■ **Spell Sounds** Give each child the following letter tiles: *a, i, g, l, n, p, v, z.* Listen to the sounds in the word *zip*: /z/ /i/ /p/, *zip*. What is the letter for /z/? It is *z*. Place your *z* tile in front of you. Continue with the remaining sounds.

Let's blend the sounds to read the word: /z/ /i/ /p/, *zip.* Continue the routine with the words *van, Val,* and *zag.*

Objectives
• Identify the common sounds that letters represent.
• Use letter-sound correspondences to spell consonant-vowel-consonant (CVC) words.

A Advanced

DAY **3**

More Reading

Use Leveled Readers or other text at children's instructional level.

For a complete lesson plan and additional practice, see the **Leveled Reader Teaching Guide**.

Independent Reader K.5.5

- **Practice High-Frequency Words** Write *where* on the board. Have volunteers say the word and use it in a sentence. Continue with the word *come*.

- **Activate Prior Knowledge** Remind children that a cab and a bus are both ways people can use to get from place to place. Encourage children to share their experiences riding in a cab or a bus.

- **Main Idea** Display the cover of *Get on the Bus!* Have children use the title and what happens in the story to tell the most important idea.

Independent Reader K.5.5

- **Reread for Fluency** After rereading with children, model reading fluently for them. I am going to read this book aloud. I will read the words with no mistakes. I want you to read it aloud with me. Try to read the words just as I do.

Use echo reading of Independent Reader K.5.5 to model reading fluently. Use your oral reading to model for children where to pause, when to change pitch, and which words to stress. Then have children reread orally three to four times, or until they can read with few or no mistakes.

- For more practice with phonics and high-frequency words and to develop fluency, have children read Kindergarten Student Reader K.5.5. Use the instruction on pp. 464–465.

Objectives
- Read at least 25 high-frequency words from a commonly used list.

Small Group Time

More Reading

Use Leveled Readers or other text at children's instructional level.

A Advanced **DAY 4**

Kindergarten Student Reader K.5.5

■ **Revisit** Display the cover of Kindergarten Student Reader K.5.5. This is a band. What is band? Tell me what you know about a band. Why do people go watch and listen to bands?

■ **Reread** Use Kindergarten Student Reader K.5.5 to practice reading fluently.

■ **Text to World** Ask children to think about music. What are different kinds of music? What do you think jazz music sounds like? What kind of music is your favorite?

■ **Read** Have children read Get Set, Roll! Reader 29, *Putt! Putt! Pop!* Use the instruction on p. 491.

Kindergarten Student Reader K.5.5

Objectives
• Read at least 25 high-frequency words from a commonly used list
• Predict what might happen next based on the illustrations.

A Advanced **DAY 5**

Fluency•Comprehension

■ **Reread for Fluency** Use the Independent Reader K.5.5 to model reading fluently for children. I am going to read this selection aloud. I will read the words with no mistakes. I want you to read it aloud with me. Try to read the words just as I do.

■ **Comprehension** After children have finished reading, have them retell what happens in the selection. Then have children draw a picture of what this selection is all about.

Independent Reader K.5.5

Objectives
• Read at least 25 high-frequency words from a commonly used list.

Concept Development

■ **Read the Concept Literacy Reader** Read *We Travel* with children. Begin by reading the title and author's name. Have children describe what they see on the cover. Then have children look at the pictures in the book. What do you see? What are the people doing? Where are the people? Read the book aloud, pausing to discuss each page. Model sentence patterns and vocabulary that describe the pictures. This is a car. People go from place to place in a car. A car can carry a small load. On a second reading, invite children to talk about the different ways people travel around the world.

■ **Develop Oral Language** Revisit *We Travel,* review the different ways that people travel. Then have children recite the following chant with you based on ways people travel:

> Up the hill and down we go,
> Skiing in the powdery snow!
> Giddy up, horse! Away we go.
> While in the boat we row, row, row.

Phonemic Awareness/Phonics

■ **Frontload Words with /v/ and /z/** Have children look at the illustration on pp. 92–93 of *My Skills Buddy.* This picture shows people and animals at a zoo. What can you do at a zoo? What can you see at a zoo? Listen to the word *zoo.* What sound does *zoo* begin with? *Zoo* begins with /z/; *zoo.* Then use this routine to introduce picture words beginning with /z/: I'm at the zoo and so are you. *Zebra, zebra, zebra* starts like *zoo.* Who can find the zebra? (Pause for an answer.) (Child's name) can find the zebra. (Have children point to the zebra in the picture.) *Zebra* begins with /z/ /z/ /z/. What does *zebra* begin with? Repeat the routine with other words in the picture that begin with /z/, including *zoom* and *zucchini.* Then repeat the chanting exercise to locate things that begin with /v/, such as *van, vest, violin, vegetable, variety,* and *vet.*

■ **Connect /v/ to *Vv* and /z/ to *Zz*** Display the words *van* and *zip.* This word is *van:* /v/ /a/ /n/, *van.* Say the word with me. Have children write *van* and circle the letter that makes /v/. Repeat with the word *zip.* Write and read aloud this sentence: *Zeke's very nice van zips to the zoo.* Point to *z* in *zips* and ask: What letter is this? Yes, this is *z.* Continue with *z* in *Zeke* and *zoo* and *v* in *very* and *van.*

Content Objective
• Develop content knowledge related to ways people travel.

Language Objectives
• Understand and use grade-level content area vocabulary.

• Recognize the sounds of English.

Concept Literacy Reader K.5.5

Daily Planner	
DAY 1	• Concept Development • Phonemic Awareness/ Phonics • Listening Comprehension
DAY 2	• Comprehension • Vocabulary
DAY 3	• Phonemic Awareness/ Phonics • Conventions
DAY 4	• Phonemic Awareness/ Phonics • Concepts and Oral Language
DAY 5	• Language Workshop • Writing

Content Objective
- Understand main idea

Language Objective
- Learn and use academic vocabulary.

My Skills Buddy, pp.94–95

Listening Comprehension: Main Idea

■ **Frontload Vocabulary** Discuss the illustrations on pp. 94–95 in *My Skills Buddy* to frontload vocabulary. What do you see in the pictures? (people going to school) Think about the pictures. Who is on the bus? (children) What things are children carrying? (backpacks) What things are people using to get to school? (bicycle, car, bus, feet)

■ **Provide Scaffolding** Look at the illustrations on pp. 94–95. Explain what is happening in the spread. Help children understand that people are going to the school in different ways. A child rides a bike, people walk, people drive a car, and some children ride on the bus.

■ **Prepare for the Read Aloud** The modified Read Aloud below prepares children for listening to the oral reading "Traveling in London" on p. 435.

Read Aloud

Traveling in London

London is a huge city. It is in England.

People in London travel in different ways. Some drive cars. Some take cabs. Many take the bus. They have double-decker buses. You climb up stairs to get on top. These buses are bright red.

London has a subway. Subways are trains. They go underground. People take stairs from the street to the subway. You buy a ticket and get on the train. There are maps to help you.

■ **First Listening** Write the title of the Read Aloud on the board. This is about ways people travel in London. Listen to find out how people travel in London. After reading, ask children to recall ways people travel in London. What are the buses called? What are these buses like? How do you get to the subway?

■ **Second Listening** Write the words *Main Idea* on the board. As you listen to the story, think about what the story is about. What do you learn from the story? After reading, help children discover the main idea of the story, or what the story is telling them.

Objectives
• Understand the main points of spoken language ranging from situations in which contexts are familiar to unfamiliar. • Understand implicit ideas in increasingly complex spoken language commensurate with grade-level learning expectations.

ELL English Language Learners

Comprehension

■ **Provide Scaffolding** Display *On the Move!* Lead a detailed picture walk through the story, naming what you see in the illustrations and describing what is happening. Use gestures and facial expressions to convey meaning. Focus on the following:

- **Set the Scene** Introduce the concepts in the Big Book by asking questions about travel. Some people use skis to travel. Where do you think people ski? Why would someone use skis instead of a car? Have children use their prior knowledge to discuss different ways people around the world travel. Use the cover of the Big Book to help them understand that this story is about ways people travel in the world.

- **Frontload Vocabulary** Use the illustrations to introduce unfamiliar words in the text. Look at this picture on page 12. This man has a llama. The llama carries things. Why would the man use a llama instead of a bicycle? These nouns can be included: *dogsled* (p. 13); *swamp, airboat* (p. 16); *helmet* (p. 19); *water, land, air* (p. 21).

Vocabulary: Compound Words

■ **Frontload Vocabulary** Have children turn to pp. 108–109 of *My Skills Buddy.* Talk about each picture, using the compound words *dogsled, raincoat,* and *mailbox.* Point to the photo of the dogsled. This is a dogsled. A dogsled pulls a load and a rider in the snow. *Dogsled* is made of two words. Point to the illustration on p. 108. Explain that *dog* and *sled* make *dogsled*, a compound word. Then use the pictures to explain how *raincoat* and *mailbox* are created.

■ **Provide Scaffolding** Write the words *dogsled, raincoat,* and *mailbox* on the board and on large cards. Read the words aloud. These words are compound words. Compound words are made up of two smaller words. Hold up the card with the word *dogsled.* What two words make up *dogsled?* Invite children to tell who might use a dogsled. Then say a sentence using the word and have children repeat the sentence: The man in Alaska rides a dogsled. Repeat with the other compound words.

■ **Practice** On the board, create a list of compound words. On note cards, write one part of each compound word listed. Mix the cards face up on a table. Read each compound word aloud as pairs find the parts of each compound. Have children say a sentence using each word.

Objectives

- Speak using learning strategies. • Use accessible language and learn new language in the process.
- Demonstrate listening comprehension of increasingly complex spoken English by collaborating with peers commensurate with content and grade-level needs.

Content Objective

- Develop background knowledge.

Language Objective

- Learn and use compound words.

Use Learning Strategies

Remind children that if they have trouble using compound words, they can consult a calendar or ask their partner for help.

Big Book

English Opportunity

Have children choose a compound word and have them illustrate it. To reinforce concept attainment, have children share the illustration with a partner by describing it in as much detail as possible.

Support for English Language Learners

Content Objective
- Use learning strategies.

Language Objectives
- Connect /v/ with *Vv* and /z/ with *Zz*.
- Use nouns in sentences.

🧩 Transfer Skills

Pronouncing /z/ In languages such as Cantonese, Portuguese, and Spanish, speakers pronounce *z* similarly to *s*. Help children understand that when they pronounce /z/, they should hear their voice, and when they pronounce /s/, they should not. Have children repeat the words *sip, zip, bus,* and *buzz* after you.

Use Learning Strategies

Help children understand that nouns name a person, place, or thing. On the board, write a list of nouns and verbs. Point to a word and ask children whether the word names a person, a place, or a thing. If the word names none of these, help students see that the word names an action and is a verb.

Phonemic Awareness/Phonics

- **Isolate Final /v/ and /z/** Introduce final /v/ and /z/. Say sentences, such as: *I gave you the pencil.* Explain that *gave* has /v/ at the end. Then say the word *jazz.* Explain that *jazz* ends with /z/. Say other words that have final /v/ and /z/, including *love, have, live, buzz, fizz,* and *fuzz.*

- **/v/ Spelled Vv and /z/ Spelled Zz** Write the word *jazz.* Point to the sounds as you segment and blend them: /j/ /a/ /z/, *jazz.* Repeat the process with the name *Bev.* Repeat the process with the words *fuzz* and *rev.*

Conventions: Nouns in Sentences

- **Provide Scaffolding** Point to the image on pp. 2–3 of *On the Move!* The girl is thinking of ways to travel. Write *girl* on the board. *The girl* is what the sentence is about. *Girl* names a person. It is a noun. Have children look for other people, places, or things in the picture and name them. Write their nouns on the board. The word *taxi* is a noun. *Taxi* names a thing.

- **Practice** What are some other nouns in this story? Page through the Big Book and have children name different naming words they see for people, places, and things. Make a list of these words on the board. Have children say sentences using the nouns they find in the pictures.

Beginning/Intermediate For each noun, have a child tell something about the word. Have the class repeat each sentence.

Advanced/Advanced-High Have students look through the illustrations in the Big Book and name nouns and verbs. While you create a list on the board, have children say a sentence that tells what type of word they have found. For example, using the photograph on pp. 6–7, a child may say the sentence *The plane flies over the city.* Plane *names a thing.*

Objectives
- Internalize new academic language by using and reusing it in meaningful ways in speaking activities that build concept and language attainment. • Develop repertoire of learning strategies commensurate with grade-level learning expectations. • Decode (sound out) words using a combination of skills.

Phonemic Awareness/Phonics

■ **Review Initial and Medial /u/** To review /u/ in words, begin by asking the following questions: Can Russ have a mug? Can Bud jump up on a bus? As children answer, have them emphasize words that begin with initial or medial /u/: *Russ, mug, Bud, jump, up, bus.* Then compare words such as *dug* and *rug.* Help children notice the same sounds (/u/ and /g/) and different sounds (/d/ and /r/).

■ **/u/ Spelled *Uu*** Write the words *up, sun, slug, under, must, gum, run, us,* and *plum.* Have children read each word as you run your hand under it. Have children point out the initial and final /u/. Check each child's progress. Monitor pronunciation for clarity but not for perfection.

Concepts and Oral Language

■ **Revisit Talk with Me Chart 29A** Display the chart. Have children describe each image on the page. Help them by describing different ways people travel.

■ **Develop Oral Language** Introduce language patterns that help describe the pictures on Talk with Me Chart 29A. Write this sentence frame on the board: *The dogsled is ____.* Let's use this sentence pattern to talk about the dogsled: *The dogsled is fast. The dogsled is in the snow.* Have children suggest other sentences using the frame. Then add this sentence frame: *The dogsled ____.* Now let's use this sentence pattern to talk about the dogsled: *The dogsled carries the man. The dogsled slides in snow.* Have children suggest other sentences using the sentence frame. Then continue the exercise to describe the other pictures on the chart.

Leveled LS Support

Beginning Have children repeat the sentences that other children make up. Let them take a turn pointing to a picture on the chart.

Intermediate Ask questions to help children notice more details about the pictures, such as: Where is the train going? What is the train carrying?

Advanced/Advanced-High Encourage children to use their prior knowledge about travel to think of other descriptive words.

Content Objectives
- Develop oral language.
- Use learning strategies.

Language Objectives
- Connect /u/ with *Uu*.
- Learn English language patterns.

Use Learning Strategies
With children, brainstorm some sentences using nouns from the Talk with Me Chart. Work with children to create a list of nouns that name people, places, or things in the pictures in the chart.

Talk with Me Chart 29A

Objectives
- Use strategic learning techniques to acquire basic vocabulary. • Speak using a variety of grammatical structures with increasing accuracy and ease as more English is acquired. • Speak using grade-level content area vocabulary in context to internalize new English words.

On the Move!   DI•84

Support for English Language Learners

Content Objectives
- Understand *On the Move!*
- Practice main idea.

Language Objectives
- Retell a selection through speaking and writing.
- Write using grade-level vocabulary.

Monitor and Self-Correct
Remind children that if they don't know how to say a word, they can ask partners for help.

Home Language Support
Invite children to share ideas in their home languages before creating their drawings and sentences.

Language Workshop: Retell *On the Move!*

■ **Introduce and Model** Turn to p. 11 of *On the Move!* Look at the man in this picture. Do you remember what he is doing? What is he traveling in? Act out the man's motions as you say: *He is paddling. His boat is called a kayak. It is small and fast.* I am acting out what the man does. I am also telling what he does. Let's act out and tell about other ways people travel.

■ **Practice** Organize children into pairs. Assign each pair two pages from *On the Move!* Explain that one child will act out some aspect of the picture. The other child will narrate, or tell about, what his or her partner is doing. Have children retell and summarize the directions you have just given them to make sure they understand what they are expected to do. Then review the actions on each page, and allow time for pairs to plan what they will do and say. Then have pairs take turns acting out and narrating their pages in the order of the book.

Writing: Write About *On the Move!*

■ **Prepare for Writing** We talked about ways people travel. We also acted out ways people travel. Now let's write about ways people around the world travel. Have each child fold a piece of paper in half to create two sections.

■ **Create Sentences About Travel** Assign a 2-page spread from *On the Move!* to each child. Have children copy the sentence starter *People use _____ to travel.* in both sections of their paper. Have children explore the main ideas of their pages by drawing the activities. Then ask children to write or dictate the mode of transportation to complete the sentence frames. When children are finished, have them share their sentences and drawings with a partner.

Leveled LS Support **Beginning** Write the sentence frames for children and have them write or dictate words to complete the sentences.

Intermediate Guide children in copying the sentence frames and writing words to complete the sentences.

Advanced/Advanced-High Encourage children to write their sentences on their own. You might also have children help less-proficient partners complete their sentences.

Objectives
• Understand the main points of spoken language ranging from situations in which contexts are familiar to unfamiliar. • Expand and internalize initial English vocabulary by retelling simple stories and basic information represented or supported by pictures.

This Week's ELL Overview

ELL Handbook

- Maximize Literacy and Cognitive Engagement
- Research Into Practice
- Full Weekly Support for Every Selection

  ### This Is the Way We Go to School
  - Routines to Support Instruction

- Transfer Activities
- Professional Development

Daily Leveled ELL Notes

ELL notes appear throughout this week's instruction and ELL Support is on the DI pages of your Teacher's Edition. The following is a sample of an ELL note from this week.

English Language Learners

Beginning Support Phonemic Awareness Have children say *quack, quick, quit, yell, yet,* and *yak* to practice /y/ and /kw/ sounds. Then have them think of silly phrases using the words, such as *ducks quack quick* or *yaks will yell.*

Intermediate Vocabulary Development Walk children through *The Quiz.* Have them find the *yak* and the *quiz* in the story. Display a word card for each of these words and have a child match each card with an appropriate picture.

Advanced Frontload Story Take children on a picture walk through the story to heighten interest and draw attention to the modes of transportation. Point out the various cultures illustrated in the book. Guide class discussion of these cultures, encouraging children with a similar cultural background to share their knowledge and experience.

Advanced High Support Retelling Guide children in retelling the stories by providing copies of Decodable Story 30, Decodable Reader 30, and Kindergarten Student Reader K.5.6. Encourage children to use the pictures in these stories to aid in their retelling.

ELL by Strand

The ELL lessons on this week's Support for English Language Learners pages are organized by strand. They offer additional scaffolding for the core curriculum. Leveled support notes on these pages address the different proficiency levels in your class. See pages DI•97–DI•102.

ELL Guy
Dr. Jim Cummins

———— The Three Pillars of ELL Instruction ————

ELL Strands	Activate Prior Knowledge	Access Content	Extend Language
Vocabulary p. DI•99	Frontload Vocabulary	Provide Scaffolding	Practice
Reading Comprehension p. DI•99	Provide Scaffolding	Set the Scene	Frontload Vocabulary
Phonics, Spelling, and Word Analysis pp. DI•97, DI•100–DI•101	Frontload Words with /y/ and /kw/	Isolate Initial /y/ and /kw/	Review Initial /v/ and /z/
Listening Comprehension p. DI•98	Prepare for the Read Aloud	First Listening	Second Listening
Conventions and Writing pp. DI•100, DI•102	Provide Scaffolding/ Introduce and Model	Practice	Leveled Practice Activities/ Leveled Writing Activities
Concept Development p. DI•97	Read the Concept Literacy Reader	Read the Concept Literacy Reader	Develop Oral Language

This Week's Practice Stations Overview

Six Weekly Practice Stations with Leveled Activities can be found at the beginning of each week of instruction. For this week's Practice Stations, see pp. 520–521.

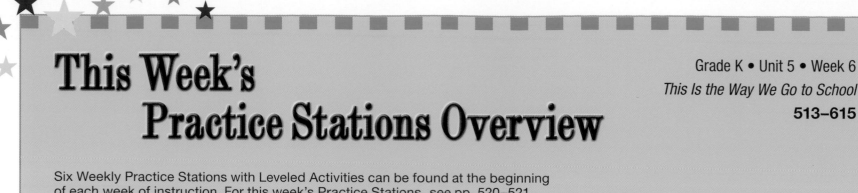

Small Group

Teacher-led

Classroom Management Handbook for Differentiated Instruction Practice Stations

Practice Stations

Daily Leveled Center Activities

⬤ Below   ▢ Advanced

△ On-Level   Ⓔ Ⓛ Ⓛ

Practice Stations Flip Charts

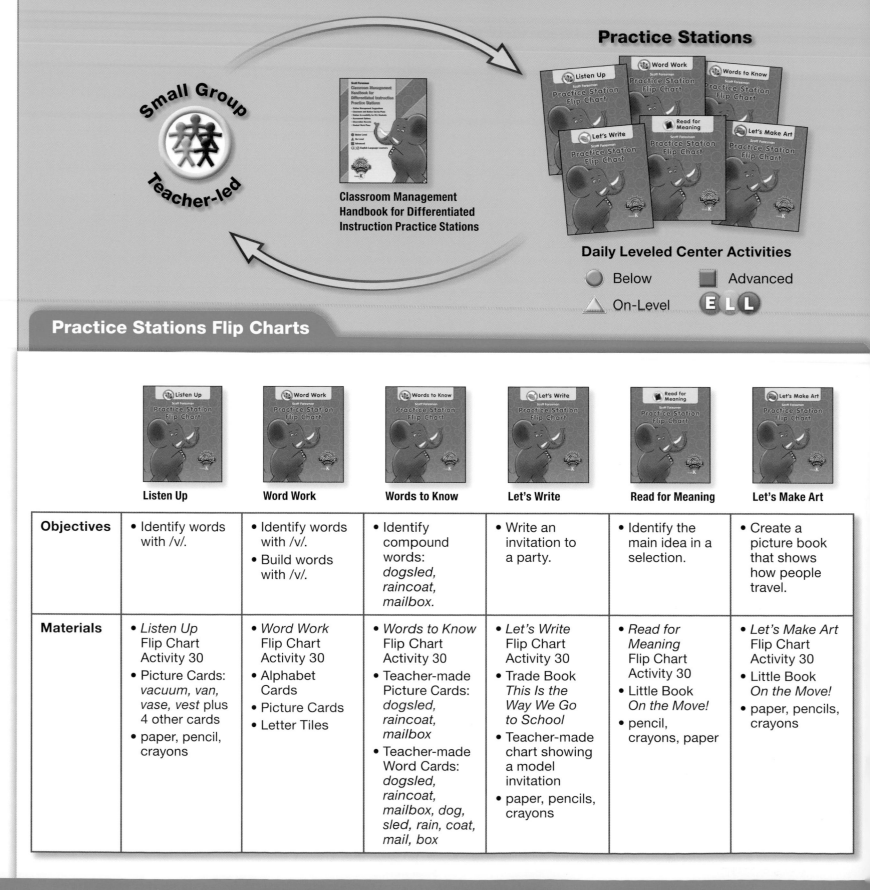

	Listen Up	Word Work	Words to Know	Let's Write	Read for Meaning	Let's Make Art
Objectives	• Identify words with /v/.	• Identify words with /v/. • Build words with /v/.	• Identify compound words: *dogsled, raincoat, mailbox.*	• Write an invitation to a party.	• Identify the main idea in a selection.	• Create a picture book that shows how people travel.
Materials	• *Listen Up* Flip Chart Activity 30 • Picture Cards: *vacuum, van, vase, vest* plus 4 other cards • paper, pencil, crayons	• *Word Work* Flip Chart Activity 30 • Alphabet Cards • Picture Cards • Letter Tiles	• *Words to Know* Flip Chart Activity 30 • Teacher-made Picture Cards: *dogsled, raincoat, mailbox* • Teacher-made Word Cards: *dogsled, raincoat, mailbox, dog, sled, rain, coat, mail, box*	• *Let's Write* Flip Chart Activity 30 • Trade Book *This Is the Way We Go to School* • Teacher-made chart showing a model invitation • paper, pencils, crayons	• *Read for Meaning* Flip Chart Activity 30 • Little Book *On the Move!* • pencil, crayons, paper	• *Let's Make Art* Flip Chart Activity 30 • Little Book *On the Move!* • paper, pencils, crayons

This Week on Reading Street!

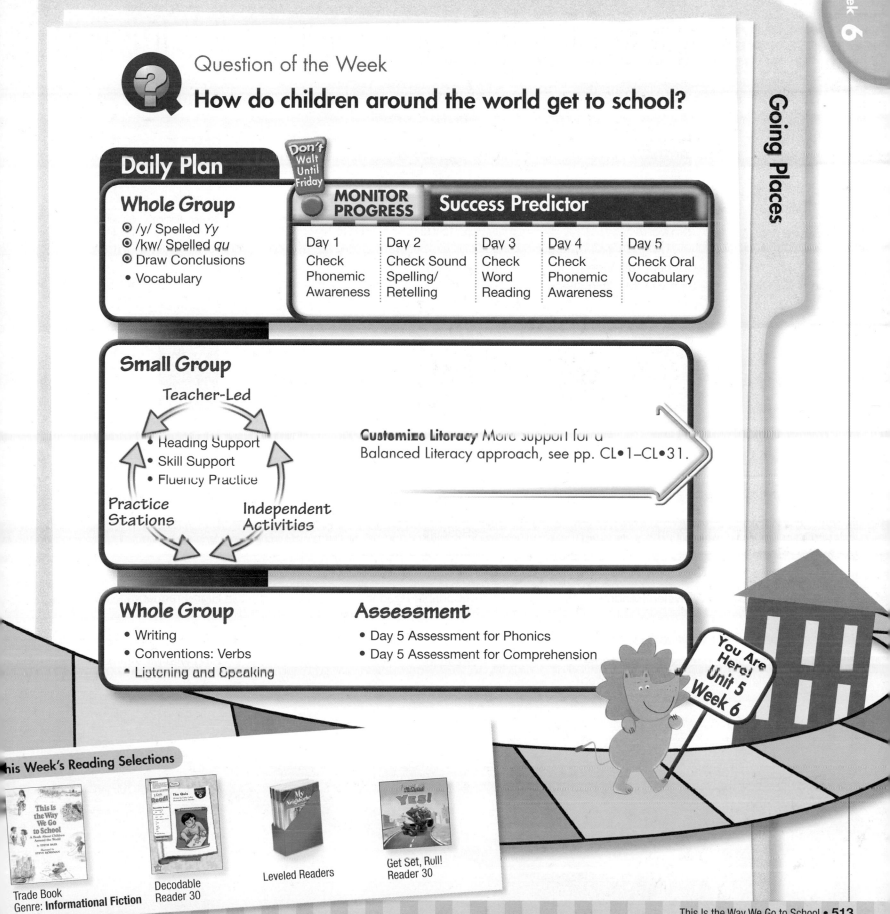

Question of the Week

How do children around the world get to school?

Daily Plan

Don't Wait Until Friday

Whole Group

- ◉ /y/ Spelled *Yy*
- ◉ /kw/ Spelled *qu*
- ◉ Draw Conclusions
- • Vocabulary

MONITOR PROGRESS **Success Predictor**

Day 1	Day 2	Day 3	Day 4	Day 5
Check Phonemic Awareness	Check Sound Spelling/ Retelling	Check Word Reading	Check Phonemic Awareness	Check Oral Vocabulary

Small Group

Teacher-Led

- • Reading Support
- • Skill Support
- • Fluency Practice

Practice Stations

Independent Activities

Customize Literacy More support for a Balanced Literacy approach, see pp. CL•1–CL•31.

Whole Group

- • Writing
- • Conventions: Verbs
- • Listening and Speaking

Assessment

- • Day 5 Assessment for Phonics
- • Day 5 Assessment for Comprehension

You Are Here! Unit 5 Week 6

This Week's Reading Selections

This Is the Way We Go to School

Trade Book Genre: **Informational Fiction**

Decodable Reader 30

Leveled Readers

Get Set, Roll! Reader 30

Resources on Reading Street!

	Build Concepts	Phonemic Awareness and Phonics	Vocabulary
Whole Group	Talk With Me/ Sing With Me	Student Edition pp. 112–113 Student Edition p. 116	Student Edition p. 117 Student Edition p. 128
Go Digital	• Concept Talk Video • Sing with Me Animations	• eReaders	
Small Group and Independent Practice	Practice Station Flip Chart Leveled Readers	Practice Station Flip Chart Decodable Reader 30 Leveled Readers Get Set, Roll! Reader 30	Practice Station Flip Chart Student Edition p. 117
Go Digital	• eReaders	• eReaders • Letter Tile Drag and Drop	
Customize Literacy	• Leveled Readers	• Decodable Reader	• High-Frequency Word Cards
Go Digital	• Concept Talk Video • Big Question Video • eReaders	• eReaders	• Sing with Me Animations

How do children around the world get to school?

Comprehension

Student Edition pp. 114–115

Trade Book

* Envision It! Animations

Practice Station Flip Chart

Leveled Readers

Get Set, Roll! Reader 30

* Envision It! Animations
* eReaders

* Leveled Readers

* Envision It! Animations
* eLeaders

Fluency

Decodable Reader 30

Kdg. Student Reader K.5.6

Get Set, Roll! Reader 30

* eReaders

Practice Station Flip Chart

Leveled Readers

* eReaders

* Leveled Readers

* eReaders

Conventions and Writing

Reader's and Writer's Notebook

* Grammar Jammer

Practice Station Flip Chart

Reader's and Writer's Notebook

* Grammar Jammer

* *Reader's and Writer's Notebook*

* Grammar Jammer

You Are Here! Unit 5 Week 6

My 5-Day Planner for Reading Street!

	Check Phonemic Awareness **Day 1** pages 522–537	Check Sound Spelling Check Retelling **Day 2** pages 538–555
Get Ready to Read	**Concept Talk,** 522 **Oral Vocabulary,** 523 *cable car, trolley, horse-and-buggy, skis, Metro line, vaporetto* **Phonemic Awareness,** 524–525 ⊙ Initial /y/ and /kw/ **Phonics,** 526–527 ⊙ /y/ Spelled *Yy*, /kw/ Spelled *Qu* **Handwriting,** 528 Letters *Y, y, Q* and *q* **High-Frequency Words,** 529 *where, come* **READ Decodable Story 30,** 530–531	**Concept Talk,** 538 **Oral Vocabulary,** 539 *cable car, trolley* **Phonemic Awareness,** 540–541 ⊙ Initial /y/ and /kw/ **Phonics,** 542–543 ⊙ /y/ Spelled *Yy*, /kw/ Spelled *Qu* **Handwriting,** 544 Words with *Yy* and *Qu* **High-Frequency Words,** 545 *where, come* **READ Decodable Reader 30,** 546–547
Read and Comprehend	**Listening Comprehension,** 532–533 ⊙ Draw Conclusions	**Listening Comprehension,** 548 ⊙ Draw Conclusions **READ Trade Book—First Read,** 548 *This Is the Way We Go to School* **Retell,** 549 **Think, Talk, and Write,** 550
Language Arts	**Conventions,** 534 Verbs **Writing,** 535 Writing Process: Plan a How-to Report **Listening and Speaking,** 536 Discuss Literary Features—Plot **Wrap Up Your Day,** 536 **Extend Your Day!,** 537	**Conventions,** 551 Verbs **Writing,** 552 Writing Process: Plan a How-to Report **Vocabulary,** 553 Action Words **Wrap Up Your Day,** 554 **Extend Your Day!,** 555

You Are Here! Unit 5 Week 6

How do children around the world get to school?

Check Word Reading	Check Phonemic Awareness	Check Oral Vocabulary
Day 3 pages 556–589	**Day 4** pages 590–601	**Day 5** pages 602–615
Concept Talk, 556 **Oral Vocabulary**, 557 *horse-and-buggy, skis* **Phonemic Awareness**, 558–559 ◉ Initial /y/ and /kw/ **Phonics**, 560–561 ◉ /y/ Spelled *Yy*, /kw/ Spelled *Qu* **READ Kindergarten Student Reader K.5.6**, 562–563	**Concept Talk**, 590 **Oral Vocabulary**, 591 *Metro line, vaporetto* **Review Phonemic Awareness**, 592 /v/ and /z/ **Review Phonics**, 593 /v/ Spelled *Vv*, /z/ Spelled *Zz* **Spelling**, 594 ◉ /y/ Spelled *Yy*, /kw/ Spelled *Qu* **READ Get Set, Roll! Reader 30**, 595	**Concept Wrap Up**, 602 **Oral Vocabulary**, 603 *cable car, trolley, horse-and-buggy, skis, Metro line, vaporetto* **Review Phonemic Awareness**, 604 ◉ /y/ and /kw/ **Review Phonics**, 605 ◉ /y/ Spelled *Yy*, /kw/ Spelled *Qu* **Assessment**, 606–607 Monitor Progress
Comprehension, 564–565 ◉ Draw Conclusions **READ Trade Book—Second Read**, 566–583 *This Is the Way We Go to School*	**Comprehension**, 596 ◉ Draw Conclusions **Review** Main Idea **READ Trade Book—Third Read**, 597 *This Is the Way We Go to School*	**Let's Practice It!**, 608–609 Fairy Tale **Assessment**, 610–611 Monitor Progress
Conventions, 584 Nouns in Sentences **Writing**, 585 Writing Process: Draft a How-to Report **Listening and Speaking**, 586–587 Discuss Literary Features—Plot **Wrap Up Your Day**, 588 **Extend Your Day!**, 589	**Conventions**, 598 Verbs **Writing**, 599 Writing Process: Revise a How-to Report **Vocabulary**, 600 Action Words **Wrap Up Your Day**, 600 **Extend Your Day!**, 601	**Review Conventions**, 612 Verbs **Writing**, 613 Writing Process: Edit and Share a How-to Report **Wrap Up Your Week!**, 614 How do children around the world get to school? **Extend Your Day!**, 615

Week 6

Grouping Options for Differentiated Instruction
Turn the page for the small group time lesson plan.

Planning Small Group Time on Reading Street!

SMALL GROUP TIME RESOURCES

DAY 1

Look for this Small Group Time box each day to help meet the individual needs of all your children. Differentiated instruction lessons appear on the DI pages at the end of each week.

Teacher-Led

SI Strategic Intervention	**OL** On-Level	**A** Advanced
Teacher-Led • Phonemic Awareness and Phonics **Reread** Decodable Story	**Teacher-Led** • Phonemic Awareness and Phonics **Reread** Decodable Story	**Teacher-Led** • Phonemic Awareness and Phonics **Reread** Decodable Story for Fluency

ELL Place English language learners in the groups that correspond to their reading abilities in English.

Practice Stations
- Listen Up
- Word Work

Independent Activities
- Read Independently
- *Reader's and Writer's Notebook*
- Concept Talk Video

ELL

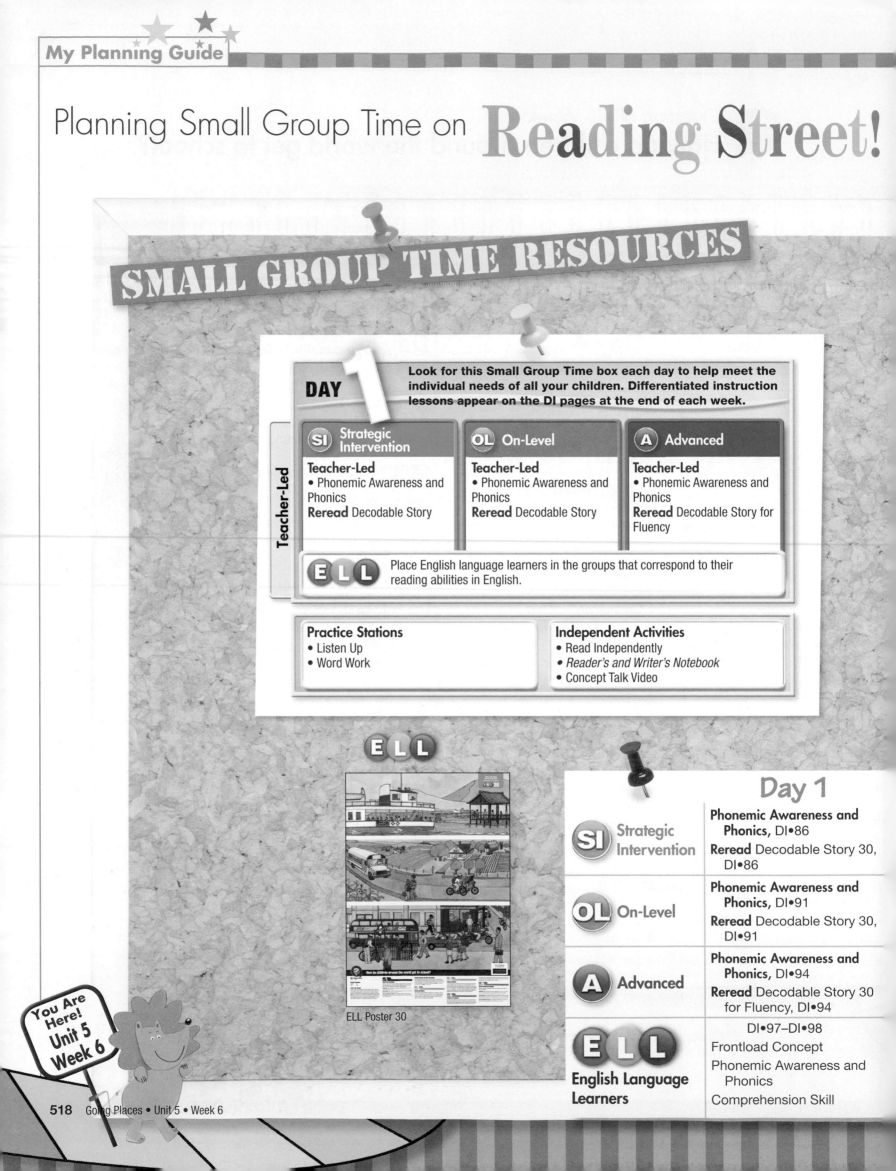

ELL Poster 30

Day 1

SI Strategic Intervention	**Phonemic Awareness and Phonics,** DI•86 **Reread** Decodable Story 30, DI•86	
OL On-Level	**Phonemic Awareness and Phonics,** DI•91 **Reread** Decodable Story 30, DI•91	
A Advanced	**Phonemic Awareness and Phonics,** DI•94 **Reread** Decodable Story 30 for Fluency, DI•94	
ELL English Language Learners	DI•97–DI•98 Frontload Concept Phonemic Awareness and Phonics Comprehension Skill	

You Are Here! Unit 5 Week 6

Reading Street Response to Intervention Kit

Reading Street Leveled Practice Stations Kit

How do children around the world get to school?

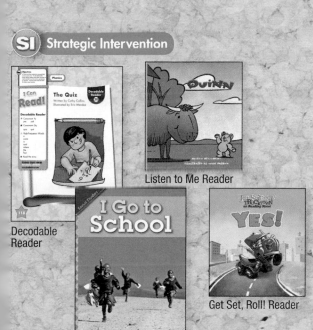

SI Strategic Intervention

Decodable Reader

Listen to Me Reader

I Go to School
Concept Literacy Reader

Get Set, Roll! Reader

OL On-Level

Kindergarten Student Reader

Decodable Reader

Get Set, Roll! Reader

A Advanced

Independent Reader

Decodable Reader

Week 6

Small Group Weekly Plan

Day 2	Day 3	Day 4	Day 5
Phonemic Awareness and Phonics, DI•87 **Reread** Decodable Reader 30, DI•87	**Phonemic Awareness and Phonics,** DI•88 **Read** Concept Literacy Reader K.5.6, DI•88	**Phonemic Awareness and Phonics,** DI•89 **Read** Get Set, Roll! Reader 30, DI•89	**Phonics Review,** DI•90 **Read** Listen to Me Reader K.5.6, DI•90
Phonemic Awareness and Phonics, DI•91 **Reread** Decodable Reader 30, DI•91	**Phonemic Awareness and Phonics,** DI•92 **Read** Kindergarten Student Reader K.5.6, DI•92	**Review Phonics and High-Frequency Words** **Read** Get Set, Roll! Reader 30, DI•93	**Phonics Review,** DI•93 **Reread** Leveled Books, DI•93
Phonics and Spelling, DI•94 **Reread** Decodable Reader 30, DI•94	**Read** Independent Reader K.5.6 or Kindergarten Student Reader K.5.6, DI•95	**Read** Get Set, Roll! Reader 30, or **Reread** Kindergarten Student Reader K.5.6, DI•96	**Fluency and Comprehension,** DI•96 **Reread** Independent Reader for Fluency, DI•96
DI•99 Comprehension Skill Frontload Vocabulary	DI•100 Review Phonemic Awareness and Phonics Scaffold Conventions	DI•101 Review Phonemic Awareness and Phonics Revisit Concept and Oral Language	DI•102 Language Workshop Writing

Practice Stations for Everyone on Reading Street!

Listen Up!
Words with /v/

Objectives
• Identify words with /v/.

Materials
• *Listen Up!* Flip Chart Activity 30
• Picture Cards: *vacuum, van, vase, vest* plus 4 other cards
• paper, pencil, crayons

Differentiated Activities

⬤ Find the Picture Card for *vase*. Say the sound you hear at the beginning. Find a Picture Card that has the same sound you hear at the beginning of *vase*.

▲ Find the Picture Card for *vase*. Say the sound you hear at the beginning. Find all the Picture Cards that have the same sound you hear at the beginning of *vase*.

■ Find the Picture Card for *vase*. Say the sound you hear at the beginning. Find other Picture Cards that begin with the sound /v/. Draw pictures to show other things that begin with /v/.

Word Work
/v/ Spelled *Vv*

Objectives
• Identify words with /v/.
• Build words with /v/.

Materials
• *Word Work* Flip Chart Activity 30
• Alphabet Cards
• Picture Cards: *vacuum, van, vase, vest,* plus 4 other cards
• Letter Tiles

Differentiated Activities

⬤ Find the Alphabet Card for the letter *Vv*. Look for Picture Cards with the beginning sound of /v/

▲ Find the Alphabet Card for the letter *Vv*. Find Picture Cards with the beginning sound of /v/. Look around the room. Find other objects that have the /v/ sound at the beginning.

■ Find the Alphabet Card for the letter *Vv*. Find Picture Cards with the beginning sound of /v/. Look around the room. Find other objects that have the /v/ sound at the beginning. Use the Letter Tiles to spell other words that begin with the sound /v/.

Technology
• Letter Tile Drop and Drag

Words To Know
Compound Words

Objectives
• Identify and compound words: dogsled, raincoat, mailbox

Materials
• *Words to Know* Flip Chart Activity 30
• Teacher-made picture cards: *dogsled, raincoat,* and a *mailbox*
• Teacher-made word cards: *dogsled, raincoat, mailbox, dog, sled, rain, coat, mail, box*

Differentiated Activities

⬤ Find a Picture Card that shows a dogsled. Say the two shorter words that make the word *dogsled*. Find a Picture Card that shows a raincoat. Say the two shorter words that make the word *raincoat*. Find a Picture Card that shows a mailbox. Say the two shorter words that make the word *mailbox*.

▲ Find a Picture Card that shows a dogsled. Find the two shorter Word Cards that make the word *dogsled*. Find the Picture Cards for raincoat and mailbox. Find the Word Cards that make the words *raincoat* and *mailbox*.

■ Match the Picture Cards and Word Cards that show *dogsled, raincoat,* and *mailbox*. Mix up the Word Cards *dog, sled, rain, coat, mail,* and *box*. Put the Word Cards back together to make the compound words *dogsled, raincoat,* and *mailbox*. Write a sentence using one of the compound words.

You Are Here! Unit 5 Week 6

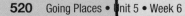

Key

◯ Below-Level Activities

△ On-Level Activities

▢ Advanced Activities

Practice Station
Flip Chart

Let's Write!
Invitation

Objectives
• Write an invitation to a party.

Materials
• *Let's Write!* Flip Chart Activity 30
• Trade Book *This Is the Way We Go to School*
• Teacher-made chart showing a model invitation
• paper, pencils, crayons

Differentiated Activities

◯ Look at the pictures in your selection. Use pictures and words to write an invitation to someone in to visit where you live.

△ Look at the pictures of people who live in different parts of the world. Write an invitation for someone to visit you where you live. Tell what you will plan for them to do.

▢ Look at the pictures of people who live in different parts of the world. Write an invitation for someone to visit you where you live. Tell when they can visit. Tell what you will do.

Read For Meaning
Main Idea

Objectives
• Identify the main idea in a selection.

Materials
• *Read for Meaning* Flip Chart Activity 30
• Little Book *On the Move!*
• pencil, crayons, paper

Differentiated Activities

A **main idea** tells the most important part, or the big idea of a book.

◯ Read your book. Think about the main idea. Point to pictures and words that tell about the main idea.

△ Read your book. Point to pictures and words that tell about the main idea. Draw a picture or write a sentence that tells the main idea.

▢ Read your book. Think about the most important part. Write a sentence that tells the main idea.

Let's Make Art!

Objectives
• Create a picture book that shows how people travel.

Materials
• *Let's Make Art!* Flip Chart Activity 30
• Little Book *On the Move!*
• paper, pencils, crayons

Differentiated Activities

◯ Look at the pictures in your story. Think about how people travel in different parts of the world. Use your art supplies to make a book that shows different ways people travel.

△ Look at the pictures in your story. How do people travel in different parts of the world? Use your art supplies to make a book that shows different ways people travel. Write a word or sentence about each page.

▢ Look at the pictures in your story. How do people travel in different parts of the world? Use your art supplies to make a book that shows different ways people travel. Write a sentence that tells something about each page.

Name _____ Date _____

My Work Plan

Put an ☒ next to the activities you complete.

Listen Up!
☐ Listen for sounds.

Let's Write!
☐ Write an invitation.

Word Work
☐ Find things with names that begin with Vv.

Words to Know
☐ Match words with pictures.

Let's Make Art!
☐ Make a picture book that shows how people go places.

Read for Meaning
☐ Tell what a book is mostly about.

Wrap Up Your Week Turn your paper over. Draw or write about what you did at school this week. What did you read? What did you learn about getting to school?

Unit 5 • Week 6 • This Is the Way We Go to School

My Weekly Work Plan

week 6

Objectives
- Share information and ideas about the concept.

Today at a Glance

Oral Vocabulary
cable car, trolley, horse-and-buggy, skis, Metro line, vaporetto

Phonemic Awareness
◉ Initial /y/ and /kw/

Phonics
◉ /y/ Spelled *Yy*
◉ /kw/ Spelled *qu*

Handwriting
Y and *y*
Q and *q*

High-Frequency Words
where, come

Comprehension
◉ Draw Conclusions

Conventions
Verbs

Writing
Plan a How-to Report

Listening and Speaking
Discuss Literary Features: Plot

TRUCKTOWN on Reading Street

Start your engines! Display p. 17 of *Truckery Rhymes.*

- Read aloud "This Little Truck" and track the print.
  - Ask children to identify repeating words. (*this, little, truck, worried*)

Truckery Rhymes

Concept Talk

Question of the Week

? How do children around the world get to school?

Introduce the concept

To build concepts and to focus their attention, tell children that this week they will talk, sing, read, and write about **ways children get to school.** Track each word as you read the question of the week.

Play the CD that features a song about going to school. What are some of the ways children get to school in the song?

💿 Background Building Audio

ROUTINE Activate Prior Knowledge [Team Talk]

① **Think** Have children think for a minute about how they get to school.

② **Pair** Have pairs of children discuss the question of the week. Remind them to take turns speaking. Have children use complete sentences in their discussions about ways to get to school.

③ **Share** Call on a few children to share their ideas with the group. Guide discussion and encourage elaboration with prompts such as: How can children get to school without a bus or a car?

Routines Flip Chart

Anchored Talk

Develop oral language

Display Talk with Me Chart 30A. These pictures show different ways you can get from one place to another place that is not very far away. They show how some children around the world get from their homes to school. Some children take a school bus. Other children ride in their parents' cars or walk to school. Do you see a picture that looks like the way you get to school? Tell children to respond in complete sentence.

This week we will talk about the different kinds of transportation children all over the world take to get to school. We are going to learn six new Amazing Words. Listen as I say each word: *cable car, trolley, horse-and-buggy, skis, Metro line, vaporetto.* Say the Amazing Words with me as I point to the picture that shows each one.

Display Sing with Me Chart 30B. Today we are going to sing a song about different ways children around the world get to school. Read the title and ask children describe the pictures. Sing the song several times to the tune of "Here We Go 'Round the Mulberry Bush." Have children sing along with you.

Talk with Me/Sing with Me Chart 30A

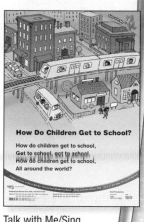

Talk with Me/Sing with Me Chart 30B

Sing with Me Audio

ELL **Preteach Concepts** Use the Day 1 instruction on ELL Poster 30 to assess and build background knowledge, develop concepts, and build oral vocabulary.

 Poster 30

Amazing Words

cable car	trolley
horse-and-buggy	skis
Metro line	vaporetto

Differentiated Instruction

SI Strategic Intervention

Build Background To help children understand words in the story such as *cable car, trolley, Metro line,* and *vaporetto,* use the art. Talk with children about how these things move people. Describe where these methods of transportation are common.

ELL

English Language Learners
ELL Support Additional ELL support and modified instruction is provided in the *ELL Handbook* and in the ELL Support lessons on pp. DI•97–102.

My Skills Buddy, pp. 112–113

Phonemic Awareness
🔄 Initial /y/ and /kw/

Introduce Today we are going to learn a new sound. Listen carefully: /y/ /y/ /y/. Say it with me: /y/ /y/ /y/. Display the *yak* Picture Card. *Yak* begins with /y/. What sound does *yak* begin with? (/y/)

Now let's learn another new sound. Listen carefully: /kw/ /kw/ /kw/. Say it with me: /kw/ /kw/ /kw/. Display the *quilt* Picture Card. *Quilt* begins with /kw/. What sound does *quilt* begin with? (/kw/)

Model Have children look at the picture on pp. 112–113 of *My Skills Buddy.* Tell them that they will be listening for /y/ and /kw/. I see a yam in the picture. What sound do you hear at the beginning of *yam*? I hear /y/ at the beginning of *yam*. What other things do you see that begin with /y/? Repeat the routine with /kw/, *quill*.

Guide practice As children name example words from the picture, guide them in stating that /y/ (or /kw/) is the beginning sound. Discuss with children some of the bulleted items on p. 112 of *My Skills Buddy*. Save the other bulleted items for discussion on Day 2.

Picture Card

Picture Card

Corrective feedback	**If...** children have difficulty naming words with /y/ and /kw/, **then...** stretch the beginning sounds on appropriate words.
Discriminate sounds	I am going to say two words. Listen carefully to the first sound in each word. One word begins with /y/, and the other word does not: *yell, bell*. Which word starts with /y/? *Yell* starts with /y/. Continue the routine with /y/ and /kw/ using the following word pairs: *bun, yum* (/y/); *quick, win* (/kw/); *yarn, vine* (/y/); *me, you* (/y/); *start, quit* (/kw/); *quiz, desk* (/kw/). I am going to say a word. Listen to the sound at the beginning of the word. What sound do you hear at the beginning of *yellow*? (/y/) Repeat the activity with *Quinn, yam, quilt, quiet,* and *yogurt*.
Corrective feedback	**If...** children cannot discriminate initial sounds, **then...** have them enunciate the initial sound in each word. When you say /y/, your tongue presses against your teeth on both sides. Say /y/ with me: /y/ /y/ /y/. Did your tongue press against your teeth on both sides? Repeat with /kw/ if necessary, pointing out that /kw/ starts at the back of the throat and then is said with pursed lips. Have children practice saying *yes* and *quiz*.
Blend	Display the *yak* Picture Card. Listen to these sounds: /y/ /a/ /k/. Say these sounds with me: /y/ /a/ /k/. Now blend these sounds to say the word *yak*. Continue the blending practice with *yet* and *quit*.

MONITOR PROGRESS

Don't Wait Until Friday

Check Phonemic Awareness   Initial /y/ and /kw/

Say *queen, zebra,* and *yo-yo*. Have children identify the words that begin with /y/ and /kw/. Continue with *taxi, yellow* and *quiet, loud*.

If... children cannot discriminate /y/ or /kw/,

then... use the small-group Strategic Intervention lesson, p. DI•86, to reteach /y/ and /kw/.

Day 1	Day 2	Day 3	Day 4	Day 5
Check Phonemic Awareness	Check Sound-Spelling/ Retelling	Check Word Reading	Check Phonemic Awareness	Check Oral Vocabulary

Success Predictor

Differentiated Instruction

SI   **Strategic Intervention**

Support Phonemic Awareness
Some young children have difficulty hearing /w/ after /k/ in /kw/. Have individual children look carefully at your mouth as you say /kw/.

ELL

English Language Learners
Support Phonemic Awareness
Point to images in the pictures on pp. 112–113 of *My Skills Buddy* as you say their corresponding words. To clarify understanding, have children point to the images as you say the words.

Objectives

• Recognize uppercase *Y* and *Q* and lowercase *y* and *q*.
◎ Associate the sound /y/ with the spelling *y*.
◎ Associate the sound /kw/ with the spelling *qu*.
• Blend and read words with /y/ and /kw/.

Skills Trace

◎ /y/ Spelled *Yy*, /kw/ Spelled *qu*
Introduce U5W6D1
Practice U5W6D2; U5W6D3
Reteach/Review U5W6D5; U6W1D4
Assess/Test Benchmark Assessment U5

KEY:
U=Unit W=Week D=Day

Phonics—Teach/Model
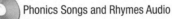 /y/ Spelled *Yy* and /kw/ Spelled *qu*

Introduce

Display the *Yy* Alphabet Card. Point to the *yo-yo* on the Alphabet Card. *Yo-yo* begins with /y/. Say the word with me, *yo-yo*. Write *yo-yo* on the board and point to the *y*. *Yo-yo* begins with /y/ spelled *y*. Now point to the letters *Yy* on the card. The sound for this letter is /y/. The name of this letter is uppercase *Y* and lowercase *y*. What is the sound for this letter? What is the name of this letter? Continue with the *Qq* Alphabet Card and a similar procedure. *Q* is a special letter because it is usually with *u*. When we see *q* words, they begin with the letters *q* and *u* and make a /kw/ sound, as in *queen*.

Alphabet Card

Model

Write *Yolla Yak* on the board. Point to the first *y*. When I see this letter, I think of the sound /y/. The first word is *Yolla*—/y/, *Yolla*. Point to *Yak*. The next word begins with *y* too. I know that the sound we have learned for *y* is /y/. The second word is /y/, *yak*. The song we will sing is "Yolla Yak."

Alphabet Card

Guide practice

Display Phonics Songs and Rhymes Chart 30. Teach children the song "Yolla Yak," sung to the tune of "Yankee Doodle." Play the CD and sing the song several times. When children are familiar with the song, tell them to clap when they hear /y/ words. Have children point to words that begin with *y*. Repeat with /kw/ spelled *qu* words.

Phonics Songs and Rhymes Audio

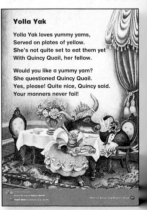

Yolla Yak

Yolla Yak loves yummy yams,
Served on plates of yellow.
She's quite set to eat them yet
With Quincy Quail, her fellow.

Would you like a yummy yam?
She questioned Quincy Quail.
Yes, please! Quite nice, Quincy said.
Your manners never fail!

Phonics Songs and Rhymes Chart 30

On their own

Tell children to use their hands as binoculars. Look around our room with your binoculars. Do you see any words that begin with *y*? How about *qu*? Say the words as you find them.

Blend Words

Review

To review sound-spellings, use Alphabet Cards *Aa, Ii, Ll, Rr,* and *Tt* and the *ant, igloo, lake, rug,* and *top* Picture Cards. Then use this routine for sound-by-sound blending to have children blend new words.

ROUTINE Sound-by-Sound Blending

① **Connect** Write the letter *y* on the board. What is the sound for this letter? The sound is /y/. Say it with me: /y/ /y/ /y/. When you see this letter in a word, what sound might you say?

② **Model** Write *yes* on the board.

- Touch under the letter *y.* What is the sound for this letter? Say it with me: /y/ /y/ /y/. Repeat the routine touching under *e* and *s.*

- Let's blend the sounds together. Listen as I blend the sounds: /y/ /e/ /s/. Say it with me: /y/ /e/ /s/, *yes.* Now say it without me.

- Listen as I use *yes* in a sentence: *Yes, you may go out to play.* Say the sentence with me. Then have children use *yes* in their own sentences.

③ **Guide Practice** Continue the routine established in step 2 with the words below:

> quit   yet   Tim   ran   past   hill   rest

Children should successfully read these words before reading Decodable Story 30 on p. 383 of *Reader's and Writer's Notebook.*

Corrective feedback If children have trouble reading a word, model blending the sounds to read the word. Then have children say it with you.

Routines Flip Chart

Handwriting

Introduce

Write *Yy* on the board. Words that begin with /y/ are written with either an uppercase *Y* or a lowercase *y*. Which letter is uppercase *Y*? Which letter is lowercase *y*? Write *Qq* on the board. Words that begin with /kw/ are written with either an uppercase *Q* or a lowercase *q*. Which letter is uppercase *Q*? Which letter is lowercase *q*?

Model uppercase Y and Q

Write *Yoko* on the board. Point to the uppercase *Y*. This is the uppercase *Y*. We use an uppercase letter at the beginning of sentences or for the first letter of a name. Watch as I trace the uppercase *Y* with my finger. Write *Quinn* on the board and repeat the routine for *Q*. Follow the stroke instructions pictured below.

Guide practice

Have children write the uppercase *Y* in the air. Use your finger to make an uppercase *Y* in the air. Now write it on the palm of your hand. Continue the routine with uppercase *Q*.

Model lowercase y and q

Write *yes* on the board. Point to the lowercase *y*. This is a lowercase *y*. Watch as I trace a lowercase *y* with my finger. Write another lowercase *y* on the board following the stroke instructions. Again, have children write *y* in the air and on their hands. Continue the routine with the word *quit* and lowercase *q*.

Guide practice

Have children use their Write-On Boards to write a row of uppercase *Y* and *Q* and a row of lowercase *y* and *q*.

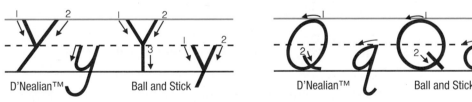

D'Nealian™   Ball and Stick   D'Nealian™   Ball and Stick

More practice

Use *Reader's and Writer's Notebook,* pp. 381, 382, for additional practice with initial *y* and *q*.

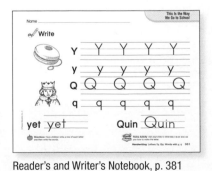

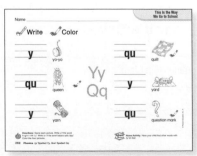

Reader's and Writer's Notebook, p. 381   Reader's and Writer's Notebook, p. 382

High-Frequency Words

Introduce   Use the routine below to teach high-frequency words *where* and *come*.

> **ROUTINE**   **Nondecodable Words**
>
> **1** **Say and Spell** Some words we must learn by remembering the letters rather than saying the sounds. We will say and spell the words to help learn them. Write *where* on the board. This is the word *where*. It has five letters. The letters in the word *where* are *w, h, e, r,* and *e.* Have children say and spell the word, first with you and then without you.
>
> **2** **Demonstrate Meaning** I can use the word *where* in lots of sentences. Here is one sentence: *Where is my hat?* Now you use the word in a sentence.
>
> Repeat the routine with the word *come.*

Routines Flip Chart

Academic Vocabulary

Write the following on the board:

conclusion	verb
how-to report	fairy tale
draft	revise

Point to the list. This week we are going to learn these important words. They are tools for learning. As we work this week, you will hear them many times. Read the words. Preteach the Academic Vocabulary at point-of-use by providing a child-friendly description, explanation, or example that clarifies the meaning of each term. Then ask children to restate the meaning of the Academic Vocabulary in their own words.

Differentiated Instruction

A **Advanced**

Words in Context Have children look through a children's magazine for words that begin with *Yy* and words that begin with *Qq.* Have them cut out the words and glue them to construction paper to make a collage of *y*-words and *q*-words.

SI **Strategic Intervention**

Support High-Frequency Words Say these sentences one at a time: *Where shall we go today? Please come to the zoo.* After each sentence, have children tell you the high-frequency words. Then have them tell you the letters in the word.

Decodable Story 30
🔊 /y/ Spelled Yy, /kw/ Spelled *qu* and High-Frequency Words

Review

Review the following high-frequency words by having children read each word as you point to it on the Word Wall.

a	said	she	the	to	you

Read Decodable Story 30

Display Decodable Story 30, *Run, Tim*. Today we will read a story about Tim running. Point to the title of the story. The title of this story is *Run, Tim*. What is the title of the story? We will read some *qu* and *y* words in this story. Have children read Decodable Story 30 on pp. 383–384 in *Reader's and Writer's Notebook*.

Use the routine for reading decodable books to read Decodable Story 30.

Reader's and Writer's Notebook, pp. 383–384

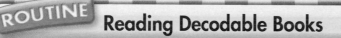

ROUTINE — Reading Decodable Books

1. **Read Silently** Have children whisper read the story page by page as you listen in.

2. **Model Fluent Reading** Have children finger point as you read a page. Then have children reread the page without you.

3. **Read Chorally** Have children finger point as they chorally read the page. Continue reading page by page, repeating steps 1 and 2.

4. **Read Individually** Have children take turns reading aloud a page.

5. **Reread and Monitor Progress** As you listen to individual children reread, monitor progress and provide support.

6. **Reread with a Partner** Have children reread the story page by page with a partner.

Routines Flip Chart

Differentiated Instruction

SI Strategic Intervention

Support Phonemic Awareness Before children read *Run, Tim,* review /y/ and /kw/ words with the following Picture Cards: *yak, yarn, yellow, quarter, queen, quilt.*

Teacher Tip

To help children who are having difficulty reading the high-frequency words, have them practice naming each letter in the words and then reading the words.

Small Group Time

DAY 1

Break into small groups after reading the Decodable Story and before the comprehension lesson.

Teacher-Led

SI Strategic Intervention	**OL** On-Level	**A** Advanced
Teacher-Led Page DI•86	**Teacher-Led** Page DI•91	**Teacher-Led** Page DI•94
• Phonemic Awareness and Phonics	• Phonemic Awareness and Phonics	• Phonemic Awareness and Phonics
• **Reread** Decodable Story 30	• **Reread** Decodable Story 30, DI•91	• **Reread** Decodable Story 30 for Fluency, DI•77

ELL Place English language learners in the groups that correspond to their reading abilities in English.

Practice Stations	**Independent Activities**
• Visit the Listen Up! Station	• Read independently
• Visit the Word Work Station	• Concept Talk Video
	• *Reader's and Writer's Notebook*

Objectives
◎ Draw conclusions.

Skills Trace

◉ **Draw Conclusions**

Introduce U3W5D1; U5W6D1; U6W6D1

Practice U3W5D2; U3W5D3; U3W5D4; U5W6D2; U5W6D3; U5W6D4; U6W6D2; U6W6D3; U6W6D4

Reteach/Review U3W5D5; U4W3D4; U5W3D4; U5W6D5; U6W1D4; U6W4D4; U6W6D5

KEY:
U=Unit W=Week D=Day

My Skills Buddy, pp. 114–115

Listening Comprehension
🎯 Draw Conclusions

Introduce   When we listen to a story and look at the pictures, we use what we know and what we hear and see to make up our minds about what is happening in the story. When we use what we know and what we read to decide things about the story, we draw conclusions.

Envision It!   Have children turn to pp. 114–115 in *My Skills Buddy* and look at the picture. We can use this picture and these words to decide how the girl is feeling. Tell children they can also think of how they feel about gifts to decide how the girl feels.

- What do you see in the picture? (a girl smiling and holding a gift)

- How would you feel if you were the girl? (happy to get a gift)

- **Point to the words.** These words say *Happy, Happy, Happy.* How are these words connected to the picture? (They tell how the girl feels.)

Model   Today I will read about ways children can get to school. Read **"Getting to School"** and model how to draw conclusions.

Think Aloud   When I read or hear a story, I think about what it tells me. I add that to what I already know to figure out an idea that makes sense. In "Getting to School," some children walk to school.

Others ride in cars or buses. If I add these details together, I can draw the conclusion that the way you get to school depends on how far away you live.

Guide practice

Have the class tell where children probably live if they take a subway to school. I think they must live in a big city that has lots of people who need to take subways, don't you?

More practice

Display the Trade Book *Mayday! Mayday!* Take a picture walk through the story. Help children draw a conclusion about why the sailors needed to be rescued. Let's look at the pictures and think about the book. I think the storm must have damaged the sailor's boat so it couldn't move anymore. Do you think that is a conclusion we can draw?

Connect to everyday life

Every day we use what we know and the details around us to make up our minds about things—we draw conclusions. What details tell you when it is time for lunch? What details tell you it's almost time to go home? You are drawing conclusions to figure out those things.

Academic Vocabulary

conclusion a decision or opinion that makes sense reached after thinking about some facts and details

Teacher Tip

Use a K-W-L chart to activate prior knowledge when discussing nonfiction or fiction that includes factual information.

**English Language Learners
Oral Comprehension** To prepare English learners for the Read Aloud, use the modified Read Aloud in the ELL Support lesson p. DI•98.

Read Aloud

Getting to School

If your school is not far away from your home, you probably walk to school.

Kids whose schools are far away from their homes usually can't walk to school. Some kids ride in cars. Some take school buses. Some take regular buses. Some kids even take trains, subways, or elevated trains.

In places where the winters are snowy, some kids may go to school using a sled or skis! Some kids who live on farms or ranches can even ride horses to school.

Kids who live really far away from school don't go to a school building at all. They use a computer. They can even talk to and see their teachers on the computer.

Conventions
Verbs

Teach verbs

Some words are action words. Action words are called verbs. Verbs are words that tell what wo do. *Walk, jump, write, think,* and *stand* are all words that tell what we do. They are verbs. What other verbs can you think of?

Model

I will say a sentence. Listen for the verb.

Lin and Tom eat spaghetti.

Lin, Tom, and *spaghetti* are nouns. They name things and people. *Lin* and *Tom* name people. *Spaghetti* names a thing. *Eat* is the verb. It shows what Lin and Tom do to the spaghetti.

Guide practice

Tell children that you will say a word. If it is a verb, they should act it out with you. If it is not a verb, they should say "not a verb." Say the following words: *jump* (verb), *tall* (not a verb), *sing* (verb), *clap* (verb), *yellow* (not a verb), *laugh* (verb), *boy* (not a verb), *smile* (verb).

Team Talk Pair children and have them take turns telling about something they like to do. Then have them draw pictures of themselves, acting out the verb.

Daily Fix-It

Use the Daily Fix-It for more conventions practice.

Writing
Writing Process:
Plan a How-to Report

Teach: Generate ideas

Talk with children about informational or expository writing. Some writing gives us information about something. Display *This Is the Way We Go to School.* This book tells us interesting information about how children in different parts of the world do things. Read aloud sentences from the book that tell how children get to school.

This week we are going to write a how-to report about how we do something here. A how-to report gives readers step-by-step instructions. It teaches them how to do or make something. Readers use a how-to report to learn a new skill.

Model: Generate ideas

When we write a how-to report, the first thing we do is choose something that we will teach our readers. I am going to think of something I would like to learn how to do or make. I would like to learn how to mail a letter. I ask myself, *What steps do I need to take to mail a letter?* Write *mail a letter* in a list titled *How do I do this?*

Guide practice: Generate ideas and choose a topic

Encourage children to generate topic ideas for the how-to report. Think about things you would like to learn how to do or make. Ask yourself a question you want to answer. Then we will choose one skill to write about.

Have children turn to p. 385 in *Reader's and Writer's Notebook* and draw pictures of themselves doing or making things as topic ideas. Then continue the skills list you began, adding children's ideas. As a class, select one skill as the how-to report topic (for example, how to check out a book from the library). Write the question on the board: *How can we check out a book from the library?*

Independent writing

Have children illustrate or copy the question on p. 386 in *Reader's and Writer's Notebook.*

Reader's and Writer's Notebook, p. 385

Write Guy
Jeff Anderson

Let Me Check My List

Encourage children to keep lists of words they find that are exciting or interesting. They can use their lists to increase their vocabulary and incorporate them in their own writing. This is a great way to improve vocabulary and word choice.

Academic Vocabulary

how-to report text that gives instructions on how to do or make something

verb a word that tells what something or someone does or is

Daily Fix-It

she runs to school
She runs to school.

This week's practice sentences appear on Teacher Resources DVD-ROM

Objectives
- Discuss plot by identifying key events of a story.
- Speak one at a time.
- Speak loudly and clearly.
- Face the speaker when listening.

Listening and Speaking
Discuss Literary Features: Plot

Teach

After we read a story, we can talk about the things that happen at the beginning, in the middle, and at the end. This is called the plot.

Model

I am going to discuss the plot of *The Little Engine That Could.* Retell the main events from the beginning, middle, and end. Remind children to face you while they listen.

- Did I talk about the beginning, the middle, and the end of the story?
- Did I speak loudly and clearly?

Guide practice

Have children briefly discuss the plot of one of the stories from Unit 5. Refer children to the Rules for Listening and Speaking on pp. 1–2 of the *Reader's and Writer's Notebook.* Remind children to speak loudly. Remind them to speak one at a time and to face the speaker when listening.

Name _____

Listening Rules
1. Face the person who is speaking.
2. Be quiet while someone is speaking.
3. Pay attention to the speaker.
4. Ask questions if you don't understand.

Listening and Speaking Rules 1

Reader's and Writer's Notebook, pp. 1–2

Wrap Up Your Day

✔ **Oral Language** Today we talked about getting to school. Let's say the Amazing Words again: *cable car, trolley, horse-and-buggy, skis, Metro line, vaporetto.*

✔ **Homework Idea** Send home the Family Times Newsletter, TR DVD•59–60.

Preview

DAY 2

Tomorrow we will read a book about children from around the world.

Extend Your Day!

Social Studies
On the School Bus
Materials: paper, crayons

Rules for Riding the Bus Tell children who ride the bus to school to explain what the rules are. List each rule on the board. After you write each one, discuss it with the whole group. Have them share what might happen if that rule were not followed. If there are specific rules for school-bus riding in your school or district, share them with children to complete the list. Have each child choose one of the rules and draw a picture of him or herself following it.

Phonics
Words with *Yy* and *Qq*
Materials: children's magazines, paper, glue, two sheets of poster board

Find *Y* and *Q* Review with children how to write the letters *Yy* and *Qq*. Distribute magazines to children. Give them time to search the magazines for words with *Yy* and *Qq*. Have children cut the words out and paste them on squares of paper.

Make a poster for each letter labeled *Yy Words* and *Qq Words*. Place squares of paper in a container. Have children select a paper, read the first letter of the word, and glue it to the appropriate poster.

Mathematics
Transportation Favorites
Materials: graph paper, marker

Way to Travel If you could choose any way to get to school, what form of transportation would you choose? Write the names of the forms of transportation children would like to take in the squares along the left side of a bar chart. Then read the different choices and have children raise their hand for their favorite. Let them color in a square on the chart next to the name of their favorite form of transportation.

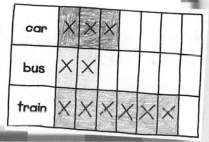

Objectives

- Discuss the concepts to develop oral language.
- Build oral vocabulary.

Today at a Glance

Oral Vocabulary
cable car, trolley

Phonemic Awareness
◉ Initial /y/ and /kw/

Phonics
◉ /y/ Spelled *Yy*
◉ /kw/ Spelled *qu*

Handwriting
Y and *y*
Q and *q*

Comprehension
◉ Draw Conclusions

Conventions
Verbs

Writing
Plan a How-to Report

Vocabulary
Action Words

TRUCKTOWN on Reading Street

Start your engines! Display p. 17 of *Truckery Rhymes*. Point to "This Little Truck." Who remembers how this little truck feels? Yes, this little truck feels worried. Let's read the rhyme together. Have children point to the repeating words as the class reads the rhyme again. Give additional children the opportunity to say the repeating words aloud and track the print.

Truckery Rhymes

Concept Talk

Question of the Week

❓ How do children around the world get to school?

Build concepts

Write the question and track the print as you read it aloud. Ask children to answer the question in complete sentences. To reinforce the concept and focus children's attention, display Talk with Me/Sing with Me Chart 30B. Tell children they are going to sing about how children get to school.

 Sing with Me Audio

Listen for Amazing Words

The Amazing Words *cable car* and *trolley* are in the song "How Do Children Get to School?" Read the title and have children describe the methods of transportation they see. Sing the song several times to the tune of "Here We Go 'Round the Mulberry Bush" until children become familiar with the words and can sing along. Have children tap their feet when they hear the Amazing Words *cable car* and *trolley*.

E L L Reinforce Vocabulary Use the Day 2 instruction on ELL Poster 30 to reinforce the meanings of high-frequency words.

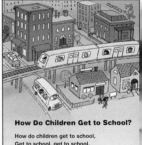

How Do Children Get to School?

How do children get to school,
Get to school, get to school,
How do children get to school,
All around the world?

Talk with Me/Sing with Me Chart 30B

E L L Poster 30

Oral Vocabulary
Amazing Words

Teach Amazing Words

Amazing Words — Oral Vocabulary Routine

1. **Introduce the Word** A *cable car* is like a train car that is pulled by a metal rope called a cable. What is our new word for a car pulled by a cable? Say the word cable car with me: *cable car.*

2. **Demonstrate** Provide examples to show meaning. *Cable cars are used on hills that are hard to climb.*

   Repeat steps 1 and 2.

   Introduce the Word A *trolley* brings us to places in the city. It is like a bus attached to electric wires overhead that send it power to move. What is our new word for an electric bus powered by wires? Say the word with me: *trolley.*

   Demonstrate *The wires that give a trolley power are only on some streets.*

3. **Apply** Tell children to use *cable car* and *trolley* in complete sentences. Have them identify *cable cars* and *trolleys* in pictures.

Routines Flip Chart

Use Amazing Words

To reinforce the concept and the Amazing Words, have children supply the appropriate Amazing Word for each sentence.

We rode a _____ up a hill in the city of San Francisco. (cable car)

My dad said there is a _____ on Main Street. (trolley)

Amazing Words

cable car	trolley
horse-and-buggy	skis
Metro line	vaporetto

Differentiated Instruction

SI Strategic Intervention

Sentence Production If children have difficulty completing the sentences, say a sentence using each Amazing Word and ask children to choose the one that makes sense. Say the sentence together.

English Language Learners
Extend Vocabulary Explain to children we use the phrase *ride on _____* for transportation (for example, *I ride on a cable car*). Say *ride on* and have children repeat. Have children share the word for *ride* in their home language.

Phonemic Awareness
↻ Initial /y/ and /kw/

Picture Card

Isolate /y/ and /kw/

Display the *quarter* Picture Card. This is a *quarter*. *Quarter* begins with /kw/. What is this? What sound does it begin with? Continue the routine with the *queen* and *quilt* Picture Cards. Follow the same routine with /y/ and the Picture Cards *yo-yo, yarn,* and *yellow*.

Model

Display the *yak* picture card. This is a *yak*. Listen carefully to the sounds: /y/ -ak. I hear /y/ at the beginning of *yak*. What is the beginning sound you hear in *yak*? Say it with me: /y/ /a/ /k/, *yak*. Continue the routine with the words *quit, yes,* and *quiz*.

Picture Card

Guide practice

Have children look at the picture on *My Skills Buddy* pp. 112–113. Remember that we saw a *yam* in the picture. *Yam* begins with /y/. We also saw a *quill* in the picture. *Quill* begins with /kw/. What other things that begin with /y/ or /kw/ did we see? Discuss with children those bulleted items on p. 112 not discussed on Day 1.

My Skills Buddy, pp. 112–113

Corrective feedback

If... children cannot discriminate /y/ or /kw/, then... have them enunciate the initial sound as they segment words.

Listen as I segment a word: /kw/ /i/ /t/. Say it with me: /kw/ /i/ /t/. What sound do you hear at the beginning? I hear /kw/ in the beginning. Continue with *quack, quick,* and *quiz*. Follow the same routine for /y/, segmenting the words *yam, yes, yet,* and *yak*.

On their own Display Phonics Songs and Rhymes Chart 30, "Yolla Yak." Remind children of the tune: "Yankee Doodle." Sing the song several times. Whenever you hear a word that begins with /y/, clap your hands. Whenever you hear a word that begins with /kw/, stomp your feet. Identify *Yolla, yak, yummy, yams, yellow, quite, yet, Quincy, Quail,* and *questioned.*

Review
Segment Listen to this word: *yes.* This word begins with /y/. Say the sound with me: /y/. The middle sound is /e/. The last sound is /s/. Say all the sounds with me: /y/ /e/ /s/. The word is *yes.* There are three sounds in *yes.* Have children segment the following words: *yam, yet, quack.*

Yolla Yak

Yolla Yak loves yummy yams,
Served on plates of yellow.
She's not quite set to eat them yet
With Quincy Quail, her fellow.

Would you like a yummy yam?
She questioned Quincy Quail.
Yes, please! Quite nice, Quincy said.
Your manners never fail!

Phonics Songs and
Rhymes Chart 30

Teacher Tip

In English, /kw/*qu* and /y/*Yy* do not occur in final position, although both can occur at the beginning of syllables that are in the middle of words such as *acquaint* or *lawyer*. The letter *y* at the end of a word spells vowel sounds such as the long *i* in *my* or the long *e* in *funny*.

English Language Learners
Support Phonemic Awareness
Have children say *quack, quick, quit, yell, yet,* and *yak* to practice /y/ and /kw/ sounds. Then have them think of silly phrases using the words, such as *ducks quack quick* or *yaks will yell.*

Objectives

◎ Practice /y/ spelled *Yy*.

◎ Practice /kw/ spelled *qu*.

• Blend /y/ and /kw/ words.

Check Sound-Spelling
SUCCESS PREDICTOR

Phonics—Teach/Model

◉ /y/ Spelled *Yy* and /kw/ Spelled *qu*

Alphabet Card

Teach /kw/ *qu*

Point to the *queen* on the *Qq* Alphabet Card. What is this? What sound does *queen* begin with? *Queen* begins with /kw/. Write *queen* on the board and point to the letters *qu* at the beginning. *Q* is a special letter because it is always with the letter *u*. When we see *q* words, they begin with the letters *q* and *u*. Continue with the *Yy* Alphabet Card and *yo-yo*.

Model

Display the *quilt* Picture Card. What is this? Say the sounds in *quilt* with me: /kw/ /i/ /l/ /t/, *quilt*. Where do you hear /kw/ in *quilt*? (at the beginning)

Write *quilt* on the board. Point to the letters as you say the corresponding sounds: /kw/ /i/ /l/ /t/, quilt. Continue the routine with the following words: *quiz, yam, yum*.

Alphabet Card

Guide practice

Envision It!

Have children open *My Skills Buddy* to p. 116. Demonstrate using the blending arrows on *My Skills Buddy*, p. 116, as you model blending the first word. Put your finger on the red arrows below the *qu*. Say the sound that *qu* stands for: /kw/. Continue with letters *i* and *t*. Now I run my finger along the blue arrow as I blend the letters quickly to read *quit*. Repeat with the word *quiz*. Explain to children that when you changed the *t* in *quit* to *z*, a new word was made, *quiz*. Have children work with a partner to blend the rest of the words on the page.

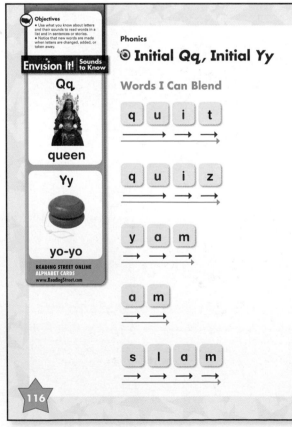

My Skills Buddy, p. 116

Blend   Use the following routine to review blending *qu* words.

ROUTINE   Sound-by-Sound Blending

①   **Connect** Write the letters *qu*. What is the sound for these letters? The sound is /kw/. Say it with me: /kw/ /kw/ /kw/. When you see these letters, what sound will you say?

②   **Model** Write the word *quit* on the board.

- Point to *qu* and ask: What is the sound for these letters? Say it with me: /kw/ /kw/ /kw/. Repeat the routine for *i* and *t*.

- Let's blend the sounds together. Listen as I blend the sounds: /kw/ /i/ /t/. Say it with me: /kw/ /i/ /t/, *quit*. Say it without me.

- Listen as I use *quit* in a sentence. *We quit eating and went outside.* Say it with me. Have children use *quit* in a sentence.

③   **Guide Practice** Continue the routine with these words:

> **quiz**   **yak**   **yes**   **Jim**   **Mom**   **can**   **him**   **sat**

Have children successfully read all of the words before reading Decodable Reader 30 on pp. 118–125 of *My Skills Buddy*.

Corrective Feedback Model blending the sounds to read the word. Then have children say it with you.

Routines Flip Chart

Differentiated Instruction

Ⓐ Advanced

Yy, Qq Display the *Yy* and *Qq* Alphabet Cards. Have children find *Yy* and *Qq* in words in *The Quiz* before reading. Have them copy these words on their Write-On Boards.

Ⓢ Strategic Intervention

/kw/ Before children read *The Quiz,* review /kw/ with the *quarter, queen,* and *quilt* Picture Cards.

Don't Wait Until Friday

MONITOR PROGRESS   ↻ Check Sound-Spelling   /y/ Spelled *Yy* and /kw/ Spelled *qu*

Have children write the letters *Yy* and *qu* on separate cards. I am going to read some words. When you hear a word that begins with /y/, hold up your *Yy* card. When you hear a word that begins with *qu,* or /kw/, hold up your *qu* card. Say: *quack, yum, quick, yam, yes, quilt, quiz, yarn.*

If... children cannot discriminate /y/ or /kw/ words,

then... use the small-group Strategic Intervention lesson, p. DI•87, to reteach /y/ and /kw/.

Continue to monitor children's progress using other instructional opportunities during the week so that children can be successful with the Day 5 Assessment.

Day 1	Day 2	Day 3	Day 4	Day 5
Check Phonemic Awareness	Check Sound-Spelling/ Retelling	Check Word Reading	Check Phonemic Awareness	Check Oral Vocabulary

Success Predictor

Sound-Spelling

Success Predictor

Objectives
- Write *Y* and *y*.
- Write *Q* and *q*.
- Read high-frequency words.

Handwriting
Write Words with *Yy* and *Qq*

Review

Write *Yoko* on the board. This is the name *Yoko*. I use an uppercase *Y* for the first letter in *Yoko's* name. Watch me make an uppercase *Y*. Write another uppercase *Y* on the board using the instructional strokes indicated on the model. Repeat the routine with the name *Quinn* for the uppercase *Q*.

Write *yak* on the board. This is the word *yak*. I use a lowercase *y* at the beginning of *yak*. Watch me make a lowercase *y*. Write another *y* on the board using the instructional strokes indicated on the model. Repeat the routine with the word *quiz* and the letter *q*, reminding children that *q* is followed by its buddy *u*.

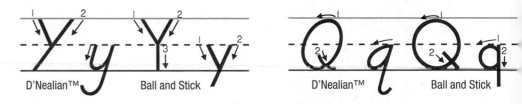

D'Nealian™   Ball and Stick   D'Nealian™   Ball and Stick

Guide practice

Have children use their Write-On Boards to make a row of uppercase *Y* and a row of lowercase *y*. Circulate around the room, assisting children as necessary. Then have children repeat the routine with uppercase *Q* and lowercase *q*. Have them write the following words: *yam, yet, yip, quack, quick, quit.*

High-Frequency Words

Model reading

Have children turn to p. 117 of *My Skills Buddy*. Read the high-frequency words *where* and *come* together. Then have children point to each word and read it themselves. Read the sentences on *My Skills Buddy* page together to read the new high-frequency words in context.

Team Talk Pair children and have them take turns reading each of the sentences aloud.

High-Frequency Words

Words I Can Read

> where

> come

Sentences I Can Read

1. Where is Quinn?
2. He did not come yet.
3. Will Quinn quit?

117

My Skills Buddy, p. 117

On their own

Use *Reader's and Writer's Notebook*, p. 387, for additional practice with this week's high-frequency words.

Reader's and Writer's Notebook, p. 387

Differentiated Instruction

A Advanced

High-Frequency Words Have children copy the high-frequency words *where* and *come* on their Write-On Boards. Tell them to use the Word Wall as reference.

English Language Learners

Support High-Frequency Words Explain to children that *where* always refers to a place. When used in a question, the answer will always be a place.

Decodable Reader 30
 /y/ Spelled *Yy,* /kw/ Spelled *qu,* and High-Frequency Words

Review Review the previously taught high-frequency words. Have children read each word as you point to it on the Word Wall.

come	said	where	the	four

Have children turn to Decodable Reader 30, *The Quiz,* on p. 118, of *My Skills Buddy*. Today we will read a story about a boy who takes a quiz. Point to the title. What is the title of the story? *The Quiz* is the title. We will read *y* and *qu* words in this story.

Use the routine for reading decodable books to read Decodable Reader 30.

My Skills Buddy, pp. 118–125

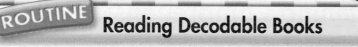

ROUTINE — **Reading Decodable Books**

1. **Read Silently** Have children whisper read the book page by page as you listen in.

2. **Model Fluent Reading** Have children finger point as you read a page. Then have children reread the book without you.

3. **Read Chorally** Have children finger point as they chorally read the page. Continue reading page by page, repeating steps 1 and 2.

4. **Read Individually** Have children take turns reading aloud a page.

5. **Reread and Monitor Progress** As you listen to individual children reread, monitor progress and provide support.

6. **Reread with a Partner** Have children reread the book page by page with a partner.

Routines Flip Chart

Small Group Time

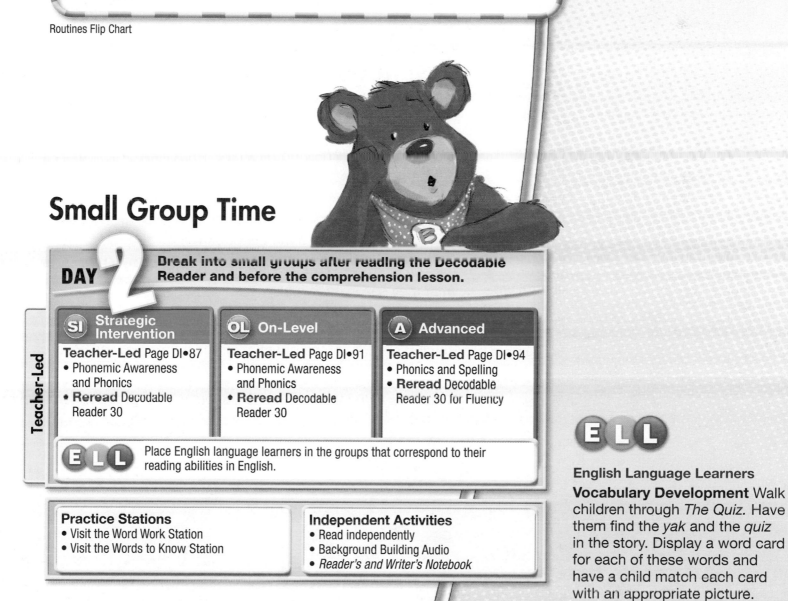

DAY 2   Break into small groups after reading the Decodable Reader and before the comprehension lesson.

Teacher-Led

SI Strategic Intervention	**OL On-Level**	**A Advanced**
Teacher-Led Page DI•87	**Teacher-Led** Page DI•91	**Teacher-Led** Page DI•94
• Phonemic Awareness and Phonics	• Phonemic Awareness and Phonics	• Phonics and Spelling
• **Reread** Decodable Reader 30	• **Reread** Decodable Reader 30	• **Reread** Decodable Reader 30 for Fluency

ELL Place English language learners in the groups that correspond to their reading abilities in English.

Practice Stations
• Visit the Word Work Station
• Visit the Words to Know Station

Independent Activities
• Read independently
• Background Building Audio
• *Reader's and Writer's Notebook*

Differentiated Instruction

A Advanced
Copy /y/ and /kw/ Words Have children copy words with /y/ and /kw/ on their Write-On Boards as they read *The Quiz.*

ELL

English Language Learners
Vocabulary Development Walk children through *The Quiz.* Have them find the *yak* and the *quiz* in the story. Display a word card for each of these words and have a child match each card with an appropriate picture.

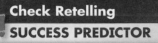

Objectives
- ◎ Practice draw conclusions.
- Preview and predict.
- Retell a story.

Check Retelling
SUCCESS PREDICTOR

Listening Comprehension
◉ Draw Conclusions

Review

Envision It!

Have children turn to p. 114 of *My Skills Buddy*. Remind children that using information they already know and the ideas and pictures in a story can help them understand what is happening. Good readers add what they already know to what they read, hear, and see in a story to draw conclusions.

My Skills Buddy, pp. 114–115

First Read—Trade Book
This Is the Way We Go to School

Concepts of print
Page through *This Is the Way We Go to School*. Have children point to the place you should begin reading on each page.

Preview and predict
 Display *This Is the Way We Go to School*. What do you see on the cover? The title of this book is *This Is the Way We Go to School*. What do you think the book will be about?

Use illustrations
Take children on a picture walk through the book. Have children tell about what they see in each picture.

Introduce genre
Informational fiction is a made-up story that also includes facts.

Set purpose
Remind children of the question of the week: *How do children around the world get to school?* Have children listen as you read.

Model
Read *This Is the Way We Go to School* with expression for enjoyment.

Read for enjoyment

Reread using Develop Vocabulary notes

Reread using Guide Comprehension notes

Retell

Check retelling

My Skills Buddy, p. 126

Have children turn to p. 126 of *My Skills Buddy*. Walk through the retelling boxes as children retell *This Is the Way We Go to School*. Let's recall what happens in the first box—the beginning of the story. We see four children walking to school. Let's retell what is happening in the second box. Continue with the rest of the boxes. After children retell the story as a group, have them draw pictures to retell a favorite part of the story. Have them write or dictate a word or sentence to go with their picture.

Top-Score Response A top-score response describes events in sequence with details.

MONITOR PROGRESS   **Check Retelling**

If... children have difficulty retelling the story,

then... go through the story one page at a time, and ask children to tell what happens in their own words.

Day 1	Day 2	Day 3	Day 4	Day 5
Check Phonemic Awareness	Check Sound-Spelling/ Retelling	Check Word Reading	Check Phonemic Awareness	Check Oral Vocabulary

Success Predictor

Differentiated Instruction

A Advanced

Extend Concept Have children draw a picture of their own answer to the question of the week and expand it to include places where children cannot walk to school and why. Have them write or dictate captions to go with their pictures.

Retelling Plan

- ☑ **Week 1** Assess Advanced students.
- ☑ **Week 2** Assess On-Level students.
- ☑ **Week 3** Assess Strategic Intervention students.
- ☑ **Week 4** Assess Advanced students.
- ☑ **Week 5** Assess On-Level students.
- ☑ **This week assess Strategic Intervention students.**

ELL

English Language Learners
Professional Development Support for Listening Comprehension According to Dr. Lily Wong Fillmore of the University of California, Berkeley: "Teachers support language development by engaging children as active participants in making sense of the texts they are working on. They do it by drawing the English learners into discussions relating to the texts. Even relative newcomers are able to participate in these discussions as long as ample scaffolding is provided."

Objectives
◎ Practice drawing conclusions.
• Confirm predictions.
• Practice using verbs.

Think, Talk, and Write

Discuss concepts

Imagine what it would be like to get to school like the children in *This Is the Way We Go to School*.

- Which way of getting to school looks like the most fun? Why?
- Which one is the way you usually get to school?
- Which one is the way other children you know get to school?

Confirm predictions

Have children recall their predictions before you read *This Is the Way We Go to School*.

- What did you think the story would be about?
- Was your prediction correct?

My Skills Buddy, p. 127

Have children turn to p. 127 of *My Skills Buddy*. Read the questions and directives and have children respond.

Text to self

1. How do you get to school? Could you get to school this way if you lived in any of the places from the story? Which place is most like where we go to school? Which place would you most like to go to school?

◉ Draw conclusions

2. Why do children in different parts of the world use different ways to get to school? Point to the children on skis. What conclusion can you draw about where these children live? (There is a lot of snow where they live.) Repeat with the other pictures.

Look back and write

3. Let's look back at our story and write about it. We remember that the way children get to school depends on how far they live from the school. We can draw conclusions about how far some of these children live from school. Read pp. 26–27 of *This Is the Way We Go to School*. Now let's write our ideas. Discuss with children why the children on p. 26 use a radio and why the children on p. 27 ride bikes. Record children's responses on chart paper. (Possible responses: Kay and Fay and Flo and Joe must live far from school. Mei and Ling must live close to school.)

Conventions
Verbs

Review
Remind children that a verb is a word that tells an action. Verbs tell what a noun—a person, animal, place, or thing—does.

Guide practice
Display the *dog* Picture Card. I am going to make up a sentence about this animal. I will use a verb in my sentence. Read the sentence: *The dog runs*. What is the verb in my sentence? (*runs*)

On their own
Use *Reader's and Writer's Notebook*, p. 388, for more practice with nouns.

Daily Fix-It
Use the Daily Fix-It exercise for more conventions practice.

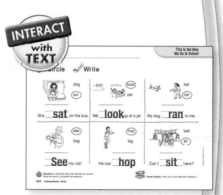

Reader's and Writer's Notebook, p. 388

Differentiated Instruction

SI Strategic Intervention

Support Conventions Remind children that some verbs take -*s* at the end, such as *listen(s), draw(s), smile(s),* and *wave(s).* We add *s* to the end when the verb is telling about what one noun is doing.

Daily Fix-It

i take the bus
I take the bus.

This week's practice sentences appear on Teacher Resources DVD-ROM.

Teacher Tip

Many present and past tense verbs are single words, but other tenses may be phrases, such as *have seen* or *have been checking*. You may wish to avoid using such tenses in examples, so as to minimize confusion.

Objectives
- Identify different media and their techniques.
- Choose and evaluate sources of information.

Writing
Writing Process: Plan a How-to Report

Teach: Choose sources

Review with children what you discussed yesterday about how-to reports. When we write a how-to report, we must find facts, or information, about how to do our skill. How do we find the facts? We can go to the library and look for books and magazines. We can get information from people, such as a librarian, a teacher, our parents, or experts on the subject. We can get information from a TV or radio show. We can also look on the Internet. These are all sources we can use. A source can be anything that gives us correct information about our topic.

Model: Choose and evaluate sources

We are going to write a how-to report about how to check out a book from the library. We need to think about sources we can use to gather information. The sources we use must have facts about checking out books from the library, so a librarian would be the perfect source. What other sources could we use? Discuss with children other possible sources and their credibility (for example, a teacher or someone else who has checked out books from the library, a brochure from the library, the library's Web site, a sibling who has checked out a book from the library).

Guide practice: Choose and evaluate sources

I got this brochure from the librarian at our library. A brochure is a very small book that contains information about something. Display a brochure from your local public library about getting a library card and checking out books. Do you think this is a good source to use for our how-to report? Do you think it will give us information to help us write our report? Yes, I think it would be a good source. It has a lot of information about checking out books.

Explain to children why one source might be better than another. For example, ask: If you do not know how to use a computer, which source might not be good for you to use? Yes, the Internet would not be a good source if you do not know how to use a computer. Then talk about sources used to get specific information. Have children suggest a source that would be helpful if they wanted to learn how to get a library card. (librarian)

Independent practice

Help children complete pp. 389–390 in *Reader's and Writer's Notebook* to review sources and media used in research. Guide them to see that the computer can be used to find the library's Web site, which should contain useful information about the hours the library is open.

Reader's and Writer's Notebook, pp. 389–390

Vocabulary
Action Words

Model

Have children turn to p. 128 of *My Skills Buddy*. Use the first Vocabulary bullet on the page to guide the discussion. Direct children to the picture of a boy riding a horse. We can *ride* on many things, such as buses, cars, or trains. This boy can *ride* on a pony. Direct children to the picture of the girl climbing. This girl can *climb*. She is using her hands and feet to go up. Demonstrate how to jump. I can *jump* up and have both my feet off the ground. Demonstrate how to hop. I can *hop*. A *hop* is like a quick jump on one leg. Skip around the room. I can *skip* by hopping on one foot and then the other. How are jumping, hopping, and skipping alike? How are they different?

My Skills Buddy, p. 128

Guide practice

Write the words *ride, jump, hop, skip,* and *climb* on the board. Point to each word as you read it.

| ride | jump | hop | skip | climb |

Let's practice our new words. Stand up. *Skip* in place. Now pretend you are *climbing* a ladder. Have children look at the pictures on p. 128 of *My Skills Buddy*. Tell me which word I am acting out: *jump* or *hop*. Jump excitedly in place. (*jump*) Show me the action word that is like *jump,* but on one leg. (*hop*) Point to the picture that shows the action word *ride*.

On their own

Have children take turns acting out the action words. Have them describe when and where they would do these action words, such as the following: *We jump rope in gym. We ride bikes in the park. We hop in hopscotch. We climb at the playground. We skip to school.*

Differentiated Instruction

A **Advanced**

Practice Vocabulary Write the action words on the board: *ride, jump, skip, hop, climb*. Have children choose one of the action words and copy it onto a piece of drawing paper. Then have them illustrate the action word and share their drawings with the class.

English Language Learners
Access Content Have children say the action words in their home languages.

Objectives
- Review skills learned and practiced today.
- Identify words that begin with /y/ or /kw/.

Wrap Up Your Day

✔ **Concept Talk** Today we read about some places where children can walk to school. Where were they?

✔ **Phonemic Awareness** I'm going to read a sentence. Clap when you hear /y/ words: *Yetta yearns for yesterday.* Now clap when you hear /kw/ words: *Quinn will not quit his quiz.*

✔ **Vocabulary Skill** Have children draw pictures of themselves performing the following action words: *ride, jump, hop, skip, climb.* Then have them act out their pictures for the class.

✔ **Homework Idea** Have children demonstrate the action words they learned this week for their families.

Preview

DAY 3

Tomorrow we will read about someone whose name is Quinn. Have you ever met anyone named Quinn?

Extend Your Day!

Social Studies
Geography and Transportation

Materials: world map or globe, four or five poster-size sheets of paper

Discuss World Geography As a class, discuss different settings around the world in *This Is the Way We Go to School*. List several in a chart on the board. Help children locate each one on the map or globe. Have children tell a kind of transportation that is used in each. Add that to a second column of the chart.

Settings and Transportation Divide the class into four or five groups, assigning each a setting. Have children draw the setting and transportation used there.

Phonics
Yy, Qq

Materials: construction paper cut into halves, glue, craft sticks, yarn, sequins, cotton balls, uncooked macaroni noodles, pencils

Make a List Have children name words that contain *Yy* or *Qq*. Write the list on the board. Give each child two halves of a sheet of construction paper. Have children write *Qq* words on one sheet and *Yy* words on the other sheet.

Decorate *Yy* or *Qq* Have children create the letters *Yy* and *Qq* on the backs of their paper using whatever craft supplies they choose.

Conventions
Verb Plates

Materials: small paper plates (one per child), yarn, drawing tools

What We Do As a class, think of many different verbs for things that children enjoy doing. Create a list of 15–20 activities on the board.

Have children draw a picture of an action on each side of a plate. Help them write the verb under each picture. Use yarn to hang the plates. Have children choose a plate and use that verb in a sentence.

Today at a Glance

Oral Vocabulary
horse-and-buggy, skis

Phonemic Awareness
◉ /y/ and /kw/

Phonics
◉ /y/ Spelled *Yy*
◉ /kw/ Spelled *qu*

Comprehension
◉ Draw Conclusions

Conventions
Nouns in Sentences

Writing
Draft a How-to Report

Listening and Speaking
Discuss Literary Features—Plot

TRUCKTOWN on Reading Street

Start your engines! Display p. 17 of of *Truckery Rhymes*. Read "This Little Truck" to children. Do you know "This Little Piggy"? Recite and repeat with children:

This little piggy went to market.
This little piggy stayed home.
This little piggy had roast beef.
This little piggy had none.
And this little piggy cried,
"Wee, wee, wee!" all the
way home.

Truckery Rhymes

Concept Talk

 Question of the Week
How do children around the world get to school?

Listen for Amazing Words

Write and read the question of the week as you track the print. Talk with children about ways to get to school. Remind children to answer the question in complete sentences and to take turns speaking.

Let's Sing Display Sing with Me Chart 30B. Remind children that yesterday they sang "How Do Children Get to School?" and listened for *cable-car* and *trolley*. Today we are going to listen for the Amazing Words *horse-and-buggy* and *skis*. Sing the song several times to the tune of "Here We Go 'Round the Mulberry Bush." Have children sing with you. Have them clap when they hear the Amazing Words *horse-and-buggy* and *skis*.

◉ Sing with Me Audio

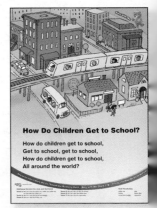

How Do Children Get to School?

How do children get to school,
Get to school, get to school,
How do children get to school,
All around the world?

Talk with Me/Sing with Me Chart 30B

Oral Vocabulary
Amazing Words

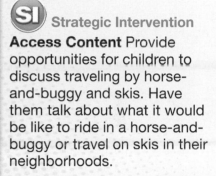

cable car	trolley
horse-and-buggy	skis
Metro line	vaporetto

Teach Amazing Words

Amazing Words · Oral Vocabulary Routine

1 Introduce the Word A horse-and-buggy is a small cart pulled by a horse. What is our new word for a cart pulled by a horse? Say it with me: *horse-and-buggy*.

2 Demonstrate Provide examples to show meaning. *The horse-and-buggy was popular before cars were made.*

Repeat steps 1 and 2.

Introduce the Word Skis are long wooden boards that people strap to their feet. They slide over the top of deep snow. What is our new word for long wooden boards that we strap to our feet? Say it with me: *skis*.

Demonstrate *People use skis to get down a snowy hill quickly.*

3 Apply Have children use *horse-and-buggy* and *skis* in complete sentences. Have them illustrate the words.

Routines Flip Chart

Differentiated Instruction

SI Strategic Intervention

Access Content Provide opportunities for children to discuss traveling by horse-and-buggy and skis. Have them talk about what it would be like to ride in a horse-and-buggy or travel on skis in their neighborhoods.

Use Amazing Words

To reinforce the concept and the Amazing Words, have children supply the appropriate Amazing Word for each sentence.

Our _____ let us slide quickly over snow. (skis)

We rode a _____ at the old-fashioned farm. (horse-and-buggy)

ELL Expand Vocabulary Use the Day 3 instruction on ELL Poster 30 to help children expand vocabulary.

ELL Poster 30

Objectives

◎ Isolate initial /y/ and /kw/.
- Discriminate initial and medial /u/.
- Segment words.
- Blend words.

Phonemic Awareness
 Initial /y/ and /kw/

Review

/y/ and /kw/ Display the *yarn* Picture Card. Listen as I say this word: *yarn*. What is the first sound in *yarn*? Say it with me: /y/ /y/ /y/, *yarn*. Display the *quilt* Picture Card. Listen as I say this word: *quilt*. What is the first sound in *quilt*? Say it with me: /kw/ /kw/ /kw/, *quilt*. Today we will continue to practice words with /y/ and /kw/.

Picture Card

Isolate initial /y/ and /kw/

Display Decodable Reader 30, *The Quiz* on p. 118. This picture shows a boy taking a quiz. What sound do you hear in the beginning of *quiz*? Say the word with me: /kw/ -iz, *quiz*. I hear /kw/. Continue the routine with the following words: *queen, quack, yum, yard.*

Discriminate sounds

Display the *queen* and *kite* Picture Cards. Point to each card as you say the word. Which word has the same beginning sound as *quiz*? Say the words with me: *quiz, queen, kite.* I hear /kw/ at the beginning of *quiz* and *queen*. Display the *yellow* and *jam* Picture Cards. Which word has the same beginning sound as *yum*? Say the words with me: *yum, yellow, jam.* I hear /y/ at the beginning of *yellow* and *yum*.

Picture Card

On their own

Display the *quarter, quilt, queen, yak, yarn, yellow,* and *yo-yo* Picture Cards. Have children choose a /kw/ Picture Card and a /y/ Picture Card and make up a sentence using those words.

Segment

Listen to the sounds in *yet*: /y/ /e/ /t/. Say them with me: /y/ /e/ /t/. How many sounds do you hear? There are three sounds in *yet*. Let's try some more words. Continue the routine with *yam, yes, yum,* and *yip.*

Listen to the sounds in *quack*: /kw/ /a/ /k/. Say them with me: /kw/ /a/ /k/. How many sounds do you hear? There are three sounds in *quack*. Let's try some more words. Continue the routine with *quick, quill, quit,* and *quiz.*

Corrective feedback

If... children cannot segment words into sounds,

then... provide practice segmenting the words into chunks /y/ -*ak*.

Blend

Remind children that they know how to blend sounds together to say a word. I am going to say some sounds and I want you to blend them to say a word. Listen carefully: /y/ /e/ /s/. Now say the sounds with me: /y/ /e/ /s/, *yes*. The word is *yes*. Continue to practice blending with *yet, yam, quit,* and *Quinn.*

Differentiated Instruction

SI **Strategic Intervention**

Supporting Blending Remind children to say each sound in a blend before blending them together. For example, there are four distinct sounds in *yelp*: /y/ /e/ /l/ /p/.

Objectives

- Practice /y/ spelled *Yy* and /kw/ spelled *qu.*
- Review sound-spellings.
- Read high-frequency words.

Check Word Reading
SUCCESS PREDICTOR

Phonics — Teach/Model
/y/ Spelled *Yy* and /kw/ Spelled *qu*

Review

/y/Yy Display the *Yy* Alphabet Card and point to the *yo-yo*. What sound do you hear at the beginning of *yo-yo?* What letter spells that sound? Point to the letters *Yy.* What is the sound for these letters? What is the name of these letters?

/kw/qu Display the *Qq* Alphabet Card and point to the *queen*. What sound do you hear at the beginning of *queen?* What letter spells that sound? Point to the letters *qu.* What is the sound for these letters together? What are the names of these letters?

Review

Letter Names and Sounds Use Alphabet Cards to review the following letter names and sounds: *Cc, Dd, Ee, Ii, Ll, Tt, Uu, Vv, Zz.*

Blend sounds

Write *yet* on the board. I am going to blend the sound of each letter together to say this word. Point to each letter as you say the sound: /y/ /c/ /t/. When I blend these sounds together, I make the word *yet*. Say the sounds with me: /y/ /e/ /t/. Now blend the sounds together: /y/ /e/ /t/, *yet*. Repeat the blending routine with *yak, quill,* and *quit*.

More practice

Use *Reader's and Writer's Notebook,* p. 391, for additional practice with /y/ and /kw/.

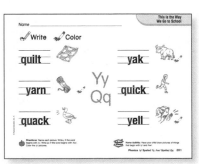

Reader's and Writer's Notebook, p. 391

Review | **Sound-Spelling** Display the *Zz* Alphabet Card. What sound do you hear at the beginning of *zigzag*? What letter spells that sound? Yes, the letter *z* spells /z/. Review the following sounds and letters with Alphabet Cards: *Aa, Cc, Dd, Ff, Gg, Ll, Nn, Oo, Tt, Uu, Ww.*

Alphabet Card

Review | **High-Frequency Words** Write *where* on the board. This is the word *where*. What is this word? Continue the routine with *come, what, said,* and *was.*

Differentiated Instruction

SI Strategic Intervention

Support High-Frequency Words Remind children that high-frequency words are not words they can sound out. Children should memorize these words so they know them when they come across them in a story.

Don't Wait Until Friday

MONITOR PROGRESS Check Word Reading High-Frequency Words

Write *where* and *come* on the board. Have children take turns reading the words.

Practice reading these words from Kindergarten Student Reader K.5.6, *Quinn Can Do It!*

Quinn	quit	yet	Dad	got	will	fun
it	can	not	get	hot	dog	

If... children cannot read the high-frequency words,
then... write the words on cards for them to practice at home.

If... children cannot blend sounds to read the words,
then... provide practice blending the words in chunks, /y/ -*et.*

If... children can successfully blend sounds to read the words,
then... have them read Kindergarten Student Reader K.5.6, *Quinn Can Do It!*

Day 1	Day 2	Day 3	Day 4	Day 5
Check Phonemic Awareness	Check Sound-Spelling/ Retelling	Check Word Reading	Check Phonemic Awareness	Check Oral Vocabulary

Success Predictor

Objectives
- Read /y/ and /kw/ words.
- Read high-frequency words.

Kindergarten Student Reader K.5.6
/y/ Spelled Yy, /kw/ Spelled qu, and High-Frequency Words

Review

Review the previously taught high-frequency words. Have children read each word as you point to it on the Word Wall.

come	here	what	look	like	you	with	for

Read Kindergarten Student Reader K.5.6

Display Kindergarten Student Reader K.5.6. Today we are going to read a new story about a boy learning to ride a bike. Point to the title of the story. The title of the story is *Quinn Can Do It!* The author's name is Evelyn Ruiz.

Use the reading decodable books routine to read the Kindergarten Student Reader.

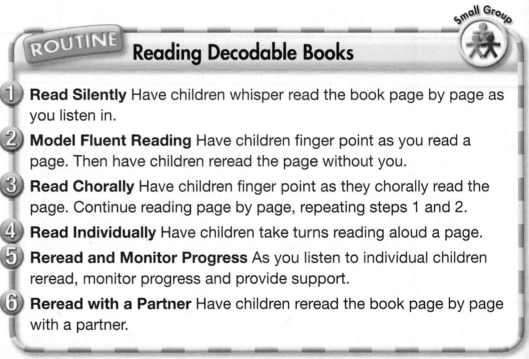

ROUTINE — **Reading Decodable Books** — *Small Group*

1. **Read Silently** Have children whisper read the book page by page as you listen in.

2. **Model Fluent Reading** Have children finger point as you read a page. Then have children reread the page without you.

3. **Read Chorally** Have children finger point as they chorally read the page. Continue reading page by page, repeating steps 1 and 2.

4. **Read Individually** Have children take turns reading aloud a page.

5. **Reread and Monitor Progress** As you listen to individual children reread, monitor progress and provide support.

6. **Reread with a Partner** Have children reread the book page by page with a partner.

Routines Flip Chart

Kindergarten Student Reader K.5.6

Differentiated Instruction

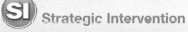

(A) Advanced

Support Retelling Have children retell *Quinn Can Do It!* in front of the class to practice their retelling and speaking skills.

(SI) Strategic Intervention

High-Frequency Words To prepare children for Kindergarten Student Reader K.5.6, have them make up sentences using the following high-frequency words: *come, here, what, look, like, is, go, do, you, he, with, me, a, for.*

Small Group Time

DAY 3 Break into small groups to read the Kindergarten Student Reader before the comprehension lesson.

Teacher-Led

(SI) Strategic Intervention	**(OL) On-Level**	**(A) Advanced**
Teacher-Led Page DI•88 • Phonemic Awareness and Phonics • **Read** Concept Literacy Reader K.5.6 or Kindergarten Student Reader K.5.6	**Teacher-Led** Page DI•92 • Phonemic Awareness and Phonics • **Read** Kindergarten Student Reader K.5.6	**Teacher-Led** Page DI•95 • **Read** Independent Reader K.5.6 or Kindergarten Student Reader K.5.6

E L L Place English language learners in the groups that correspond to their reading abilities in English.

Practice Stations
• Visit the Words to Know Station
• Visit the Let's Write! Station

Independent Activities
• Read independently
• Audio Text of Big Book
• *Reader's and Writer's Notebook*

Objectives
- Recall and retell a selection.
- ◎ Practice drawing conclusions.
- Develop and use vocabulary.
- Develop and apply comprehension skills.

Comprehension

Retell the story

Have children turn to p. 126 of *My Skills Buddy* and use the retelling boxes to retell the story *This Is the Way We Go to School*.

Envision It!

Direct children to the first retell box. This part of the story shows one way that children get to school: walking. Tell me one conclusion you can draw about how far these children live from their school.

Continue reviewing the retelling boxes and having children retell the story.

My Skills Buddy, p. 126

Review

Draw Conclusions Display illustrations in *This Is the Way We Go to School*. Sometimes when we read a story, we figure out more on our own by combining what we already know with what the story says. Let's practice drawing some conclusions about the story.

- Why would some children ride a boat to school? **(They need to cross a river or body of water.)**

- Why can some children go on skis to school? **(They have a lot of snow where they live.)**

- Why do some children get to stop and play on their way to school? **(They live very close to their school.)**

More practice

Use *Reader's and Writer's Notebook,* p. 392, for additional practice with drawing conclusions.

Reader's and Writer's Notebook, p. 392

Second Read—Trade Book
This Is the Way We Go to School

Develop vocabulary

Reread *This Is the Way We Go to School*. Follow the Day 3 arrow beginning on p. 566, and use the Develop Vocabulary Notes to prompt conversations about the story.

Have children use the Amazing Words *cable car, trolley, horse-and-buggy, skis, Metro line,* and *vaporetto* to talk about the story.

DAY **2**
Read for enjoyment

DAY **3**
Reread using Develop Vocabulary notes

DAY **4**
Reread using Guide Comprehension notes

English Language Learners
Frontload Story Take children on a picture walk through the story to heighten interest and draw attention to the modes of transportation. Point out the various cultures illustrated in the book. Guide class discussion of these cultures, encouraging children with a similar cultural background to share their knowledge and experience.

Develop Vocabulary

DAY 3

Wh- question

Where are these four children going? (school)

- The children are going to school. How are these children getting to school? (They are walking.)

> One by one or two by two—
> Come along, it's fun to do!

Trade Book, p. 5

Guide Comprehension

DAY 4

Inferential

What does "one by one" mean? (one at a time) What does "two by two" mean? (two at a time)

Wh- question

How does Ellen get to school? (by walking)

- Ellen walks to school. What does she see on her way?

Trade Book, pp. 6–7

Draw Conclusions

Do you think that Ellen lives close to her school? (yes) What makes you think so? (She probably lives close by because she walks to school and has time to go slow on her way there.)

Develop Vocabulary, continued

DAY 3

Distancing

Liz and Larry are jogging. What is this boy doing? (roller skating)

- The boy is roller skating. Have you ever gone roller skating?

Liz and Larry, as a rule, wear their jogging shoes to school.

But at twenty minutes past, roller skates are twice as fast.

Trade Book, pp. 8–9

Guide Comprehension, continued

DAY 4

Draw Conclusions

Use what you know about getting to school plus what this page says to figure out what "twenty minutes past" means. (It means that the boy skating probably needs to get to school very soon, perhaps 25 or 30 minutes past 8:00 A.M.)

Open-ended

What else can take children to school? (a bus or a car)

- Children can ride in a bus or car. Why would children take a bus or go in a car?

Develop Vocabulary car

And the fastest way by far   is by school bus or by car!

Trade Book, pp. 10–11

Connect to personal experience

How do most of the children you know get to school? Do some take the school bus? Do some come by car? Do some walk?

Develop Vocabulary, continued

DAY 3

Wh- question

What place does this picture show?
(a city with a river)

- This city is on a river. What do these children take to get to school? (a boat, the Staten Island ferry)

Jenny, Jerry, Pete, and Perry   ride the Staten Island Ferry.

Trade Book, pp. 12–13

Guide Comprehension, continued

DAY 4

Draw Conclusions

Look at the picture on these pages. Use what you know about children who live in big cities. Do you think all the children in this city take the ferry to school? Why or why not? (Some children may walk, bike, or ride in a car or train.)

Wh- question

Wow! This is a big hill. What are children using to get to school here? **(a cable car)**

- The children are riding on a cable car. How many cable cars do you see? **(two)**

Cable cars take Jack and Jill up the hill—

and down the hill.

Trade Book, pp. 14–15

Inferential

Why do you think the children take a cable car instead of a bus? **(Buses cannot go up such steep hills, but cable cars can.)**

Develop Vocabulary, continued

DAY 3

Distancing

What are these boys riding? (a train)

- The boys are on the El, which is a train on tracks high above the street. *El* is short for *elevated*. This train is elevated because it rides above the street. What other stories about trains have we read?

Expand Vocabulary the El

Michael and his friend Miguel see the rooftops from the El.

Horse-and-buggy rides, it's plain, start the day for Jake and Jane.

Trade Book, pp. 16–17

Guide Comprehension, continued

DAY 4

Activate prior knowledge

What does "the El" stand for?
(It is short for "the Elevated train."
For Spanish speakers, "the El"
translates into "the the," so translate
the phrase for them first.

Open-ended

Look very carefully at the picture. What makes the trolley different from a normal bus? **(It is attached to wires at the top.)**

• The trolley is a bus powered by these electric wires. Why are the children running toward the trolley?

And in Philly, Mitch and Molly go to school by trackless trolley!

Bianca, Beppo, Benedetto ride aboard the *vaporetto*.

Trade Book, pp. 18–19

Recall

It looks like the vaporetto is a kind of boat. What other kind of boat did we read about? (the Staten Island ferry on pp. 12–13)

Develop Vocabulary, continued

Open-ended

DAY 3

What are these children wearing?
(hats, mittens, and jackets)

• Niels and Solveig are wearing
hats, mittens, and jackets. Why
are they wearing winter clothes?
(It is cold and snowy where they
live. It is probably winter.)

Bundled up against the breeze,   Niels and Solveig go on skis.

Trade Book, pp. 20–21

Guide Comprehension, continued

DAY 4

Draw Conclusions

How do you suppose Niels and
Solveig get to school when there
is no snow? What makes you think
so? (They probably walk. Although
skiing might be faster, they must be
close enough to school to walk if
necessary.)

Recall

Is this a warm or cold place? **(a warm place)**

- This is a warm place. How is this boy keeping cool? **(He is walking in the shade.)**

Mira takes time out to play,
school's a hop and skip away.

Palm trees help keep Ahmed cool
on his sunny walk to school.

Trade Book, pp. 22–23

Recall

Ahmed walks to school, and it looks like Mira does too. What other children have we read about who also walk to school? **(the children on p. 5; Ellen on p. 6)**

Develop Vocabulary, continued

DAY 3

Open-ended
What is the background of both of these pictures? (mountains)

- These children live near mountains. What is another way to get down the mountain?

Develop Vocabulary train

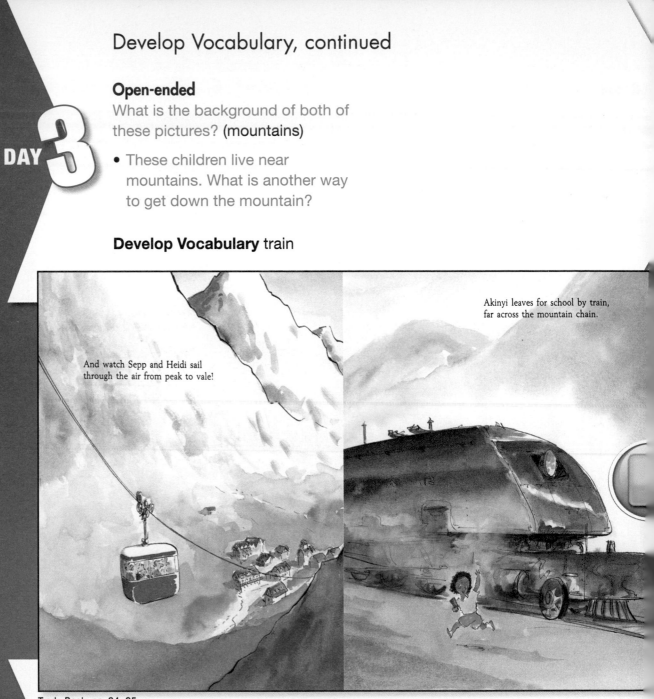

And watch Sepp and Heidi sail through the air from peak to vale!

Akinyi leaves for school by train, far across the mountain chain.

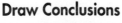
Trade Book, pp. 24–25

Guide Comprehension, continued

DAY 4

Draw Conclusions
Use what you know and what you see in these pictures to tell whether these children live far away from school or near it. (They live far away from school.)

Open-ended

What are these children using? **(a radio)**

- These children are using a radio to speak to their teacher. Why do they use the radio? **(They live very far from school.)**

Develop Vocabulary bicycles, radio

Kay and Fay and Flo and Joe go to school by radio.

Bicycles bring Mei and Ling through the traffic of Nanjing.

Trade Book, pp. 26–27

Wh- question

What other kind of machine could these children use instead of a radio? **(They might use a computer.)**

Develop Vocabulary, continued

Open-ended

How can someone in this rainy picture get to school? **(by bus or car)**

DAY 3

- You could ride in a car or a double-decker bus. What could you see from the top level of that bus?

And beneath the dripping sky, Ram is riding high and dry.

William comes ashore by boat, counting sea gulls while afloat.

Trade Book, pp. 28-29

Guide Comprehension, continued

DAY 4

Compare and Contrast

Here is another boat. How is it like the others we've seen? How is it different? **(It's like the others because it carries children to school over water. It's different because it is smaller.)**

Open-ended

How does Carlos get to school? (He is running.)

- Carlos is running. Why do you think he is running?

Luz prefers the countryside.

Carlos takes the town in stride.

Trade Book, pp. 30–31

Contrast

Look at the town on p. 30 and the countryside on p. 31. How are these places different? (The town is crowded with buildings, but the countryside seems open.)

Develop Vocabulary, continued

Wh- question

What are all these people waiting for? (a train)

DAY 3

- The people are waiting for a train. What kind of train is this? (an underground train, or subway)

And the famous Metro line suits Igor and Ilyana fine.

Trade Book, pp. 32–33

Guide Comprehension, continued

DAY 4

Draw Conclusions

Where is this train? (in a city) A train like this that goes in a tunnel underground is called a subway. Do you think a small town would have a subway? Why or why not? (I do not think a small town would have a subway. There would not be enough people to ride it.)

Open-ended

These look like fun ways to go to school.
What are these children riding to school?
(helicopter, sled)

• These children ride in a helicopter and the
  others are on a sled behind a snowmobile.
  Could you walk to school In thls weather?

Go by Copter?

By Skidoo?
Somewhere, sometimes, some kids do!

Trade Book, pp. 34–35

Recall

What other way of getting to school in the
snow have we read about? (skiing, pp. 20–21)

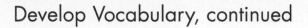

Develop Vocabulary, continued

Open-ended

Where do you think these children are going? (to school)

DAY 3

- I think these children are going to school. How do you get to school?

You come, too! We'll look for you.

THIS IS WHERE WE LIVE

Ellen lives in Hawaii, U.S.A.
Liz and Larry and the skater live in California, U.S.A.
The bus and car riders live in Raytown, Missouri, U.S.A.
Jenny, Jerry, Pete, and Perry live in Staten Island, New York, U.S.A.
Jack and Jill live in San Francisco, California, U.S.A.
Michael and Miguel live in Chicago, Illinois, U.S.A.
Jake and Jane live in Lancaster, Pennsylvania, U.S.A.
Mitch and Molly live in Philadelphia, Pennsylvania, U.S.A.
Bianca, Beppo, and Benedetto live in Venice, Italy.
Niels and Solveig live in Norway.
Ahmed lives in Egypt.
Mira lives in Israel.
Sepp and Heidi live in Switzerland.
Akinyi lives in Kenya.
Kay, Fay, Flo, and Joe live in Australia.
Mei and Ling live in China.
Ram lives in India.
William lives in Maine, U.S.A.
Carlos and Luz live in Mexico.
Igor and Ilyana live in Moscow, Russia.
The Copter passengers live in Siberia, Russia.
The Skidoo passengers live in Canada.

Trade Book, pp. 36–37

Guide Comprehension, continued

DAY 4

Draw Conclusions

What are the children carrying? (books) How does that help you figure out that they are on the way to school? (Books are used at school.)

Open-ended

This is a map of the world that shows where the children in the story live. What is written on the map? (numbers)

• This map has numbers marking where the children live. Find North America. Which children live near you?

Continue with DAY 3
Conventions p. 584

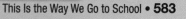

① Ellen	⑦ Jake and Jane	⑬ Sepp and Heidi	⑲ Carlos
② Liz and Larry and the skater	⑧ Mitch and Molly	⑭ Akinyi	⑳ Luz
③ The bus and car riders	⑨ Bianca, Beppo, and Benedetto	⑮ Kay, Fay, Flo, and Joe	㉑ Igor and Ilyana
④ Jenny, Jerry, Pete, and Perry	⑩ Niels and Solveig	⑯ Mei and Ling	㉒ The Copter passengers
⑤ Jack and Jill	⑪ Ahmed	⑰ Ram	㉓ The Skidoo passengers
⑥ Michael and Miguel	⑫ Mira	⑱ William	

Trade Book, pp. 38–39

Open-ended

Who can find where we live on this map?

Skip to DAY 4
Conventions p. 598

Objectives

- Review nouns in sentences.
- Develop and write a first draft of a how-to report.

Conventions
Nouns in Sentences

Review

Remind children that nouns name people, animals, places, and things. Write these words and sentence on the board:

> car   bus   boat
>
> We can travel to school in a _____.

Guide practice

Let's use some nouns in sentences. We can put our nouns into the same sentence, one at a time. I have written a sentence on the board. I will read the sentence and AlphaBuddy will call on someone to use a noun to complete the sentence. Write the noun each child suggests on the line. Read the sentence aloud, pointing to the noun and reading it with children. Have children add other nouns to use in the sentence.

Team Talk Pair children and have them take turns making up **sentences**. Have children identify the noun in their partners' sentences and tell if it is a person, animal, place, or thing. Then have children write their nouns.

On their own

Use *Reader's and Writer's Notebook*, p. 393, for more practice with nouns in sentences.

Daily Fix-It

Use the Daily Fix-It for more conventions practice.

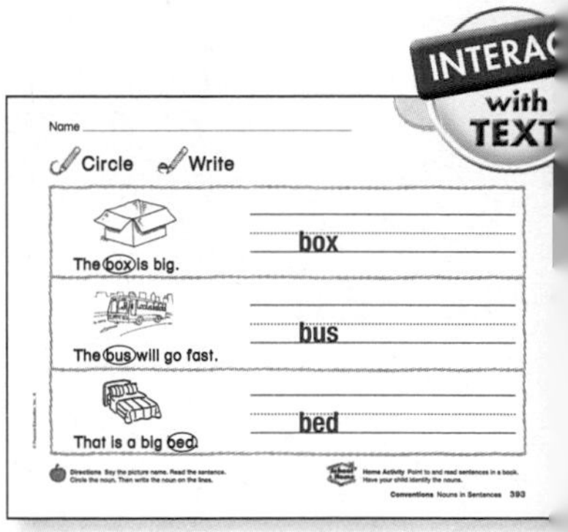

INTERAC with TEXT

Reader's and Writer's Notebook, p. 393

Writing

Writing Process:
Draft a How-to Report

Teach: Gather evidence

Today we will gather the information for our how-to report on how to check out a book from the library. Then we will start writing a draft of our report. A draft is a first try at writing. We'll come back to our draft later and make it better. Right now we just want to get the main words down on the paper in the right order.

Model: Gather evidence

Display the library brochure about checking out books that you discussed yesterday. Here's the brochure we thought would be a good one for gathering facts about checking out books.

Read aloud information about how to get a library card. In this brochure, we learn that before we can check out a book, we must sign up for a library card. Record this information using words and an illustration. Write the number 1 next to them. (Possible sentence: *First, sign up for a card.*)

Guide practice: Gather evidence

Listen for the next thing we need to do to check out a book. Read aloud information from the brochure about finding a book to check out. What should we write next? Write and illustrate children's suggestions. Write the number 2 next to them. (Possible sentence: *Next, find a book you want to read.*)

Listen for the last thing you need to do to check out a book. Read aloud information about showing your library card to the librarian before leaving. Again, write and illustrate children's suggestions about what you just read. Write the number 3 next to them. (Possible sentence: *Last, show your new card.*)

Independent writing

Reread and discuss what you wrote, underlining key words in your draft. Have children write or dictate the group draft or copy the underlined key words on p. 394 in *Reader's and Writer's Notebook.*

Reader's and Writer's Notebook, p. 394

Academic Vocabulary

draft a first version of a piece of writing

Daily Fix-It

do you walk to school
<u>D</u>o you walk to school<u>?</u>

This week's practice sentences appear on Teacher Resources DVD-ROM.

- Practice discussing plot.
- Speak loudly and clearly.
- Speak one at a time.
- Face the speaker when listening.

Listening and Speaking
Discuss Literary Features: Plot

Review

Remember, when we talk about a story, we can talk about the plot, or what happens at the beginning, in the middle, and at the end of the story.

Model

Tell children this story: AlphaBuddy is walking along, singing "This is the way we go to school, go to school, go to school; this is the way we go to school so early in the morning." Suddenly, AlphaBuddy stops and says, "Oh look! It's such a nice day! I think I'll ride my scooter to school because it is more fun than walking!"

Have children turn to p. 129 of *My Skills Buddy.* These pictures at the top show the first part of my story. Follow along with pictures as I tell the rest of the story. Continue the story, telling how AlphaBuddy meets a friend riding a bicycle. He and his friend trade rides and now AlphaBuddy is riding the bike. Then he sees a friend skipping to school, so AlphaBuddy decides to skip too. By the time he gets to school, he is tired from trying so many fun ways to get to school.

Guide practice

Use the Listening and Speaking bullets on p. 128 of *My Skills Buddy* to guide the discussion about plot. Think about what happens first to AlphaBuddy. Then what happens? What happens next? What happens last? Continue to discuss the story's plot.

My Skills Buddy, p. 129

Independent practice

Divide the class into three groups and have each group discuss the plot of Decodable Story 30, *Run, Tim*, Decodable Reader 30, *The Quiz,* or Kindergarten Student Reader K.5.6, *Quinn Can Do It!* Monitor small group discussion to check that children are retelling the beginning, the middle, and the end of the story in the correct sequence. Refer children to their Rules for Listening and Speaking from pp. 1–2 of *Reader's and Writer's Notebook.* Tell children to speak one at a time during discussions. Remind them to face the speaker as they listen.

Name _____

Listening Rules

1. Face the person who is speaking.
2. Be quiet while someone is speaking.
3. Pay attention to the speaker.
4. Ask questions if you don't understand.

Reader's and Writer's Notebook, pp. 1–2

Be a Good Listener

1. Face the speaker.
2. Ask questions if you don't understand.
3. Be quiet when others are speaking.
4. Speak one at a time.

Teacher Tip

Watch for children's tendencies to repeat too much detail and to follow tangents while retelling and discussing plot.

English Language Learners
Support Retelling Guide children in retelling the stories by providing copies of Decodable Story 30, Decodable Reader 30, and Kindergarten Student Reader K.5.6. Encourage children to use the pictures in these stories to aid in their retelling.

Wrap Up Your Day

✔ **Concept Talk** Today we talked more about ways children get to school. Did one of them ever ride a *quiet yak* to school? What would that be like?

✔ **Respond to Literature** Today we read about Quinn learning to ride a bike. Have you learned to ride a bike? What was it like?

✔ **Conventions** Have children write or dictate a sentence about the way they go to school. Have them circle any nouns in their sentence.

✔ **Homework Idea** Have children draw and label a picture of something they see at home whose name begins with a *q* or *y*.

Preview DAY 4

Tomorrow we will read about one of our Trucktown friends.

Extend Your Day!

Conventions
Getting to School
Materials: paper, crayons

Learn a Song Teach children the song "Going to School," sung to the tune of "She'll Be Coming 'Round the Mountain."

All the children ride the bus to school,

All the children ride the bus to school.

They'll be walking, they'll be riding,

They'll be floating, they'll be flying, oh.

All the children ride the bus to school!

Add New Verbs and Nouns Replace lyrics in the song with several different ways children get to school, such as *walk on foot, take the train, row a boat,* or *ride on skis.* Point out that each group of words includes a verb and a noun. Ask children to add other phrases with a verb and a noun. Have children illustrate one of the verses.

All the children ride the bus to school.

Science
Mountain and Valley
Materials: Trade Book *This Is the Way We Go to School*, paper plates, modeling clay

Peak and Vale Display p. 21 of *This Is the Way We Go to School*. The mountain peak is the top of the mountain. Mountain peaks often have snow on them. The place between mountains is called a vale or valley.

Make Mountains Have groups use clay to build models of two mountains with a valley between them, using paper plates as a base. Have children place their models on the tray. Pour water on them to simulate snow melting on the mountain and flowing down to form streams.

Social Studies
Where in the World?
Materials: construction paper, crayons, world map

Ways to Get to School Let's list ways to get to school in different parts of the world. Write children's responses on the board. Have them illustrate and label a form of transportation from the list. Have children show their pictures and let the class conclude where the scene could take place. Help children find that location on a world map.

Objectives

- Discuss the concept to develop oral language.
- Build oral vocabulary.

Today at a Glance

Oral Vocabulary
Motro lino, vaporotto

Phonemic Awareness
/v/ and /z/

Phonics
/v/ Spelled *Vv*
/z/ Spelled *Zz*
Spell Words

Comprehension
◉ Draw Conclusions

Conventions
Verbs

Writing
Revise a How-to Report

Vocabulary
Action Words

TRUCKTOWN on Reading Street

Start your engines!

- Display "This Little Truck" and lead the group in saying the rhyme a few times.
- Have the group clap the rhythm as they recite the rhyme.
- When children master the rhythm, have them march around the room as they say the rhyme.

Truckery Rhymes

Concept Talk

Question of the Week

How do children around the world get to school?

Build concepts

Write and read the question of the week as you track the print. Have children answer the question in complete sentences. Display Sing with Me Chart 30B.

Listen for Amazing Words

We are going to sing this song again. Listen for the Amazing Words *Metro line* and *vaporetto*. Sing the song several times with children to the tune of "Here We Go 'Round the Mulberry Bush." Have them clap when they hear *Metro line* and *vaporetto*.

🔘 Sing with Me Audio

ELL Produce Oral Language Use the Day 4 instruction on ELL Poster 30 to extend and enrich language.

How Do Children Get to School?

How do children get to school,
Get to school, get to school,
How do children get to school,
All around the world?

Talk with Me/Sing with Me Chart 30B

Poster 30

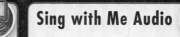
Oral Vocabulary
Amazing Words

Amazing Words

cable car	trolley
horse-and-buggy	skis
Metro line	vaporetto

Teach Amazing Words

> ### ★ Amazing Words ★ Oral Vocabulary Routine
>
> **1 Introduce the Word** The *Metro line* is a train that travels underground to take people around the city. What is our new word for an underground train that runs through a city? Say it with me: *Metro line*.
>
> **2 Demonstrate** *In some large cities, a Metro line is needed to help everyone travel quickly.*
>
> Repeat steps 1 and 2.
>
> **Introduce the Word** A *vaporetto* is a boat that is like a bus and carries people over water in the city of Venice, Italy. What is our new word for a boat that takes people around Venice? Say it with me: *vaporetto*.
>
> **Demonstrate** *If you visit Venice, you can take a vaporetto to your hotel.*
>
> **3 Apply** Have children use *Metro line* and *vaporetto* in complete sentences. Have them illustrate the words.

Routines Flip Chart

Use Amazing Words

To reinforce the concept and the Amazing Words, have children supply the appropriate Amazing Word for each sentence.

A _____ **is like a bus that goes on water.** (vaporetto)

The _____ **is a train that goes underground.** (Metro line)

ELL

English Language Learners

Access Content Explain to children that *vaporetto* is the name of a special Italian boat. Have them share any names for special boats in their home language.

Access Content Explain to children that some words stay the same in any language. *Metro* is an English word and remains the same even when translated into other languages.

Objectives
- Review /v/ spelled *Vv*.
- Review /z/ spelled *Zz*.

Check Phonemic Awareness
SUCCESS PREDICTOR

Phonemic Awareness
Review /v/ and /z/

Review

Display the *van* Picture Card. This is a *van. Van* begins with /v/. What sound does *van* begin with? Continue with the Picture Cards *vacuum, vase,* and *vest.* Then display the *zebra* Picture Card. This is a *zebra. Zebra* begins with /z/. What sound does *zebra* begin with? Continue with the Picture Cards *zipper* and *zoo.*

I am going to say three words. Tell me which word doesn't begin with the same sound. Listen carefully: *van, vest, zip.* Which word doesn't belong? *Zip* doesn't belong because it begins with /z/. *Van* and *vest* begin with /v/. Continue with the following word groups: *zoom, volcano, zip; veggies, zinnias, violets; valentine, violin, zebra; zipper, vine, zoo.*

Picture Card

Corrective feedback

If... children cannot discriminate /v/ or /z/, **then...** say each sound several times and have children watch you closely as you do so.

When you say /v/, your bottom lip buzzes across your top teeth. When you say /z/, your teeth are close together and your tongue buzzes against them. Have children practice saying /v/ and /z/. Then repeat the discrimination activity.

Picture Card

Phonics
/v/ Spelled Vv and /z/ Spelled Zz

Review

Display the *Vv* Alphabet Card. This is a *volcano*. *Volcano* begins with /v/. What letter spells this sound /v/? Yes, the letter *v*. Display the *Zz* Alphabet Card. This is a *zigag*. *Zigzag* begins with /z/. What letter spells this sound /z/? Yes, the letter *z*.

Write the word *vest* on the board. Help me blend this word. Listen as I say each sound: /v/ /e/ /s/ /t/. Now let's blend the sounds together to read the word: /v/ /e/ /s/ /t/, *vest*. What is the word? (*vest*) Let's try more. Repeat the routine with *Val, zip,* and *zap*.

Alphabet Card

Alphabet Card

Don't Wait Until Friday

MONITOR PROGRESS | Check Phonemic Awareness

Phoneme Segmentation I am going to say a word. I want you to tell me the sounds in the word.

| quit | quick | yak | quiz | yes | quilt | yel | yum |

If... children cannot segment the sounds,

then... use the small-group Strategic Intervention lesson, p. DI•89, to reteach segmentation skills.

Continue to monitor children's progress using other instructional opportunities during the week so that they can be successful with the Day 5 Assessment. See the Skills Trace on p. 526.

Day 1	Day 2	Day 3	Day 4	Day 5
Check Phonemic Awareness	Check Sound-Spelling/ Retelling	Check Word Reading	Check Phonemic Awareness	Check Oral Vocabulary

Success Predictor

Teacher Tip

The spoken English language has several pairs of consonant sounds that are formed identically in the mouth, with one being voiced and the other unvoiced:

/b/ is voiced /p/

/d/ is voiced /t/

/v/ is voiced /f/

/j/ is voiced /ch/

/g/ is voiced /k/

/z/ is voiced /s/

/zh/ is voiced /sh/

 ELL

English Language Learners

Support Phonics Speakers of Japanese, Korean, and Spanish may have a hard time distinguishing /b/ and /v/. Show how the lips and teeth are used differently to produce each sound. Provide additional practice with /v/ words.

Phonemic Awareness

Success Predictor

Objectives
- Spell words.
- Blend and segment words.

Spelling
/y/ Spelled Yy and /kw/ Spelled qu

ROUTINE Spell Words

1. **Review Sound-Spellings** Display the *Yy* Alphabet Card. This is a *yo-yo. Yo-yo* begins with /y/. What is the letter for /y/? (*y*) Continue the routine with the following Alphabet Cards: *Qq, Vv,* and *Zz.*

2. **Model** Today we are going to spell some words. Listen to the three sounds in *yak:* /y/ /a/ /k/.

   - What is the first sound in *yak?* (/y/) What is the letter for /y/? (*y*) Write *y* on the board.
   - What is the middle sound in *yak?* (/a/) What is the letter for /a/? (*a*) Write *a* on the board.
   - What is the last sound in *yak?* (/k/) What is the letter for /k/? (*k*) Write *k* on the board.
   - Point to *yak.* Help me blend the sound of each letter together to read this word: /y/ /a/ /k/. The word is *yak.* Repeat with the word *quiz.*

3. **Guide Practice** Now let's spell the word *quit* together. Listen to the sounds in *quit:* /kw/ /i/ /t/. What is the first sound in *quit?* (/kw/) What are the letters for /kw/? (*qu*) Write *qu* on the board. Remember that the letter *q* has its buddy *u* with it. Now write *q* and *u* on your paper. What is the middle sound in *quit?* (/i/) What is the letter for /i/? (*i*) Write *i* on the board. Now write *i* on your paper. What is the last sound in *quit?* (/t/) What is the letter for /t/? (*t*) Write *t* on the board. Now write *t* on your paper. Now we can blend the sounds of the letters together to read the word: /kw/ /i/ /t/. What is the word? (*quit*) Continue spell and blend practice with the following words: *yes, vet, zip.*

4. **On Your Own** This time I am going to say a word. I want you to write the word on your paper. Remember, first say the word slowly in your head and then write the letter for each sound you hear. Listen carefully. Write the word *yet.* Give children time to write the word. How do you spell the word *yet?* Listen to the sounds: /y/ /e/ /t/. The first sound is /y/. What is the letter for /y/? Did you write *y* on your paper? What is the letter for /e/? Did you write *e* on your paper? What is the letter for /t/? Did you write *t* on your paper? Name the letters in *yet.* *Yet* is spelled *y, e, t.* Continue the activity with the following words: *yam, yes, yum, quit, quiz, vet, van, zip, zap.*

Routines Flip Chart

Get Set, Roll! Reader 30
🔊 Practice /y/ Spelled *Yy* and /kw/ Spelled *qu*

Review
Review the high-frequency words *is, go, where,* and *come.* Have children read each word as you point to it on the Word Wall.

Read Get Set, Roll! Reader 30
Today we will read a story about a race between Max and Jack. Point to the title of the story. What is the title of the story? *Yes!* is the title of the story. We will read some /y/ and /kw/ words in this book.

Use the routine for reading decodable books found in the Routines Flip Chart to read Get Set, Roll! Reader 30.

Get Set, Roll! Reader 30

Differentiated Instruction

A Advanced
Practice High-Frequency Words Have children copy the high-frequency words *is, go, where* and *come* on their Write-On Boards. Have them use the Word Wall as reference.

Small Group Time

DAY 4 Break into small groups to read the Get Set, Roll! Reader before the comprehension lesson.

Teacher-Led

SI Strategic Intervention	**OL** On-Level	**A** Advanced
Teacher-Led Page DI•89 • Phonemic Awareness and Phonics • **Read** Get Set, Roll! Reader 30	**Teacher-Led** Page DI•93 • Get Set, Roll! Reader 30	**Teacher-Led** Page DI•96 • **Read** Get Set, Roll! Reader 30 or **Reread** Kindergarten Student Reader K.5.6

ELL Place English language learners in the groups that correspond to their reading abilities in English.

Practice Stations
• Visit the Let's Write! Station
• Visit the Read for Meaning Station

Independent Activities
• Read independently
• Audio Text of the Trade Book
• *Reader's and Writer's Notebook*

English Language Learners
Frontload Reader Take a picture walk with children to preview the reader before starting the routine.

Comprehension
Draw Conclusions

Practice draw conclusions

 Envision It!

Have children turn to the Draw Conclusions picture on p. 114 of *My Skills Buddy.* As you look at the picture, remind children that they can use pictures, words, and what they already know to decide things about stories.

My Skills Buddy, pp. 114–115

Team Talk Pair children and have them take turns drawing conclusions about where children live based on how they get to school in *This Is the Way We Go to School.* Remind them to use both pictures and plot elements in drawing their conclusions.

Main Idea: Theme

Review

Direct children to the Main Idea picture on pp. 94–95 of *My Skills Buddy.* Main idea is the most important idea a story tells. Another word for main idea is *theme.* You can tell about a story's theme in just a few words. Good readers pay attention to the main idea, or theme, of what they read. This helps them understand and remember stories.

Display AlphaBuddy. AlphaBuddy is going to tell you a story about this picture. Listen for main idea, or theme, in the story. It is morning and the bell rings for school to start. Tim rides his bike to get to school. Ann and Ben walk to get to school. Tina rides in a car to get to school. Other children ride in a bus to get to school. They all get to school on time!

• What is the main idea, or theme, of this story? (Children get to school in different ways.)

• How do you know? (The pictures show children getting to school. The words tell how each child gets to school. I know how I get to school.)

More practice

For more practice with main idea, use *Reader's and Writer's Notebook,* p. 395.

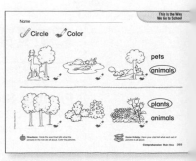

Reader's and Writer's Notebook, p. 395

Third Read—Trade Book
This Is the Way We Go to School

Guide comprehension

Display *This Is the Way We Go to School.* Remember, sometimes a clue to the main idea of a story is in its title.

- According to this book, where do all children go? (to school)

- Why don't all children go to school the same way? (They live in different countries where the weather, land, and water are different.)

- Why do some children get to school faster while others get there slower? (different distances, different ways of getting there)

- What is the main idea, or theme, of this story? (There are many different ways to get to school.)

Reread *This Is the Way We Go to School.* Return to p. 566. Follow the Day 4 arrow and use the Guide Comprehension notes to give children the opportunity to gain a more complete understanding of the story.

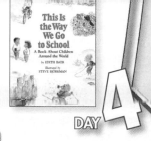

DAY **2**
Read for enjoyment

DAY **3**
Reread using Develop Vocabulary notes

DAY **4**
Reread using Guide Comprehension notes

Objectives
- Practice using verbs.
- Revise a class how-to report by adding details and sentences.

Conventions
Verbs

Review   Remind children what they learned about verbs. Some words are action words, or verbs. Verbs tell what nouns do. Remember, nouns are words for people, animals, places, and things. There are nouns to name each one of us, and there are verbs to tell what each of one of us can do! What are things we can do? Listen for verbs in these sentences: *We can run. We can sit. Run* is a verb. *Sit* is a verb. *Run* and *sit* tell what we can do, so they are verbs.

Guide practice   I will say another sentence. Raise your hand when you hear the verb in my sentence: *I write on the board.* Continue with these sentences: *Pam jumps rope. Nan plays in the park. Rob runs the fastest. We race to the store.* Have children make up a sentence and then identify its verb.

On their own   Use *Reader's and Writer's Notebook,* p. 396, for more practice with verbs.

Daily Fix-It   Use the Daily Fix-It for more conventions practice.

INTERAC with TEXT

Reader's and Writer's Notebook, p. 396

Writing
Writing Process:
Revise a How-to Report

Teach

Yesterday we wrote a draft of our how-to report on how to check out a book from the library. We put the steps in order. Today we're going to revise our report. When we revise our writing, we make it better. One way to make our writing better is to add more information. How can adding information make writing better? **Encourage children to share their thoughts and ideas.** (Adding more information can make the report more interesting by giving the reader more to learn and think about.)

Model

Let's look at the writing we did yesterday. We learned three steps we need to take to check out a library book. **Review with children the information you documented.** Yesterday we wrote down the steps, but we forgot to tell them what the steps would teach them to do! Let's add a sentence explaining what skill we are teaching them. Who remembers the topic of our how-to report? **(how to check out a book from the library)** Let's add that information to the beginning of our report. (Possible sentences: *You want to check out a library book. How do you do it?*)

Guide practice

What do you do with a library book once you are done reading it? Do you get to keep it? No, you have to return it so that other people can read it. Let's go back to our source—the brochure from the library—to find that information. **Read aloud text that tells how long materials from your local library can be checked out.** Let's add that information into our report. Where should we add it? Yes, that should go at the end of our how-to report. (Possible sentence: Do not forget to bring the book back.)

Independent writing

On p. 397 in *Reader's and Writer's Notebook,* have children draw pictures of and write or dictate additional information that could be included in the how-to report. Then children can write or draw and dictate the entire report on p. 398 in *Reader's and Writer's Notebook.*

Reader's and Writer's
Notebook, p. 397

Academic Vocabulary

revise look over and improve

Daily Fix-It

kids run to school
Kids run to school.

This week's practice sentences appear on Teacher Resources DVD-ROM.

English Language Learners Support Writing Have English learners share their ideas with you aloud before writing. Restate ideas when necessary to model syntax and word usage.

Objectives
• Practice using action words.

Vocabulary
Action Words

| ride | jump | skip | hop | climb |

My Skills Buddy, p. 128

Teach

Write the words *ride, jump, skip, hop,* and *climb* on the board. Point to each word as you read it. These words name actions we can do. They are verbs. Have children turn to p. 128 of *My Skills Buddy.* Use the last three Vocabulary bullets on the page in the discussion. Direct children to the picture of the boy jumping. Does this boy *jump* or does he *hop?* Then direct them to the girl skipping. Does this girl *skip* or does she *hop?* Point to the picture that shows the word *hop.* Then have children point to the child that *climbs* and the child that *rides.*

Team Talk Pair children and have them take turns acting out one of the action words. Have each child's partner guess which action word he or she is acting out.

Wrap Up Your Day

✔ **Oral Language** Let's sing "How Do Children Get to School?" again. Clap when you hear one of the Amazing Words—*cable car, trolley, horse-and-buggy, skis, Metro line,* and *vaporetto.*

✔ **Phonemic Awareness** I'm going to say some sentences. Clap when you hear a /z/ or /v/ word. *Zelda the zebra lives in the zoo. Violet plays the violin very well.*

✔ **Conventions** Have children think of a verb and act it out for the class. After children correctly guess each verb, write it on the board.

Preview DAY 5 Tell children that tomorrow they will review some of the books and stories they have read this week.

Extend Your Day!

Social Studies
Colorful Continents

Materials: globe, world map, photocopies of a world outline map, crayons, Trade Book *This Is the Way We Go to School*

Globe Versus Map Display the globe. What is this called? It is a globe. What is a globe? (a very small model of Earth) Display the world map. This is a flattened version of a globe. It is a picture of our world. What is it called? (a map) Is there more land on Earth or more water? How do you know? What are the pieces of land called? (continents) What are the big areas of water called? (oceans or seas)

Find the Continents Distribute copies of a world outline map. Let's count how many continents there are. Who knows the name of one of the continents? Identify each continent and connect them with continents in *This Is the Way We Go to School.* As you identify each continent, list its name on a chart with a different colored marker. Instruct children to color the oceans blue and the continents other colors of their choosing.

Conventions
A Verb Game

Follow the Leader Choose a leader and have children line up behind him or her. Instruct children that the leader will call out a verb and that the other children must follow the command. The leader gives one command and then goes to the end of the line. The next child in line then becomes the leader. After each child has had a turn, have the next leader silently act out one command and the other children follow.

Social Studies
Kids Around the World

Materials: Trade Book *This Is the Way We Go to School*, drawing paper, crayons

Cultural Differences Guide children in a discussion of the cultural differences illustrated by the story. What can you tell about these children's lives from where they live and how they dress? All the children in the book have something in common with each other and with us: We all go to school.

Exchange Students Have children choose a child from the book. Tell them to draw pictures of themselves going to school with the child.

Objectives
- Review the concepts.
- Build oral vocabulary.

Today at a Glance

Oral Vocabulary
cable car, trolley, horse-and-buggy, skis, Metro line, vaporetto

Phonemic Awareness
◉ /y/ and /kw/

Phonics
◉ /y/ Spelled *Yy*
◉ /kw/ Spelled *qu*

Comprehension
◉ Draw Conclusions

Conventions
Verbs

Writing
Edit and Share a How-to Report

Check Oral Vocabulary
SUCCESS PREDICTOR

TRUCKTOWN on Reading Street

Start your engines!

- Display "This Little Truck" and lead the group in saying the rhyme a few times.
- Have half the group recite the rhyme while the other half acts it out.
- Then have the groups change roles.

Truckery Rhymes

Concept Wrap Up

Question of the Week

? How do children around the world get to school?

Listen for Amazing Words

Write the question of the week on the board. Track the print as you read it to children. Have them use Amazing Words in their responses (*cable car, trolley, horse-and-buggy, skis, Metro line, vaporetto*) and remind them to answer in complete sentences. Display Sing with Me Chart 30B. Let's sing "How Do Children Get to School?" I want you to listen for the Amazing Words we learned this week. Say them with me: *cable car, trolley, horse-and-buggy, skis, Metro line, vaporetto.* Sing the song several times to the tune of "Here We Go 'Round the Mulberry Bush." Have the children sing with you.

How Do Children Get to School?

How do children get to school,
Get to school, get to school,
How do children get to school,
All around the world?

Sing with Me Chart 30B

 Sing with Me Audio

ELL Check Concepts and Language Use the Day 5 instruction on ELL Poster 30 to monitor children's understanding of the lesson concept.

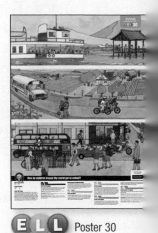

ELL Poster 30

Oral Vocabulary
Amazing Words

Review

Let's Talk Display Talk with Me Chart 30A. We learned six new Amazing Words this week. Let's say the Amazing Words as I point to the pictures on the chart. Point to each picture and give children the chance to say the appropriate Amazing Word before offering it.

> A _____ is a kind of boat used in Italy. (vaporetto)
>
> A _____ goes up and down steep hills. (cable car)
>
> A _____ has an electric line at the top of the bus. (trolley)
>
> Some people ride slowly in a _____. (horse-and-buggy)
>
> It can be fun to go on _____ down a snowy hill. (skis)
>
> The _____ is a city train that runs under ground. (Metro line)

Amazing Words ★

cable car	trolley
horse-and-buggy	skis
Metro line	vaporetto

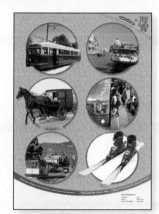

Talk with Me/Sing with Me Chart 30A

Differentiated Instruction

(A) Advanced

Amazing Words Have children illustrate and dictate their own sentence using one of this week's Amazing Words.

It's Friday

MONITOR PROGRESS | **Check Oral Vocabulary**

Demonstrate Word Knowledge Monitor the Amazing Words by asking the following questions. Have children use the Amazing Word in their answer.

- **What can you ride to school in Italy?** (vaporetto)
- **What can you put on your feet to move downhill in winter?** (skis)
- **What has an electric line overhead?** (trolley)
- **What do you ride up and down steep hills?** (cable car)
- **What is a small cart pulled by a horse?** (horse-and-buggy)
- **What is a train that goes underground?** (Metro line)

If… children have difficulty using the Amazing Words,

then… reteach the words using the Oral Vocabulary Routine on the Routines Flip Chart.

Day 1	Day 2	Day 3	Day 4	Day 5
Check Phonemic Awareness	Check Sound-Spelling/ Retelling	Check Word Reading	Check Phonemic Awareness	**Check Oral Vocabulary**

Success Predictor

Oral Vocabulary

Success Predictor

Objectives
• Review /y/ Spelled *Yy*.
• Review /kw/ Spelled *qu*.

Phonemic Awareness Review
🎯 /y/ and /kw/

Isolate /y/ and /kw/

Display the *yarn* Picture Card. What is the first sound in *yarn*? Say tho word with me: /y/ /y/ /y/, *yarn*. Review /y/ with *yak, yellow,* and *yo-yo* Picture Cards.

Display the *quilt* Picture Card. What is the first sound in *quilt*? Say the word with me: /kw/ /kw/ /kw/, *quilt*. Review /kw/ with *quarter* and *queen* Picture Cards.

Picture Card

Discriminate initial sounds

I am going to read some words. When you hear words that begin with /y/, clap your hands. Listen carefully: *yard* (clap), *yellow* (clap), *bell, set, yet* (clap), *can, yum* (clap). Now I am going to read some more words. This time, I want you to tap your feet when you hear words that begin with /kw/. Listen carefully: *yak, quack* (tap), *quick* (tap), *kick, quit* (tap), *sit, question* (tap). Combine the activities by having children clap for /y/ words and tap for /kw/ words when you read the following list: *quit* (tap), *yip* (clap), *sip, yellow* (clap), *quilt* (tap), *quiet* (tap), *yap* (clap), *quack* (tap), *sack, quarter* (tap), *lawn, yawn* (clap), *yell* (clap), *question* (tap), *Ken*.

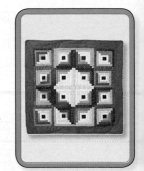

Picture Card

Phonics **Review**

⟲ /y/ Spelled *Yy* and /kw/ Spelled *qu*

Teach /y/Yy and /kw/qu

Display the *Yy* Alphabet Card. This is a *yo-yo*. What sound do you hear at the beginning of *yo-yo*? What letter spells that sound? Repeat the routine with the *Qq* Alphabet Card.

Alphabet Card

High-frequency words

Write the word *where* on the board. This is the word *where*. What is this word? Repeat the routine with *come*.

Apply phonics in familiar text

Let's Reread Have children reread one of the books specific to the target letter sound. You may wish to review the decodable words and the high-frequency words that appear in each book prior to rereading.

Decodable Reader 30
My Skills Buddy, p. 118

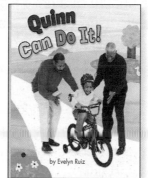

Kindergarten Student
Reader K.5.6

Get Set, Roll!
Reader 30

Small Group Time

DAY 5 Break into small groups after phonics and before the phonics and word reading assessment.

Teacher-Led

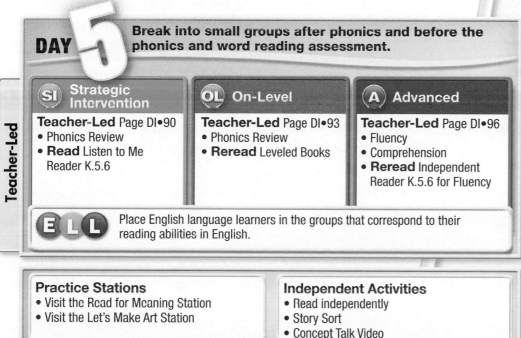

SI Strategic Intervention	**OL On-Level**	**Ⓐ Advanced**
Teacher-Led Page DI•90	**Teacher-Led** Page DI•93	**Teacher-Led** Page DI•96
• Phonics Review	• Phonics Review	• Fluency
• **Read** Listen to Me Reader K.5.6	• **Reread** Leveled Books	• Comprehension
		• **Reread** Independent Reader K.5.6 for Fluency

ELL Place English language learners in the groups that correspond to their reading abilities in English.

Practice Stations	**Independent Activities**
• Visit the Read for Meaning Station	• Read independently
• Visit the Let's Make Art Station	• Story Sort
	• Concept Talk Video

Assessment
Monitor Progress

/y/ Spelled Yy and /kw/ Spelled qu

Whole Class Have children number a sheet of paper from 1 to 6. Have children write a *y* next to the number if they hear /y/ or a *qu* if they hear /kw/ at the beginning of the word. Read the following words:

> **1. yarn   2. quit   3. quack   4. yes   5. yak   6. quilt**

MONITOR PROGRESS	Check Word and Sentence Reading

If... children cannot complete the whole-class assessment, **then...** use the Reteach lesson in *First Stop*.

If... you are unsure of a child's grasp of this week's skills, **then...** use the assessment below to obtain a clearer evaluation of the child's progress.

/y/ Spelled Yy, /kw/ Spelled qu, and high-frequency words

One-on-One To facilitate individual progress monitoring, assess some children on Day 4 and the rest on Day 5. While individual children are being assessed, the rest of the class can reread this week's books and look for words with /y/ and /kw/.

Word reading

Use the word lists on reproducible p. 607 to assess a child's ability to read words with /y/, words with /kw/, and high-frequency words. We're going to read some words. I'll read the first word, and you read the rest. The first word is *quit*, /kw/ /i/ /t/. For each child, record any decoding problems.

Sentence reading

Use the sentences on reproducible p. 607 to assess a child's ability to read words in sentences. Have the child read two sentences aloud. Have each child read different sentences. Start over with sentence one if necessary.

Record scores

Monitor children's accuracy by recording their scores using the Word and Sentence Reading Chart for this unit in *First Stop*.

Name _____

Read the Words

quit	☐	yam	☐
yell	☐	Quinn	☐
quiz	☐	where	☐
yak	☐	yet	☐
come	☐	quill	☐
quilt	☐	yes	☐

Read the Sentences

1. Yes, you can come and see the quilt.

2. Quinn, where is the yam?

3. Yes, I like where the quiz is.

4. Come and see the yak with a quill.

5. Come and see that Dad will not quit yet.

Note to Teacher: Children read each word. Children read two sentences.

Scoring for Read the Words: Score 1 point for each correct word.

/y/Yy (yell, yak, yam, yet, yes) _____ /__5__
/kw/qu (quit, quiz, quilt, Quinn, quill) _____ /__5__
High-Frequency Words (come, where) _____ /__2__

MONITOR PROGRESS
- /y/ Spelled Yy
- /kw/ Spelled qu
- High-frequency words

Objectives
- Recognize a fairy tale.
- Identify the common elements of fairy tales.

My Skills Buddy, pp. 130–131

Let's Practice It!
Fairy Tale

Teach

Tell children that today they will listen to a fairy tale. A fairy tale is a type of story. Review the features of a fairy tale with children.

- A fairy tale has magical characters.
- A fairy tale has magical events.
- Fairy tales have similar characters and words.

Have children turn to p. 130 of *My Skills Buddy.* I am going to read a fairy tale called "The Dragon Test." Look at the pictures as I read. Read the text of "The Dragon Test." As you read, direct children to look at the appropriate picture.

Guide practice

Discuss the features of a fairy tale and the bulleted text on *My Skills Buddy* p. 130.

- A fairy tale has magical characters. Which character from "The Dragon Test" is magical? (the dragon) Why is a dragon a magical character? (There are no dragons in real life.)

- A fairy tale has magical events. Which events from "The Dragon Test" are magical? (the dragon flying, burning fields, and snatching cattle)

- Fairy tales have similar characters and words. Have you seen characters like these characters in other fairy tales? (Yes. Other fairy tales have a king, a clever character, or a dragon.) Have you heard any of these words in other fairy tales? (yes; "once upon a time," "happily ever after")

- Help children use plot to make inferences. The middle son is cowardly and afraid. Do you think he would make a good king? Why or why not? (No, he would not make a good king. A king needs to be brave.)

Retell Have children retell important events in the story in the correct sequence with details. Go through the story one picture at a time, and ask children to retell what happens in their own words.

Differentiated Instruction

A Advanced

Fairy Tale Have children name and retell other fairy tales they have heard with a dragon. Then have them discuss if the dragons from their fairy tales are alike or different from the dragon in "The Dragon Test." Is your dragon a scary dragon? Does your dragon fly away without a fight? Does your dragon talk?

Academic Vocabulary

fairy tale a folk story with magical characters and events

Read Aloud

The Dragon Test

Once upon a time, there was a king who had three sons. He wanted to know which of his sons should inherit his kingdom. So he decided to give them a test.

There were reports of a dragon causing trouble in the mountains to the north. The king called his sons together and told them that whoever got rid of the dragon would be the next king.

The eldest son wanted to be king, but he was very lazy, and getting rid of a dragon sounded like a hard job. So he paid five men to do it. The men rode out to the mountains, but they were never seen again.

The middle son wanted to be king, but he was very cowardly and afraid, and getting rid of a dragon sounded like a scary job. So he paid ten men to do it. The men rode out to the mountains, but they were never seen again.

The youngest son didn't really care about being king, but he was very curious, and getting rid of a dragon sounded like a great adventure. So he rode out to the mountains. He watched as the dragon flew around, burning fields and snatching cattle. When at last the dragon landed, the youngest son walked up to it and said quite firmly, "Go away, you annoying beast!"

No one had ever dared to speak to the dragon like that. Shocked and offended, the dragon flew away over the mountains, and it was never, ever seen again.

As promised, the king chose the youngest son to be the next king. The son married a princess from the next kingdom. In time, they became king and queen, and they lived happily ever after.

Objectives
◎ Review drawing conclusions.

Assess
◉ Draw conclusions.

Comprehension Assessment
Monitor Progress

Review ◉ **Draw Conclusions** Remember that when we read or listen to stories, we can use what we already know plus what the story tells us to figure out something else about the story. This is called drawing conclusions. What do we call figuring things out? (drawing conclusions) Good readers use what they already know and what the story tells them to draw conclusions.

Read "Henry Hikes to Fitchburg" Tell children that you are going to read them a story about two friends going on a journey. Tell them to listen carefully and think about what they already know. After I read the story, I will ask you to draw some conclusions about it. Read "Henry Hikes to Fitchburg" on p. 72 of the *Read Aloud Anthology*.

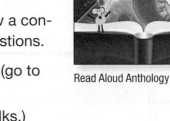

Read Aloud Anthology

Check draw conclusions After you read the story, ask children to draw a conclusion by asking the following series of questions.

- What do Henry and his friend want to do? (go to Fitchburg)

- How does Henry get to Fitchburg? (He walks.)

- How does Henry's friend get to Fitchburg? (He rides the train.)

- What does Henry do along the way? (He has many adventures and sees many things.)

- What does Henry's friend do in the meantime? (He works to pay for his ticket.)

- Henry and his friend go to Fitchburg to see the country. Which character's journey allows him to see the country better? Why? (Henry sees the country better because he spends the whole day walking through the country.)

Corrective feedback **If...** children cannot draw conclusions,
then... reteach drawing conclusions using the Reteach lesson in *First Stop.*

Assess draw conclusions Use the blackline master on p. 611. Make one copy for each child. Have children draw conclusions about what they think will happen to the bears next. Have them draw their conclusions in the empty boxes.

Name _____

Draw Conclusions

Draw conclusions about what might happen next.

Note to Teacher: Review the illustrations with children. Have the children decide and draw what might happen next.

Conventions
Verbs

Review   Remind children of what they learned about verbs. *This week we talked about action words, or verbs. Verbs tell what someone or something is doing.*

Model   Write on the board: *Jan ran to school.* Read the sentence aloud as you track the print. *In this sentence, the verb* ran *tells what Jan did. Jan is the noun—the "someone or something" that is doing something. Ran is the verb.*

Guide practice   Write and read the following sentences aloud: *Tim walks to school. Bob rides in a car. Ann skips in the park.* Have children identify the verb in each sentence. Then ask children to suggest their own sentences. Write their suggestions on the board and guide the class in identifying the verbs.

On their own   Show children how to fold their papers to make four sections. Have them write a verb in each section and draw a picture to illustrate the verb. Have children share their pictures and act out their verbs, if possible.

Daily Fix-It   Use the Daily Fix-It exercise for more conventions practice.

Writing
Writing Process: Edit and Share a How-to Report

Teach: Edit

What steps in the writing process have we done so far in writing our how-to report? (We chose a topic; we decided which sources to use; we wrote down and/or drew the information, in order; we added information, or revised, our report.) Today we will edit our report, or check to make sure we've written it correctly. Did we use correct spacing between words and letters? Did we use uppercase letters correctly? Remind children that we leave small spaces between letters in a word and bigger spaces between words in a sentence. Point out that we also begin each sentence with an uppercase letter and end with a period or question mark.

Model: Edit

Reread the how-to report you wrote. Point out the correct spacing between letters and words as well as the correct use of uppercase letters and end punctuation. Have children point out anything they think needs to be fixed. Show them how to mark the corrections.

Guide Practice: Edit

Work with children to complete the editing activity on p. 399 in *Reader's and Writer's Notebook*.

Teach: Share

Display the how-to report you have written together. Now it's time to share our work with others. First we will rewrite our report using our best handwriting. We will correct any mistakes we found during editing. We can add pictures if we choose, and we can make a cover. Then our report will be ready to share with others.

Reader's and Writer's Notebook, p. 399

Model: Share

Now I will rewrite our how-to report using my best handwriting. Quickly check letter and word spacing, capitalization and punctuation.

Guide Practice: Share

Work with children to write their how-to reports on a separate sheet of paper. Encourage them to personalize their reports by drawing pictures to accompany the text and adding a cover with a title and their name. Make each child's report into a booklet.

After they have completed their report and shared it with others, have children complete p. 400 in *Reader's and Writer's Notebook*. As a group, discuss reviewers' reactions to the how-to report. Have children save their reports to add to the classroom library.

Differentiated Instruction

SI Strategic Intervention

Support Writing Have children identify verbs by looking through familiar books and identifying the action words. Tell them to act the words out.

Daily Fix-It

do you ride your bike to school
D̲o you ride your bike to school?

This week's practice sentences appear on Teacher Resources DVD-ROM.

ELL

English Language Learners
Poster Preview Prepare children for next week by using Week 1 ELL Poster 31. Read the Poster Talk-Through to introduce the concept and vocabulary. Ask children to identify and describe objects and actions they see.

Objectives
- Review weekly concept.
- Review plot.

Wrap Up Your Week!

Amazing Words

You've learned
0 0 6
words this week!

You've learned
1 8 0
words this year!

Question of the Week

How do children around the world get to school?

Illustrate drawing conclusions

This week we talked about how children around the world get to school.

- Make a four-column chart like the shown below and fill it with children's responses about the different forms of transportation in *This Is the Way We Go to School.*
- Have children identify one way from the book that children around the world get to school. Write it in the first column.
- Have children describe the illustration(s) that corresponds to the way in the first column.
- Have children describe what they already knew about the subject in the third column.
- Help the class draw a conclusion about the subject and write it in the last column.

What we read...	What we saw...	What we knew...	Conclusion

Next Week's Question

How is a school built?

Discuss next week's question. Guide children in making connections between building a school and going to school.

Preview NEXT WEEK

Tell children that next week they will read about how a school is built.

Extend Your Day!

Social Studies
Where in the World?

Materials: world map or globe, sticky notes

Identify a Location Display the world map and help children compare it to the map on pp. 38–39 of *This Is the Way We Go to School*. Help children write sticky notes identifying several of the children mentioned in the book and affix them to the map in the appropriate area. Add a sticky note that shows where your school is located.

Tell children to find out where they were born and share that information with the class. Help individuals locate their birthplace on the map and mark it with a sticky note.

- Who was born the farthest away?
- Who was born near one of the children from the book?
- How many were born near where we live now?

Social Studies
Where Are We From?
Materials: graph paper

Country Graph Tell children to ask their parents from which country their families originally came. List the countries on graph paper. Have children enter their information by coloring a square on the graph next to the name of the country from which their families came. Help children total the number in the class whose families are from each country.

Canada				
Colombia				
England				
Greece				
Japan				
Mexico				
Puerto Rico				
South Africa				
	1	2	3	4

Math
Count Ways to Travel

Tally Transportation Display pages of *This Is the Way We Go to School*. Have children identify different forms of transportation. Write their responses in a column on the board. When all the forms have been listed, show children the pages again, counting and tallying how many times that form of transportation appears in the illustrations.

boat	III	helicopter	I
walking	IIIII II	snowmobile	I
car	I	radio	I
bus	III	skates	I
train	III	bike	I
cable car	II	horse-and-buggy	I
skis	I		

UNIT 5

The Big Question

How do people and things get from here to there?

Understanding By Design

Grant Wiggins, Ed. D.
Reading Street Author

" . . . an understanding is not a straightforward given, but a conclusion inferred using givens . . . . What might seem like something the learner can simply accept actually demands analysis (breaking it up into bits) and synthesis (putting it back together in the learner's own words or representations) before true understanding can occur. "

Unit Wrap-Up

WEEK 1

Question of the Week
What are different ways of going places?

Concept Knowledge

Children understand that transportation:

• can take many different forms

• helps people get from one place to another

WEEK 2

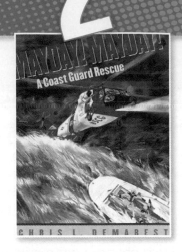

Question of the Week
What kinds of transportation help us in an emergency?

Concept Knowledge

Children understand that the Coast Guard:

• provides help during a storm or in other emergencies

• uses emergency vehicles to assist in a rescue

Discuss the Big Question

Help children relate the theme question for this unit to the selections and their own experiences. Write the big question and prompt discussion with questions such as the following:

What kinds of transportation did we learn about in the stories we read? Possible responses:

• Max uses many forms of transportation to get to the ice cream store.

• The Coast Guard uses a helicopter for rescues.

• Trucks are important in moving goods to where they need to go.

• A small blue engine gets the toys to the other side of the mountain.

• Traveling around the world, we see different forms of transportation.

• We learn how children around the world get to school.

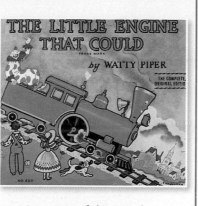

Question of the Week	Question of the Week	Question of the Week	Question of the Week
What kinds of transportation help people do their jobs?	**What kind of work do trains do?**	**How do people in different parts of the world travel?**	**How do children around the world get to school?**
Concept Knowledge	**Concept Knowledge**	**Concept Knowledge**	**Concept Knowledge**
Children understand that trucks:	**Children understand that trains:**	**Children understand that transportation:**	**Children understand that school children all around the world:**
• are an important form of transportation • help move goods from one place to another	• are important in moving people and things from one place to another • sometimes need help to get where they are going	• is important to people all over the world • exists everywhere in many different forms	• need to get to school • use different forms of transportation depending on where they live and what the climate is like

How many different types of transportation have you taken?

Responses will vary.

What jobs need transportation in order to do them? Possible responses:

• Emergency workers, such as an ambulance drivers or firefighters, need vehicles.

• Truck drivers need trucks to move products.

• Messengers and delivery people need bikes or cars.

• Police officers need cars, motorcycles, or horses.

Weekly Assessment

Use the whole-class assessment on pages 606–607 and 610–611 in this Teacher's Edition to check:

✔ 🔊 **/y/ Spelled** *Yy*

✔ 🔊 **/kw/ Spelled** *Qu*

✔ 🔊 **Comprehension Skill** *Draw Conclusions*

✔ **High-Frequency Words**   where   come

Teacher's Edition, Day 5

Managing Assessment

Use the Assessment Handbook for:

✔ **Observation Checklists**

✔ **Record-Keeping Forms**

✔ **Portfolio Assessment**

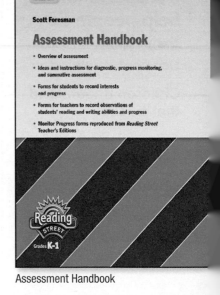

Assessment Handbook

Unit Assessment

Use the Unit 5 Assessment to check progress in:

✔ **Phonemic Awareness**

✔ **Phonics**

✔ **High-Frequency Words**

✔ **Comprehension** *Plot*

✔ **Conventions in Writing**

Unit Assessment

Teacher Notes

Pacing Small Group Instruction

20–30 mins.

5 Day Plan

DAY 1	• Phonemic Awareness/ Phonics • Decodable Story 30
DAY 2	• Phonemic Awareness/ Phonics • Decodable Reader 30
DAY 3	• Phonemic Awareness/ Phonics • Concept Literacy Reader K.5.6 or Kindergarten Student Reader K.5.6
DAY 4	• Phonemic Awareness/ Phonics • Get Set, Roll! Reader 30
DAY 5	• Phonics Review • Listen to Me Reader K.5.6

3 or 4 Day Plan

DAY 1	• Phonemic Awareness/ Phonics • Decodable Story 30
DAY 2	• Phonemic Awareness/ Phonics • Decodable Reader 30
DAY 3	• Phonemic Awareness/ Phonics • Concept Literacy Reader K.5.6 or Kindergarten Student Reader K.5.6
DAY 4	• Phonemic Awareness/ Phonics • Get Set, Roll! Reader 30

3 Day Plan: Eliminate the shaded box.

Phonemic Awareness•Phonics

■ **Isolate /y/ and /kw/** Display the *yak* Picture Card. This is a *yak. Yak* begins with /y/. Say it with me: /y/ /y/ /y/, *yak.* Repeat with *yarn* and *yellow.* Display the *queen* Picture Card. Queen begins with /kw/. Say it with me: /kw/ /kw/ /kw/, *queen.* Repeat with *quilt* and *quarter.*

■ **Connect /y/ to *Yy* and /kw/ to *qu*** I am going to say three words. I want you to tell me which word begins with /y/. Listen carefully: *yarn, fox, hat.* Say the words with me: *yarn, fox, hat.* Which word begins with /y/? *Yarn* begins with /y/. Write the letters *Yy* on the board and have children make the letters in the air. Point out that the letter *y* stands for /y/ at the beginning of *yarn.* Continue with the following sets of words: *net, yet, bet; yam, ham, Sam; gum, sum, yum.* Repeat the routine with /kw/ spelled *qu* with these sets of words: *quiz, lips, tap; bit, sit, quit; built, quilt, tilt.*

Decodable Story 30

■ **Review** Review the previously taught high-frequency words by writing each of the words and having children say the words with you.

she	said	you	a	the

If... children have difficulty reading the words,
then... say a word and have children point to the word and say the word. Repeat several times, giving assistance as needed.

■ **Read** Have children read *Run, Tim* orally. Then have them reread the story several times individually.

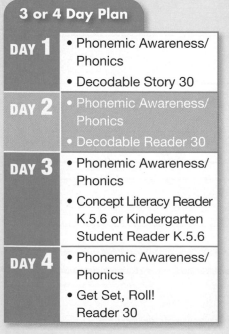

Reader's and Writer's Notebook, pp. 383–384

Objectives
• Identify the common sounds that letters represent.
• Read at least 25 high-frequency words from a commonly used list.

SI Strategic Intervention

DAY 2

Phonemic Awareness•Phonics

■ **Discriminate /y/ and /kw/** Display Phonics Songs and Rhymes Chart 30. Sing "Yolla Yak" to the tune of "Yankee Doodle" several times with children. Have children clap their hands when they hear a word with /y/ or /kw/.

■ **Connect /y/ to Yy and /kw/ to qu** Review "Yolla Yak" on Phonics Songs and Rhymes Chart 30. Have children find the words with /y/ and circle the letter that stands for /y/. Continue with /kw/. Then ask children to name other words that have /y/Yy or /kw/qu.

Decodable Reader 30

■ **Review** Review the high-frequency words by writing *come* on the board. This is the word *come*. What word is this? Continue with the following words: *a, is, said, where, the, four*.

> **If...** children have difficulty reading the words,
> **then...** say a word and have children point to the word. Repeat several times, giving assistance as needed.

■ **Read** Display the cover of *The Quiz* on p. 118 of *My Skills Buddy*. Ask a volunteer to read the first page of the story. Have children tell the questions Jim was asked. Does Jim pass the quiz?

My Skills Buddy

More Reading
Use Leveled Readers or other text at children's instructional level.

SI Strategic Intervention

DAY 3

Phonemic Awareness•Phonics

- **Isolate /y/ and /kw/** Show the *queen* Picture Card. This is a *queen. Queen* begins with /kw/. Say it with me: /kw/ /kw/ /kw/, *queen.* When you hear a word that begins with /kw/, quack like a duck. Use the following words: *quit, play, quiz, quite, race, quote.* Continue with the yak card and these words: *yellow, yes, girl, yarn, fish, monkey.*

- **Discriminate /y/ and /kw/** Listen to this word: *yes. Yes* begins with /y/. Write the letters *Yy* on the board. The letter *y* stands for /y/. Say it with me: /y/ /y/ /y/, *yes.* When you hear a word that begin with /y/, I want you to say "yes!" Use these words: *yak, pack, you, yellow, red, yarn, year, jam, yam.* Repeat with /kw/ and these words: *queen, king, quit, quick, take, quiz.*

- **Blend Sounds** Write *yet* on the board. Have children blend the sound of each letter to read the word: /y/ /e/ /t/, *yet.* Repeat the routine with the following words: *quit, yes.*

- **Review High-Frequency Words** Write *come* on the board. Have volunteers say the word and use it in a sentence. Continue with the words *where, was, what, said.*

- To practice phonics and high-frequency words, have children read Kindergarten Student Reader K.5.6. Use the instruction on pp. 562–563.

For a complete lesson plan and additional practice, see the **Leveled Reader Teaching Guide.**

Concept Literacy Reader K.5.6

- **Preview and Predict** Display the cover of the Concept Literacy Reader K.5.6. Point to the title. The title of the book is *I Go to School.* What do you think this book is about? Have children tell about the picture and what they think the book might be about.

- **Set a Purpose** We talked about the title of the book. Let's read the book to learn about different ways children get to school. Have children read the Concept Literacy Reader.

- **Read** Provide corrective feedback as children read the book orally. During reading, ask them if they are able to confirm any of the predictions they made prior to reading.

If... children have difficulty reading the book individually,
then... read a sentence aloud as children point to each word. Then have the group reread the sentences as they continue pointing to the words.

- **Retell** Have children retell the content as you page through the book. Help them identify what the book is about. Also call attention to the different ways children around the world dress when they go to school.

Concept Literacy Reader K.5.6

Objectives
- Identify the common sounds that letters represent. • Predict what might happen next based on the cover.
- Predict what might happen next based on the title. • Retell important facts in a text, heard or read.

SI Strategic Intervention

DAY **4**

More Reading

Use Leveled Readers or other text at children's instructional level.

Phonemic Awareness•Phonics

■ **Segmenting** Say *yip.* I hear three sounds in *yip,* /y/ /i/ /p/, *yip.* How many sounds do you hear in *yell?* What are they? (three, /y/ /e/ /l/) Continue with *yes, quit, quick,* and *quiz.*

■ **Recognize** *Yy* **and** *Qq* Write uppercase *Y* on the board. Name the letter as you write it several times. Have children write the letter on a sheet of paper. Then write a lowercase *y* on the board. Name the letter and ask a volunteer to write the letter on the board. Then ask children to name words that begin with /y/. Repeat with the letters *Qq.*

Get Set, Roll! Reader 30

■ **Review** Review the following high-frequency words with children prior to reading the story: *is, go, where, come.*

■ **Read** Display Get Set, Roll! Reader 30, *Yes!* Today we will read a story about a race between Max and Jack. The title of the story is *Yes!* Look at the picture and think about the title. What do you think this story will be about?

> **If...** children have difficulty reading the story individually, **then...** read a sentence aloud as children point to each word. Then have the group reread the sentences as they continue pointing to the words.

Get Set, Roll! Reader 30

■ **Reread** Use echo reading of Get Set, Roll! Reader 30 to model fluent reading. Use your oral reading to model for children where to pause, when to change pitch, and which words to stress. Then have children reread orally three to four times, or until they can read with few or no mistakes.

Objectives
• Identify the common sounds that letters represent.
• Read at least 25 high-frequency words from a commonly used list.
• Predict what might happen next based on the cover.

Small Group Time

More Reading

Use Leveled Readers or other text at children's instructional level.

SI *Strategic Intervention*

DAY 5

Phonics Review

■ **Listen for /y/ and /kw/** Write *Yy* on the board. The sound we learned for *Yy* is /y/. Write *qu* on the board. The sound we learned for these two letters is /kw/. Tell children you will tell them a story and they should listen for /y/ and /kw/. When you say a word that begins with /y/, children should yawn and repeat the word. When you say a word that begins with /kw/, children should say "quick" and repeat the word. Tell a simple story, emphasizing the /y/ and /kw/ words and pausing to give children a chance to respond. *Yolanda* woke up *quietly* this morning. She had *quite* a *quiz* yesterday. Today she eats *yummy yogurt.* Then she *quickly* studies for another *quiz* in a *quiet* room!

Listen to Me Reader K.5.6

■ **Preview and Predict** Display the cover of the book. The title of this story is *Quinn.* It is written by Zak Belahmira. It is illustrated by John Patrick. Look at the cover. What do you think will happen in this story?

Listen to Me Reader K.5.6

■ **Set a Purpose** Review children's ideas. Point out that after they read, they will know more about Quinn. Tell children that you will read the story with them. Follow along with your finger as I read. Then we will take turns reading this page. Repeat this routine through all of the pages. Guide children to decode words.

■ **Reread for Fluency** Use echo reading of Listen to Me Reader K.5.6 to model reading fluently. Use your oral reading to model for children when to pause, when to change pitch, and which words to stress. Then have children reread orally three to four times, or until they can read with few or no mistakes.

Objectives
- Identify the common sounds that letters represent.
- Predict what might happen next based on the cover.

OL On-Level

DAY 1

Phonemic Awareness•Phonics

■ **Connect /y/ to Yy and /kw/ to qu** Draw seven squares on the board. Collect twelve Picture Cards, including the following cards: *yak, yarn, yellow, yo-yo, quarter, queen, quilt.* Mix the cards and display them one at a time. Have a child name the picture. If the name has /y/ or /kw/, have the child write a lowercase *y* or *qu* in one of the squares.

Objectives
- Isolate the initial sound in spoken one-syllable words.
- Identify the common sounds that letters represent.

OL On-Level

DAY 2

Phonemic Awareness•Phonics

■ **Discriminate /y/ and /kw/** Display the *yo-yo* Picture Card. This is a *yo-yo. Yo-yo* begins with /y/. Say it with me: /y/ /y/ /y/, *yo-yo.* Does *go* begin with the same sound as *yo-yo*? No, *go* does not begin with /y/. Continue with *yard, yellow, tent, yawn, mask,* and *yarn.* Repeat the procedure with the *queen* Picture Card for /kw/. Use the following words: *quiet, leaf, question, top, quack, quart, fish, quarter.*

■ **Connect /y/ to Yy and /kw/ to qu** Write the letters *Yy* on the board. Have children identify the letters. Then write the word *yet.* Say the word emphasizing /y/: /y/ /y/ /y/, *yet.* Repeat with the letters *qu* and the word *quit.* Then say the following words and have children point to the word on the board that begins with the same sound: *yarn, quiet, quart, yard, yellow, queen.*

Objectives
- Isolate the initial sound in spoken one-syllable words.
- Identify the common sounds that letters represent.
- Read at least 25 high-frequency words from a commonly used list.

Pacing Small Group Instruction

20–30 mins.

5 Day Plan

DAY 1	• Phonemic Awareness/ Phonics • Decodable Story 30
DAY 2	• Phonemic Awareness/ Phonics • Decodable Reader 30
DAY 3	• Phonemic Awareness/ Phonics • Kindergarten Student Reader K.5.6
DAY 4	• Get Set, Roll! Reader 30
DAY 5	• Phonics Review • Reread Leveled Books

3 or 4 Day Plan

DAY 1	• Phonemic Awareness/ Phonics • Decodable Story 30
DAY 2	• Phonemic Awareness/ Phonics • Decodable Reader 30
DAY 3	• Phonemic Awareness/ Phonics • Kindergarten Student Reader K.5.6
DAY 4	• Get Set, Roll! Reader 30

3 Day Plan: Eliminate the shaded box.

More Practice

For additional practice with this week's phonics skills, have children reread the Decodable Story (Day 1) and the Decodable Reader (Day 2).

Small Group Time

Phonemic Awareness•Phonics

■ **Yell Yellow!** *Yellow* begins with /y/. When I say a word that has /y/, "Yell yellow!" Say these words: *yard, young, junk, water, yard, yesterday, yak.*

Ask a Question Draw a question mark on the board. Write the word *question*. This is the word *question*. *Question* begins with /kw/. Say it with me: /kw/ /kw/ /kw/, *question*. The letters *qu* stand for /kw/. When I say a word that begins with /kw/, point to the question mark. Say: *yarn, quit, quiet, zebra, quarrel, quote.*

Kindergarten Student Reader K.5.6

■ **Preview and Predict** Display the cover of the book. The title of this story is *Quinn Can Do It!* Look at the cover. What is Quinn doing? Who is helping him? Do you think Quinn will learn how to ride a bike? Let's read to find out.

Kindergarten Student Reader K.5.6

■ **Set a Purpose** Review the list of things children think might happen in the story. Remind children they will read to find out if Quinn learns to ride a bike.

■ **Read** Have children follow along as they read the story with you. After reading p. 2, ask children to tell what Quinn's dad got for him. Continue with each page. Ask the following questions:

• What does Quinn wear when rides the bike?

• What do the other people say to Quinn?

• Does Quinn learn to ride the bike?

■ **Summarize** Have children retell the story to a partner and tell what Quinn thinks about at the end.

■ **Text to Self** Help children make personal connections to the story as they tell how they learned to do something.

Objectives
• Identify the common sounds that letters represent.
• Predict what might happen next based on the cover.
• Respond to questions about text.

OL On-Level   DAY **4**

Get Set, Roll! Reader 30

■ **Review** Review the high-frequency words *is, go, where,* and *come* by writing each word on the board and saying the word with children.

■ **Read** Display Get Set, Roll! Reader 30, *Yes!* Today we will read a story about a race between Max and Jack. Look at the title. Who can read the title? Have children work together to say the sound for each letter and blend the sounds to read the word. *Yes!* is the title of the story. Look at the picture. What do you think will happen in this story? Let's read the story together.

Objectives
- Read at least 25 high-frequency words from a commonly used list.
- Predict what might happen next based on the cover.

OL On-Level   DAY **5**

Phonics Review

■ **Hail to the Queen** Collect a set of Picture Cards and include pictures that begin with /y/ and /kw/. Cut out a shape of a crown from construction paper. Show the crown. A *queen* wears a crown. What sound does *queen* begin with? Yes, *queen* begins with /kw/. Say it with me: /kw/ /kw/ /kw/, *queen*. Give the crown to one child. Show a Picture Card and ask the child to name the picture and the letter for the beginning sound. Have the child give the crown to another child to continue the game.

Objectives
- Identify the common sounds that letters represent.

More Reading

Use Leveled Readers or other text at children's instructional level to develop fluency.

Small Group Time

Pacing Small Group Instruction

5 Day Plan

DAY 1	• Phonemic Awareness/ Phonics • Decodable Story 30
DAY 2	• Phonics • Spelling • Decodable Reader 30
DAY 3	• Independent Reader K.5.6 or Kindergarten Student Reader K.5.6
DAY 4	• Get Set, Roll! Reader or Kindergarten Student Reader K.5.6
DAY 5	• Fluency/Comprehension • Independent Reader K.5.6

3 or 4 Day Plan

DAY 1	• Phonemic Awareness/ Phonics • Decodable Story 30
DAY 2	• Phonics • Spelling • Decodable Reader 30
DAY 3	• Independent Reader K.5.6 or Kindergarten Student Reader K.5.6
DAY 4	• Get Set, Roll! Reader or Kindergarten Student Reader K.5.6

3 Day Plan: Eliminate the shaded box.

More Practice

For additional practice with this week's phonics skills and to develop fluency, have children reread the Decodable Story (Day 1) and the Decodable Reader (Day 2).

A   **DAY 1**

Phonemic Awareness•Phonics

■ **Sound Riddle!** Say a short riddle to children and ask them to name the word that answers the riddle. Use riddles such as the following:

> It begins with /y/. It is a color.
>
> It begins with /kw/. It means fast.
>
> It begins with /y/. It is a place to play.
>
> It begins with /y/. It is used to knit.
>
> It begins with /kw/. It is a ruler of a country.

■ **Connect /y/ to Yy and /kw/ to qu** After children identify the answers to the riddles, have them identify the letter or letters that stand for the first sound in each word.

Objectives
• Isolate the initial sound in spoken one-syllable words.
• Identify the common sounds that letters represent.

A Advanced **DAY 2**

Phonics•Spelling

■ **Connect /y/ to Yy and /kw/ to qu** Display the *Yy* Alphabet Card. What is the name of this letter? What is the sound we learned for this letter? Trace the uppercase *Y* and lowercase *y* with your fingers in the air. Repeat with the *Qq* Alphabet Card. Explain that *Qq* is always followed by *u* to make /kw/.

■ **Spell Sounds** Give each child the following letter tiles: *e, i, f, q, s, t, u, y, z.* Listen to the sounds in the word *yes:* /y/ /e/ /s/, *yes.* What is the letter for /y/? It is *y.* Place your *y* tile in front of you. Continue with the remaining sounds. Repeat the routine with the following words: *quit, yet, quiz.*

Objectives
• Identify the common sounds that letters represent.
• Use letter-sound correspondences to spell consonant-vowel-consonant (CVC) words.

A Advanced

DAY 3

More Reading

Use Leveled Readers or other text at children's instructional level.

For a complete lesson plan and additional practice, see the **Leveled Reader Teaching Guide**.

Independent Reader K.5.6

Independent Leveled Reader K.5.6

- **Practice High-Frequency Words** Write *where* on the board. Have volunteers say the word and use it in a sentence. Continue with the word *come.*

- **Activate Prior Knowledge** Tell children that the book *Catch the Ball!* is about a group of children playing a game of catch. Encourage children to share their experiences playing catch.

- **Draw Conclusions** Display the cover of *Catch the Ball!* Why do people need to pay attention to what they are doing when they are playing catch?

- **Reread for Fluency** After rereading with children, model reading fluently for them. I am going to read this book aloud. I will read the words with no mistakes. I want you to read it aloud with me. Try to read the words just as I do.

Use echo reading of Independent Reader K.5.6 to model reading fluently. Use your oral reading to model for children where to pause, when to change pitch, and which words to stress. Then have children reread orally three to four times, or until they can read with few or no mistakes.

- For more practice with phonics and high-frequency words and to develop fluency, have children read Kindergarten Student Reader K.5.6. Use the instruction on pp. 562–563.

Objectives
- Read at least 25 high-frequency words from a commonly used list.

Small Group Time

More Reading

Use Leveled Readers or other text at children's instructional level.

A Advanced DAY **4**

Kindergarten Student Reader K.5.6

- **Revisit** Display the cover of Kindergarten Student Reader K.5.6. What is Quinn doing? Do you think Quinn will be able to learn how to ride a bike?

- **Reread** Use Kindergarten Student Reader K.5.6 to practice reading fluently.

- **Text to World** Quinn is learning to ride a bike. Where is good place to learn how to ride a bike? What should you wear while learning to ride a bike?

- **Read** Have children read Get Set, Roll! Reader 30, *Yes!* Use the instruction on p. 595.

Kindergarten Student
Reader K.5.6

Objectives
- Read at least 25 high-frequency words from a commonly used list.
- Predict what might happen next based on the illustrations.

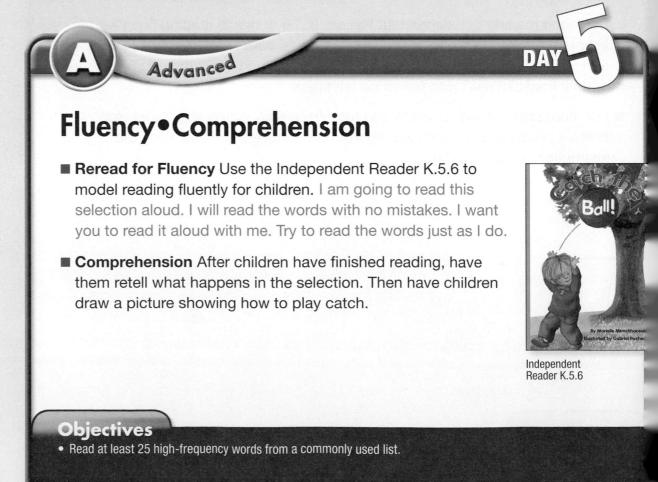

A Advanced DAY **5**

Fluency•Comprehension

- **Reread for Fluency** Use the Independent Reader K.5.6 to model reading fluently for children. I am going to read this selection aloud. I will read the words with no mistakes. I want you to read it aloud with me. Try to read the words just as I do.

- **Comprehension** After children have finished reading, have them retell what happens in the selection. Then have children draw a picture showing how to play catch.

Independent
Reader K.5.6

Objectives
- Read at least 25 high-frequency words from a commonly used list.

Concept Development

■ **Read the Concept Literacy Reader** Read *I Go to School* with children. Begin by having children look at the pictures in the book. What do you see? What are the children doing? How are they getting to school? Read the book aloud, pausing to discuss each page. Model sentence patterns and vocabulary that describe the pictures. This is a school bus. How is this bus different from school buses you have seen? On a second reading, invite children to talk about the different ways children go to school. This is a boat. Some children live where there is a lot of water. They ride to school in boats.

■ **Develop Oral Language** Revisit *I Go to School*, reviewing the different ways that people travel. Then have children sing the following song with you to the tune of "Here We Go 'Round the Mulberry Bush":

> This is the way we go to school,
> Go to school, go to school.
> This is the way we go to school,
> So early in the morning.

Phonemic Awareness/Phonics

■ **Frontload Words with /y/ and /kw/** Have children look at the illustration on pp. 112–113 of *My Skills Buddy*. This picture shows animals at a yard sale. What kinds of things do you see at a yard sale? Listen to the word *yard*. What sound does *yard* begin with? *Yard* begins with /y/; *yard*, /y/. Then use this routine to introduce picture words beginning with /y/ and /kw/: Come on down to the sale with me. Tell me, tell me, what do you see? (Ask children to find something that begins with /y/.)

Repeat the chant with other words in the picture, alternating between words that begin with /y/ and /kw/. Include words such as *quilt, quarter, quill, yarn, queen, yam, yacht, question mark,* and *yell.*

■ **Connect /y/ to Yy and /kw/ to qu** Use letter tiles to display the words *yam* and *quit* or write them on the board. This word is *yam*: /y/ /a/ /m/, *yam*. Say the word with me. Have children write the word *yam* and circle the letter that makes /y/. Repeat with the word *quit*. Write and read aloud the following sentence: *Quinn, quit yelling for yarn.* Point to Q in *Quinn* and ask: What letter is this? Yes, this is uppercase Q. Continue with *quit, yelling,* and *yarn.*

Content Objective
• Develop content knowledge related to ways children get to school.

Language Objectives
• Understand and use grade-level content area vocabulary.

• Recognize the sounds of English.

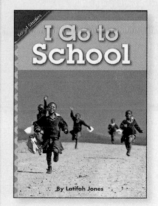

Concept Literacy Reader K.5.6

Daily Planner

DAY 1	• Concept Development • Phonemic Awareness/ Phonics • Listening Comprehension
DAY 2	• Comprehension • Vocabulary
DAY 3	• Phonemic Awareness/ Phonics • Conventions
DAY 4	• Phonemic Awareness/ Phonics • Concepts and Oral Language
DAY 5	• Language Workshop • Writing

Support for English Language Learners

Content Objective
- Understand drawing conclusions.

Language Objective
- Learn and use academic vocabulary.

My Skills Buddy, pp. 114 115

Listening Comprehension: Draw Conclusions

■ **Frontload Vocabulary** Discuss the illustration on pp. 114–115 in *My Skills Buddy* to frontload vocabulary. Cover p. 115 so that only p. 114 is showing *What do you see in the picture?* (a girl) *What is the girl holding?* (a present) *Look at the girl's face. What is she doing?* (smiling) *How do you think she feels?* (happy) Now uncover p. 115 and discuss the illustration. *This page says Happy Happy Happy. The equal sign tells us that the first picture "equals" the second picture. So, smiling girl with present equals Happy Happy Happy.*

■ **Provide Scaffolding** Look at the illustrations on pp. 114–115. Explain to children that, when they looked at the smiling girl and guessed that she felt happy, they were drawing a conclusion about the girl. Help them understand that drawing conclusions means using what you already know to make a statement about something. *When we see a girl smiling, we can conclude that she is happy.*

■ **Prepare for the Read Aloud** The modified Read Aloud below prepares children for listening to the oral reading "Getting to School" on p. 533.

Getting to School

If you live near school, you might walk.

Some children live far from school. They can't walk to school. Some kids ride in cars. Some take school buses. Some take other buses. Some kids take trains or subways.

Some places have a lot of snow. Some kids ride a sled to school. Some kids ride skis. Some kids live on farms or ranches. They can ride horses to school.

Some kids live too far from school. They stay home. They use a computer. They talk to their teachers on the computer.

■ **First Listening** Write the title of the Read Aloud on the board. This is about ways children go to school. Listen to find out how they get to school. After reading, ask children to recall ways children go to school. Who might walk to school? How might you get to school in the snow? Who rides a horse to school?

■ **Second Listening** Write the words *Draw Conclusions* on the board. As you listen to the story, think about why children get to school in different ways. After reading, help children draw a conclusion about how certain children go to school.

Objectives
- Understand the main points of spoken language ranging from situations in which contexts are familiar to unfamiliar. • Expand reading skills by employing inferential skills commensurate with content area needs.

ELL *English Language Learners*   **DAY 2**

Comprehension

■ **Provide Scaffolding** Display *This Is the Way We Go to School.* Lead a detailed picture walk through the story, naming what you see in the illustrations and describing what is happening. Use gestures and facial expressions to convey meaning. Focus on the following:

• **Set the Scene** Use the cover of the Trade Book to help children understand that this story is about children from many different places and how they get to school. Children live in small towns. Many live in big cities. Some children live on islands or by the sea. Some live in the country or in the mountains. Where else do children live?

• **Frontload Vocabulary** Use the illustrations to introduce unfamiliar words in the text. Include some of the verbs. This girl walks slowly to school. She walks through a forest. Look at the picture on pages 6–7. Would you like to walk through a forest to school? Include some of the following verbs: *grow* (p. 7); *ride* (p. 13); *take* (p. 14); *leaves* (p. 25); *bring* (p. 27).

Vocabulary: Action Words

■ **Frontload Vocabulary** Have children turn to p. 128 of *My Skills Buddy.* Talk about each picture and illustration, using the action words *ride, jump, hop, skip,* and *climb.* Point to the illustration of the boy on horseback. The boy rides the horse. Is the word *ride* a person, place, or thing? No, *ride* is an action. *Ride* tells what the boy does. It is an action word, or a verb. Then invite children to talk about the pictures using the action words.

■ **Provide Scaffolding** Write the words *ride, jump, hop, skip,* and *climb* on the board and on large cards. Read the words aloud. These words tell about actions, or things we do. Hold up the card with the word *jump.* Show me how you jump. Invite children to demonstrate jumping. Then say a sentence using the word and have children repeat the sentence: We jump high in the air. Repeat with the other action words.

■ **Practice** Have children work in pairs. Assign one of the action words (*ride, jump, hop, skip,* or *climb*) to each pair. One child should act out one of the action words, such as by pretending to ride a bicycle. The partner should say a sentence about what the first child is doing: *Mia can ride.* Encourage partners to work together to add details to their sentences, such as *Mia can ride a bike very fast.*

Content Objective

• Develop background knowledge.

Language Objective

• Learn and use action words.

Use Learning Strategies

Remind children that if they have trouble adding details to their sentences, they can ask their partner for help.

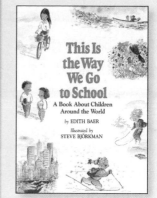

This Is the Way We Go to School
A Book About Children Around the World
by EDITH BAER
Illustrated by STEVE BJÖRKMAN

Trade Book

Objectives
• Seek clarification [of spoken language] as needed. • Share information in cooperative learning interactions.
• Use support from peers and teachers to develop background knowledge needed to comprehend increasingly challenging language.

Support for English Language Learners

Content Objective
- Use learning strategies.

Language Objectives
- Connect /y/ with *Yy* and /kw/ with *Qu*.
- Use verbs.

Transfer Skills

Have children discuss different ways children in their native country get to school.

Use Learning Strategies

Help children understand that action words name an action. An action is something that happens or something a person can do. On the board, write a 2-column chart for nouns and verbs. Say and write a word and ask children whether the word names something a person can do or if it names a person, a place, or a thing. Then write the word in the correct column in the chart.

Phonemic Awareness/Phonics

- **Isolate Initial /y/ and /kw/** Help children hear /y/ and /kw/ in the words *quack, quick, quit, yell, yet,* and *yak*. Say the words aloud, emphasizing /y/ and /kw/ in each word. Have children say *quack* several times, emphasizing initial /kw/. Repeat for each word listed above.

- **/y/ Spelled *Yy* and /kw/ Spelled *qu*** Use letter tiles to show the words *quick, quit, yet,* and *yak* or write them on the board. Read the words aloud. Say new phrases, such as *quit quacking* and *quick, yell.* Point to *qu.* What letters are these? Yes, these are *q* and *u.* Point to *y.* What letter is this? Yes, this is *y.*

Conventions: Verbs

- **Provide Scaffolding** Point to the image on p. 5 of *This Is the Way We Go to School.* The children walk to school. Write *walk* on the board and repeat the sentence. What do the children do? (walk to school). They walk to school. *Walk* is an action word, or a verb. It tells what the children do.

- **Practice** What are some other action words in this story? Have children look through the pictures in the story and name other actions they see. Write their action words on the board and have children use the words in sentences. The word *run* is an action word.

Leveled LS Support **Beginning/Intermediate** For each verb, have a child demonstrate the action. While the child is acting out the verb, explain what is happening: (Child's name) runs. Have children repeat the sentences after you and then make up their own sentences using the action words.

Advanced/Advanced-High Include some of the more challenging action words in the story, such as *counting* (p. 29), *prefers* (p. 31), and *suits* (p. 33). Have children use each verb in a sentence to deepen their understanding.

Objectives
• Expand repertoire of learning strategies commensurate with grade-level learning expectations. • Use visual and contextual support to develop grasp of language structures needed to comprehend increasingly challenging language.

ELL English Language Learners

DAY 2

Comprehension

■ **Provide Scaffolding** Display *This Is the Way We Go to School.* Lead a detailed picture walk through the story, naming what you see in the illustrations and describing what is happening. Use gestures and facial expressions to convey meaning. Focus on the following:

• **Set the Scene** Use the cover of the Trade Book to help children understand that this story is about children from many different places and how they get to school. Children live in small towns. Many live in big cities. Some children live on islands or by the sea. Some live in the country or in the mountains. Where else do children live?

• **Frontload Vocabulary** Use the illustrations to introduce unfamiliar words in the text. Include some of the verbs. This girl walks slowly to school. She walks through a forest. Look at the picture on pages 6–7. Would you like to walk through a forest to school? Include some of the following verbs: *grow* (p. 7); *ride* (p. 13); *take* (p. 14); *leaves* (p. 25); *bring* (p. 27).

Vocabulary: Action Words

■ **Frontload Vocabulary** Have children turn to p. 128 of *My Skills Buddy.* Talk about each picture and illustration, using the action words *ride, jump, hop, skip,* and *climb.* Point to the illustration of the boy on horseback. The boy rides the horse. Is the word *ride* a person, place, or thing? No, *ride* is an action. *Ride* tells what the boy does. It is an action word, or a verb. Then invite children to talk about the pictures using the action words.

■ **Provide Scaffolding** Write the words *ride, jump, hop, skip,* and *climb* on the board and on large cards. Read the words aloud. These words tell about actions, or things we do. Hold up the card with the word *jump.* Show me how you jump. Invite children to demonstrate jumping. Then say a sentence using the word and have children repeat the sentence: We jump high in the air. Repeat with the other action words.

■ **Practice** Have children work in pairs. Assign one of the action words (*ride, jump, hop, skip,* or *climb*) to each pair. One child should act out one of the action words, such as by pretending to ride a bicycle. The partner should say a sentence about what the first child is doing: *Mia can ride.* Encourage partners to work together to add details to their sentences, such as *Mia can ride a bike very fast.*

Content Objective

• Develop background knowledge.

Language Objective

• Learn and use action words.

Use Learning Strategies

Remind children that if they have trouble adding details to their sentences, they can ask their partner for help.

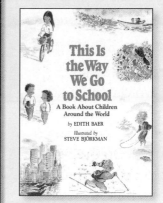

Trade Book

Objectives
• Seek clarification [of spoken language] as needed. • Share information in cooperative learning interactions.
• Use support from peers and teachers to develop background knowledge needed to comprehend increasingly challenging language.

Support for English Language Learners

Content Objective
• Use learning strategies.

Language Objectives
• Connect /y/ with *Yy* and /kw/ with *Qu*.
• Use verbs.

Transfer Skills
Have children discuss different ways children in their native country get to school.

Use Learning Strategies
Help children understand that action words name an action. An action is something that happens or something a person can do. On the board, write a 2-column chart for nouns and verbs. Say and write a word and ask children whether the word names something a person can do or if it names a person, a place, or a thing. Then write the word in the correct column in the chart.

Phonemic Awareness/Phonics

■ **Isolate Initial /y/ and /kw/** Help children hear /y/ and /kw/ in the words *quack, quick, quit, yell, yet,* and *yak.* Say the words aloud, emphasizing /y/ and /kw/ in each word. Have children say *quack* several times, emphasizing initial /kw/. Repeat for each word listed above.

■ **/y/ Spelled *Yy* and /kw/ Spelled *qu*** Use letter tiles to show the words *quick, quit, yet,* and *yak* or write them on the board. Read the words aloud. Say new phrases, such as *quit quacking* and *quick, yell.* Point to *qu.* What letters are these? Yes, these are *q* and *u.* Point to *y.* What letter is this? Yes, this is *y.*

Conventions: Verbs

■ **Provide Scaffolding** Point to the image on p. 5 of *This Is the Way We Go to School.* The children walk to school. Write *walk* on the board and repeat the sentence. What do the children do? (walk to school). They walk to school. *Walk* is an action word, or a verb. It tells what the children do.

■ **Practice** What are some other action words in this story? Have children look through the pictures in the story and name other actions they see. Write their action words on the board and have children use the words in sentences. The word *run* is an action word.

LS **Beginning/Intermediate** For each verb, have a child demonstrate the action. While the child is acting out the verb, explain what is happening: (Child's name) runs. Have children repeat the sentences after you and then make up their own sentences using the action words.

Advanced/Advanced-High Include some of the more challenging action words in the story, such as *counting* (p. 29), *prefers* (p. 31), and *suits* (p. 33). Have children use each verb in a sentence to deepen their understanding.

Objectives
• Expand repertoire of learning strategies commensurate with grade-level learning expectations. • Use visual and contextual support to develop grasp of language structures needed to comprehend increasingly challenging language.

Phonemic Awareness/Phonics

- **Review initial /v/ and /z/** Help children review /v/ and /z/ in words by saying sentences such as the following: *Val vents in the van. Zack zips into a zebra costume.* Emphasize /v/ and /z/ in the words. Repeat the sentences in parts (such as *Val vents*) so children can repeat the words. Then have them blend sounds, such as /v/ /a/ /l/ = *Val*.

- **/v/ Spelled *Vv* and /z/ Spelled *Zz*** Show words from sentences, such as *Val vents in the van* and *Zack zips into a zebra costume.* Model reading the words, isolating v and pointing out /v/ and /z/. Show all the sound-letter correspondences (for example, /v/ /a/ /l/ = *Val*). Repeat the modeling for z and /z/.

Concepts and Oral Language

- **Revisit Talk with Me Chart 30A** Display the chart. Have children describe each image on the page. Help them by describing ways children around the world go to school.

- **Develop Oral Language** Introduce language patterns that help describe the pictures on Talk with Me Chart 30A. Write this sentence frame on the board: *The cable car _____.* Now let's use this sentence pattern to talk about what the cable car does: *The cable car rolls. The cable car carries passengers.* Have children suggest other sentences using the sentence frame. Repeat the exercise using the other pictures on the chart. Then play a game with students in which you ask a question about the pictures, such as: *Which picture shows a vaporetto?* Have children point to the correct picture and then answer your question with a sentence, such as *This picture shows a vaporetto floating.*

 Beginning Have children repeat the question you ask. Let them take a turn pointing to a picture on the chart.

Intermediate Ask questions to help children notice more details about the modes of travel in the pictures, such as *What sounds do you hear in a horse-and-buggy?*

Advanced/Advanced-High Have children use their prior knowledge about travel to think of other action words, such as *glide, work,* or *pull.*

Content Objectives
- Develop oral language.
- Use learning strategies.

Language Objectives
- Connect /v/ with *Vv* and /z/ with *Zz*.
- Learn English language patterns.

Use Learning Strategies
With children, brainstorm some sentences using action words from the Talk with Me Chart. Work with children to create a list of verbs that name actions and events in the pictures in the chart.

Talk with Me Chart 30A

Support for English Language Learners

Content Objectives

- Understand *This Is the Way We Go to School.*
- Make a chart.

Language Objectives

- Make comparisons through speaking and writing.
- Write using grade-level vocabulary.

Monitor and Self-Correct

Remind children that if they don't know how to write the words, they can see if the words in the class chart will help them.

Home Language Support

Invite children to share ideas in their home languages before creating their sentences.

Language Workshop: Make Comparisons

■ **Introduce and Model** Turn to p. 5 of *This Is the Way We Go to School.* These children walk to school. Do you think they live close to school? Ask children if they walk to school. Invite them to share their opinions about walking to school. Would some children prefer to ride the bus? How do you get to school? (car, bus, bike) Which way do you like best? What is the best part about going this way? Which way do you think is fastest? When we talk about how things are the same and different, we compare and contrast. When we compare, we tell how things are alike. When we contrast, we tell how things are different.

■ **Practice** Think about ways children in the story get to school. Then think about how you get to school. What are some ways they are the same? What are some ways they are different? List answers in a T-chart with columns labeled *Alike* and *Different.* Have children share their charts with the class.

Writing: Make Comparisons

■ **Prepare for Writing** We talked about how children around the world have different ways of getting to school. Now let's write about them.

■ **Create Sentences About Going to School** Have children title their papers *Going to School.* Then have them copy this sentence frame at the bottom of the first section: _____ *is better than walking.* Have them copy this sentence frame at the bottom of the second section: _____ *is the best way.* In the first section, have children draw a way to get to school that they feel is better than walking. Have them draw what they feel is the best way to get to school in the second section. Have them complete the sentence frames. Have them read their sentences to a partner several times. Display their papers for the class to see.

Beginning Provide the sentence frame in each section, and have children dictate or write words to complete the sentences.

Intermediate Guide children in writing words to complete the sentences.

Advanced/Advanced-High Encourage children to write their sentences on their own. Have children help less-proficient partners complete their sentences.

Objectives

• Expand and internalize initial English vocabulary by learning and using high-frequency English words necessary for identifying and describing people, places, and objects. • Write using a variety of grade-appropriate sentence lengths in increasingly accurate ways as more English is acquired.

Customize Literacy in Your Classroom

Table of Contents
for Customize Literacy

Customize Literacy is organized into different sections, each one designed to help you organize and carry out an effective literacy program. Each section contains strategies and support for teaching comprehension skills and strategies. *Customize Literacy* also shows how to use weekly text sets of readers in your literacy program.

Weekly Text Sets
to Customize Literacy

The following readers can be used to enhance your literacy instruction.

	Decodable Reader	Concept Literacy Reader	Below-Level Reader	On-Level Reader	Advanced Reader
Unit 5 WEEK 4	Jan at the Fair	Trains Work Hard	Six Cubs	Bud Likes Mud	The Big Train
Unit 5 WEEK 5	Zip Up, Val!	We Travel	Bev and Vin	The Big Jazz Band	Get On the Bus!
Unit 5 WEEK 6	The Quiz	I Go to School	Quinn	Quinn Can Do It!	Catch the Ball!

Customize Literacy
in Your Classroom

Instruction in comprehension skills and strategies provides readers with avenues to understanding a text. Through teacher modeling and guided, collaborative, and independent practice, children become independent thinkers who employ a variety of skills and strategies to help them make meaning as they read.

Mini-Lessons for Comprehension Skills and Strategies

Envision It!
A Comprehension Handbook

Unit 1	Character, Setting, Classify and Categorize, Predict and Set Purpose, Recall and Retell
Unit 2	Compare and Contrast, Setting, Main Idea, Realism and Fantasy, Sequence, Predict and Set Purpose, Recall and Retell
Unit 3	Compare and Contrast, Plot, Cause and Effect, Draw Conclusions, Main Idea, Predict and Set Purpose, Recall and Retell
Unit 4	Sequence, Cause and Effect, Character, Classify and Categorize, Setting, Predict and Set Purpose, Recall and Retell
Unit 5	Realism and Fantasy, Cause and Effect, Compare and Contrast, Plot, Main Idea, Draw Conclusions, Predict and Set Purpose, Recall and Retell
Unit 6	Compare and Contrast, Character, Main Idea, Plot, Setting, Draw Conclusions, Predict and Set Purpose, Recall and Retell

Envision It! | Visual Skills Handbook

Author's Purpose
Categorize and Classify
Cause and Effect
Compare and Contrast
Draw Conclusions
Fact and Opinion
Generalize
Graphic Sources
Literary Elements
Main Idea and Details
Sequence

Envision It! | Visual Strategies Handbook

Background Knowledge
Important Ideas
Inferring
Monitor and Clarify
Predict and Set Purpose
Questioning
Story Structure
Summarize
Text Structure
Visualize

Anchor Chart Anchor charts are provided with each strategy lesson. These charts incorporate the language of strategic thinkers. They help students make their thinking visible and permanent and provide students with a means to clarify their thinking about how and when to use each strategy. As children gain more experience with a strategy, the chart may undergo revision.

See pages 97–113 in the *First Stop on Reading Street* Teacher's Edition for additional support as you customize literacy in your classroom.

Good Readers DRA2 users will find additional resources in the *First Stop on Reading Street* Teacher's Edition on pages 100–102.

Contents

Pacing Guide

This chart shows the instructional sequence from *Scott Foresman Reading Street* for Grade K. You can use this pacing guide as is to ensure you are following a comprehensive scope and sequence. Or, you can adjust the sequence to match your calendar, curriculum map, or testing schedule.

Grade K — LANGUAGE ARTS

UNIT 1

	Week 1	Week 2	Week 3	Week 4	Week 5	Week 6
Phonological/ Phonemic Awareness	Rhyming Words	Syllables Sound Discrimination	Discriminate Sounds Segment Syllables	Discriminate Sounds	Isolate /m/ Discriminate Sounds	Isolate /t/ Discriminate Sounds Rhyme
Phonics	Letter Recognition: *Aa, Bb, Cc, Dd, Ee*	Letter Recognition: *Ff, Gg, Hh, Ii, Jj, Kk, Ll, Mm, Nn*	Letter Recognition: *Oo, Pp, Qq, Rr, Ss*	Letter Recognition: *Tt, Uu, Vv, Ww, Xx, Yy, Zz*	/m/ Spelled *Mm*	/t/ Spelled *Tt*
High-Frequency Words	*I, am*	*I, am*	*the, little*	*the, little*	*a, to*	*a, to*
Listening Comprehension	Character	Setting	Sequence	Classify and Categorize	Character	Classify and Categorize
Comprehension Strategies	Preview and Predict, Retell					

UNIT 2

	Week 1	Week 2
Phonological/ Phonemic Awareness	Isolate /a/ Oral Blending	Isolate /s/ Oral Blending
Phonics	/a/ Spelled *Aa*	/s/ Spelled *Ss*
High-Frequency Words	*have, is*	*have, is*
Listening Comprehension	Compare and Contrast	Setting

UNIT 4

	Week 1	Week 2	Week 3	Week 4	Week 5	Week 6
Phonemic Awareness	Isolate /h/ Oral Blending Segment Phonemes	Isolate /l/ Oral Blending Segment Phonemes		Isolate /g/ Segment Phonemes	Isolate /e/ Segment Phonemes Discriminate Phonemes	Isolate /e/ Segment Phonemes Discriminate Phonemes
Phonics	/h/ Spelled *Hh*	/l/ Spelled *Ll*	Consonant Blends	/g/ Spelled *Gg*	/e/ Spelled *Ee*	/e/ Spelled *Ee*
High-Frequency Words	*are, that, do*	*are, that, do*	*one, two, three, four, five*	*one, two, three, four, five*	*here, go, from*	*here, go, from*
Listening Comprehension	Sequence	Cause and Effect	Sequence	Character	Classify and Categorize	Setting
Comprehension Strategies	Preview and Predict, Retell					

UNIT 5

	Week 1	Week 2
Phonemic Awareness	Isolate /j/, /w/ Oral Blending Segment Phonemes	Isolate /ks/ Oral Blending Segment Phonemes
Phonics	/j/ Spelled *Jj* and /w/ Spelled *Ww*	/ks/ Spelled *Xx*
High-Frequency Words	*yellow, blue, green*	*yellow, blue, green*
Listening Comprehension	Realism and Fantasy	Cause and Effect

> **Are you the adventurous type? Want to use some of your own ideas and materials in your teaching? But you worry you might be leaving out some critical instruction kids need? Customize Literacy can help.**

Week 3	Week 4	Week 5	Week 6
Isolate /p/ Oral Blending	Isolate /k/ Oral Blending	Isolate /i/ Discriminate Sounds Oral Blending	Isolate /i/ Discriminate Sounds Oral Blending
/p/ Spelled *Pp*	/k/ Spelled *Cc*	/i/ Spelled *Ii*	/i/ Spelled *Ii*
we, my, like	*we, my, like*	*he, for*	*he, for*
Main Idea	Realism and Fantasy	Sequence	Realism and Fantasy
Preview and Predict, Retell			

UNIT 3

Week 1	Week 2	Week 3	Week 4	Week 5	Week 6
Isolate /n/, /b/ Oral Blending Segment Phonemes	Isolate /r/ Oral Blending Segment Phonemes	Isolate /d/, /k/ Oral Blending Segment Phonemes	Isolate /t/ Oral Blending Segment Phonemes	Isolate /o/ Oral Blending Segment Phonemes	Isolate /o/ Oral Blending Segment Phonemes
/n/ Spelled *Nn* and /b/ Spelled *Bb*	/r/ Spelled *Rr*	/d/ Spelled *Dd* and /k/ Spelled *Kk*	/f/ Spelled *Ff*	/o/ Spelled *Oo*	/o/ Spelled *Oo*
me, with, she	*me, with, she*	*see, look*	*see, look*	*they, you, of*	*they, you, of*
Compare and Contrast	Plot	Cause and Effect	Plot	Draw Conclusions	Main Idea
Preview and Predict, Retell					

Week 3	Week 4	Week 5	Week 6
Isolate /u/ Oral Blending Segment Phonemes	Isolate /u/ Oral Blending Segment Phonemes	Isolate /v/, /z/ Oral Blending Segment Phonemes	Isolate /y/, /kw/ Oral Blending Segment Phonemes
/u/ Spelled *Uu*	/u/ Spelled *Uu*	/v/ Spelled *Vv* and /z/ Spelled *Zz*	/y/ Spelled *Yy* and /kw/ Spelled *qu*
what, said, was	*what, said, was*	*where, come*	*where, come*
Compare and Contrast	Plot	Main Idea	Draw Conclusions
Preview and Predict, Retell			

UNIT 6

Week 1	Week 2	Week 3	Week 4	Week 5	Week 6
Isolate /a/ and /i/ Blend Phonemes Segment Phonemes	Isolate /o/ Blend Phonemes Segment Phonemes	Isolate /e/ Blend Phonemes Segment Phonemes	Isolate /u/ Blend Phonemes Segment Phonemes	Consonant and Vowel Sounds	Consonant and Vowel Sounds
/a/ Spelled *Aa* and /i/ Spelled *Ii*	/o/ Spelled *Oo*	/e/ Spelled *Ee*	/u/ Spelled *Uu*	Consonants and Short Vowels	Consonants and Short Vowels
here, do, little, with, what	*where, is, go, that, come*	*the, was, to, like, from*	*for, of, my, we, yellow*	*have, they, four, two, blue*	*you, said, see, look, three*
Compare and Contrast	Character	Main Idea	Plot	Setting	Draw Conclusions
Preview and Predict, Retell					

Pacing Guide

Grade K

UNIT 1 — LANGUAGE ARTS

	Week 1	Week 2	Week 3	Week 4	Week 5	Week 6
Speaking and Listening	Follow Directions	Drama—Respond to Literature	Listen for Rhyme and Rhythm	Talk About Me	Announcements and Messages	Drama—Respond to Literature
Grammar/Conventions	Say Our Names	Write Our Names	What We Look Like	What We Can Do	Nouns for People and Animals	Nouns for Places and Things
Writing	Song	Invitation	Poem	Instructions	Caption	Personal Narrative

UNIT 2

	Week 1	Week 2
Speaking and Listening	Listen for Sequence	Listen for Directions
Grammar/Conventions	Nouns for More Than One	Proper Nouns
Writing	Label	List

UNIT 4

	Week 1	Week 2	Week 3	Week 4	Week 5	Week 6
Speaking and Listening	Give Directions	Compare and Contrast	Listen for Sequence	Discuss Authors and Illustrators	Listen for Story Elements: Character	Listen to Poems
Grammar/Conventions	Subjects (Naming Parts)	Predicates (Action Parts)	Complete Sentences	Telling Sentences	Capital Letters and Periods	Pronouns *I* and *me*
Writing	Directions	Poem	Description	List	Informal Letter	List

UNIT 5

	Week 1	Week 2
Speaking and Listening	Ask and Answer Questions	Drama—Respond to Literature
Grammar/Conventions	Questions	Question Marks and Capital Letters
Writing	Caption	Rhyme

Week 3	Week 4	Week 5	Week 6
Discussions	Listen for Setting	Give a Description	Listen for Plot
Adjectives: Colors and Shapes	Adjectives: Sizes and Numbers	Adjectives: Opposites	Adjectives
Notes	Poem	Caption	Story

UNIT 3

Week 1	Week 2	Week 3	Week 4	Week 5	Week 6
Respond to Literature	Sequence	Recite Rhymes	Oral Presentation	Messages and Letters	Ask and Answer Questions
Verbs	Verbs for Now and the Past	Verbs That Add -s	Verbs for Now and the Future	Meaningful Word Groups	Sentences
Summary	Invitation	Persuasive Statement	Caption	List	Poem

Week 3	Week 4	Week 5	Week 6
Discuss Literature	Sequence	Oral Presentation —Description	Discuss Literary Elements: Plot
Prepositions	Nouns	Nouns in Sentences	Verbs
Poem	Formal Letter	Invitation	How-to Report

UNIT 6

Week 1	Week 2	Week 3	Week 4	Week 5	Week 6
Recite Language	Discuss Fact and Opinion	Interpret Information	Discuss Literary Elements: Character	Oral Presentation —Book Report	Discuss Literary Elements: Setting
Pronouns I and me	Prepositional Phrases	Telling Sentences	Questions	Exclamations	Complete Sentences
List	Song	Rhyme	Rhyme	Poem	Report

Teaching Record Chart

This chart shows the critical comprehension skills and strategies you need to cover. Check off each one as you provide instruction.

Reading/Comprehension	DATES OF INSTRUCTION		
Predict what might happen next in text based on the cover, title, and illustrations.			
Ask and respond to questions about texts read aloud.			
Identify elements of a story including setting, character, and key events.			
Discuss the big idea (theme) of a well-known folk tale or fable and connect it to personal experience.			
Recognize sensory details.			
Recognize recurring phrases and characters in traditional fairy tales, lullabies, and folk tales from various cultures.			
Respond to rhythm and rhyme in poetry through identifying a regular beat and similarities in word sounds.			
Retell a main event from a story read aloud.			
Describe characters in a story and the reasons for their actions.			
Identify the topic of an informational text heard.			

" Tired of using slips of paper or stickies to make sure you teach everything you need to? Need an easier way to keep track of what you have taught, and what you still need to cover? Customize Literacy can help. "

Reading/Comprehension	DATES OF INSTRUCTION		
Identify the topic and details in expository text heard or read, referring to the words and/or illustrations.			
Retell important facts in a text, heard or read.			
Discuss the ways authors group information in text.			
Use titles and illustrations to make predictions about text.			
Follow pictorial directions (e.g., recipes, science experiments).			
Identify the meaning of specific signs (e.g., traffic signs, warning signs).			
Discuss the purposes for reading and listening to various texts (e.g., to become involved in real and imagined events, settings, actions, and to enjoy language).			
Ask and respond to questions about text.			
Monitor and adjust comprehension (e.g., using background knowledge, creating sensory images, re-reading a portion aloud).			
Make inferences based on the cover, title, illustrations, and plot.			
Retell or act out important events in stories.			
Make connections to own experiences, to ideas in other texts, and to the larger community and discuss textual evidence.			

Plot

Mini-Lesson

Understand the Skill

Student Edition K.5, pp. 74–75

The **plot** is the series of events in a story. Children learn that the events happen in a certain order. They talk about what happens in the beginning, middle, and end of a story.

Teach

Use the **Envision It!** lesson on K.5, pages 74–75 to visually teach plot.

Remind children that stories have a beginning, middle, and end. Ask: What is the first thing that happens in this story about the tortoise and the hare? What happens next? What happens at the end of the story? Use a story chart to record children's responses.

Practice

Tell children that stories happen in order. Retell a familiar story, such as "The Three Little Pigs" or "Goldilocks and the Three Bears." Show children picture cards of story events and have them put the cards in story order. Retell the story using the picture cards and the words *beginning, middle,* and *end.*

If... children have difficulty describing the order of story events,
then... give children two events from the story and ask: *Did the pig build the brick house before the pig built the house of straw?* Use pictures to help children as necessary.

Apply

Tell children to listen carefully as you read to know what happens in the beginning, middle, and end of a story. They can use the pictures to help them. Have children retell the story using *beginning, middle,* and *end*. You may wish to use a story char to help children retell the story.

Writing

Children can write and/or draw what happens in the beginning, middle, and end of a story.

Objectives:

- Children know that a story is made up of events that happen one after another.
- Children know that a story has a beginning, middle, and end.

Texts for Teaching

- *Little Quack*
- *Farfallina and Marcel*
- *The Little Engine That Could*
- *Alistair and Kip's Great Adventure*

Leveled Readers

- See pages CL16–CL17 for a list of Leveled Readers.

Objectives:
- Children tell the one big idea in a story or a selection.
- Children tell what they used to identify what a story or article is about.

Texts for Teaching
- *Animal Babies in Grasslands*
- *The Lion and the Mouse*
- *On the Move!*
- *Building Beavers*

Leveled Readers
- See pages CL16–CL17 for a list of Leveled Readers.

Main Idea

Mini-Lesson

Student Edition K.5, pp. 94–95

Understand the Skill

The **main idea** is what a story or nonfiction article is about. Children tell what the big idea in a story or article is after hearing it read aloud. They retell the story or are able to say in a word or two what the big idea of an article is.

Teach

Use the **Envision It!** lesson on K.5, pages 94–95 to visually teach main idea. Remind children that the big idea of these pages is that people go to school in different ways.

Tell children that every story tells about a big idea. They will know what the big idea is because most of the sentences will tell about it. Most of the pictures will also be about the big idea. Think aloud as you model finding the big idea. *This story is all about a jungle. I see pictures of different kinds of baby animals and their mothers. The sentences tell me the names of all the baby animals. The big idea of this story is that lots of different animals live in the jungle.*

Practice

Read or retell a familiar tale or selection to children and have them listen and think about what the story is mostly about. (For example, *Goldilocks* is mostly about a girl who causes trouble in a bears' house.) When you are finished, talk about what the story is mostly about and ask: *What helps us figure out what the story is mostly about?* Help them understand that what happens in a story helps us figure this out. In *Goldilocks*, the little girl causes trouble by eating the porridge, breaking a chair, and by sleeping in a bed. We put these events together to see what the story is mostly about.

If... children have difficulty telling what a story is mostly about,

then... retell the story with them and then ask: *What is this story mostly about?*

Apply

Ask children to listen carefully to the stories you read to hear the big ideas. Have them ask questions: *What is this story about? What are all the sentences about? Do the pictures help me think about what the big idea is? What do the pictures show?* Talk with children about the big ideas in the story.

Writing

Have children write a story and give it a title that tells what their story is mostly about. Children can illustrate their stories.

Objectives:

- Children use what they already know to make decisions about what happens in pictures and books.
- Children make decisions about characters based on text and pictures.
- Children support their decisions.

Texts for Teaching

- *Then and Now*
- *This Is the Way We Go to School*
- *Ants and Their Nest*

Leveled Readers

- See pages CL16–CL17 for a list of Leveled Readers.

Draw Conclusions

Mini-Lesson

Understand the Skill

Student Edition K.5, pp. 114–115

Drawing conclusions means taking what you already know and what you see in the world, see in a picture, or hear from a story to make a decision about something. Children learn that they have many experiences that can help them make decisions about characters or books.

Teach

Use the **Envision It!** lesson on K.5, pages 114–115 to visually teach draw conclusions. Help children conclude that the present will make the girl happy.

Tell children that they can use clues from the pictures to figure out what is happening in a story. Think aloud as you model drawing conclusions from pictures. Show children a familiar book.

This book is about a girl who makes a present for her mom. I can use the pictures figure out how the girl feels about making the present. In this picture she is smiling know that I smile when I am happy. The girl must be happy.

Talk about other emotions that children know, such as sadness or anger. Ask: How do you know when someone is sad or angry?

Practice

Tell children that they can use what they know to figure out how a character feels. Show children a familiar book and use clues from the pictures to make decisions about characters. Ask: What do you think the character feels in this story? What is the character doing in this picture? Why? Have children tell you why they think as they do.

If... children have difficulty drawing conclusions,

then... talk about what they do when they feel sad, happy, or excited, and help children connect what they do to what the character is doing in the pictures.

Apply

Tell children to listen carefully to the story and look at the pictures as you read so they can make decisions about the characters. Ask questions about the characters such as What did the characters do that was kind? mean? Do you think this character is strong? brave? friendly? Have children tell you why they think as they do.

Writing

Children can complete sentences: *When I am _____, I _____.*

Objectives:
- Children identify important ideas in a story.
- Children recall facts and details in a book.
- Children retell story events in their own words.

Texts for Teaching

- *Recall/Retell is a strategy that can be applied to any selection. Encourage children to recall and retell after they read.*

Recall/Retell

Mini-Lesson

Understand the Strategy

Recall/retell is related to summarizing, which children begin in Grade 1. This strategy means picking out the important ideas in a story or an article and restating them in one's own words. Being able to recall/retell enables readers to organize information and evaluate the importance of what they read.

Teach

Tell children that they can retell what happens in a book. They should not tell everything that happened. They should think about the important ideas. They should put the important ideas in their own words. Using a familiar fiction or nonfiction book, model asking questions to help determine the important ideas. (Use a fiction book one day, and a nonfiction book another.) Then summarize in a sentence or two.

This book is about winter and how animals get ready for it. Some animals hibernate during winter and some go where it's warmer.

The main character wants to earn money to buy his Mom a gift. Instead of buying something, he ends up baking cookies for her with his Dad.

Questions for Fiction
• What happened first in this book?
• What did the main character want to do?
• Did he or she do it? How?
• What happened at the end of this book?

Questions for Nonfiction
• What is this book mostly about?
• What is one thing you learned in this book?

Practice and Apply

Read a story together and use the questions to talk about the story. Then use pictures and have children retell the story.

If... children have difficulty retelling,

then... talk about what happened first, next, and last.

Anchor Chart

Anchor charts help children make their thinking visible and permanent. With an anchor chart, the group can clarify their thinking about how to use a strategy. You might make a chart of the questions to help children recall and retell and hang it in the classroom.

Glossary of Literacy Terms

This glossary lists academic language terms that are related to literacy.
They are provided for your information and professional use.

A

alliteration	the repetition of a consonant sound in a group of words, especially in poetry
animal fantasy	a story about animals that talk and act like people
antonym	a word that means the opposite of another word
author's purpose	the reason the author wrote the text
autobiography	the story of a real person's life written by that person

B

background knowledge	the information and experience that a reader brings to a text
biography	the story of a real person's life written by another person

C

cause	why something happens
character	a person, an animal, or a personified object in a story
classify and categorize	put things, such as pictures or words, into groups
compare and contrast	tell how things are the same and different
comprehension	understanding of text being read—the ultimate goal of reading
comprehension strategy	a conscious plan used by a reader to gain understanding of text. Comprehension strategies may be used before, during, or after reading.
context clue	the words, phrases, or sentences near an unknown word that give the reader clues to the word's meaning

D

details	small pieces of information
dialogue	written conversation
draw conclusions	arrive at decisions or opinions after thinking about facts and details and using prior knowledge

E

effect	what happens as the result of a cause
expository text	text that contains facts and information. Also called *informational text.*

F

fable	a story, usually with animal characters, that is written to teach a moral, or lesson
fact	piece of information that can be proved to be true
fairy tale	a folk story with magical characters and events
fantasy	a story that could not really happen
fiction	writing that tells about imaginary people, things, and events
folk tale	a story that has been passed down by word of mouth
foreshadowing	the use of hints or clues about what will happen later in a story

Instruction

generalize	make a broad statement or rule after examining particular facts
graphic organizer	a drawing, chart, or web that illustrates concepts or shows how ideas relate to each other. Readers use graphic organizers to help them keep track of and understand important information and ideas as they read. Story maps, word webs, Venn diagrams, and KWL charts are graphic organizers.
graphic source	a chart, diagram, or map within a text that adds to readers' understanding of the text

G

historical fiction	realistic fiction that takes place in the past. It is an imaginary story based on historical events and characters.
humor	writing or speech that has a funny or amusing quality

H

idiom	a phrase whose meaning differs from the ordinary meaning of the words. *A stone's throw* is an idiom meaning "a short distance."
imagery	the use of language to create beautiful or forceful pictures in the reader's mind
inference	conclusion reached on the basis of evidence and reasoning
inform	give knowledge, facts, or news to someone
informational text	writing that contains facts and information. Also called *expository text*.
interview	a face-to-face conversation in which someone responds to questions

I

legend	a story coming down from the past about the great deeds of a hero. Although a legend may be based on historical people and events, it is not regarded as historically true.
literary elements	the characters, setting, plot, and theme of a narrative text

L

main idea	the big idea that tells what a paragraph or a selection is mainly about; the most important idea of a text
metacognition	an awareness of one's own thinking processes and the ability to monitor and direct them to a desired goal. Good readers use metacognition to monitor their reading and adjust their reading strategies.
monitor and clarify	a comprehension strategy by which readers actively think about understanding their reading and know when they understand and when they do not. Readers use appropriate strategies to make sense of difficult words, ideas, or passages.

M

M

moral	the lesson or teaching of a fable or story
mystery	a story about mysterious events that are not explained until the end, so as to keep the reader in suspense
myth	a story that attempts to explain something in nature

N

narrative	a story, made up or true, that someone tells or narrates
narrator	the character in a selection who tells the story
nonfiction	writing that tells about real things, real people, and real events

O

onomatopoeia	the use of words that sound like their meanings, such as *buzz* and *hum*
opinion	someone's judgment, belief, or way of thinking
oral vocabulary	the words needed for speaking and listening

P

personification	a figure of speech in which human traits or actions are given to animals or inanimate objects, as in *The sunbeam danced on the waves.*
persuade	convince someone to do or to believe something
play	a story that is written to be acted out for an audience
plot	a series of related events at the beginning, middle, and end of a story; the action of a story
poem	an expressive, imaginative piece of writing often arranged in lines having rhythm and rhyme. In a poem, the patterns made by the sounds of the words have special importance.
pourquoi tale	a type of folk story that explains why things in nature came to be. *Pourquoi* is a French word meaning "why."
predict	tell what a selection might be about or what might happen in a text. Readers use text features and information to predict. They confirm or revise their predictions as they read.
preview	look over a text before reading it

Q

questioning	a reading strategy in which readers ask and answer questions to help make sense of what they read

R

reading vocabulary	the words we recognize or use in print
realistic fiction	a story about imaginary people and events that could happen in real life

repetition	the repeated use of some aspect of language
rhyme	to end in the same sound(s)
rhythm	a pattern of strong beats in speech or writing, especially poetry

R

science fiction	a story based on science that often tells what life in the future might be like
semantic map	a graphic organizer, often a web, used to display words or concepts that are meaningfully related
sequence	the order of events in a selection or the order of the steps in which something is completed
sequence words	clue words such as *first, next, then,* and *finally* that signal the order of events in a selection
setting	where and when a story takes place
stanza	a group of lines in a poem
steps in a process	the order of the steps in which something is completed
story map	a graphic organizer used to record the literary elements and the sequence of events in a narrative text
story structure	how the characters, setting, and events of a story are organized into a plot
summarize	give the most important ideas of what was read. Readers summarize important information in the selection to keep track of what they are reading.
supporting detail	piece of information that tells about the main idea

S

tall tale	a humorous story that uses exaggeration to describe impossible happenings
text structure	the organization of a piece of nonfiction writing. Text structures of informational text include cause/effect, chronological, compare/contrast, description, problem/solution, proposition/support, and ask/answer questions.
theme	the big idea or author's message in a story
think aloud	an instructional strategy in which a teacher verbalizes his or her thinking to model the process of comprehension or the application of a skill
topic	the subject of a discussion, conversation, or piece of text

T

visualize	picture in one's mind what is happening in the text. Visualizing helps readers imagine the things they read about.

V

Instruction

Leveled Readers Skills Chart

Scott Foresman Reading Street provides more than six hundred leveled readers. Each one is designed to:

- Practice critical skills and strategies
- Build fluency
- Build vocabulary and concepts
- Develop a lifelong love of reading

Grade K

Title	Level*	DRA Level	Genre
Max the Duck	A	1	Fantasy
Fun for Us	B	2	Informational Text
Nick the Fix-It Man	B	2	Informational Text
Red and Blue	B	2	Realistic Fiction
We Have Fun Together	B	2	Fantasy
Two or Three?	B	2	Realistic Fiction
Buds for Mom	B	2	Realistic Fiction
A Walk in the Forest	B	2	Realistic Fiction
Looking for Animals	D	2	Realistic Fiction
Skip and Run	C	3	Fantasy
A Winter Home	C	3	Informational Text
A Yard for All	C	3	Fantasy
The Fawn	C	3	Realistic Fiction
We Can Do It!	C	3	Realistic Fiction
Fun with Gram	C	3	Realistic Fiction
They Will Grow	C	3	Realistic Fiction
What Can You Do?	C	3	Informational Text
Sad and Glad	C	3	Realistic Fiction
The Trip	C	3	Informational Text
Pigs	C	3	Informational Text
Frog's New Home	C	3	Informational Text
Five Bears	C	3	Fantasy
My Walk in Antarctica	C	3	Realistic Fiction
A Trip to Washington, D.C.	C	3	Informational Text
The Bus Ride	C	3	Realistic Fiction
The Boat Ride	C	3	Realistic Fiction
Ming on the Job	C	3	Realistic Fiction
The Big Train	D	4	Realistic Fiction
Get On the Bus!	D	4	Realistic Fiction
Catch the Ball!	D	4	Realistic Fiction
Homes	D	4	Informational Text
The Best Club Hut	D	4	Realistic Fiction
A Small Trip	D	4	Informational Text
The Box	D	4	Informational Text
Our Camping Trip	D	4	Realistic Fiction
Safe Places for Animals	D	4	Informational Text

* Suggested Guided Reading Level. Use your knowledge of children's abilities to adjust levels as needed.

This chart lists titles of leveled readers appropriate for children in Kindergarten. Use the chart to find titles that meet your children's interest and instructional needs. The books in this list were leveled using the criteria suggested in *Matching Books to Readers: Using Leveled Books in Guided Reading, Grades K–3* by Irene C. Fountas and Gay Su Pinnell. For more on leveling, see the *Reading Street Leveled Readers Leveling Guide*.

Comprehension Strategy	Target Comprehension Skill	Additional Comprehension Instruction	Vocabulary
Recall/Retell	Character	N/A	N/A
Recall/Retell	Setting	N/A	N/A
Recall/Retell	Sequence	N/A	N/A
Recall/Retell	Classify and Categorize	N/A	N/A
Recall/Retell	Character	N/A	N/A
Recall/Retell	Classify and Categorize	N/A	N/A
Recall/Retell	Compare and Contrast	N/A	N/A
Recall/Retell	Setting	N/A	N/A
Recall/Retell	Main Idea	N/A	N/A
Recall/Retell	Realism and Fantasy	N/A	N/A
Recall/Retell	Sequence	N/A	N/A
Recall/Retell	Realism and Fantasy	N/A	N/A
Recall/Retell	Compare and Contrast	N/A	N/A
Recall/Retell	Plot	N/A	N/A
Recall/Retell	Cause and Effect	N/A	N/A
Recall/Retell	Plot	N/A	N/A
Recall/Retell	Draw Conclusions	N/A	N/A
Recall/Retell	Main Idea	N/A	N/A
Recall/Retell	Sequence	N/A	N/A
Recall/Retell	Cause and Effect	N/A	N/A
Recall/Retell	Sequence	N/A	N/A
Recall/Retell	Character	N/A	N/A
Recall/Retell	Classify and Categorize	N/A	N/A
Recall/Retell	Setting	N/A	N/A
Recall/Retell	Realism and Fantasy	N/A	N/A
Recall/Retell	Cause and Effect	N/A	N/A
Recall/Retell	Compare and Contrast	N/A	N/A
Recall/Retell	Plot	N/A	N/A
Recall/Retell	Main Idea	N/A	N/A
Recall/Retell	Draw Conclusions	N/A	N/A
Recall/Retell	Compare and Contrast	N/A	N/A
Recall/Retell	Character	N/A	N/A
Recall/Retell	Main Idea	N/A	N/A
Recall/Retell	Plot	N/A	N/A
Recall/Retell	Setting	N/A	N/A
Recall/Retell	Draw Conclusions	N/A	N/A

What Good Readers Do

You can use the characteristics and behaviors of good readers to help all your children read better. But what are these characteristics and behaviors? And how can you use them to foster good reading behaviors for all your children? Here are some helpful tips.

Good Readers enjoy reading! They have favorite books, authors, and genres. Good readers often have a preference about where and when they read. They talk about books and recommend their favorites.

Develop this behavior by giving children opportunities to respond in different ways to what they read. Get them talking about what they read, and why they like or dislike it.

This behavior is important because book sharing alerts you to children who are somewhat passive about reading or have limited literacy experiences. Book sharing also helps you when you select books for the class.

Good Readers select books they can read.

Develop this behavior by providing a range of three or four texts appropriate for the child and then letting the child choose.

This behavior is important because children gain control over reading when they can choose from books they can read. This helps them become more independent in the classroom.

Good Readers use text features to help them preview and set purposes.

Develop this behavior by having children use the title and illustrations in fiction texts or the title, contents, headings, and other graphic features in nonfiction texts to make predictions about what they will be reading.

This behavior is important because previewing actually makes reading easier! Looking at features and sampling the text enables readers to predict and set expectations for reading.

Good Readers predict and ask questions before and while they read.

Develop this behavior by asking questions. After reading a passage, ask children what they think will happen next in a fiction text. Have them ask a question they think will be answered in a nonfiction text and read on to see if it is.

This behavior is important because when children predict and ask questions as they read, they are engaged. They have a purpose for reading and a basis for monitoring their comprehension.

> Want to improve your children's performance by fostering good reading behaviors? **Customize Literacy can help.**

Good Readers use effective strategies and sources of information to figure out unknown words.

Develop this behavior by teaching specific strategies for figuring out unknown words, such as sounding out clusters of letters, using context, reading on, and using references.

This behavior is important because when readers have a variety of strategies to use, they are more able to decode and self-correct quickly. Readers who do these things view themselves as good readers.

CH- QU- ST-

Good Readers construct meaning as they read and then share or demonstrate their understanding.

Develop this behavior by having children retell what they read or write a summary of what they read in their own words.

This behavior is important because the ability to retell or write a summary is essential for success in reading. It shows how well a child has constructed meaning.

Good Readers make connections.

Develop this behavior by asking questions to help children make connections: *What does this remind you of? Have you ever read or experienced anything like this?*

This behavior is important because making connections helps readers understand and appreciate a text. Making connections to self, the world, and other texts supports high-level thinking.

Matching Books & Readers

Conversation Starters

Asking Good Questions Children want to read and listen to interesting and thought-provoking books! You can help them talk about these books. Use questions such as the following to assess listening comprehension and help children think about books. As you read longer books, pause often to ask questions about past and future events.

Cause and Effect

- What happens in this story?

- Why does it happen?

Classify and Categorize

- How are these things alike?

- Do these things belong in the same group?

- Is this thing like the others? Does it belong in the group?

- How do you know that it is like/not like the others?

- How would you group these things?

Character

- Who is in this story?

- What does this character like to do?

- How did the character feel in this part of the book?

- What does this character think about what happens in the book?

- Does this character seem real or made-up? What makes you think so?

- What character would you like to be? Why?

Compare and Contrast

- How are these things/characters/stories alike?

- How are these things/characters/stories different?

Draw Conclusions

- What happens in the story?

- What did the characters do to show you that they are kind/mean/strong?

- Which character do you like best? Why?

- Do you like this story? What makes you like it or dislike it?

Main Idea

- What is this story all about?

- What is the big idea of this story?

- What clues help you know what the story is about?

Plot

- In the story, what happens at the beginning? in the middle? at the end?

- What are other important things that happen in the story?

- What do you think is the most exciting/ important thing that happens?

- What is the problem that the character must solve/fix?

- How is that problem solved or fixed?

Realism and Fantasy

- Could this story happen in real life? Why do you think as you do?

- What things in the story could happen in real life?

- Do the people in this story act like people you know?

- How do you know if a story is make-believe or could really happen?

Sequence

- In this story, what happened first? next? last?

Setting

- What do the pictures tell you about when and where this story happened?

- What is this place like? What do you think it would be like?

- Does the place seem real or made-up? How can you tell?

- Do you want to visit this place? Why?

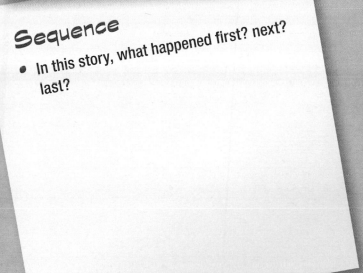

Matching Books & Readers

Connecting Science and Social Studies

Scott Foresman Reading Street Leveled Readers are perfect for covering, supporting, or enriching science and social studies content. Using these books ensures that all students can access important concepts.

Grade K Leveled Readers

Science

Earth and Space Science

Fiction Books
- *We Can Do It!*

Life Science

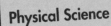

Nonfiction Books
- *A Winter Home*
- *What Can You Do?*
- *The Trip*
- *Pigs*
- *Frog's New Home*
- *A Small Trip*
- *Safe Places for Animals*

Fiction Books
- *A Walk in the Forest*
- *Looking for Animals*
- *Skip and Run*
- *A Yard for All*
- *The Fawn*
- *Fun with Gram*
- *They Will Grow*
- *Sad and Glad*

Physical Science

Fiction Books
- *Catch the Ball!*
- *The Best Club Hut*

Grade K Leveled Readers

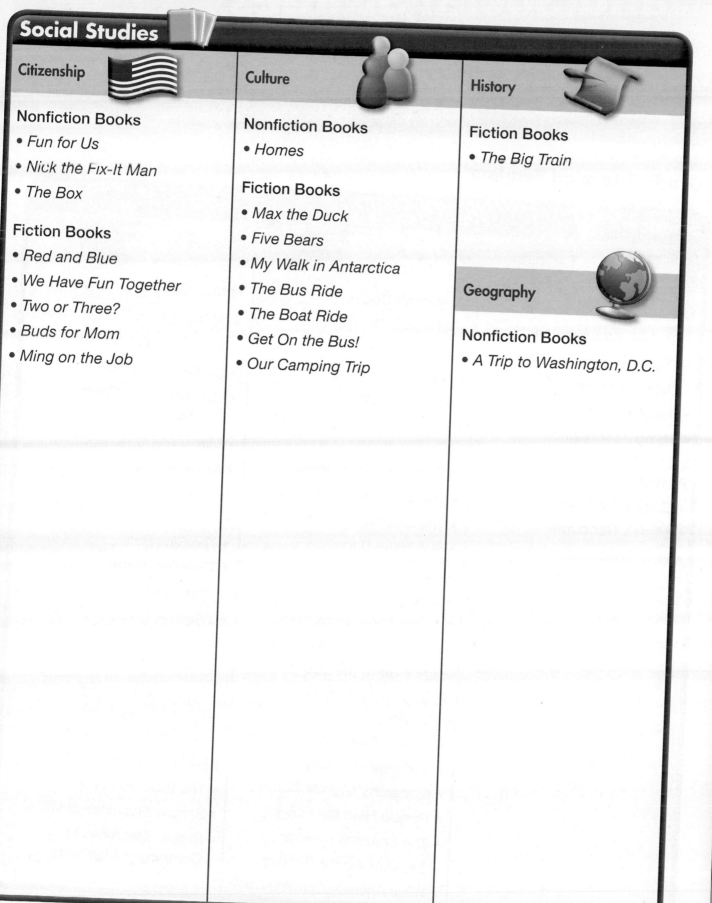

Social Studies

Citizenship

Nonfiction Books
- *Fun for Us*
- *Nick the Fix-It Man*
- *The Box*

Fiction Books
- *Red and Blue*
- *We Have Fun Together*
- *Two or Three?*
- *Buds for Mom*
- *Ming on the Job*

Culture

Nonfiction Books
- *Homes*

Fiction Books
- *Max the Duck*
- *Five Bears*
- *My Walk in Antarctica*
- *The Bus Ride*
- *The Boat Ride*
- *Get On the Bus!*
- *Our Camping Trip*

History

Fiction Books
- *The Big Train*

Geography

Nonfiction Books
- *A Trip to Washington, D.C.*

Matching Books & Readers

Connecting Science and Social Studies

Grade 1 Leveled Readers

Science

Earth and Space Science

Nonfiction Books
- All About the Weather
- The Communication Story
- Over the Years
- Ready for Winter?
- Using the Telephone

Fiction Books
- Cody's Adventure
- Marla's Good Idea
- What a Detective Does

Life Science

Nonfiction Books
- All About Food Chains
- Animals Change and Grow
- Around the Forest
- Around the World
- Baby Animals in the Rain Forest
- Bees and Beekeepers
- The Dinosaur Detectives
- The Dinosaur Herds
- Fun in the Sun
- Honey
- In My Room
- Learn About Butterflies
- Learn About Worker Bees
- Let's Go to the Zoo
- Let's Visit a Butterfly Greenhouse
- Look at Dinosaurs
- A Mighty Oak Tree
- Monarchs Migrate South
- People Help the Forest
- The Seasons Change
- Seasons Come and Go
- What Animals Can You See?

Life Science

Fiction Books
- Bix the Dog
- Britton Finds a Kitten
- Carlos Picks a Pet
- Cary and the Wildlife Shelter
- Mac Can Do It!
- Mack and Zack
- Plans Change
- Sam
- The Sick Pets
- Time for Dinner
- What Brown Saw
- Which Animals Will We See?
- Which Fox?

Physical Science

Nonfiction Books
- The Inclined Plane
- Simple Machines at Work
- Simple Machines in Compound Machines

Grade 1 Leveled Readers

Social Studies

Citizenship

Nonfiction Books

- *A Class*
- *A Garden for All*
- *Great Scientists: Detectives at Work*
- *Here in My Neighborhood*
- *A New Library*
- *Puppy Raiser*
- *The Story of the Kids Care Club*
- *Ways to Be a Good Citizen*

Fiction Books

- *The Art Show*
- *At Your Vet*
- *Big Wishes and Her Baby*
- *Double Trouble Twins*
- *Fly Away Owl!*
- *Grasshopper and Ant*
- *Hank's Song*
- *Let's Build a Park!*
- *Look at My Neighborhood*
- *My Little Brother Drew*
- *On the Farm*
- *Paul's Bed*
- *A Play*
- *Rules at School*
- *Space Star*
- *Squirrel and Bear*
- *That Cat Needs Help!*

Culture

Nonfiction Books

- *Cascarones Are for Fun*
- *My Babysitter*
- *Special Days, Special Food*
- *We Are a Family*
- *What Makes Buildings Special?*

Fiction Books

- *Go West!*
- *Grandma's Farm*
- *Gus the Pup*
- *Jamie's Jumble of Junk*
- *A New Baby Brother*
- *A Party for Pedro*
- *A Visit to the Ranch*
- *Where They Live*

History

Nonfiction Books

- *School: Then and Now*
- *Treasures of Our Country*

Fiction Books

- *Loni's Town*

Government

Nonfiction Books

- *America's Home*
- *Our Leaders*

Fiction Books

- *Mom the Mayor*

Planning Teacher Study Groups

Adventurous teachers often have good ideas for lessons. A teacher study group is a great way to share ideas and get feedback on the best way to connect content and students. Working with other teachers can provide you with the support and motivation you need to implement new teaching strategies. A teacher study group offers many opportunities to collaborate, support each other's work, share insights, and get feedback.

Think About It

A weekly or monthly teacher study group can help support you in developing your expertise in the classroom. You and a group of like-minded teachers can form your own study group. What can this group accomplish?

- Read and discuss professional articles by researchers in the field of education.

- Meet to share teaching tips, collaborate on multi-grade lessons, and share resources.

- Develop lessons to try out new teaching strategies. Meet to share experiences and discuss how to further improve your teaching approach.

Let's Meet!

Forming a study group is easy. Just follow these four steps:

1. **Decide on the size of the group.** A small group has the advantage of making each member feel accountable, but make sure that all people can make the same commitment!

2. **Choose teachers to invite to join your group.** Think about whom you want to invite. Should they all teach the same grade? Can you invite teachers from other schools? Remember that the more diverse the group, the more it benefits from new perspectives.

3. **Set goals for the group.** In order to succeed, know what you want the group to do. Meet to set goals. Rank goals in order of importance and refer often to the goals to keep the group on track.

4. **Make logistical decisions.** This is often the most difficult. Decide where and when you will meet. Consider an online meeting place where group members can post discussion questions and replies if people are not able to meet.

What Will We Study? Use the goals you set to help determine what your group will study. Consider what materials are needed to reach your goals, and how long you think you will need to prepare for each meeting.

How Will It Work? Think about how you structure groups in your classroom. Use some of the same strategies.

- **Assign a group facilitator.** This person is responsible for guiding the meeting. This person comes prepared with discussion questions and leads the meeting. This could be a rotating responsibility dependent on experience with various topics. This person might be responsible for providing the materials.

- **Assign a recorder.** Have someone take notes during the meeting and record group decisions.

- **Use the jigsaw method.** Not everyone has time to be a facilitator. In this case, divide the text and assign each portion to a different person. Each person is responsible for leading the discussion on that particular part.

Meet Again Make a commitment to meet for a minimum number of times. After that, the group can reevaluate and decide whether or not to continue.

> " Have some great teaching tips to share? Want to exchange ideas with your colleagues? Build your own professional community of teachers. **Customize Literacy** gets you started. "

Building Community

Trial Lessons

Use your colleagues' experiences to help as you think about new ways to connect content and students. Use the following plan to create a mini-lesson. It should last twenty minutes. Get the support of your colleagues as you try something new, and then reflect on what happened.

Be Creative! As you develop a plan for a mini-lesson, use these four words to guide planning: *purpose, text, resources,* and *routine.*

- **Purpose:** Decide on a skill or strategy to cover. Define your purpose for teaching the lesson.

- **Text:** Develop a list of the materials you could use. Ask your colleagues for suggestions.

- **Resources:** Make a list of the available resources, and consider how to use those resources most effectively. Consider using the leveled readers listed on pages CL16–CL17 and CL22–CL25 of Customize Literacy.

- **Routine:** Choose an instructional routine to structure your mini-lesson. See the mini-lessons in Customize Literacy for suggestions.

Try It! Try out your lesson! Consider audio- or videotaping the lesson for later review. You may wish to invite a colleague to sit in as you teach. Make notes on how the lesson went.

How Did It Go? Use the self-evaluation checklist on page CL29 as you reflect on your trial lesson. This provides a framework for later discussion.

Discuss, Reflect, Repeat Solicit feedback from your teacher study group. Explain the lesson and share your reflections. Ask for suggestions on ways to improve the lesson. Take some time to reflect on the feedback. Modify your lesson to reflect what you have learned. Then try teaching the lesson again.

Checklist for Teacher Self-Evaluation

How Well Did I ...	Very Well	Satisfactory	Not Very Well
Plan the lesson?			
Select the appropriate level of text?			
Introduce the lesson and explain its objectives?			
Review previously taught skills?			
Directly explain the new skills being taught?			
Model the new skills?			
Break the material down into small steps?			
Integrate guided practice into the lesson?			
Monitor guided practice for student understanding?			
Provide feedback on independent practice?			
Maintain an appropriate pace?			
Assess student understanding of the material?			
Stress the importance of applying the skill as they read?			
Maintain students' interest?			
Ask questions?			
Handle student questions and responses?			
Respond to the range of abilities?			

Building Community

Books for Teachers

Children aren't the only ones who need to read to grow. Here is a brief list of books that you may find useful to fill your reading teacher basket and learn new things.

A Professional Bibliography

Adams, M. J. "Alphabetic Anxiety and Explicit, Systematic Phonics Instruction: A Cognitive Science Perspective." *Handbook of Early Literacy Research.* The Guilford Press, 2001.

Adams, M. J. *Beginning to Read: Thinking and Learning About Print.* The MIT Press, 1990.

Afflerbach, P. "The Influence of Prior Knowledge and Text Genre on Readers' Prediction Strategies." *Journal of Reading Behavior,* vol. XXII, no. 2 (1990).

Armbruster, B. B., F. Lehr, and J. Osborn. *Put Reading First: The Research Building Blocks for Teaching Children to Read.* Partnership for Reading, Washington, D.C., 2001.

Bear, D. R., M. Invernizzi, S. Templeton, and F. Johnston. *Words Their Way.* Merrill Prentice Hall, 2004.

Beck, I., M. G. McKeown, and L. Kucan. *Bringing Words to Life: Robust Vocabulary Instruction.* The Guilford Press, 2002.

Biemiller, A. "Teaching Vocabulary in the Primary Grades: Vocabulary Instruction Needed." *Vocabulary Instruction Research to Practice.* The Guilford Press, 2004.

Blachowicz, C. and P. Fisher. "Vocabulary Instruction." *Handbook of Reading Research,* vol. III. Lawrence Erlbaum Associates, 2000.

Cunningham, P. M. and J. W. Cunningham. "What We Know About How to Teach Phonics." *What Research Says About Reading Instruction,* 3rd ed. International Reading Association, 2002.

Daniels, H. *Literature Circles.* 2nd ed. Stenhouse Publishers, 2002.

Dickson, S. V., D. C. Simmons, and E. J. Kame'enui. "Text Organization: Instructional and Curricular Basics and Implications." *What Reading Research Tells Us About Children with Diverse Learning Needs: Bases and Basics.* Lawrence Erlbaum Associates, 1998.

Diller, D. *Making the Most of Small Groups: Differentiation for All.* Stenhouse Publishers, 2007.

Duke, N. K., V. S. Bennett-Armistead, and E. M. Roberts. "Bridging the Gap Between Learning to Read and Reading to Learn." *Literacy and Young Children: Research-Based Practices.* The Guilford Press, 2003.

Duke, N. K. and C. Tower. "Nonfiction Texts for Young Readers." *The Texts in Elementary Classrooms.* Lawrence Erlbaum Associates, 2004.

Ehri, L. C. and S. R. Nunes. "The Role of Phonemic Awareness in Learning to Read." *What Research Has to Say About Reading Instruction.* 3rd ed. International Reading Association, 2002.

Fountas, I. C. and G. S. Pinnell. *Guided Reading: Good First Teaching for All Children.* Heinemann, 1996.

Fountas, I. C. and G. S. Pinnell. *Matching Books to Readers: Using Leveled Books in Guided Reading,* K-3. Heinemann, 1999.

Harvey, S. and A. Goudvis. *Strategies That Work: Teaching Comprehension to Enhance Understanding.* 2nd ed. Stenhouse Publishers, 2007.

Hiebert, E. H. and L. A. Martin. "The Texts of Beginning Reading Instruction." *Handbook of Early Literacy Research.* The Guilford Press, 2001.

Indrisano, R. and J. R. Paratore. *Learning to Write, Writing to Learn. Theory and Research in Practice.* International Reading Association, 2005.

Juel, C., G. Biancarosa, D. Coker, and R. Deffes. "Walking with Rosie: A Cautionary Tale of Early Reading Instruction." *Educational Leadership* (April 2003).

National Reading Panel. *Teaching Children to Read.* National Institute of Child Health and Human Development, 1999.

Pressley, M. *Reading Instruction That Works: The Case for Balanced Teaching,* 3rd ed. The Guilford Press, 2005.

Smith, S., D. C. Simmons, and E. J. Kame'enui. "Word Recognition: Research Bases." *What Reading Research Tells Us About Children with Diverse Learning Needs: Bases and Basics.* Lawrence Erlbaum Associates, 1998.

Snow, C., S. Burns, and P. Griffin, eds. *Preventing Reading Difficulties in Young Children.* National Academy Press, 1998.

Vaughn, S., P. G. Mathes, S. Linan-Thompson, and D. J. Francis. "Teaching English Language Learners at Risk for Reading Disabilities to Read: Putting Research into Practice." *Learning Disabilities Research & Practice,* vol. 20, issue 1 (February 2006).

Building Community

Acknowledgments

Acknowledgments

Illustrations

Cover Rob Hefferan
12, 50–65 Natalia Vasquez
19–25 Maria Mola
30 Julia Woolf
32 Paul Meisel
39–43 Cale Atkinson
50–51 Rob Hefferan
52 Mary Sullivan
70 Jan Bryan Hunt
72, 108 George Ulrich
79–85 Dani Jones
90–91 Ana Ochoa
92 Carol Koeller
99–105 Bobbie Short
110 Leslie Harrington
112 Jamie Smith
119–125 Wednesday Kirwan
128 Anthony Lewis
130–131 Viviana Garofoli

Photographs

Every effort has been made to secure permission and provide appropriate credit for photographic material. The publisher deeply regrets any omission and pledges to correct errors called to its attention in subsequent editions.

Unless otherwise acknowledged, all photographs are the property of Pearson Education, Inc.

Photo locators denoted as follows: Top (T), Center (C), Bottom (B), Left (L), Right (R), Background (Bkgd)

10 (B) ©Tim Bird/Corbis

20 ©Alex Segre/Alamy Images, ©moodboard/Corbis, ©Randy Faris/Corbis, ©Corbis/Jupiter Images

29 ©JG Photography/Alamy

48 Getty Images

68 ©Peter Titmuss/Alamy Images, ©Picture Contact/Alamy Images, Brand X Pictures, Jupiter Images.

144

Teacher Editions

KWL Strategy: The KWL Interactive Reading Strategy was developed and is used by permission of Donna Ogle, National-Louis University, Skokie, Illinois, co-author of *Reading Today and Tomorrow*, Holt, Rinehart & Winston Publishers, 1988. (See also the *Reading Teacher*, February 1986, pp. 564–570.)

Understanding by Design quotes: Wiggins, G. & McTighe, J. (2005). *Understanding by Design.* Alexandria, VA: Association for Supervision and Curriculum Development.

Illustrations

Cover Rob Hefferan

Running Header Steven Mach

Photos

Every effort has been made to secure permission and provide appropriate credit for photographic material. The publisher deeply regrets any omission and pledges to correct errors called to its attention in subsequent editions.

Unless otherwise acknowledged, all photographs are the property of Pearson Education, Inc.

Teacher Notes

Teacher Resources

Looking for Teacher Resources and other important information?

In the **First Stop**
on Reading Street

Teacher Resources

Looking for Teacher Resources and other important information?

In the **First Stop** on Reading Street